THE M WORD
Real Mothers in Contemporary Art

THE M WORD

Real Mothers in Contemporary Art

EDITED BY

MYREL CHERNICK AND JENNIE KLEIN

DEMETER PRESS
BRADFORD, CANADA

Demeter Press
c/o Motherhood Initiative for Research and
Community Involvement (MIRCI)
140 Holland St. West, P.O. 13022
Bradford, ON, L3Z 2Y5
Telephone: 905.775.5215
Email: info@demeterpress.org
Website: www.demeterpress.org

Demeter Press logo based on the sculpture *Demeter* by Maria-Luise Bodirsky <www.keramik-atelier.bodirsky.de>

Cover Art: Myrel Chernick, *Mommy Mommy*, 1994. Video still.

Printed and Bound in Canada

Library and Archives Canada Cataloguing in Publication

The M word : real mothers in contemporary art / edited by Myrel Chernick and Jennie Klein.

Includes bibliographical references.
ISBN 978-0-9866671-2-1

1. Motherhood and the arts. 2. Motherhood in art. 3. Women artists—Interviews. I. Chernick, Myrel, 1952– II. Klein, Jennie, 1964–

NX180.M68M86 2011 700.852 C2011-900432-1

To our mothers:

Sue Klein

and

Anne Chernick
(1918–2006)

IN MEMORIAM

Valérie Roy
(1965–2010)

Black Children's Shoes, 2008. Acrylic and pastel on Kraft paper, 53 × 43 inches.

Artist, Mother, Friend

Sailor Jacket Size 4, 2009. Acrylic and pastel on Kraft paper, 43 × 53 inches.

Acknowledgements

A LIFE CHANGE (MOTHERHOOD) GENERATED an exhibit and catalog—*Maternal Metaphors*—and a second exhibit, *Maternal Metaphors II*—that expanded into *The M Word: Real Mothers in Contemporary Art*. During its years of development and execution, the children have grown older and some have become adults. We begin by acknowledging the dedication of Elizabeth McDade and Sarah Webb at the Rochester Contemporary, and Petra Kralickova at Ohio University, whose invitations to present, and whose persistence and hard work produced two stunning exhibits. We are extremely grateful to be able to see this project through to its publication by Demeter Press. We thank all of the artists and writers for their contributions. We appreciate the effort that went into preparing and submitting their work, much of it for tight deadlines. We are indebted to the editing skills of Nina Lewallen Hufford and Tanya Llewellyn. We thank the reviewers for their close readings and perceptive comments. A faculty development grant from Pratt Institute contributed in the early stages to the acquisition and preparation of materials, and we are extremely grateful for the generous financial support of the Morgan Phoa Family Foundation. We thank Perry Bard for coining the M Word, our spouses for their aesthetic and practical assistance, and last but not least, our children, without whose existence this project could not have been possible.

Mary Kelly's excerpts from *Post-Partum Document* were originally printed in *Post-Partum Document* (London: Routledge, 1983).

"My Mother's Silver Pin" by Susan Rubin Suleiman was originally printed as "The Silver Pin," in *Evocative Objects*, ed. Sherry Turkle (Cambridge: MIT Press, 2007).

An earlier version of "The Body in Question: Rethinking Motherhood, Alterity and Desire" by Andrea Liss appeared in *New Feminist Criticism: Art, Identity, Action*, eds. Joanna Frueh, Cassandra L. Langer and Arlene Raven (New York: HarperCollins, 1994).

A previous version of Nancy Gerber's "We Don't Talk About Mothers Here: Seeking the Maternal in Holocaust Memoir and Art" was published in the *Journal of the Association for Research on Mothering* 12.1 (Spring/Summer 2010).

Mignon Nixon's "Epilogue" was first published as the final chapter of her book *Fantastic Reality: Louise Bourgeois and a Story of Modern Art* (Cambridge: MIT Press, 2005).

Maria Assumpta Bassas Vila's essay "S.O.S.: Searching for the Mother in the Family Album" was first published in *n.paradoxa* 16 (July 2005).

An earlier version of Michelle Moravec's "Make Room for Mommy: Feminist Artists and My Maternal Musings" was published as "Mother Art: Feminism, Art, Activism," in the *Journal of the Association for Research on Mothering: Mothering, Popular Culture, and the Arts* 5.1 (Spring/Summer 2003).

"Observations of a Mother" by Jane Gallop and Dick Blau was originally published in *The Familial Gaze,* ed. Marianne Hirsch (Hanover: University Press of New England, 1999).

An earlier version of "Art Between Us" by Ellen McMahon was published in *The Oldest We've Ever Been: Seven True Stories of Midlife Transitions*, ed. Maud Lavin (Tucson: University of Arizona Press, 2008).

"BabyLove" by Christen Clifford was originally published online at nerve.com.

Contents

II. *MATERNAL METAPHORS I*

III. CONTEMPORARY ART AND THE MATERNAL: ARTICULATING THE MATERNAL METAPHOR IN FEMINIST ART

MYREL CHERNICK AND JENNIE KLEIN

Introduction

> *Motherhood within early feminist struggles and still today interferes with retrograde myths of the avant-garde. Motherhood, especially feminist motherhood, confuses the normalized order of gender and power. Feminist motherhood complicates the dominant institutionalized idea of motherhood.*
>
> —Andrea Liss[1]

AS ANDREA LISS TRENCHANTLY ARGUES, from its inception the feminist art movement has at best ignored mothers and at worst been downright hostile to motherhood and maternity. In the mid-1970s Laura Silagi was one of many women who moved to Los Angeles in order to study at the Feminist Studio Workshop (FSW), the first educational program devoted exclusively to the education of feminist artists. The Feminist Studio Workshop was located in the Los Angeles Woman's Building, an institution that housed the Sisterhood Bookstore and the FSW, as well as women's art galleries and artists' studios. Silagi had previously been part of a group that successfully lobbied the University of California, San Diego, to provide childcare. When she arrived at the Woman's Building, she was shocked to discover that an institution supposedly founded on egalitarian feminist principles was so unwelcoming to mothers and their children: "While there was support for art dealing with certain issues, support for those of us, both lesbian and heterosexual, who had children was totally lacking. In fact, we faced overt hostility when it came to the subject of motherhood and children."[2]

This attitude towards motherhood stood in stark contrast to the philosophy of cultural feminism espoused by the Building's founders and participants. An important tenet of cultural feminism was that women's bodies were sacred because of their connection to nature, the goddess, and a prehistoric matriarchal society. Childbirth was a central component of the celebration of the female body. In reality, though, the actual child, with his or her constant needs and demands, was not part of this celebration. It is telling that Judy Chicago, one of the founders of the Woman's Building and the creator of a large-scale tapestry series about childbirth (*Birth Project* 1980–1985), told another mother at the FSW, Helen Million Ruby, that Ruby had to choose between her children and her art.[3] Chicago believed that she was only stating a fact, not giving an ultimatum. Silagi and the other women with small children—Ruby, Christy Kruse, Suzanne Siegel, and Gloria Hajduk—responded by founding Mother Art in 1974, one of the first collectives to come out of the Woman's Building. Their first project was to build a playground in the parking lot. Their second project for the Woman's Building, in 1975, was to organize the exhibition *By Mothers*. The intent was to demonstrate to the other women artists (most of whom were childless and in their early twenties) that motherhood was a legitimate subject for feminist art.

In the United States in 1975, there was little support in either the feminist or art worlds for women who were both mothers and artists. Two classic feminist texts about motherhood, creativity, and ambivalence —Adrienne Rich's *Of Woman Born: Motherhood as Experience and Institution* and Jane Lazarre's *The Mother Knot*—would not be published until the following year.[4] While there were a few prominent women artists who had children, such as Louise Nevelson and Sheila de Bretteville, the fact that they were mothers was not evident in their artwork. Although feminism has made radical incursions into the male-dominated art world during the past thirty years, mothers and the representation of motherhood remain on the margins of art practice. As recently as 1992, when Susan Bee and Mira Schor, the editors of the art journal *M/E/A/N/I/N/G*, organized a forum on motherhood and art, although they received a high percentage of responses to their request for participation, more than one artist wondered how the editors had found out that they had children, "so separate had children been kept from art world life."[5] The contributions to the forum that Bee and Schor did receive all concerned the difficulty of balancing one's career as an artist with one's identity as a mother. "Being a mother and an artist: hard," responded Joan Snyder, a well-known painter. She continued, "Being a mother is being a mother is being a mother. Being an artist means doing your work. You need time and you need help, years and years of help."[6]

It has taken a surprising amount of time for motherhood to be regarded as a serious topic for feminists and feminist artists.[7] In comparison with other feminist topics such as lesbian identity, feminism and popular culture, and female sexuality, in art the subject of maternity is only beginning to receive attention. A number of women artists who make work about their experience as mothers, many of them included in this book, are now being awarded prestigious gallery shows, reviews in art publications, and tenure. There is a growing bibliography, of which Andrea Liss's 2009 book, *Feminist Art and the Maternal,* is the most recent example, which deals with the (sometimes uneasy) alliance among feminism, feminist art, and the representation of motherhood. Journals such as *Hypatia, Genders,* and *n.paradoxa* have published articles on the representation of motherhood in film and popular culture.[8] Routledge recently published a monograph on Bobby Baker, a British artist who has made objects and performances about middle-class motherhood, depression, and cooking since the 1970s.[9] *The Journal of the Association for Research on Mothering* devoted an issue to "Mothering, Popular Culture, and the Arts" (Spring/Summer 2003). At the 2009 meeting of the College Art Association, several panels were devoted to motherhood, including two intriguingly titled "Mothers of Innovation I and II." Art historian Rachel Epp Buller is presently compiling an anthology of historical writing and artists' writing entitled *Reconciling Art and Motherhood.*[10] There have also been several exhibitions of artwork that deal with the representation of motherhood in the past ten years.[11] This anthology, in development since 2006, thus contributes to the growing interest in examining the relationship between the maternal and the practice of art and also documents the changing reception of motherhood in the visual arts.

* * *

The M Word: Real Mothers in Contemporary Art is a reflection—or mirror—of the possibilities for mothering today. It includes personal essays, critical and historical writing, interviews, and artwork that explore how women artists and writers have grappled in their work with their identity as mothers. The women in this anthology attempt an honest portrayal of motherhood in a society where mothers are either sanctified for their selfless love or blamed for their children's problems. In examining the effect of motherhood on their work, these artists and writers explore the complex and ambivalent emotions associated with motherhood, countering the pervasive and popular myth of unconditional, all-sacrificing mother love. The title "M Word" alludes to the fact that many artists, such as those approached by Bee and Schor for inclusion in the special issue of *M/E/A/N/I/N/G*, actually conceal their identity as mothers in order to be taken seriously in an art world that does not value motherhood.

The predominantly white and middle-class feminists who came to study at the Woman's Building in the 1970s assumed that their experiences were shared by most women. The assumptions of those second-wave feminists have since been challenged on a number of fronts: by women of color, by critics informed by postmodern and postcolonial theories of identity and subjectivity, and by the rapid communication among cultures enabled by our globalized, electronically connected world. Advances in reproductive technologies have also enabled a wider spectrum of people to become parents, especially gay and lesbian couples. Today, there exists a plethora of feminisms and a conception and construction of motherhood that takes into account the diverse nature and experiences of mothers and families in an interconnected global society.[12]

The M Word promotes multiple visual, historical, and critical readings of motherhood as well as international and historical perspectives on motherhood and the visual arts. The writers and artists included in this book represent a diverse group of ages, races, ethnicities, and socio-economic backgrounds, united by a commitment to feminist mothering. We have actively recruited artists and writers that practice outside of the United States, and we are pleased to include international artists such as Silvia Ziranek (United Kingdom), Johanna Tuukkanen (Finland), Leslie Reid (Canada), Signe Theill (Germany), Mónica Mayer and Patricia Cué (Mexico), Youngbok Hong (Korea), Maria Assumpta Bassas Vila (Spain), and Margaret Morgan and Denise Ferris (Australia). *The M Word* includes work by and about artists of color, artists who have lost custody of their children, artists who identify as lesbian, and artists who have struggled with infertility or are dealing with the process of adoption.

The M Word reflects the growing interest in the role that motherhood and maternity have played in contemporary feminist visual representation, as both a metaphor for creation and creativity and as lived experience informing the artist's work. The crucial precedent for the work presented in this anthology is Mary Kelly's *Post-Partum Document*. A chronicle of the first four years of her son's life, written and represented through the prism of Lacanian psychoanalytic theory, *Post-Partum Document* was a watershed when it was first exhibited and later published in a book version in the early 1980s. In this rigorously conceptual artwork, Kelly's experience of raising a child from infancy to the age at which he was able to write his own name was used as a foil to interrogate psychoanalytic theory regarding maternal desire, normative psycho-social development, and the entry into the symbolic/linguistic order. Kelly, as many of the artists included here, eschewed images of the maternal body and instead displayed objects (diapers, baby vests, plaster casts, and found objects), drawings and written words to document the intersubjective mother-child relationship. A dual discourse resulted, with Kelly's maternal fantasies and anxieties reflecting the social position of women as primary caregivers. She then wrote her own psychoanalytically informed critique of this discourse, creating a detailed examination of the complexities of maternal subjectivity that demonstrated how motherhood, far from shutting down the creative process, could be a catalyst for art making.

The contributors to this book, almost all working from the mother's perspective, have explored, documented, repudiated, confronted and analyzed aspects of the multifaceted and divided category of maternal subjectivity, a subject position that, even now, has not been fully theorized in psychoanalytic discourse.[13] By representing through their work the range, complexity and contradictions of their conscious and unconscious desires, artist mothers contribute to the recognition of multiple maternal subjectivities, to help counter the cultural ideology of motherhood as an idealized selflessness.

The M Word expands on earlier work on maternal representation, gaze, and desire. The artists and writers included in this book have been influenced by the disciplines of film, literature, and theory. E. Ann Kaplan's *Motherhood and Representation* (1992) and *Representations of Motherhood* (1994), edited by Donna Bassin, Margaret Honey, and Meryle Mahrer Kaplan, while concerned primarily with filmic representation, both explored areas that had important implications for feminist artists interested in a critical practice of art making, including maternal desire and analysis of the mother as sign.[14] Susan Rubin Suleiman's writings on the ambivalence that women feel when torn between the demands of their creative activity and those of their children in her two seminal essays "Feminist Intertextuality and the Laugh of the Mother" (1990), and "Writing and Motherhood" (presented in 1979 and published in 1985) are echoed by much of the work included in this book.[15] Equally vital is Suleiman's eloquent argument, in the form of a published letter exchange with Raquel Portillo Bauman published in *Signs*, for the relevance of psychoanalysis as a critical tool in understanding language and representation, even as she acknowledges its limitations.[16]

Along with Suleiman, we feel that psychoanalytic theory, which has informed many of the writings about motherhood and maternity, is central to any understanding of motherhood and maternity. The debate within psychoanalysis over an innate, essential femininity versus a sexuality constructed and defined by culture began in the early twentieth century. Psychoanalysts and theorists such as Julia Kristeva and Luce Irigaray in

France and Nancy Chodorow in the U.S. criticized Freud as phallocentric, while others—including Kelly, Suleiman, Gallop, and other writers in this volume—found that Jacques Lacan's exploration of sexual difference as never fixed, but based on an unfulfilled desire for the phallus by both sexes, opened up a space for feminist critique and revision.[17] In Lacan's theory there is no unified, pre-given subject. The sexual subject is constructed, created through loss, and defined by a patriarchal language and culture that he called the symbolic. Other key Lacanian terms referred to directly and indirectly in this book—and diagrammed by Kelly in *Post-Partum Document*—include his concept of the mirror stage, where the child's fictional mirror image becomes the model for its future identifications; the imaginary, which represents the original mother/child dyad that is broken by the introduction of the oedipal father; and the real as the locus of unfulfilled desire.[18] The work of Melanie Klein, a major psychoanalyst and theorist on the other side of the debate, has also been important for feminists. In this volume, Mignon Nixon refers to Kleinian theory in examining the powerful and complicated work of Louise Bourgeois, who herself had considered studying child analysis. Although feminists have disagreed with aspects of Klein's depiction of femininity as innate, she is important for her stress on the pre-oedipal relationship, allowing for the introduction of aggression and destruction into the picture of the self-sacrificing mother.[19]

Marianne Hirsch has examined the relationship between the family, the mother, the child, and photography in her book, *Family Frames: Photography, Narrative, and Postmemory* (1997) and in the edited volume *The Familial Gaze* (1999).[20] Hirsch's essay "Maternal Exposures," included in *Family Frames*, examines the implications of transforming a child into an image through the work of photographer Sally Mann and the short story "Good Housekeeping" by Rosellen Brown. Many of the artists included in *The M Word* are aware of the potential repercussions of their depictions of their children through their cameras, through the mediums of painting or sculpture that result in the objects presented here.

The artists in this book are also responding to more recent work on motherhood and culture that has been motivated by the increased visibility of the maternal in the late twentieth century. In the past several years, there have been a number of books interrogating the construction of the maternal in popular culture. Informed by a number of disciplines that evolved from postmodern feminist theory such as gender and disability theory, media studies, and post-colonial theories of identity construction, this work has examined the representation of the maternal and of motherhood as it is imbricated within popular culture. Books such as *Motherhood Misconceived*, edited by Heather Addison, Mary Kate Goodwin-Kelly, and Elaine Roth include articles that use cultural studies to locate maternity in specific ideological and socio-economic contexts in order to argue that the cinematic and tabloid representation of motherhood has remained remarkably static.[21] Other scholars, such as Imogen Tyler, have addressed the relationship between class, representation, and maternity in articles that look to tabloids and television in order to construct the ideology of motherhood in the twenty-first century.[22] In the past ten years Demeter Press has published or will publish anthologies on the politics and ideology of breast milk, motherhood and blogging, online communities, Aboriginal mothering, and mothering and hip-hop culture.[23]

* * *

Following the example set by Mary Kelly, who insisted that her personal experience be read against a conceptual, psychoanalytic framework, *The M Word* aims to foreground the relationship among theory, practice, and imagery. We have included as much artwork as possible. In our selection of work, we have tried to avoid the traditionally sentimental images in favor of work that is rigorously conceptual. With that in mind, we have included artists' pages with images and statements in three sections, text/image pieces made specifically for this book, and performance scripts written by artists whose work is informed by late twentieth-century conceptual practices taught in art schools. We have illustrated the stories, articles, and reflections with additional images. Throughout the book, we have done our best to maintain the balance between the theorization and representation of motherhood and the use of the maternal in contemporary art.

The book is organized into three sections of writing and three of artwork. The artwork sections, II, IV and VI, consist of artists' statements and multiple reproductions of each artist's work. These sections also include a selection of work from four exhibitions on art and motherhood: *Maternal Metaphors I* and *II*, on which we collaborated; *Doublebind*, presented in Germany and Australia in 2003 and 2004, and described here by curator Signe Theill; and *Mother/mother-**, curated by Jennifer Wroblewski and presented at A.I.R. in 2009, the first exhibit at the feminist gallery (since its inception in 1972) that focuses on maternal work. Additions to the original exhibition checklist include Wroblewski, the performance artist Johanna Tuukkanen, and the filmmaker Caroline Koebel.

The first section, "Conversations and Questions," presents selections of previously published works by Mary Kelly, Susan Rubin Suleiman, and Andrea Liss as well as new, recent interviews with Kelly and Suleiman and a 2009 postscript by Liss. Kelly, Suleiman, and Liss first published important articles theorizing motherhood and representation around the same time that several artist mothers admitted to Susan Bee and Mira Schor that they didn't acknowledge to the art world that they had children. In this section, as with much of the work included in this book, we wanted to both revive the initial debates around motherhood, subjectivity, and maternal desire and to look back at those debates from the vantage point of twenty years of work on maternity and maternal subjectivity.

Section I reprints excerpts from *Post-Partum Document*, including the series of Rosetta Stone images and accompanying text that document the entry of Kelly's son, Kelly Barrie, into the symbolic order—his ability to write his own name. These excerpts are paired with two interviews, the first an exclusive interview with Mary Kelly by Margaret Morgan, and the second an interview with both Mary Kelly and Kelly Barrie by Ruth Skilbeck. The latter took place on the occasion of a collaborative installation at the 2008 Sydney Biennale that included Kelly's Super 8 film, *Antepartum*, made in 1973, and Barrie's video-recording *Astral Fields* made 35 years later, in 2008. Morgan's interview is particularly significant because it situates Kelly as one of the first artists to interrogate the subjectivity of motherhood and to engage conceptually with the linguistic structures that characterize the mother/child dyad. Skilbeck's interview brings the mother/child dyad full circle, establishing Kelly Barrie as an artist who is as versant in the meaning and signification of language and representation as was his mother thirty years earlier.

The first section also includes an interview conducted by Myrel Chernick with Suleiman as well as Suleiman's personal essay "My Mother's Silver Pin."[24] These two pieces establish Suleiman's own history as a Holocaust survivor and child of the Diaspora; her family moved from Budapest to Vienna, to Paris, then Haiti, New York City, and finally Chicago, all before Suleiman was twenty years of age. Suleiman, as mentioned above, has been important to contemporary theorizations of motherhood and representation due to her articulation of the ambivalence that a mother feels when she ignores a crying child in order to pursue her own creativity and her theorization of a laughing, playful maternal subjectivity that stands in contradistinction to the avant-garde construction of the mother as narrow-minded upholder of the Lacanian Law of the Father. In both the short story and the interview included here, Suleiman acknowledges another ambivalence—that of the daughter towards the mother. Suleiman's mother was in many ways an "impossible person," yet at the same time, she embodied the laughing mother that Suleiman had initially championed, a mother whose discourse is often silenced or brutally punished in art, literature, and popular culture. Chernick's interview situates Suleiman and her theorization of motherhood within the particular context of the displaced Hungarian Jewish refugee who is also a survivor of the Holocaust.

In the final essay in this section, Andrea Liss, who is of a younger generation than Kelly and Suleiman, situates and resituates herself in relationship to the idea of the maternal. Liss's essay, "The Body in Question: Rethinking Motherhood, Alterity, and Desire," explores the relationship between Elizabeth Grosz's re-reading of Emmanuel Levinas's ethical mother and her own inability to completely give up selfhood in relationship to her child. Arguing for an acceptance of maternal giving and a deployment of the same outside of the realm of the private, Liss proposes a way of being both a feminist and a mother. At the time Liss wrote "The Body in Question," her son Miles was a student at Seven Songs Preschool. In her 2009 postscript, Liss both returns to the questions raised by the essay and anticipates an impending separation—Miles is eighteen and leaving home to attend college. Liss's postscript is both an elegy to her own maternal ethos as well as a commentary on the continued marginality of the mother in psychoanalysis and capitalist culture. Liss notes that "since the first publication of this essay in 1994 to its second appearance in 2004 and its gracious inclusion in this crucial book, it is still against the norm in the field of cultural theory and visual art writing for a feminist to proclaim herself a mother or a mother to name herself a feminist."

Section III, "Contemporary Art and the Maternal: Articulating the Maternal Metaphor in Feminist Art," and Section V, "Finding the Maternal in the Visual Field: Practice, Narratives, Images," contain writing, artwork, text/image pieces, artists' statements, and performance scripts by women from all over the world who insist that they can be both mothers and feminists; the experience of feminist mothering is one that is so central to who they are that they deliberately choose to build a body of work around and about that identity. Section III includes art-historical writing and writings by artists about the articulation in art of subjectivity by mothers who are also artists. We felt it was fitting to begin this section with Nancy Gerber's reading of the work of Francine Christophe and Alice Lok Cahana, two daughters of the Holocaust whose written and visual work recovers the legacy of the lost mothers of the Holocaust. Fitting, because the experience of being a second-generation survivor of the

Holocaust influenced Suleiman, Hirsch, and Liss (whose first book was on Holocaust memorials) to write about motherhood and maternity.[25] In Mignon Nixon's epilogue to her 2005 book *Fantastic Reality: Louise Bourgeois and a Story of Modern Art,* Nixon discusses Bourgeois's relationship to Melanie Klein's theories, in her ability to depict the death drive within the mother-child relationship, and to use this as a rich resource for her art.[26] Nixon makes the important point that Bourgeois developed a body of work that drew upon—rather than denied—the dynamic of mothering children. For Nixon, Bourgeois's work that depicts maternal aggression from both the daughter's and mother's position exemplifies maternal ambivalence as a psychic position.

Many of the selections in Section III deal with art made about or during the 1970s, the era of second-wave feminism in which the personal was deemed political. Michelle Moravec's "Make Room for Mommy: Feminist Artists and My Maternal Musings" tells the story of Mother Art. Barbara T. Smith's "The Coffins" is a painful reflection on the breakup of her marriage and subsequent loss of custody of her children in the late 1960s, events that inspired her to make a number of Xerox books with her children's pictures.

We are pleased to include in this section writing by and about female artists outside of the United States. These demonstrate that the urge to create art about maternal identity was not limited to American artists but was an international phenomenon during this period. Mónica Mayer's "¡Madres!" describes the feminist artists' collective that she founded with Maris Bustamante in Mexico in the early 1980s, after completing the Feminist Art Program at the Woman's Building in Los Angeles, and less than a decade after Mother Art. This collective was known as Polvo de Gallina Negra (Black Hen Powder), a popular remedy for the evil eye, a curse often directed at nursing mothers and pampered babies whose supposed plenitude and satisfaction inspired envy. Using popular humor, the collective's agenda included the promotion of women's participation in contemporary art and the creation of feminist images in order to transform the visual world. Their most ambitious project, "¡Madres!," consisted of a series of mail art pieces and performances that took place over three years, beginning with Mayer's and Bustamante's pregnancies, and culminated in an appearance on Guillermo Ochoa's *Nuestro Mundo*, a popular daytime television show, where the host was dressed as a pregnant woman and named Mother for One Day. Assumpta Bassas Vila's article, very different in tone, discusses three Catalonian artists who began working in the 1970s—Fina Miralles, Eugenia Balcells, and Cori Mercadé—who approach maternal subjectivity from both the mother's and the daughter's position. Feeling the need to redress the absence of the mother in Franco's fascist patriarchal family, these women read between the lines of the traditional family album to document the violence and restraints against women, as they recover the grandmother, the sister and what Bassas Vila calls the maternal symbolic order. Both Jennie Klein and Margaret Morgan treat contemporary maternal art practices in their respective essays "Visualizing Maternity in Contemporary Art: Race, Culture, Class," and "Home Truths." In the former, Klein analyzes the accounts of African American, immigrant, Jewish and working-class mothers in the formally diverse work—ranging from handcrafted artists books to video and computer installations—of Youngbok Hong, Patricia Cué, Gail Rebhan, Myrel Chernick, and Camille Billops. Referencing popular culture and sociological studies, Klein discusses the conflicts between the immigrant mother's desire to assimilate while simultaneously maintaining ethnic and/or racial identity as well as the difficulty of being a "good" mother when one is neither white nor middle class. Complementing Klein's article are film stills from Camille Billops' *Finding Christa* (1991), a film about Billops' reunion with her daughter, whom she gave up for adoption at age four. The film attempts to preclude closure, even though Christa's need for closure is what motivated her to contact Billops in the first place. Morgan's essay considers how the work of Catherine Opie (*Self Portrait/Nursing* 2004 and the series *In and Around Home* 2005) and Andrea Bowers (*Nothing is Neutral* 2006) "speak the truth," countering and exposing the increasingly conservative political and social environment of the waning years of the Bush administration. Morgan uses the work of Bowers and Opie to imbricate maternity and domesticity into the specific socio-political context from which they draw their meaning.

Jane Gallop, author of *The Daughter's Seduction* (1982), concludes Section III with her essay "Observations of a Mother," a collaborative piece with her partner, the photographer Dick Blau.[27] Gallop situates her self-examination as a photographed mother within a group of family pictures. Working through a reading of Roland Barthes's description of the "subject becoming an object" in his book *Camera Lucida*, she moves back and forth between the feminist theorist as spectator and the mother as photographed subject. Her detailed observations describe both her pleasure in and resistance to adopting the role of "She who is photographed."[28]

Section V, "Finding the Maternal in the Visual Field: Practice, Narratives, Images," focuses on the mother-as-subject with a collection of writings and text-image pieces by mothers who are artists and feminists. We have attempted to include a multiplicity of voices, perspectives, and life stages since too often the ideological portrayal of motherhood is confined to mothers with young children and excludes those with adopted children. The writing included here suggests that one's identity as a mother is mutable and subject to reinterpretation. Section V includes a number of pieces that pick up where *Post-Partum Document* left off—the moment at which the child writes his name and establishes an identity within the symbolic order. Appropriately, much of this work deals with language, or the use of language. British performance artist Sylvia Ziranek, who has been doing work on domesticity, maternity, family life, and the color pink since the 1970s, is represented here by five performance poems that use language that is as wildly inventive as her pink performances. Ziranek is terribly normal, worrying about getting her son away from the screen, or feeding her finicky children (TAKE OMELETTES—WE DO, ONCE A WEEK OR SO, 2006). Sherry Millner and her daughter Nadja Millner-Larsen have collaborated on a piece created for this book, *Naming Nadja*, in which the grown-up Nadja responds to Millner's process of naming her after the character created by André Breton.

Myrel Chernick's short story "The Studio Visit" and text/image piece *Time Passes* are bookends to her experience as an artist and mother. In "The Studio Visit" the protagonist reflects on her work and domestic life as she struggles with the tensions of preparing her studio for a curator's visit. She manages to both punish and reward herself for her persistence in making art. In *Time Passes*, Chernick takes a nine-hour round-trip bus ride to Boston, where her son is at university, to see him for three brief hours. As he walks her back to the subway stop, it is clear to Chernick that the separation she both longed for and dreaded is now complete. In Ellen McMahon's "Art Between Us," a narrative about her daughter Alice's creative but stormy adolescence, we see McMahon torn between her roles as artist and mother. While she finds her daughter's extraordinary creativity fascinating, it also demonstrates how troubled Alice is; one night, after staying up late working, Alice overdoses on Tylenol and has to be rushed to the hospital. McMahon fears for her daughter's health and sanity yet admires, almost to the point of envy, Alice's extreme passion and creativity, which is so all-consuming it prevents McMahon from doing her own work.

Many of the pieces included in the book are concerned with the relationship between maternity, which is life-giving, and the death drive. Mignon Nixon has suggested that the power of Bourgeois's imagery lies in its embrace of the image of the mother as an aggressive and ambivalent figure. Maternal ambivalence rises as a psychic position from which the feminist artist can act. Maternal ambivalence is tied to the death drive, for "in extremis, Maternal ambivalence assumes the guise of mother death" (276). In Rachel Hall's memoir, "After Long Winter," illustrated with Sarah Webb's *Fat and Blood* series (2004), she grapples with the ambivalence of tending for a sick child, while remembering her own childhood experience of illness. Sarah Webb's "Milk and Tears: Performing Maternity" is about the meaning of breasts for Webb as she nursed her infant son while simultaneously nursing her mother-in-law through her unsuccessful battle with breast cancer. Webb discusses the work of Sarah Hutt and Sarah Slavick as well as her own *Milk and Tears*, an installation of diapers delicately embroidered in red thread with the words of Anne Sexton's poem "Dreaming the Breast."

Leslie Reid's affective writing mourns her sons' lost youth and expresses her deep ambivalence about their need and desire to grow and separate from her. Her photographs and paintings of ambiguous images of her children in light and shadow "evoke a dark side of her connectedness to her sons ... and recognition of both external and internal danger." Danielle Abrams, a New York-based artist and the lesbian daughter of an African-American father and a Jewish mother, channels both her black Southern grandmother and her Jewish grandmother in her performance script "On Mommas and Mothers." In "Pigeon Co-op or How I learned to respect my Mama," Abrams alternates between her father's point of view and her own, careening through pigeon coops and old photographs as she goes in search of the women who raised her father, Great and Aunt Liz. Abrams's tributes in these pieces to her grandmothers, including one she never knew, and to a mother her father barely knew, suggest the power of maternal desire, a desire that exceeds the culturally conditioned imperative to have a baby and become a mother.

The M Word includes three essays that directly address the topic of maternal desire. Christen Clifford, who writes about sex and maternity, exemplifies the mother as an aggressive and ambivalent figure. This version of her script for "BabyLove: How My Infant Son Became the Other Man," a ribald and hilarious performance she gave during the first few years of her son's life, is funny and ironic, but also unsettling in its frankness, especially when Clifford describes the all-consuming and overwhelming passion she has for her son, who replaces her husband as the object of her intense desire: "He knows I'm too into him. When I feed him, he pushes my face away. He wants the breast and the milk, not the mother." Laura Larson's "Hidden Mother" is a poignant meditation on the death of the artist's mother and the impending—but not yet finalized—adoption of Gadisse Larson, who quite possibly shares a birthday with Larson's mother. Larson knows Gadisse only from photographs and descriptions and writes to her as the not-yet-known child that she is now and as the teenager that she will become. As a photographer, Larson has documented Gadisse's absence, photographing ghostly arms and pubescent spiritual manifestations. In the winter of 2010, Larson was able to bring Gadisse home. She is presently working on a book about her experience, entitled *Hidden Mother*.

* * *

The M Word: Real Mothers in Contemporary Art is about the work of artists who are mothers and feminists and have made this the subject of their work. It is about maternal ambivalence, but it is also about maternal desire, a desire that plays itself out from outside of the institution of motherhood. When Laura Silagi first organized Mother Art, there were no other artist/mothers with whom she and the members of Mother Art could make common cause. When putting together this book, we felt that it was important to include as many artists as we could, in order to highlight the depth and diversity of work being created. The images reproduced in the book show the process of becoming—becoming-mother for the artists and becoming-other for the children. As such, they provide a counter-narrative to the texts included in this book—a counter-narrative that both supports and exceeds these texts.

The genesis of this book began many years ago, when both of us still had children living at home. At the time we collaborated on *Maternal Metaphors I* and *II*, we felt that we wanted to do something more lasting than a temporary exhibition. We wanted to put together an unconventional book that acknowledged the work that had been done on motherhood and visual culture in the years since Mother Art was founded, Mary Kelly finished *Post-Partum Document* (1978), and Susan Suleiman wrote her essay "Writing and Motherhood (1979).[29] As we worked on the book and as our children grew older, we thought it fitting to conclude with an essay written from the perspective of one of those children: Chernick's daughter Tanya Llewellyn, now grown up and herself a writer. In "Artist Mom," Llewellyn writes articulately about what it was like to have a mother who was an artist and a feminist. Llewellyn's text is echoed elsewhere in the book—whether it be the call and response of Millner and Nadja Millner-Larsen, the collaborative work between Mary Kelly and Kelly Barrie or Patricia Cué and her daughter Julia, the wisdom of Andrea Liss's son Miles, or the invocation of the mother through the daughter/granddaughter in the work of Abrams and Suleiman. These children are able to acknowledge the complicated maternal subjectivities presented here. It is our hope that this book will be the first of many on this topic and that mothers everywhere can relish their roles as speaking (and painting, drawing, photographing, and sculpting) subjects.

—Jennie Klein and Myrel Chernick, August 2010

Notes

[1]Andrea Liss, *Feminist Art and the Maternal* (Minneapolis: University of Minnesota Press, 2009), xvi.
[2]Laura Silagi, email to author, April 15, 2009.
[3]Ibid.
[4]Adrienne Cecile Rich, *Of Woman Born: Motherhood as Experience and Institution*, tenth anniversary ed. (New York: Norton, 1986); Jane Lazarre, *The Mother Knot* (1976; reprint Boston: Beacon Press, 1986). Adrienne Rich subsequently did a poetry reading at the Woman's Building in 1979.
[5]Susan Bee and Mira Schor, "*M/E/A/N/I/N/G* Forum: On Motherhood, Art, and Apple Pie" (1992), reprinted in *Mother Reader: Essential Writings on Motherhood*, ed. Moyra Davey (New York: Seven Stories Press, 2001), 200.
[6]Ibid., 205.
[7]Adrienne Rich's important book was published when second-wave feminism had already been around for more than a decade.
[8]Rosemary Betterton, "Promising Monsters: Pregnant Bodies, Artistic Subjectivity, and Maternal Imagination," *Hypatia* 21.1 (Winter 2006): 80-100; Mary Thompson, "Third Wave Feminism and the Politics of Motherhood," *Genders* 43 (2006): http://www.genders.org/g43/g43_marythompson.html, accessed 11/27/09. Tracy LeMaster, " M/Othering the Children," *Genders* 47 (2008): http://www.genders.org/g47/g47_lemaster.html, accessed 11/27/09; Shelly Cobb, "Mother of the Year," *Genders* 48 (2008): http://www.genders.org/g48/g48_cobb.html, accessed 11/27/2009: Jordana Aamalia, "Mad, Bad Mothers and the Deviant Event: Catherine Bell and the Maternal Instinct," *n.paradoxa* 22 (July 2008): 69-75; Andrea Liss, "Maternal Rites: Feminist Strategies," *n.paradoxa* 14 (July 2002): 24-31.
[9]Michèle Barrett and Bobby Baker, eds., *Bobby Baker: Redeeming Features of Daily Life* (Abingdon, Oxon: Routledge, 2007).
[10]Epp Buller's anthology includes essays by art historians, curators and artists and covers nineteenth- and twentieth-century art and visual culture.
[11]In 2003, Signe Theill curated *DoubleBind: Art/Children/Career* for Künstlerhaus Bethanien, Berlin. Myrel Chernick curated *Maternal Metaphors* for the Rochester

Contemporary Art Center in Rochester, New York. *Maternal Metaphors II*, which was expanded considerably from the original exhibition, was mounted at the Ohio University Art Gallery, Athens, Ohio, in 2006. In December 2009, A.I.R. Gallery in New York City mounted an exhibition on motherhood and the visual arts, *Mother/mother-**, curated by Jennifer Wroblewski (whose work with, and the work of several presenting artists, is included in this book).

[12]Sarah Earle and Gayle Letherby, eds., *Gender, Identity and Reproduction: Social Perspectives* (Basingstoke, Hampshire and New York: Palgrave Macmillan, 2003); Heléna Ragoné and France Winddance Twine, eds., *Ideologies and Technologies of Motherhood: Race, Class, Sexuality, Nationalism* (New York: Routledge, 2000); Sarah Boykin Hardy and Caroline Alice Wiedmer, eds., *Motherhood and Space: Configurations of the Maternal through Politics, Home, and the Body* (New York: Palgrave Macmillan, 2005).

[13]Suzanne Juhasz, "Mother-Writing and the Narrative of Maternal Subjectivity," *Studies in Gender and Sexuality* 4.4 (2003): 395-425.

[14]E. Ann Kaplan, *Motherhood and Representation* (London/New York: Routledge, 1992); Donna Bassin, Margaret Honey, and Meryle Mahrer Kaplan, eds., *Representations of Motherhood* (New Haven: Yale University Press, 1994).

[15]"Feminist Intertextuality and the Laugh of the Mother" was published in Susan Rubin Suleiman, *Subversive Intent* (Cambridge, MA: Harvard University Press, 1990), 141-180. "Writing and Motherhood" was included in Suleiman's collection of essays *Risking Who One Is: Encounters with Contemporary Art and Literature* (Cambridge, MA: Harvard University Press, 1994), 13-37.

[16]Suleiman, "On Maternal Splitting: A Propos of Mary Gordon's 'Of Men and Angels'," *Signs* 14.1 (Autumn 1988): 25-41; Raquelle Portillo Bauman, "Comment on Suleiman's 'On Maternal Splitting,'" *Signs* 15.3 (Spring 1990): 653-655; Susan Rubin Suleiman, "Reply to Bauman," *Signs* 15.3 (Spring 1990): 656-659. Suleiman included the exchange under the title "Motherhood and Identity Politics: An Exchange," in *Risking Who One Is*, 55-66.

[17]Ibid.

[18]Juliet Mitchell and Jacqueline Rose, eds., *Feminine Sexuality: Jacques Lacan and the école freudienne* (New York: W.W. Norton & Company, 1982), 31-32.

[19]Elizabeth Wright, ed., *Feminism and Psychoanalysis: A Critical Dictionary* (Oxford: Blackwell, 1992), 191-193.

[20]Marianne Hirsch, *Family Frames: Photography, Narrative, and Postmemory* (Cambridge, MA: Harvard University Press, 1997); Marianne Hirsch, ed., *The Familial Gaze* (Hanover, University Press of New England, 1999).

[21]Heather Addison, Mary Kate Goodwin-Kelly, and Elaine Roth, eds., *Motherhood Misconceived: Representing the Maternal in U.S. Films.* (Albany: State University of New York, 2009), 5.

[22]Imogen Tyler, "'Chav Mum, Chav Scum': Class Disgust in Contemporary

Britain," *Feminist Media Studies* 8.2 (June 2008): 17-34; "'Celebrity Chav': Fame, Femininity and Social Class," *European Journal of Cultural Studies* 13.3 (August 2010): 375-393.

[23]Dawn Memee Lavell-Harvard and Jeannette Corbiere Lavell, eds., *Until Our Hearts Are On the Ground: Aboriginal Mothering, Oppression, Resistance and Rebirth* (Bradford, ON: Demeter Press, 2006); May Friedman and Shana L. Calixte, eds., *Mothering and Blogging* (Bradford, ON: Demeter Press, 2009); Gina Wong, ed., *Moms Gone Mad* (Bradford, ON: Demeter Press, forthcoming 2011); Michelle Moravec, ed., *Mothers Online: How Online Communities Shape Modern Motherhood* (Bradford, ON: Demeter Press, forthcoming 2011); and Maki Motapanyane and Shana L. Calixte, eds., *Mothering and Hip-Hop Culture* (Bradford ON: Demeter Press, forthcoming 2011). For a complete list of Demeter Press titles, see http://www.demeterpress.org/.

[24]Originally published in *Evocative Objects*, Sherry Turkle, ed. (Cambridge, MA: MIT Press, 2007), 184-193.

[25]Andrea Liss, *Trespassing Through Shadows: Memory, Photography, and the Holocaust* (Minneapolis: University of Minnesota Press, 1998).

[26]Mignon Nixon, *Fantastic Reality: Louise Bourgeois and a Story of Modern Art* (Cambridge, MA: MIT Press, 2005).

[27]"Observations of a Mother" was originally published in Hirsch, ed., *The Familial Gaze*, 67-84. Gallop's by now infamous book, which engaged with the writing of Lacan and various texts by French feminists, was published by Cornell University Press as *The Daughter's Seduction: Feminism and Psychoanalysis* (1982) and by London Macmillan as *Feminism and Psychoanalysis: The Daughter's Seduction*. We thought it was fitting that Gallop's article ends with Gallop's daughter Ruby, who has so seduced her mother that Gallop includes Ruby's image in spite of having no particular reason to do so.

[28]Roland Barthes, *Camera Lucida: Reflections on Photography*, trans. Richard Howard (New York: Hill and Wang, 1981), 14.

[29]Susan Suleiman first presented "Writing and Motherhood" at the MLA convention in San Francisco in December 1979, the first time she wrote (or even thought seriously) about motherhood in a personal way. The essay was first published in 1985, in a volume titled *The (M)other Tongue: Essays in Feminist Psychoanalytic Interpretation*, ed. Shirley Nelson Garner, Claire Kahane and Madelon Sprengnether (Ithaca, NY: Cornell University Press, 1985), 352-377. E-mail to Myrel Chernick, September 9, 2009.

I.

Conversations and Questions

MARY KELLY AND MARGARET MORGAN

On Love, Politics and Fallen Shoes

Margaret Morgan in Conversation with Mary Kelly

MARGARET MORGAN: IN REEXAMINING YOUR work, I was struck by how important the maternal is to all of it, not just *Post-Partum Document*,[1] but also the work that is ostensibly far removed from the maternal. I was also struck by how varied the maternal's configuration is throughout. So that the *Document* seems the most intensely, and intimately, inward-looking, if you like, and at different points the work then expands outwards, as in the case of *Interim* (1984–89), or *The Ballad of Kastriot Rexhepi* (2001), yet there's always this recurring relationship to the maternal. Do you agree?

MARY KELLY: Absolutely. The maternal is at the center of what I would call the critical inquiry. Kristeva suggests that one of the meanings of "revolt" is *a return*, in the psychoanalytic sense; you return to the past to engage in a process of self-reflection or self-criticism. And when I started working, which was in the wake of excitement produced by the "events of 1968," I remember thinking—I was in art school at the time—that the idea of interrogating the object was inevitably leading to questions that went beyond this to the interrogation of the interrogation itself, and, well, I thought the other shoe would simply fall: subjectivity was going to be part of that project.

MM: So, if Joseph Kosuth and Terry Atkinson and other conceptual artists were at the time addressing the structures of art and language and the role of social and institutional contexts, it seemed self-evident, to you, that subjectivity, and the fundamental role of language in forming it, would be interrogated.

MK: Yes, but as it turned out, this wasn't evident in the art context at all. The questions of sexuality, identity, were informed mainly by the politics of the women's movement.

MM: It was ironic that the artists who were interrogating the interrogation, by addressing linguistic structure, were unable to "take the next step," if you like, in their own logic and look at the acquisition of language as integral to the mother-child dyad, which was the basis of the *Document.*

MK: In your opening remarks, you described the *Document* as being somehow less in the world than later works. I can see where that comes from, because you're left historically with the physical forms, the material forms of the work, in which the autobiographical narrative is a central part of the signifying system. But I might think of that moment myself as being *more* in the world, you know, in the sense that the urgency of the question was immediately felt, as something imposed by a much broader context: *I was in it with other women, it was bigger than we were*, and *why hadn't anyone thought about what this meant?* Most women had children and their lives were totally determined by it, but if you looked at art history, representations of the mother-child relationship were *always* from the point of view of an observer. Even with (Mary) Cassatt, you would *look* at the woman; it would be part of the *picture* of maternal femininity.

MM: Cassatt painted and drew portraits of women and children, though she herself was not a mother.

MK: There was no interrogation of that subjectivity, nothing that gave a voice to the woman as *subject.* So my interest in psychoanalysis really came from that political urgency, you know, from trying to find a discourse that had as its appropriate object something like feminine sexuality. I mean, the object of psychoanalysis is the unconscious, but you have no unconscious without sexuality. In *Post-Partum Document*, running parallel to the autobiographical narrative, there is always another kind of interrogation, one that is informed by what I call the "discursive site." At that time, it was the debate about psychoanalysis in the women's movement in London, where I was living then. So the esoteric reworkings or revisions of the Lacanian diagrams represent a moment when we were trying to describe what was being experienced here, in that symbiotic relationship with the child, and how the trauma of separation, once it was mapped onto the traditional schema of the subject unfolding in the field of the other—identification, castration, and so on—would reveal something unique about the way maternal femininity is formed. What is unique about maternal femininity?

MM: Can I ask what it meant for you personally? At that time?

MK: Well, it all hangs out. I mean, in the *Document* I didn't exactly bury my subjective investment. I let the theoretical reworking run parallel to the diaries rather than explain or obscure them. Once my son said, when he read the *Document*, "That doesn't sound like the mother that

I knew." I guess there's a lot of worrying in the narrative. "Did I get it right?" and "Oh, this school is absolutely horrible!" and "I haven't got enough money to protect him from this." Every parent knows you don't tell the child that. You just say, "Trust me, everything will be all right," even though you think it's all going to fall apart the next day. So that fragile sense of being able to protect, control, or make the child "be what I want him to be" is always being negotiated. What it meant for me is obvious. You can read it in the diaries.

MM: Yes, I would like to touch upon this. You lived in a commune then, didn't you?

MK: Yes, three other women and myself set up this household, and their partners, men included, could live there if they abided by the collective rules. You know, we thought the family was going to wither away like the state in those days! We shared the housework and, to some extent, childcare responsibilities. One of my friends had a child, and we would help each other, but those in the commune without children definitely didn't pull their weight. And here was the most interesting discovery: I didn't want them to anyway. Everyone was saying, "You have to wean him because we can't help if you're breastfeeding," and "You can't sleep all night unless he has a bottle"—this sort of thing. So I did wean him, but I think kind of prematurely, you know, after about four months, and then, I cried. But of course that helped me to understand there was more to it than the sociologically oriented tendency within the women's movement had claimed (I mean those who thought it was just about demanding wages for housework). They argued that discrimination was an effect of the sexual division of labor, but the psychological dimension was missing. So the commune was important because it helped me to ask why, if someone else was willing to get up in the middle of the night, well, why didn't I want him to? Why did I want to be the privileged other? What kind of pleasure was at stake here? Then, there it was in Lacan: the earliest moment of the mirror phase, which he describes in the developmental sense as an Imaginary captation. And I thought, yes, that's exactly how it is for the mother, too. The world doesn't seem real. Here I am trying to read the newspaper, but it makes no sense to me.

MM: In that period, especially before weaning from the breast, there is a palpable physiological link, an incredibly powerful force, in the mother-child dyad that seems almost to produce the mother as fragmented, broken up, *not herself.*

MK: Verging on a kind of psychosis.

MM: It is.

MK: Of course, that's where Freud first found the symptoms of the neuroses and psychoses: in everyday life. There's a very fine line here. You know, I didn't start *Post-Partum Document* until he was six months. I couldn't do anything before that.

MM: It's retrospective. Could you talk about that process?

MK: Well, with *Documentation I*, I took down what I was feeding him, as the doctors told me, but I made that more obsessive—every hour, every day for three months. Then it took me about two years after the event to look at it from a distance, to try to analyze it and give it a visual form. It was the same process for all six parts, and I didn't predict the ending. It was only in *Documentation VI*, when he wrote his name, that I felt I couldn't go on. I thought: he's the author of his own text now—a kind of superstition that to pursue this would be madness.

MM: For both parties.

MK: Not that your attachment to the child suddenly ends, but it's transformed, radically—more like watching at a distance.

MM: Yes, that's right.

MK: So this separation is, classically, I suppose, what you would call castration. The demand for which there is no object, you know, there's nothing you can specularize. Probably the most profound discovery, from a theoretical point of view, if I could claim anything like that, is found in *Documentation IV*, where I describe something like the *fort-da* game for the mother, that is, how she tries to conceptualize the child's absence. First, she hangs on—"you're still my baby"—then lets go—"you're so grown-up now." But, I asked myself, what is it that she's really afraid of losing, you could say, beyond the child's body? It seemed to be about the pleasure of being like her own mother. And more. There's an imagined closeness to the body of another woman that produces a kind of incestuous *jouissance*. Around this time, Montrelay published an article in which she proposed a concentric, or archaic, oral/anal organization of the drives as the woman's stake in symbolic castration and the condition for her access to sublimated pleasure.[2] This made a lot of sense, at the time, in terms of my understanding of maternal femininity, because it made a distinction between repression of the mother's body and a form of censorship in which she retains an anxious proximity to the first object. So I thought I was onto something.

MM: Formally speaking, what was the most difficult part of the *Document*?

MK: *Documentation V* was a hard one. He would bring me a snail and say, "Do you have a hole in your tummy?" I couldn't figure it out. What did they have to do with each other? Finally, I juxtaposed the questions and the specimens with a kind of non-answer in the form of fragments of a diagram representing a full-term pregnancy and a list of medical terms. You know, Piaget says children always ask sexual questions first, and then they try to figure out the order of the universe. But what it meant in my universe, I guess, is that he was finding out that I didn't have the phallus; in other words, I wasn't this powerful person who could meet all his demands, and in fact, I probably was going to be *demoted* once he put me in the social order of things [laughter]. And that did happen. You know, at school they asked him what his father did and he said, "He's an artist." But when they asked him what his mother did, he said, "I don't know."

MM: [laughter] Oh, that's fascinating.

MK: Then I started to think about the mother as the "Real Other," the unrepresentable supplement that breeds the *object a* as Lacan says. No one occupies this position, but it's the site of many projections. Say, if you go home to see your mother and she doesn't listen to *you* and talks about herself instead, you're so pissed off.

MM: Right, right. And, for many people, that's taken up by the therapist or the analyst.

MK: [laughter] I guess we all have to make our peace with the impossibility of forging a path back to the first object.

MM: So can you talk a little about your current experience of this maternal role—I mean, your son is a grown man—and if we can project a little bit, the role of your students in *Love Songs* (2005–07), the work you exhibited in *Documenta XII*. Do you think it represents, perhaps in displaced form, your relationship with the adult child?

MK: Certainly, the issue of generations is central to that work. I was archiving the recollections of women like me who were activists in the late sixties and comparing them with the comments of those like my students, my son, and you, of course, who were born around '68 and after. I started to notice their preoccupation with social movements of that time, what they seemed to know about it intuitively, what they thought they missed, and then I began to see the past more from the point of view of its construction in the present.

MM: A fictive past?

MK: Not exactly ... more like an imaginary investment in the political legacy. This provoked me to ask what, if anything, is passed on from one generation to the next after the *specific* demands of that moment have passed. I wouldn't describe this as nostalgia either. It's more like a form of intuitive knowledge based on words, gestures, or even silences in the family's interactions that the child somehow decodes as parental desire.

Mary Kelly, *Love Songs*, 2005–07. Installation, Neue Galerie, *Documenta XII,* Kassel.

There's the sexual mystery of conception, Freud's *primal scene,* which prompts the child's question: "Where did I come from?" I thought, in a similar way, this return to the sixties concerned a myth of origins in the social and historical sense, so I decided to call the psychic disposition that underlies it the *political primal scene.* As I went on in my work, I got more interested in the phylogenetic contents of the unconscious. After all, Freud said it was sometimes legitimate to consider the way the child fills in the gaps in his or her own experience with the events of "ancestors." Perhaps this is also what Benjamin had in mind when he referred to "a secret agreement between past generations and the present one."[3] But I'm not suggesting some notion of a collective unconscious here. You could say *Post-Partum Document* deals with the endogenous or developmental sense of the subject taking a place within the order of language and culture, and in later works like *Mea Culpa* [1999], and the *Ballad of Kastriot Rexhepi* [2001], which deal with war and trauma, you see the impression of the past, I mean an exogenous system of meaning pre-existing the subject, what comes to you from the outside world. For instance, in one of the narratives of *Mea Culpa*, about Sarajevo, a mother asks, "What will we do?" And her son, who is only four, says, "Slit their throats." I thought, well, how does a child get this precise terminology at that age?

MM: Perhaps beliefs and attitudes a child gleans informally, are expressed in more extreme form by the child precisely because they are not subject to the usual taboos or constraints around expression as when, say, a parent actively teaches a child and in doing so also teaches the child the bounds of propriety, of either good manners or caution.

MK: That's true, and I recall Lacan pointing out that it's not so much what the parents actively teach or what they say that intrigues the child, but "Why are they telling me this?" I've collected a lot of things people have told me that illustrate the phantasmatic way we "fill in the gaps." For example, someone said, "My grandmother never held me when I was a baby, and I knew it was because my mother was Polish," and another, referring to orthodox Judaism, told me, "There were these books we weren't supposed to read as kids, but we all knew what was in them, anyway." But how? Not from *reading*, hardly even through gestures and innuendo, but something is *passed on,* probably as the enigma of the parental desire and, inevitably, as a scenario of failure because the Other is always found "lacking." Let's take, for example, the moment of '68: a young woman I was working with on the *Multi-Story House* project [2007] said, "I'm sorry that my parents weren't part of the German student movement, but now I'm trying to be more revolutionary."

So I wasn't only interested in how *this* generation constructed the past, but what that meant for mine.

MM: In constructing the future?

MK: No, no, in *my* return. This traces a path back to what I was initially saying about continual self-critique. When I return to the past, it's not that I go back there and say this was the greatest thing that ever happened, although I *would* say there's something really ecstatic about being with other women, a sense of...

MM: Possibility, agency.

MK: Yes, possibility *and* pleasure. But when I look back at this moment of euphoria in the present context, I have to ask myself how it's really that different from other fanatical or messianic experiences. It has many of the same features. So what was specific about feminism? When Rancière talks about becoming a political subject, he emphasizes the importance of a process called disidentification.[4] Let's just think of this as something like: "Okay, I'm no longer going to be the woman who stays at home or the worker who accepts those wages," and this process is followed by making a demand on behalf of all women, all workers. Some people have problems with this, but the best example I can give in the current context—because you can't *make* this happen, it depends on so many things—is that of Cindy Sheehan when she says, "I am not going to be a 'good mother' and accept my son's death in Iraq." And then, "*We,* as mothers, do not want our sons to go to war." So suddenly she becomes the center of the anti-war protest because she can make a demand on behalf of the Other. To get back to my question about feminism, I think there was something very specific about the way demands were formulated within the women's movement because there was an insistence on everyone having a voice and an aversion to hierarchical forms of organization. In this sense, it differed significantly from the usual tactics on the left.

MM: In the film loop, *WLM Demo Remix* [2005] that was shown in the *Love Songs* installation, I see the clearest evidence of this.

MK: Yes, the demonstration we were restaging took place in New York City in 1970. It was the 50th Anniversary of the 19th Amendment. When we were talking during the set-up—I think of this not only as a physical location, but also an emotional point that exists in the space between the original archival image and its technical reproduction—talking about the demands of the movement at that time, everyone agreed there was no way we could go out there and say, "Abortion on demand," right now. Who would we be representing? And we weren't going to say, "Free childcare for all," either. I mean, we couldn't imagine anything "free" in this economy! But what does endure has much more to do with the transformative potential of that event—a certain relation to what you might call knowledge or truth.

MM: In the restaging?

MK: No, no, I mean, what's left. What's left of that moment in the women's movement is a legacy of personal transformation, which I call epistemological so that I can separate it from trauma and effects of the unconscious order. Here I'm thinking of Alain Badiou's concept of "event."[5] Something out of the ordinary "happens." You're aware of being changed by it, but don't know where it's going. In spite of this, you feel committed to the consequences, and that he calls "fidelity." Going back to the beginning of our talk, you remember I said that in the *Document* there was this commitment to a conceptualist notion of interrogation, but one informed by feminism, and that proposing subjectivity as the object of that inquiry was like letting the other shoe fall. Well, the shoes continued to fall—from maternal femininity to the question of masculinity and then, from war and trauma to resistance and political euphoria. But then I discovered that I had come full circle, so to speak, back to the origin of my project, and saw its trajectory as a certain kind of fidelity to the consequences of an event. The logic of that trajectory is really encapsulated in the famous slogan of May '68: "No right to speak without *les enquêtes*." So you could say what happens with *Love Songs* is like an interrogation of the etiology of my project, where all the earlier stuff came from, at least that's what it means for me.

MM: Oh, that's really interesting. So my sense of the *Document* being a very internal, inward-looking, intense thing is actually opened up. Could you say more here to connect with *Love Songs*?

MK: I tell my students, "I am not your mother, my love is conditional," [laughter] but secretly I absolutely adore them. And so there's a lot of transference going on here. My feelings towards the group of women I was working with on the remixes (*WLM Demo* and *Flashing Nipple* [2005]) was ... ah, intensely personal. You know, I brought some of my '70s clothes in for props and ended up giving my favorite jacket to one of them!

MM: That's hilarious. A literal sort of passing on of the mantle.

MK: Yes, that's right. And you know in the work how I—in the DVD, I changed the placard in the fade-out from "Unite for women's emancipation" to an obscure line from Sylvia Plath: "From stone to cloud."

MM: From "Love Letter"?

MK Yes, the last stanza goes:

Tree and stone glittered, without shadows.
My finger-length grew lucent as glass.
I started to bud like a March twig:
An arm and a leg, an arm, a leg.
From stone to cloud, so I ascended.
Now I resemble a sort of god,
Floating through the air in my soul-shift.
Pure as a pane of ice. It's a gift.[6]

MM: It is extraordinary. Is it elegiac for them or for you?

MK: In a way, for me, their coming of age as feminists is like a gift.

MM: Yes, yes, absolutely.

MK: I was also thinking about the pleasure, for women, of being together, both now and in the past, and wondering what kind of function this had in the realm of the political.

MM: You thought it was funny though, too: the show, the work, *Love Songs*.

MK: You're right. The humor *is* important in all the works, but especially in the drawings for the *Happening* [2008]. They made me laugh out loud when I was making them. But it's the kind of laughter that's sheer joy.

MM: Yes, yes. And it puts "love" smack-dab into the center of the political.

MK: You know, it's just ridiculous. But often, when you're in love it's like that. I mean, you can't stop smiling, and you feel like an idiot really.

MM: That's right, that's right.

—January 19, 2007

Notes

[1]Mary Kelly, *Post-Partum Document* (London: Routledge, 1983).

[2]Michele Montrelay, "Inquiry into Femininity," *m/f* 1 (1978): 83-101.

[3]Walter Benjamin, *Walter Benjamin: Selected Writings*, Vol. 4, eds. Howard Eiland and Michael W. Jennings (Cambridge: Belknap Press, 1940), 390.

[4]Jacques Rancière, *The Politics of Aesthetics*, trans. Gabriel Rockhill (London: Continuum: 2004).

[5]Alain Badiou, "The Matheme of the Event," in *Being and Event*, trans. Oliver Feltham (London: Continuum, 2006), 178-184.

[6]Sylvia Plath, *Collected Poems*, ed. Ted Hughes (London: Faber and Faber, 2002), 129.

MARY KELLY

Excerpts from *Post-Partum Document*

PPD 1976 REF. I–8T

Documentation IV
Transitional objects, diary and diagram

In this document, 'transitional objects' refer to the child's comforter ('blankie') and to the plaster 'hand plaques' which constitute part of the mother's 'memorabilia' (reminiscent of baby's first photos, shoes, lock of hair, etc.). The clay imprints were initiated as an extension of the child's play activities at the nursery school between the age of 2.5–2.9. The diary texts, inscribed on the comforter fragments, were recorded at irregular intervals between January and May 1976. They functioned on the one hand as a confessional, expressing the mother's ambivalence about 'working outside the home,' and on the other, as a polemic, interrogating the familiar theme of 'separation anxiety' by placing emphasis on the consequences for the mother rather than the child.

The inclusion of Schema R within the discourse of Documentation IV summarises and, to a certain extent subverts, its use in Experimentum Mentis I-III. The diagram, which is stamped on the hand imprints, does not correspond literally to the diary texts in the sense of illustrating the subject's history. It unfolds as a representation of the static states of the subjects (S) within the fields of the Imaginary, the Symbolic and the Real.

- (I) the Imaginary; including (a) the figure of the Imaginary other of the Mirror stage, (a´) the paternal imago (ø) the Imaginary object, i.e., the phallus.
- (S) the Symbolic; including (M) the signifier of the primordial object (I) the Ideal of the ego (P) the Name-of-the-Father in the locus of the Other (A)
- (R) the Real; framed and maintained by the relations of the Imaginary and the Symbolic (the Real cannot be articulated but remains as a kind of residue of articulation, fore-closed to representation as such).

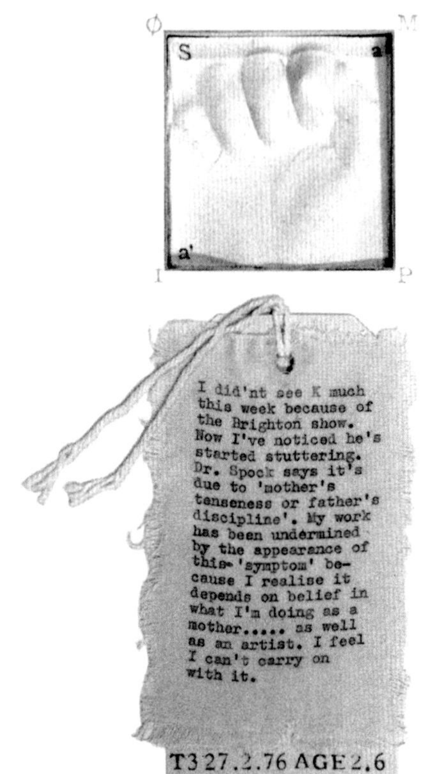
Ø
M
S
a
a'
I
P
I did'nt see K much
this week because of
the Brighton show.
Now I've noticed he's
started stuttering.
Dr. Spock says it's
due to 'mother's
tenseness or father's
discipline'. My work
has been undermined
by the appearance of
this 'symptom' be-
cause I realise it
depends on belief in
what I'm doing as a
mother..... as well
as an artist. I feel
I can't carry on
with it.
T3 27.2.76 AGE 2.6

PPD 1977 REF. I–8T

Experimentum Mentis IV
On femininity

At the Oedipal moment, the mother, father and child inhabit a closed field of desire. But for the mother, the distancing function of the father uncovers the source of narcissistic satisfaction which is sustained by her Imaginary object, the child as phallus. This is the pleasure of maternal femininity. *The site of this excavation is precisely the corporeal reality of the child's body (the soft, round, perfectly formed body of* her *baby), because the pleasure she derives from it must be relinquished. This loss is pre-ordained on the one hand by the natural process of maturation, and, on the other, by the prohibitions of the Father and the Law. The Oedipal melodrama is staged as a maternal version of the Fort/Da game, 'How grown up you are' / 'You're still my baby,' or elided as in Documentation* IV, *T1, 'You're not a baby but a grown-up boy' (i.e., 'I* wish *you were still my baby but…').*

This moment is decisive if her child is a boy since the prohibition to incest is insured by the threat of castration. However, the mother-daughter relationship is more ambivalent because the girl enters the Oedipal situation in retreat rather than in confrontation, in hope of receiving the phallus from her father, eventually in the form of a child. To achieve this end, she must identify herself with her own mother and take up a position of lack. *This process of identification with the ideal type of her sex makes it possible for a woman to see herself as desirable, to enter into a sexual relationship with a man and to satisfy the needs of the child produced by this relationship; but it also introduces her to the pleasure of having the mother's body, cathecting her own body as that of her mother (or of another woman). Beyond the pleasure of the real of the child's body lies the pleasure of the maternal body experienced as real through it; the loss of this pleasure constitutes the ultimate threat to the mother's narcissism. Her 'memorabilia' and the child's 'transitional objects' are* emblems *which testify to the threatened loss of mutual enjoyment, but the desire in which they are grounded can only be caused in the unconscious by the specific structure of the phantasy.*

When the mother anxiously poses the question, 'What do you want?(!)' in response to her child's whining, aggressive or clinging complaints, she is essentially asking herself, 'What does he/she want of me?' The child's demand constitutes the mother as the Other who has the privilege of satisfying his/her needs and, at the same time, the whimsical power of depriving him/her of this satisfaction. To a certain extent the mother recognises the unconditional element of demand as a demand for love. It is this recognition which underlies her feeling of 'ultimate responsibility' for the child even when the sexual division of labour in childcare is radically altered to include the father.

But there is another cause for this asymmetry which is not necessarily given at the level of consciousness. This is the mother's desire to remain the privileged Other of the pre-Oedipal instance, in so far as the child's demands are the guarantee of her maternal femininity. *Thus, she transforms the child's gifts into proofs of love and his/her indiscretions into denials. In this situation it is difficult for the child to locate his/her desire. Finally, it is the Law, of which the Father is the original representative, that intervenes to insure the autonomous status of desire; i.e., to substitute for the unconditional element in the demand for love, the absolute condition of desire. Paradoxically this implies a detachment which is the minimum condition for the Oedipal child's unsolicited expression, as in Documentation* IV, *T5, 'I love you, Mummy.' Through the child's words, 'the real' of the mother's body is represented as signifier of the real Other in the register of the Symbolic.*

PPD 1977–8 REF. 3.50Ix–4.515B

Documentation VI
Pre-writing alphabet, exerque and diary

The formative phase in which the child began to read and write was documented over a period of 18 months from January 1977 to April 1978. During this time (age 3.5–4.8) he started to identify certain letter shapes and map out a system of markings related to the traditional alphabet. Notations were made on his observations following 'ABC sessions' (i.e., reading from favourite alphabet books as part of the bed-time story repertoire), and the documentation was concluded when he began to write his own name. At the same time he entered infants' school, an event which was equally significant for the mother because the learning process, once assumed to be a 'private' discourse, was then clearly seen to be determined by an institutional context.

This documentation is inscribed on slates and set out in chronological order. Each inscription is divided into three registers (analogous to the Rosetta Stone (with the Child's 'hieroglyphic' letter-shapes (pre-writing alphabet) in the upper portion; the mother's print-script commentary (exerque) in the middle section and her type-script narrative (diary) in the lower part.

Alphabet

The letter shapes deciphered in these inscriptions do not constitute a logical alphabet (there are 15 figures beginning with x and ending in B rather than 26 from A to Z); but they do demonstrate the child's propensity to develop a system of graphic representation.

Pre-writing succeeds a mode of purposeful scribbling which already includes diagrammatic markings such as crosses and circles. At this moment the significant difference is that the child's expressed intention in making these marks is *writing*. The x, called 'a cross,' ref. 3.501x constitutes a kind of universal grapheme class. It is virtually the functional equivalent of all letters, as the commentary indicates, 'he substitutes different letter names for the same mark'; as yet, the child does not recognise the distinctive features which are necessary to distinguish one letter or grapheme class from another. In ref. 6.6020, the distinctive feature of o, curvedness, displays an optimal contrast with the straight lines (ascenders) of x. o is generally associated with anything round, but at the same time it designates a more specific letter category than x in so far as when he writes o, he calls it 'a round **and an o.**' The development of a graphemic system follows from this initial opposition of marks, but it is ultimately dependent upon filling in the gaps between x and o. The first split occurs on the side of curvedness between the closedness of o and the openness of e, ref. 3.6030. At this point an extensive number of variations or graphs are included in the grapheme class e but together with x and o, they comprise a triangle defining the distinctive features closedness-openness on the horizontal axis and straightness-curvedness on the vertical axis.

x

o e

In turn, straightness is distinguished by symmetry, x, versus asymmetry, r. The grapheme r, called 'a hook,' ref. 3.704r, also introduces curvedness into this category and by an extension of the 'hook' produces n and m. Next the ascender l is marked by the addition of a feature-i which he calls 'a dot and an i,' ref. 3.805i, and c, significantly unnamed, ref. 3.806c, is marked by the addition of ascenders and descenders b, d, p, q, 'a round and a straight,' ref. 3.908p, thus combining the distinctive features of bothes axes of the triangle.

Then capital letter configurations arise from combinations, additions or substractions of ascenders; first placing an emphasis on the distinctive feature straightness as in E, F, 'a straight one and another straight one,' ref. 3.909E, and later introducing curvedness as in R, ref. 4113R. This is followed by the letters K and B, ref. 4.414K–4.515B, which are constructed with the specific intention of writing his own name. By this time the child's discrimination of distinctive features is adequate enough to categorise most letters of the alphabet and designate them by a spoken name. In addition, he recognises that letters such as E and e constitute alternatives for a single grapheme class and that although they have no distinctive features in common, they are equated when identifying a letter category in reading. The concept of reading also implies directionality; as is evidenced in ref. 4.515K, the child's name is insistently printed from left to right, and significantly, previous inversions and reversals of letters such as ə q ɔ are corrected in this process. As a result his letters effectively represent the minimal contrasts necessary to distinguish a word in writing and at this moment his 'writing' articulates the letter as a material locus, a visual configuration, a concept and a category name.

Exerque

The commentary and quotations set out below the child's inscription, identify the letter as material support of a concrete discourse. Within this space emphasis is placed on the intersubjective relations between mother and child in the act of reading and writing. Thus the gaps, omissions and inversions of the pre-writing alphabet are crucial for the mother in deciphering the child's text. His incipient agraphia—the provocative ə, ref. 3.603e, the unspoken ɔ, ref. 3.806c, the overstated E, ref. 4.012H, in so far as it is symptomatic of a resistance to the repression of Oedipal sexuality, implicates the mother and gives a place to her phantasies as well as those of the child. In this sense the intertextuality of alphabet and exerque efface the distinction between an object-letter and a subject who deciphers it. The hieroglyphic residue of the child's letter-shapes—the ideographic x, ref. 3.051x, the pictographic i, ref. 3.805i, the phonographic s, ref. 3.1111s—undermine a notion of the alphabet as absolute representation, i.e., as a system of arbitrary signs purged of all figurative regressions.

On the one hand, the repression, condensation and displacement of graphemic signifiers in the child's text suggest a writing anterior to speech, an insistence of the letter in the discourse of the unconscious which is resistant to signification as such. And on the other hand, the graphic rhetoric of children's books referred to in the mother's annotations to the child's script, such as A is for apple, B is for balloon, C is for cake, etc., implies a certain coagulation of the signified, underlining the logocentric bias of the system of language to which the letter ultimately subscribes; a system that privileges naming and the proper name and that pronounces the beginning of writing with the child's inscription of his father's name.

Diary

The diary narrative inserts the intersubjective discourse of the letter into a complex of institutional practices and systems of representation which produce the social subordination of the mother. First, there is the representation of a specific socio-economic category. The diary events surrounding the child's entry into infants' school 'take place' in an urban, industrial, multi-racial, working-class area of the inner city often designated as disadvantaged or 'deprived,' ref. 3.8060c. In sociological rhetoric, 'disadvantage' is constituted by a signifying chain of percentages concerning one-parent families, working mothers, low income, poor housing, inadequate transport, overcrowded schoools, accidents, disease, pollution, illiteracy and crime. The place the mother occupies as an effect of the signifying chain is inevitably that of failure or at best a victim of circumstance; but the position she takes up in the process of representing this place to herself is by no means fixed as one of resignation; in ref. 3.704r, it is resistance, in ref. 3.908p, denial, in ref. 3.1111s, disassociation. Ultimately, it is not the mother's hopes, aspirations and ambitions for her child that are lacking, but the possibility of their realisation which is circumscribed by the economic constraints, social practices and political effects of separation from the means of production, possession and 'advantage.'

Second, there is the construction of the agency of the mother/housewife. In this position the mother is assigned certain responsibilities, moral attributes and legal statuses by the education authority. For instance, in ref. 4.414K, the form of address employed by the headmistress, i.e., 'Mrs,' at once confirms the parent's legal status as wife and her moral attribute as mother, implying the child's 'legitimacy.' It is to this agent/addressee that the school sends all memoranda concerning the dates of term, of holidays, the requirements for school outings, bazaars and benefits, the cost of school dinners, the rules and regulations concerning absenteeism, tardiness, fires, floods, the lending of library books, and the lending of a helping hand, such as supervising the playgroup, ref. 3.501x.

In addition the local health authority, in collaboration with the school, administer a medical service which consists primarily of monitoring the child's health (illnesses, immunisation, physical growth, mental progress and general social adjustment), and which designates the mother as guarantor of his well-being. This process of surveillance is epitomised by the yearly check-up, ref. 3.909E, and the mother's attendance is 'strongly advised.' Unavoidably the child's symptom is read as a sign of her capacity/incapacity to fulfill the agency of the mother/housewife at the level of the attributes deemed essential to that agency such as common sense, practicality and discipline mediated by an intimate, 'natural' bond with the child. However, the mother never sufficiently corresponds to the agency this institutional discourse defines and that is demonstrated by the father's participation in the realisation (also always partial) of those capacities, for instance when the mother is working, ref. 4.113R. Nor does the father ever conform to the agency of the father/husband fulfilling the function of the breadwinner or possessing a 'natural' aptitude for authority, etc. On the one hand, there is often conflict between the husband and wife over responsibility for the child, ref. 4.414K, but on the other hand there is unmitigated deference shown by both parents towards the assumed authority of the headmistress/teacher in matters concerning childcare, ref. 3.807m. Thus the mother's secondary social status is not necessarily a result of the subordination of women by men, but rather it is an effect of the position occupied as the agent of childcare within the legal, moral, medical and pedagogic discourses of the educational institution. But there is a difference for the mother with respect to that position because these discourses also assign a place to the child which radically displaces her representation of him as part of herself. Consequently, the school becomes the site of a struggle for 'possession' of the child; it is a struggle the mother always loses and it is this sense of 'loss' which produces a specific form of subordination for the woman in her capacity as the mother/housewife.

(age 3.6) e IS FOR ELEPHANT. He calls it
the "curvy one" and pronounces it – "eeh".
He often forgets it and sometimes writes
it upside-down "ə". When he sees an e,
a present or a breast, he says, "What's that?"
Something at once lost, forgotten, remembered
and hoped for. "ə" as in "me." E IS FOR AL-
LIGATORS ENTERTAINING ELEPHANTS. E IS
FOR AN EAGLE ON AN ELEPHANT IN AN EGG
AND SPOON RACE. GOOD NIGHT EDWARD ELMER
ELEPHANT. GOOD NIGHT LITTLE E.
22.1977: I noticed the general conditions
then the children this time, like the rubbish
outside the building and the dust inside. When I washed
the cups the rag looked so grey I couldn't bring myself
to use it. But I suppose they do the best they can,
it isn't their own space, its only rented during the
day from a boys club. There's no playground and the
children have to stay indoors. All but about 20 mins
of the 2 hrs. is 'unstructured' and seems to get out of
hand. I'm afraid they'll get hurt. I can't stand the bad
grammar after about an hour of it – I can't believe I
could be so uptight and pretentious. I feel inadequate
because I can't offer Kelly more. I wish he could
to a good school, but it's hopeless in this area.
went to the Social Services Dept.
demanded the addresses of proper nursery schools.
They just smiled and refused, saying it would be of no
use since all of them had at least a 2 yr. waiting list.
3.603e

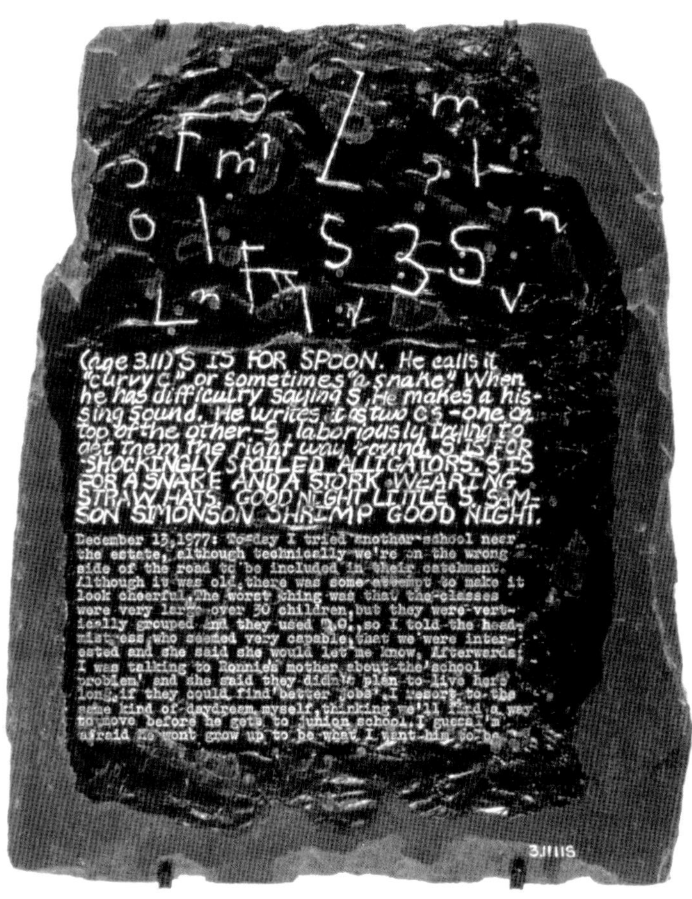
(age 3.11) S IS FOR SPOON. He calls it
"curvy c" or sometimes "a snake" When
he has difficulty saying S, He makes a his-
sing sound. He writes it as two C S - one on
top of the other - S laboriously trying to
get them the right way 'round. S IS FOR
SHOCKINGLY SPOILED ALLIGATORS. S IS
FOR A SNAKE AND A STORK WEARING
STRAW HATS. GOOD NIGHT LITTLE S. SAM-
SON SIMONSON SHRIMP GOOD NIGHT.
December 13, 1977: To-day I tried another school near
the estate, although technically we're on the wrong
side of the road to be included in their catchment.
Although it was old, there was some attempt to make it
look cheerful. The worst thing was that the classes
were very large over 30 children, but they were vert-
ically grouped and they used T.O., so I told the headmistress who seemed very capable, that we were interested and she said she would let me know. Afterwards
I was talking to Ronnie's mother about the 'school
problem' and she said they didn't plan to live here
long, if they could find 'better jobs'. I resort to the
same kind of daydream myself, thinking we'll find a way
to move before he gets to junior school. I guess I'm
afraid he wont grow up to be what I want him to be.

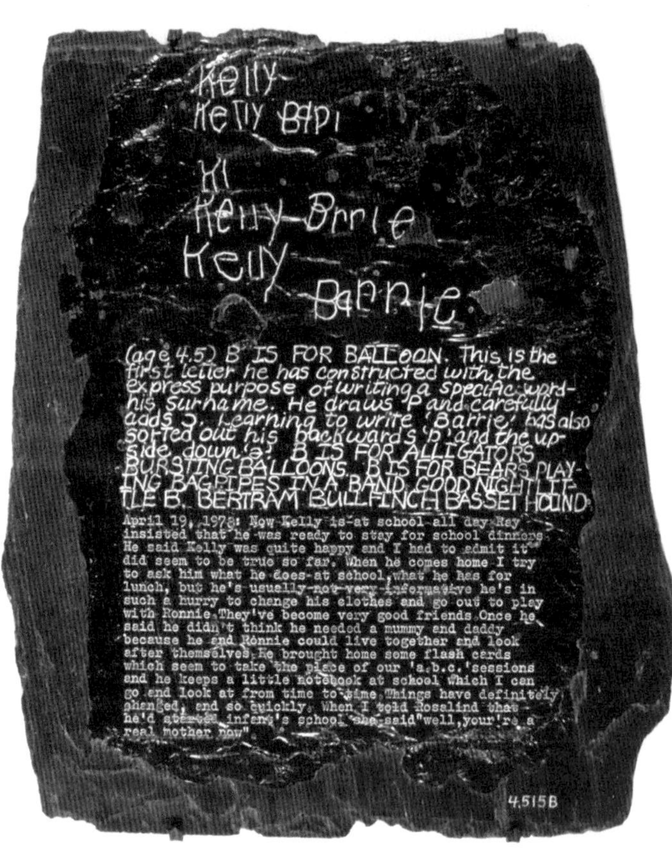
Kelly
Kelly Bapi
Ki
Kelly Brrie
Kelly
Barnie
(age 4.5) B IS FOR BALLOON. This is the first letter he has constructed with the express purpose of writing a specific word–his surname. He draws P and carefully adds Ↄ. Learning to write 'Barrie' has also sorted out his backwards 'b' and the upside down 'ə'. B IS FOR ALLIGATORS BURSTING BALLOONS. B IS FOR BEARS PLAYING BAGPIPES IN A BAND. GOOD NIGHT LITTLE B. BERTRAM BULLFINCH BASSET HOUND
April 19, 1978: Now Kelly is at school all day Ray insisted that he was ready to stay for school dinners. He said Kelly was quite happy and I had to admit it did seem to be true so far. When he comes home I try to ask him what he does at school, what he has for lunch, but he's usually not very informative he's in such a hurry to change his clothes and go out to play with Ronnie. They've become very good friends. Once he said he didn't think he needed a mummy and daddy because he and Ronnie could live together and look after themselves. He brought home some flash cards which seem to take the place of our 'a.b.c.' sessions and he keeps a little notebook at school which I can go and look at from time to time. Things have definitely changed, and so quickly. When I told Rosalind that he'd started infant's school she said "well, your're a real mother now"
4.515B

PPD 1979 REF. 3.501X–R/515B

Experimentum Mentis VI
On the insistence of the letter

Pre-writing emerges as post-script to the Oedipus complex and as preface to the moment of latency. In so far as the child's sexual researches are repressed by the Law and the Father, they are sublimated in the body of the letter; *but it is the mother who first censors the look, who wipes the slate clean with her silence and prepares the site of inscription. For the mother, the child's text is a fetish object; it desires her. The polymorphous perversity of the letter explores the body beyond the limit of the look. The breast (e), the hook (r), the lack (c), the eye (i), the snake (s); forbidden anatomies, incestuous morphologies; the child's alphabet is an anagram of the maternal body. For the child the grapheme-as-body-in-the-position-of-the-signifier plays with difference, not the difference of the founding moment of castration, the ultimatum of being or having, but rather a re-play of differences and separations already sanctioned in the structuring and dissolution of the Oedipus complex. A cross (x), a round (o), an up and a down (n and m), a straight and a round (p, b, d, q): pairs of graphemic oppositions designate the symbolic function of presence and absence in a double movement of memory and forgetting. Faeces, mark, imprint, utterance; a residue of corporality subtends the letter and overflows the text. The gift unfolds the child's desire to-be-what-she-wants-him-to-be; but the letter constructs the cannot-be of his autonomy and instigates the unexpected pleasure of deferment.*

With the inscription of his proper name, the child is instituted as the author of his text. Each purposeful stroke disfigures the anagram, dismembers the body. The mother is dispossessed of the phallic attributes of the pre-Oedipal instance, but only as if re-tracing a vague figure of repletion on a distant screen. Fading, forgetting; she cannot remember although 'it seems like only yesterday.' This wound to her narcissism is now a caricature: a tearful bliss, a simulated ecstasy, a veritable stigmata in the Name-of-the-Father. With the child's insistent repetition of the Name, he appropriates the status of the Father, the dead Father, the absent Father, the pre-condition of the 'word.' The incestuous meaning of the letter is ciphered by the paternal metaphor. But at the same time this introduces the possibility of 'truth,' the truth of the mother; that is, the fiction of the 'real mother,' not the Madonna, but the Pietà, dispelling imputations of guilt with patience, self-sacrifice, long-suffering and resignation. Resignation punctuated with protests: 'he is too little ... he is too young ... they are too rough ... it's too far.' In phantasy, the mother endures an endless series of threats to the child's well-being; sickness, accident, death. Her castration fears take the form of losing her loved objects, primarily her children; but underlying this is the fear of losing love, that is, the fear of being unable to reconstitute her narcissistic aim, of being unable to see herself as infinitely good and unconditionally loved. Ultimately, it is the fear of her mother's death and her own death as the imaginary stake in the representation of that loss. This negation is constituted by a recognition of unbearable dependence; but it is also an affirmation of life since the child's independence is implicated in the renunciation he imposes on her desire.

The effects of repressing Oedipal pleasure for both the mother and the child are evaded through sublimation, that is, through their mutual inscription in an order of extra-familial discourse and social practice. But the very movement towards a non-parental ideal that prompts the child's creative initiatives or indiscretions and constructs the representation of his social place, returns the mother to the site of the family, to the parental ideal of her own mother and to the representation of maternal femininity. Such a circuitous passage is problematic; being the phallus, she cannot have it; not having it, she cannot represent herself as an object of desire. She finds it difficult to assume responsibility for her pleasure without guilt; to provoke her sexual partner, to slight her child. Fearing failure, she is distracted from the projects which interest her most. There is a reprieve; another child, the fullness of the dyad, the sweetness of that imaginary encapsulation which reduces the 'outside world' to absurdity. But there is also the inevitable moment of separation reiterating a lack *always already inscribed and impossible to efface. She asks herself, 'What will I do ... when he starts shool ... when he grows up ... when he leaves home ... when he leaves me...?' This moment signifies more than separation; it articulates a rupture, a rent, a gap and a confrontation—a confrontation not only because of the way in which her desire, as desire of the child, to-be-what-she-wants-him-to-be, is produced within a field of social and economic constraints; but also because of the way in which the dialectic of desire, the movement of subject and object with its insistence on bisexuality, continually transgresses the system of representation in which it is founded. The construction of femininity as essentially natural and maternal is never finally fixed but forever unsettled in the process of articulating her difference, her loss. And it is precisely at such moments, that it is possible to desire to speak and to dare to change.*

Excerpts from *Post-Partum Document*

Documentation IV	Transitional objects and diary, 1976 1 unit 29.78 x 35.6 cm mixed media	1–3
Documentation VI	Pre-writing alphabet, exerque and diary, 1978 3 units 20.3 x 25/.4 cm resin and slate	4–15

MARY KELLY AND KELLY BARRIE

Ruth Skilbeck in Conversation with Mary Kelly and Kelly Barrie

IN 2008 MARY KELLY AND HER SON, Kelly Barrie, created a collaborative installation for the Sydney Biennale. In the following excerpt from a conversation with Ruth Skilbeck at Sydney's Museum of Contemporary Art, they discuss their personal and artistic relationship.

RUTH SKILBECK: I have some questions I'd like to ask you about your practice as artists, mother and son, working together and separately. I'm interested in the ideas in your work, in your creative processes, your methodologies, how these intersect with your lives and are articulated in your collaborative installation at Sydney's Museum of Contemporary Art, at the Sydney Biennale: Mary's Super 8 film, *Antepartum*, made in 1973, and Kelly's video-recording *Astral Fields*, made 35 years later in 2008. So, how long have you been collaborating as artists?

MARY KELLY: Well, consciously we haven't been collaborating at all! But of course we had collaborated on one of my first and perhaps most well-known works, *Post-Partum Document*, in the '70s. Carolyn [Christov-Bakargiev] thought that it would be interesting to return to the work now with Kelly being an artist and for him to respond to it. At first we thought, well that's a little weird—can we do it right? But then it generated a lot of really interesting conversations, and Kelly actually came up with the installation plan, juxtaposing an animated version of one of his still photographs from the *Astral Fields* series with my film loop, *Antepartum*, so that the kind of rhythm of the child's movements was synchronized with the actions in his projected image. I thought it was really interesting and wanted to go ahead with the project. [To Kelly] What would you say?

KELLY BARRIE: When I was looking at both images together on the smaller scale of the computer screen, the aspect of Mary's work that I wanted to respond to directly was the sort of live action of the movements within the womb which appear as intermittent bumps on the surface of a sphere. At the same time, I wanted to retain a strong presence of my own practice within that, so taking a still per se and animating it was one way to reactivate that space with Mary's. Because the image itself, the photograph, is formed from multiple exposures laid on top of each other, the video is reanimating it even further by reactivating these layers and allowing them to mesh and fragment and spin and twist and engage in these moments of synchronicity with Mary's piece—where there would be a movement internally in the belly, and it would correspond in certain ways with my piece.

RS: Mary, could you talk a little about *Post-Partum Document* and the context in which it was made, in terms of the context of your life, and, more widely, in terms of the social context of the time?

MK: Well, when I started *Post-Partum Document* it was at the high point of the social movements of the late '60s and particularly the women's movement. I brought it into my own procedures in terms of the work itself and embarked on this project-based, art-as-life thing. I didn't know when it was going to end, but when I started out I thought it would be clear that it had come out of conceptualism, but it just ended up making everybody uneasy [laughs]. The critics and theorists said, well, they liked the theory but why did it have to have that "stuff" like the, you know, so-called dirty nappies [laughs], and the feminists said, oh, well, we like the narratives and the "stuff," but why do you have to have the theory? So on every front it seemed to be confrontational at the time. Although perhaps I can't completely take credit for consciously causing a scandal at the ICA [Institute of Contemporary Art in London] in 1976, when I look back on it, the way that that moment in history came together with my practice as an artist, I would say something of a breakthrough took place then in terms of gender and the way that art could no longer be viewed as perfectly neutral. When I came to Sydney in 1982—this was the Biennale Bill Wright directed and he included the entire *Post-Partum Document*—it marked an historic moment here for identity politics in the art world. All the debates about identity and difference were very much debated at that time—you know, it was a hot topic. So that was the context for PPD, which carried on from 1973 until '79. When Kelly wrote his name, I always say that was the end [laughs], because it was something like, he's the author of his own text now, and I'd better not go further than that. And I never had any intention of doing anything with him again [laughs]—going to keep my distance—so this was an interesting way to come back and reconsider certain things, a personal as well as political history.

RS: That's interesting about the writing of the name. That's the Lacanian idea of the individual subject emerging through entering into the symbolic order of language?

MK: That's right.

KB: Yes, and in a way some of my practice is at least engaged photographically in these subject relations in terms of the camera specifically having such a powerful presence when it's just documenting and recording things, and I was consciously aware of the dilemma of that subject-object position. So it was very natural for me to make myself the subject of my own gaze in that sense, because I only felt comfortable producing that examination or conducting that experiment on myself, so to speak. By occupying both positions, I was able to sort of examine those relationships, especially in the format of the still and in terms of doing these sorts of very basic gestures of making hand casts and documenting this almost pre-verbal utterance—you know, this sort of action—that was in the process of becoming. I also made a series of photographs before in which I used my own saliva, ejecting it into space, and some of them have a direct relationship as sort of archaic precedents to a self-portrait. I'm taking the pictures blindly, spitting out towards the camera and essentially over time building up this perceived pattern of saliva that's evacuated of all materiality because it becomes translucent as the light passes through it.

MK: We were talking about the way Julia Kristeva describes the child's earliest relationship with the mother as introjection and projection, something prior to full identification. Well, Kelly and I were joking about spitting out the mother [laughs], in a sense. And then as we thought more about those psychic processes it seemed like spitting was an obvious projection, which in your image expands to suggest an infinite universe, and then in mine there's introjection of the child in terms of the symbiotic relation to the mother's body and in the imaginary space of maternal identity. But when we thought about it again things reversed, right? And how did it go? We were saying that there's projection on the side of my piece and then introjection on the side of yours....

KB: That articulation—when you move your hands—it's very much about the surface, yet for me there's a projection past the surface into an interior, so in a way it is a reversal, an externalized interiority. That's also what I'm dealing with in the image of my literal video projection: a sort of imagined space. I try to draw out this idea of interior space, and the idea of blindness and the idea of not being able to actually reach that vanishing point—you know, what's real for whom—so then, what's imagined is just as poignant for me in terms of trying to articulate that space.

RS: And it relates to Julia Kristeva's notion of the pre-linguistic "chora"?

KB: Yes, very much so, absolutely.

MK: This is interesting for me too, because I'm known as a text-based artist and my piece does not have any words, but of course it has gestures which are semiotically loaded [laughs], and the "chora"—Kristeva's realm of rhythms and intonations anterior to the phoneme—is further evoked in Kelly's photographic manipulations. Would you go with that?

KB: What's fascinating for me about the photographic process is that the performance of casting and dispersing the hand imprints in flour is based on an impulsive, repetitive act, the goal being to capture that one still moment where the sculpture has been frozen in time and remains intact, but of course that's absolutely impossible, it's constantly failing. The photograph is made up of mutant waves of refracted light, which give it an odd structure, commonly seen as a mistake in technical photographic practice. So it becomes not only about how light transforms these fragile, would-be sculptures in mid-air, but also about their inevitable failure because they collapse and disintegrate and fracture and transform into other sorts of bodies. They all exist on the same plane, so to speak, so they are all competing with each other equally, I mean they're all in that together...

MK: ...in a space of "psycho-graphic equilibrium." Kristeva talks about this in an article on Giotto, I think, something to do with the way color, or in your case light, inscribes instinctual residues that disturb that balance because they're difficult to symbolize. Of course the photographic processes you use are so complex compared with those in the '70s when I made my film, originally in Super 8, later transferred to DVD. It was shot in real time, only 90 seconds, but has a sense of infinite duration. Very little happens in it, just one gesture, which is repeated in an endless loop. When it was shown in the context of work from that period, though, you could see how the bottom-line simplicity of my minimal form, or receptacle—the meaning of "chora" in Greek and, according to Plato, the mother of all things—produces a kind of humor in relation to something like, say, Tony Smith's *Black Box*. In one sense there's a return to the past as one meaning of revolution in this exhibition, which is quite obviously historical. And I thought this touched on what was really at stake in my work and why it goes beyond the exhibition to invoke an almost existential sense of return to the past, I mean everyone's wish to return to that impossible place—that unmediated relation to the mother.

RS: It's a simple image, a very profound image: a minimal close-up of the circular abdomen at full term, caressed by the maternal hands.

KB: That was one of the prime things in terms of the installation. It was quite an elaborate, more complicated spatial arrangement initially, and I think it became problematic, and there was a kind of a reversal again in terms of deconstructing it and bringing the two projections back down to their raw, minimal base. This became more poignant as we went on with the project, as we realized that the images were so loaded that it would make more sense to allow the beams to simply cross over through each other and exist as these two positions within one installation.

MK: I think that was brought out by the curatorial overview too, because there's an emphasis on simplicity, anti-spectacle in a way, which we appreciated when we had to work within that directive. And I do understand that it's not necessarily a valorization of the maternal, but I feel there was something anti-phallocentric as a whole, a certain kind of interrogation that you don't usually see in large international theme shows and places like the art fairs.

RS: Is this the first time this has been shown?

MK: My film has been shown many times before, but the collaboration with Kelly makes it a new work.

—Sydney, Australia, June 20, 2008

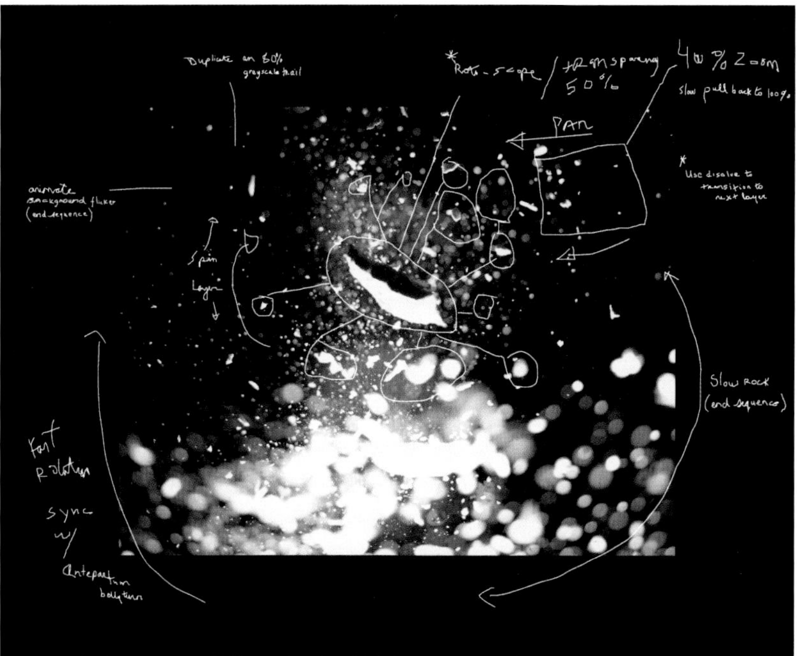

Kelly Barrie, *Sketch for Astral Fields video*, 2008. Archival inkjet print, 13 × 19 inches.

SUSAN RUBIN SULEIMAN AND MYREL CHERNICK

"Good Enough Mothers"

Myrel Chernick in Conversation with Susan Rubin Suleiman

SUSAN RUBIN SULEIMAN IS THE C. Douglas Dillon Professor of the Civilization of France and Professor of Comparative Literature at Harvard University. Among her extensive writing on literature and art, she has published several important essays that address maternal subjectivity, including "Writing and Motherhood" and "Maternal Splitting" (reprinted in "Conflicts of a Mother," *Risking Who One Is,* Part One)[1] and "Playing and Motherhood" (adapted from "Feminist Intertextuality and the Laugh of the Mother," *Subversive Intent*, Chapter Seven).[2]

When I first encountered *Subversive Intent* as an artist and mother of young children struggling with multiple professional identities and the demands of my family, it was a revelation for me to read about maternal subjectivity in a scholarly work devoted to contemporary literary theory and art criticism. There I found many affinities to my own life and work that became even more apparent in Suleiman's subsequent book *Risking Who One Is*, which interweaves her personal and professional lives and begins to relate her history as a child born at the beginning of World War II in Hungary. In Suleiman's most personal work, *Budapest Diary*, recounting her return to Budapest for the first time since she fled as a child thirty-five years earlier, she begins to examine her past with the kind of intensity and deep analysis that she brings to her theoretical writing. In her more recent work, she explores the terrain of memory and the Holocaust.

In 1995, as a response to questions on recent feminist theory and practice and "elitism vs. accessibility" (in a forum in *October* 71, *feminist issueS*, edited by Silvia Kolbowski and Mignon Nixon), Susan Rubin Suleiman wrote: "Personally ... my critical trajectory since the early 1980s has been toward greater accessibility. But this has less to do with thoughts ... about theory than with thoughts about language and about audience. I have felt an increasing need, or desire, or longing, to be read by more than a few people.... It is ... a matter of speaking in a common language. So yes, there has been a refusal in my work: I would call it a refusal of, even a revulsion against, the excesses of metalanguage."[3] This ability to connect is reflected in Suleiman's style, in the quality of her writing, and in the mingling of the theoretical and the lived experience in her work. As I have always been interested in the story behind the story, I have appreciated a style of feminist writing, perhaps inspired by that original tenet of "the personal is the political" that interweaves theory and anecdote, and which contributed to my original attraction to Suleiman's work. In these excerpts from our informal conversation in January 2006, she describes some of the formative experiences that produced the intrepid scholar and writer.

MYREL CHERNICK: One of the things I found interesting when I first inquired about your essay "Writing and Motherhood"[4] for our book, *The M Word: Real Mothers in Contemporary Art,* was that you asked if it was still relevant. I actually wish it were less relevant, but in observing the situation that exists for mothers today, I find the exhibit *Maternal Metaphors* still relevant, as well as the questions women ask themselves.

SUSAN RUBIN SULEIMAN: Is it because our society hasn't gotten any better or because this is a permanent structural feature of the human psyche or the maternal psyche?

MC: That's an important question, and I believe that the answer is "both." In some ways I do think the society's gotten worse.

SRS: I agree with that.

MC: Especially when you read about these women now deciding to abandon their careers completely...

SRS: After getting a law degree at Harvard.

MC: And that decision is celebrated in an article on the front page of the *New York Times*.[5]

SRS: In one of my other essays, "Maternal Splitting,"[6] which has to do with the mother thinking of herself as somehow guilty, or torn between conflicting demands (I guess even in "Writing and Motherhood" I was talking about that), I argued that if the society were more supportive of mothers by providing really top-notch childcare, and by generally making it easier for a woman to move in and out of mothering and careering or to have support while she was a mother, so that she could also satisfy her other commitments, then some of that ambivalence would disappear or at least be lessened. But obviously things have not gotten better in that respect since the 1980s.

MC: I don't believe we've had a chance to test that theory, because the kind of help and childcare you're talking about is not there in the United States, other than for very wealthy women. What about France, where they have better childcare?

SRS: I think in France there is generally less pressure. In the United States, one of the reasons that mothers have terribly torn feelings is that they are sent a message by the culture that a good mother is always there with cookies and milk when the child comes home from school, and a good mother doesn't have any other interests besides her child or her family. That's still a very powerful message. In France, first of all they have a very good childcare system, but also for centuries women have sent their babies off to wet nurses, or to their own mothers to be taken care of—many kids have grown up with their grandmothers. Mind you, I'm not advocating this as a solution; I think children should grow up with their parents, if at all possible. But it shows that the societal expectation in France is generally less stringent about what a "good" mother does. The paradox is that in the United States, despite this sort of Perfect Mommy image we also have the most appalling degree of child abuse. I haven't read of things like this in France—the number of children who get killed every year by their parents is just mind-boggling. Violence against children exists in Europe too, that's undeniable, but the numbers are not comparable at all. It's a truly exceptional event for a child to be killed there, whereas it's all too depressingly frequent in the United States. So there's a strange thing: on the one hand we're told you have to sacrifice yourself completely to your child, and on the other hand we tolerate, literally tolerate, children being beaten to death by their parents. Clearly things are not getting any better.

MC: That says something about the structure of American society, where the government won't provide programs to help mothers cope—and that makes the contradiction greater. You feel worse if you're not a conventionally good mother because there's no tolerance of the less-than-perfect mother in the popular culture.

SRS: Or even of the "good enough" mother, as D.W. Winnicott called her. There is an ideal out there, which real mothers, as you put it in your title, are constantly having to measure themselves against. To get back to Europe for a minute, there's maybe less of that ideal image there, and therefore real mothers don't have to be beating themselves on the head so much for being just good enough.

MC: I would like to lead in with that to your early experience with Europe. I wanted you to talk about your life because I think your trajectory is relevant to all your interests and the variety of work that you write about.

SRS: I was born in Hungary, a month before the outbreak of World War II into a Jewish Hungarian family. That means that technically I am a child survivor of the Holocaust, although I don't particularly love that label. Like many other Jewish children who survived the war in Europe without being taken to concentration camps, I haven't thought of myself as "a Holocaust survivor." But technically, this relatively new term of "child survivor" does apply to me, so what does that mean? It means that some of my earliest memories have to do with being scared. Hungary was on the side of the Germans in World War II, entering the war in 1941. Paradoxically, that meant that Hungarian Jews were somewhat less threatened in the beginning than Jews in Poland or in occupied Europe.

Even though Jews were doing well, relatively speaking, until 1944, Jewish men were being drafted into forced labor service. The mass deportations of Jews didn't begin until the spring of 1944, when the Germans invaded Hungary. Of course the Hungarian government cooperated fully. They cleared out the Jews from the provinces, and then turned to Budapest. But luckily, meanwhile the Allies landed in Normandy, and the Hungarian leader Horthy stopped the deportations in mid-July—too bad the idea didn't occur to him earlier, before 400,000 Jews were shipped to Auschwitz.

My first memories date from the spring of 1944 when the Germans occupied Hungary. I was not yet five years old, and this sort of panic was all around me. It certainly must have influenced me, but I was among the very lucky ones, I guess. The other main event during that time was that my parents, like many other Jews in various countries, thought they would keep me safe by taking me to a farm and leaving me there by myself with people I didn't know. That was traumatic, for a child so young. After a while they came back to get me, and my mother always claimed they didn't leave me there for long. But it was long enough to be imprinted in my memory, and it's an event I keep coming back to when I think about my childhood. After the farm I was with my parents in Budapest, and we spent that winter hiding with false papers, pretending to be Christians. That was pretty scary too, but at least we were together and we survived, that's why I say I'm lucky. Then after the war, things were really good for a few years. I started school in September 1945, and it felt like a normal childhood despite all the enormous losses—both my parents' extended families were almost entirely wiped out. In '48 the Hungarian Communist Party came to power and stopped emigration. My family had to do what many other families did in 1949: walk across the border illegally, into Austria. We spent eight months in Vienna, then started moving west. We spent a few weeks in Paris, then boarded a ship in Le Havre and ended up in Haiti.

MC: Where did you stay in all these places? How did your family survive?

SRS: Interesting question. We got to Vienna in August 1949, and we certainly didn't have much, no more than a suitcase or two. But I think my father had brought out some money with him. Somehow or other we managed, like all the other refugees at the time who were in Vienna. Vienna at that time was divided into four sectors: the American, the French, the British and the Russian. We rented half of an apartment from a widow who was living there. I remember my parents had a whole circle of friends, other refugees from Hungary, with whom we went on Sunday hikes. It was a kind of artificial existence, since everyone was on their way somewhere else, using Vienna as a way station. Then in Paris we were already on our way to Haiti, and we stayed in the apartment of an aunt of mine, who had emigrated to France in the 1930s with her husband and daughter.

And then we were really on our way. We were again among the lucky ones because my mother had a younger brother, my uncle Nick, who was the fabled *oncle d'Amérique*, the American uncle who had left Europe as a young man and made his fortune. He had a factory in Haiti and he said, "Come and spend time in Haiti, and from there you can see about entering the U.S. or Canada." The other alternative would have been to go to a displaced persons camp in Europe, and my parents considered it for a while, but then when he came up with this offer they realized it would be much better not to be in a displaced persons camp. We spent six months in Haiti, and then got visas for the United States—my sister was born prematurely in Haiti, so the first thing we did when we entered the States was to spend a few weeks in Miami while she grew. She was in an incubator, and we'd visit her every day.

MC: How did this affect your education? How much was the total time?

SRS: We left Hungary in August 1949, and we entered the United States at the end of December 1950, so the whole trip was about 15 or 16 months, of which eight were spent in Vienna, and I went to a French school there. I had already started to learn French in Budapest, then did the school in Vienna, and in Haiti I went to a French school too, run by *les bonnes soeurs*, the nuns of Saint Rose of Lima. The French education system was fabled for its strictness, and I certainly learned grammar and arithmetic very well. It also added another layer to my identity. Having had to pretend to be Catholic at age five for several months and then going to school with the nuns in Haiti, all that produced a certain vacillation, especially considering that my father was trained as a rabbi and we kept kosher, even in Haiti! It was not clear to me exactly who or what I was, or who I wanted to be.

MC: I can imagine that the entire experience, moving around that way, was difficult for a child of your age, although you were with your parents.

SRS: Right, I was with my parents, and so throughout that time it was a kind of alternation between feeling very disoriented and feeling that I was living a great adventure. You know, I remember in a strange way turning the whole war experience into an adventure tale: having to pretend to be a little Christian girl whose name was Mary, and we couldn't say who we were. Hitler was a monster and we were trying to protect ourselves from him, and we must sing "Holy Night" at Christmas. One of the first pieces of autobiography I wrote many years later was a short piece titled "My War in Four Episodes," where I describe that adventure. I especially remember going out at night with my parents and the other people we lived with to collect snow, around December 1944, so that we would have water to drink—I described it as an almost magical moment, though it must have been frightening too. I began to tell this story when I was about seven or eight to anybody who would listen, and later there was the story of leaving Hungary. I had two adventures, the war and leaving Hungary on foot. So on the one hand there was disorientation and fear, and on the other a kind of swagger: Hey, we were able to do this, we are invincible, or at least we have managed to live through this adventure and tell about it, live to tell the tale.

MC: Did you stay in New York very long?

SRS: About two and a half years—we arrived there in January 1951. My father got a job as a rabbi in a summer community, which was very nice for us. For two summers we went up to the Catskills, but still, during the year what was he going to do? Eventually he got a job in Chicago, which was why we moved to Chicago.

MC: How old were you at that point?

SRS: I was just about to turn 14. We moved to Chicago in the summer of '53, less than three years after we arrived in New York. They had put me into sixth grade when I first got there: I knew not a word of English, you realize, but with all my training from the *bonnes soeurs* I was really good in math. The other thing that helped me was that I discovered the public library, and I just read voraciously. I also loved comic books, *Little Lulu* and *Archie* and all those comics, that's how I learned English. After a few months in school they did some kind of testing—this was the

New York City public schools—and I guess I was able to perform on this test, which made the powers that be decide that I should be in a special class. They had a system where you did seven special-nine special, so you skipped a grade in middle school, and that was great because I was in this special class with other girls; it was an all-girls' school.

They gave us the test in the spring of '51, and in the fall I went to a junior high school on York Avenue and 81st Street—it no longer exists. We lived on 83rd and York, and for two years I was in the special class with other "smart girls." I became part of a little circle of very good friends which included a girl who lived on Central Park West and whose mother was an art critic for the *New York Times*. I'll never forget the apartment they had overlooking the park, full of modern art. And then there was another girl who was Jewish too, who lived on York Avenue—both of these women got in touch with me in later years because of *Budapest Diary,* and they're still living in New York. There was another girl in our group who was Puerto Rican, Lila Rodriguez. We had meetings every week at Connie the rich girl's apartment on Central Park West. In those days a girl like Constance was going to public school. Nowadays that would just not be possible; a girl whose parents are an investment banker and an art critic for the *New York Times* simply would never meet a girl like Lila Rodriguez or me unless we were scholarship students in some private school. So I was really happy. And I remember that the teachers in this junior high school were just marvelous women. One was our social studies teacher, or maybe she did social studies and English—she was the least good, but I liked her. Our science teacher was a really dedicated, hard-as-nails woman—it was unbelievable how good she was. She would have those of us who were her little favorites, or who wanted to be, stay over during lunch hour and share her Wheat Thins, talking about science. Then there was our math teacher, Miss Crowley, who drilled us like crazy because we all had to get into either Bronx High School of Science or Hunter High School; those were our two choices. I was admitted to both schools, it was marvelous, and because of the influence of that science teacher I decided to go to Bronx Science. But, disaster, that was the summer of 1953, when my father got his job in Chicago. My mother said, "We're driving to Chicago" and we drove to Chicago. I went off to Barnard in the fall of 1956, and that was the beginning of my brilliant career! [laughter]

MC: And it has been, too. When did you get interested in French again?

SRS: I was taking French in high school, and I also got very involved in the school paper and was seriously considering doing journalism. When I got to Barnard, since I was very good in chemistry, I became a chemistry major—this was still the influence of my science teacher from junior high school, and Barnard had a wonderful woman chemistry teacher as well, Helen Downing. But I still kept up my French, took one or two French literature courses. I was very interested in literature, yet somehow felt that I should study chemistry. I guess this had to do with my identity question, not knowing whether I was a scientist or a humanist. But in my second semester of junior year I took a literature course with a visiting professor from England. These strong women, now that I think of it, have certainly played a role in my intellectual evolution. Her name was Elizabeth Wilkinson, she was a professor of German literature, and she was the first Gildersleeve Visiting Professor at Barnard, so there was big excitement when she got there. She gave a course on the Faust myth in literature, and I was just totally enthralled by this course and by her way of teaching, which somehow assumed that we were all mature thinkers and lovers of ideas—although in fact we were just young women muddling along. I remember very clearly: it was after writing a paper on Thomas Mann's *Doctor Faustus* that I decided to switch my major and become a literature major. In the end I didn't formally switch, but the rest of my courses that year were all in English and French literature, and I again had a number of teachers who were wonderful women and who encouraged me tremendously, including one who was Dean of the Faculty as well as a French professor. She was great, she kept telling me, "You need to apply for a Woodrow Wilson Fellowship to go to graduate school." After graduation I was given a small traveling scholarship by Barnard, and my dear uncle Nick gave me a present: a monthly allowance in Paris for a year, which changed my life. After that, I did get a Woodrow Fellowship and came to Harvard to do graduate work.

MC: What was the year like for you in Paris?

SRS: I had dreams of being a writer. I had published a poem in the Barnard literary journal, and had started to write fiction. The poem was okay but the fiction wasn't going very far. Again I was trying to live an adventure, the Paris adventure, reading *Tropic of Cancer* and sitting in smoke-filled cafes. For the first month and a half I stayed in a hotel in Montparnasse, on the rue Delambre, which was a total fleabag as well as maybe an *hotel de passe*, where prostitutes came with their clients, but it was all I could afford.

And soon after that, when it turned cold and dark and the hotel had only 40-watt bulbs and no heat, I realized that I should give up leading the bohemian life and try to do something a little more reasonable. So I applied for a room at the Pavillon des Etats Unis at the Cité Universitaire in November, and the rest of the year I lived there. I was there in the spring of 1961 when a bomb went off; this was during the height of the Algerian war.

MC: I wanted to bring the conversation to when you began to write about motherhood. I believe that there is a relationship between your life, which formed the basis for your intellectual drive, and your broad interests that range from literary theory to Surrealism, to artists writing about motherhood, to your personal writing, and to your more recent work about memory and the Holocaust. I find it a fascinating story, particularly your account of the women who encouraged you.

SRS: Actually I'm finding this quite fascinating too, in some ways, because I want to do more personal writing and was wondering what to write about. In that piece about my mother's silver pin[7] [reprinted here], the focus was more on the United States, the experience of being immigrants in the United States. I think I should emphasize that now, rather than the Budapest years. Even though *Budapest Diary* does not systematically talk about my childhood in Budapest, in a way that is the book about "over there." If I want to write another book, it has to be more about "there and here."

MC: I found myself wanting to fill in the gaps, when I was reading that book, because at a certain point your academic and theoretical writing comes to the fore, although you have a way of integrating your life into your writing even in *Subversive Intent*, where you let us know in the introduction that you're a mother.[8]

SRS: Yes, I let the reader know that I'm a mother in *Subversive Intent*. In the next to the last chapter where I talk about motherhood and about the laughing mother, my own image does come in.[9]

MC: What are the origins of that piece? Can you talk about that? I find it an intriguing concept, especially in terms of the work that is in this show, where we do have some ironically humorous work, although there's not so much that's "playful." I think the idea of the mother being afraid of her own power, and her ability to harm her child, is a conflict that's very strong, certainly for creative women who are trying to decide between their children and their artwork. I think it would be extremely helpful if it could be understood more through art. It seems to me that in certain cultures there's more of a circle of mothers around a child, and in that situation a woman does feel secure in leaving her child with other people.

SRS: This goes back to the idea of more support for mothers, whether the support is institutionalized because you no longer have the extended family, or whether in fact it is the extended family. My daughter-in-law, my younger son's wife, whom I really love, maybe because I have no daughters, comes from a very large family in Venezuela, and her mother had eight siblings, most of them girls. So she has all these *tías,* these aunts, and all these cousins, and she knows the inner/outer workings of this whole bevy of women she's surrounded by. [laughter] I think it's very nice to have the possibility of other mothers, who are like second and third mothers. I can see that some of the women I've mentioned, all those women in the early years in New York and then at Barnard, were kinds of mother figures, older or middle-aged women who became models for what I could become or what a mothering type could be. I think that had something to do with the fact that my relation to my own mother was so fraught and contradictory. I didn't want to be like her, so I found all these other women to model myself on.

MC: I think that's not uncommon, especially among strong women, and now you're going back and exploring that relationship more.

SRS: I definitely want to. Because in spite of everything, and although, as I write in that silver pin piece, my mother was in some ways totally impossible, utterly devoid of tact and of the ability to gauge a situation and not say the first thing that came into her head, she nevertheless played a huge role in both my and my sister's lives, and in a good way. She played a huge role because she too had a wonderful way of laughing; she was a very fun-loving person. She was the one who took me hiking when I was a little girl, the one who played games with me, and she also had great ambitions, even though she herself didn't achieve any huge thing. Still, after my father died, she was able to support herself and to make a life for herself in Florida, with the help of her brothers and sister.

MC: And how did you come to writing about the mother?

SRS: It's interesting, because I realize that in my intellectual development I haven't followed a straight line but more like overlapping waves. I always use the famous example of the hedgehog and the fox that Isaiah Berlin put into circulation. Tolstoy was a fox and Dostoevsky was a hedgehog, according to Berlin. The hedgehog keeps digging in the same hole and goes deeper and deeper, while the fox is all over the place, covering a lot of ground. And the funny thing that Berlin pointed out was that hedgehogs never want to be anything other than hedgehogs—they like being hedgehogs—but the fox is always saying "I wish I were a hedgehog, I wish I could go deeper." I'm all over the map, definitely a fox, but I also do things overlappingly. In the mid-1970s, I was in New York, teaching at Columbia, and I was struggling over my first book. You mentioned *Subversive Intent,* which was the first *for you* but, for me, my first book was *Authoritarian Fictions: The Ideological Novel as a Liter-*

ary Genre,[10] which was a real struggle, but in some ways I think it's my most original book. It deals with the thesis novel, *roman à thèse*, a kind of fiction that hits you on the head with whatever you're supposed to be thinking. So there I was writing this very rigorous, structuralist study of "authoritarian fictions," but suddenly I got an invitation to participate in one of the Barnard feminist conferences, one of the very first ones, in 1975. I told myself I was definitely *not* going to speak about the *roman à thèse*, no way! Instead, I wrote a paper that later became a chapter in *Subversive Intent*, the chapter on Robbe-Grillet, which dealt with the way that the "new novel" in France made use of the mother's body by a total "othering" of it, using it as something to step on. There already was the seed of *Subversive Intent*, but I still had to finish *Authoritarian Fictions*, which was not published until 1983. I finally finished it in 1979, but I had written it in French because it was so influenced by French structuralism that I felt I had to. As if it wasn't already hard enough to write your first book on a topic that nobody had written about, that you were creating out of whole cloth more or less (that's not quite true, the *roman à thèse* is a term that we know, but nobody had really studied it), I was writing in French! Even though it was my language before English, I still write more easily in English, and did even then. So it was just another hoop to jump through. Then when I translated it, I actually rewrote it in English, and transferred some of the changes to the French manuscript as well. It was a crazy process, but in a way it was also fun to see the process of translation at work. And as the author, I had the right to change the text, not just translate it! But back in 1975, while I was struggling with this book, writing the essay on Robbe-Grillet had an incredibly liberating feel, because his work was the exact opposite of "authoritarian fictions." It was not a realist novel: it was an avant-garde piece of writing that looked, at least theoretically, like the opposite of the kind of work I was writing about. And the other liberating thing was that it really got me to read Freud, for the first time. I had read some Freud, obviously, but not in a deep way, or not in a sustained way, and it was exhilarating. You know people say that Freud is like a bogeyman for feminists, but I don't think that's true. I think that even though we might consider him dead wrong and just a Viennese Victorian sexist on many things, nevertheless he was a brilliant and fascinating writer, and not wrong about everything.

The next step along this path was in 1979, when I wrote the "Writing and Motherhood" essay for an MLA panel on motherhood. I started to read a whole lot of books that a French professor doesn't necessarily read, at least not professionally: Margaret Drabble, more Freud, and

Adrienne Rich who had just published *Of Woman Born*[11] not long before then, and that too was very significant, a huge leap forward. That was before I had even finished *Authoritarian Fictions*, so I was preparing the way for a lot of other work. I was writing then about the painfulness and all the problems of motherhood. The idea of the laughing mother, on the other hand, came about because of my interest in Surrealism. I had always been interested in the Surrealists, but I hadn't come to them via poetry, like some of my friends who are Surrealist scholars. I came to Surrealism through visual art and prose narratives, such as Breton's *Nadja*. Above all, I was very interested in Surrealist politics because they were so involved, as a group, in revolutionary politics. Writers and politics, that's what *Authoritarian Fictions* is really about, but unlike the "thesis novelists" the Surrealists were also playful. Somehow all of that came together in *Subversive Intent*. My argument in that book was that the historical European avant-garde, although heavily male and male-oriented, and sometimes misogynist, did have something terrific that could be very useful for women: invention and irreverence, the refusal or downgrading of authority, and parody and humor. Then I discovered Leonora Carrington, who was perfect, a wonderful artist and writer—and a mother, unlike many other women involved with Surrealism. She was also very funny, in some of her writing. And that's how I got to the idea of the playful mother, the laughing mother.

MC: I find the idea of the laughing mother intriguing. I think it's also extremely liberating in terms of the mother's subjectivity, and it's something that you don't see often, even in my exhibit, where most of the work is very serious.

SRS: Including yours.

MC: Including mine. I've been thinking of an installation that I'd like to do now that my children are out of the house. I actually had already thought of using humor, which would be a struggle in some ways but also of course liberating. Rereading your essay recently has been extremely helpful, and I'm hoping to move on with this work. It's very important too, as a way of undermining a structure, and reaching people.

SRS: Yes, and from Schiller on, the concept of play is very much linked to art. Art is play, art is the freedom of the imagination, it's the possibility of allowing yourself to roam. Art is freedom, and play is freedom—one is never freer than when one is at play, because of the gratuitousness of play. There's that sentence of Freud's that I absolutely adore, and I quote it whenever I can: "The opposite of what is playful is not what is serious, but what is real." Play can be very serious, but at the same time, it has the unfetteredness of not being linked to the demands of reality—of things as they are—so it allows enormous freedom, that's what I mean by gratuitousness. Play can be very important, but it's gratuitous too, because it is not bound by the real.

MC: Yes, and I think a pleasurable aspect of motherhood is to witness one's children playing, because for me not only did it remind me of my own ability to play, but also how reality is filtered through play, and that that's how children process it.

SRS: That's true. But then the question is: if play is so important to artistic activity, and to creative activity of every kind, then why is it so rarely associated with the mother? There's that other image I often mention, Roland Barthes's beautiful image of a child playing around the mother. That's his idea of himself, of his writing, that image of the little boy running around, bringing little pebbles to his mom, who sits there quietly and says, "Yes dear, that's very nice." What would happen if she got up and joined the game? My idea was that many things would change. Now, maybe, looking back on it from the crazy world we're living in, you could say, "This was the high point of postmodernism, when everybody wanted to play." But I think a certain amount of humor is very useful even in tragic times, right?

MC: Yes, absolutely. And I find your discussion of writing and motherhood, particularly maternal ambivalence and the laughing mother, as relevant now as when I first came upon it, and refreshing to reread as well. There is still a very negative reaction when mothers are willing to make their ambivalence public, like in the Rosellen Brown story that you talk about in "Writing and Motherhood." From my own experience with my work and the exhibit, I think it's still very much with us, with plenty of room for more work on the subject. The fact that books and journals are being published on the topic right now supports that idea.

SRS: Maybe we should end on the note of dear old Winnicott: it's enough if we're "good enough mothers." We don't have to be perfect mothers, a good enough mother is just fine.

—January 30, 2006

Notes

---

[1]Susan Rubin Suleiman, *Risking Who One Is* (Cambridge, MA: Harvard University Press, 1994), 13-38.

[2]Suleiman, *Subversive Intent: Gender, Politics, and the Avant-Garde* (Cambridge,

MA: Harvard University Press, 1990), 179-180. Suleiman, "Playing and Motherhood; or, How to Get the Most Out of the Avant-Garde," in *Representations of Motherhood*, ed. Donna Bassin, Margaret Honey, and Meryle Mahrer Kaplan (New Haven: Yale University Press, 1994), 272-282.

[3]Suleiman, "Questions of Feminism: 25 Responses," *October* 71 (Winter 1995): 39.

[4]Suleiman, *Risking Who One Is*, 13-37.

[5]Louise Story, "Many Women at Elite Colleges Set Career Path to Motherhood." *New York Times*, September 20, 2005, A1+.

[6]Suleiman, *Risking Who One Is*, 38-54.

[7]Suleiman, "The Silver Pin," in *Evocative Objects*, ed. Sherry Turkle (Cambridge, MA: MIT Press, 2007), 184-193.

[8]Suleiman, *Subversive Intent: Gender, Politics, and the Avant-Garde*, XVI-VXII.

[9]Ibid., 179-180.

[10]Suleiman, *Authoritarian Fictions: The Ideological Novel as a Literary Genre* (New York: Columbia University Press, 1983).

[11]Adrienne Rich, *Of Woman Born* (New York: W.W. Norton & Company, 1976).

SUSAN RUBIN SULEIMAN

My Mother's Silver Pin

FOR A LONG TIME, I thought of it as a precious thing: a flower pin, long and slender, the sculpted leaves spreading on both sides of the stylized petals, with two symmetrically placed pearls in the middle. My mother wore it on the collar of her black dress in the photos we posed for before we left Hungary. It was in the spring of 1949, a few months before we crossed the border into Czechoslovakia. I still recall the session with the fancy photographer, who came to our house and had me leaning against doorposts in "casual" girlish poses (I was nine years old). He also took more formal pictures of my parents and me, including the one of my mother in her black dress, sitting at a table with her arms resting on an open book. Her left hand, very white and smooth, stands out against the black of her sleeves. Her head is slightly tilted, and around her mouth there plays a slight, sweet smile. She looks kind and beautiful, her eyes shining, her dark hair a halo—an elegant, still young woman of leisure. One would hardly believe, looking at her manicured hands, that a few years earlier she had been working as a maid in Buda, hiding from the Nazis with false papers. My father and I had been there too.

On the back of the photo, which I now hold in my hand, its edges slightly frayed, is an inscription in flowing black ink: *Sok szeretettel, Lilly*—with much love, Lilly. She had sent this photo to her mother, my grandmother *Rézi nagymama,* who had left Hungary the previous year with my uncle Lester, her eldest son. They were allowed to take the train, no need to walk across the border—that was before the Communist regime in Hungary cracked down on emigration. Rézi was in New York City, where we eventually joined her. Her youngest son, my "American uncle" Nick, who was doing well in the shoe business, had set her up in a one-bedroom apartment on York Avenue not far from the Mayor's mansion, in a tall brick box that was the latest thing in those years, with doorman and elevators, and air conditioners visible in all the windows as you looked up at the blank facade. It was in her apartment that I was introduced to the wonders of television: we watched Molly Goldberg and Milton Berle religiously, and *Dragnet* too ("Just the facts, Ma'am"). How strange America was, and how green I felt!

Curiously, I have no memory of my mother ever wearing that pin after we came to the United States. She held on to it, that's certain. I have it in front of me right now, on the desk next to the photo, and keep glancing at it as I write: the pearls are slightly yellowed, and if I look closely I see many imperfections on their surface. The sculpted leaves, too, show signs of decrepitude, dotted with small gaping holes that were once filled in with glittery stones—"not diamonds," the jeweler told me recently when I took it to him for his opinion. The holes look almost as if they were there on purpose, as if the designer had wanted to alternate empty spaces with filled-in ones. It's an old pin, graceful in shape and commercially worthless. "Enjoy it, it's pretty," the jeweler said.

So why didn't she wear it? Was this modest relic of postwar Budapest unworthy in her eyes? (I think my father bought it for her shortly before the photography session, a sign of prosperity and survival.) Or was it perhaps associated with a country, and a city, that she had no desire to remember? She had lost most of her extended family in 1944, deported with the help of the Hungarian government. She never spoke about those uncles and aunts and cousins, and I have no memories of them since almost all of them lived in the provinces, far from Budapest, but when I was writing my book *Budapest Diary*, I made a pilgrimage to the city where she was born, where some of the family had lived. She spent her summer vacations there as a child. I can't even begin to imagine what it felt like for her to learn, at war's end, that all those people were dead.

Some immigrants retain their ties to the old country. I know Hungarian Jews in Boston who still refer to Budapest as "home," decades after they just barely escaped being shot into the Danube by Hungarian Nazis—that was quite the sport in the fall of 1944. Some left the country soon after the war, like us; others waited until 1956, fleeing when the borders became temporarily crossable after the failed revolution. They all started going back for visits in the 1960s and 1970s, when "goulash Communism" made life in Hungary quite pleasant again, especially for Hungarians with American passports and dollars. My uncle Lester returned to Budapest every summer for more than twenty years, right up to his death. Communism or no, the Gerbeaud pastry shop on Vörösmarty Square still served the best sour cherry strudels, and you could dine outdoors on chicken paprikas with *nockerli* at the Duna Corso restaurant on the bank of the Danube, late into the night. Not to mention music and theater, the best in the world, according to him.

My mother had no truck with such nostalgia. She never went back to Budapest, and reminisced about her youth in that great European capital only if I pushed her hard, with photos spread out before us. "The Gellért baths, I went there often when I was courting," or: "Do you remember our Sunday hikes in Buda, when you were little? You loved the cog railway." Generally, she sought advancement and novelty, not memories. She had a talent for small talk with strangers, and within a few weeks after we arrived in New York, she had established several outposts of acquaintances in the neighborhood. I especially recall the children's clothing shop on 86th Street near York Avenue, where she would go to chat with the owners in a mixture of German, Hungarian, and broken English as she looked for outfits for my baby sister. She didn't hesitate to ask them for a discount, given our status as new immigrants. Often I felt embarrassed when I went with her, especially when she pushed me forward to translate for her or when she started telling people she had just met about her most intimate concerns: her worries about money, her anxiety about our future, her doubts about my hair! ("You must do something about your hair," the refrain of my adolescence.) It was around that time that I began to feel she and I had nothing in common.

It occurs to me that maybe she did wear the pin in America, and it is I who have blocked it from memory. Was I ashamed of her for not being American? Was the pin, which I had thought splendid and precious in Budapest, now merely a reminder of foreignness?

After the first two years of struggle in New York, we moved to Chicago, where I went to high school—another displacement, another round of feeling like an outsider. For a short while, I had an intense friendship with a girl I thought of as the perfect American. She lived in a large frame house on the North Side, with her parents and a sister and brother (he was older, already in college, but came home for the holidays). At Christmas, they put a big tree in the middle of their living room and went caroling in the snow. I don't remember what her mother looked like, but I recall wishing my mother were more like her: she never yelled, never nagged her daughter about her appearance. She was calm, not excitable and embarrassingly familiar with strangers. After a few weeks, my friend and I drifted apart, or maybe she snubbed me. Today, I recall only the yearning I felt to be like her, to have a family like hers.

Looking back on this now, I realize how desperate I was to be an "insider," not different, just like other Americans. And how ashamed I must have been of my immigrant mother, who never learned to speak English properly and never learned to speak calmly. But the drive for assimilation came from her as well; in a curious way, I was fulfilling her desire by wanting to have little to do with her. Success in school was my escape, my chance to leave her and foreignness behind. I was offered a scholarship to Barnard College in New York, and jumped at it. My mother was happy too, knowing I was in a fancy school. Sometimes a new acquaintance would notice an accent and ask me about it, but most people I met in college thought of me as a girl from Chicago. I had a little black dress for parties, and my hair was finally in shape.

Back in Chicago, my father gradually made his way to a job he was proud of, as the executive director of a Hebrew day school. In the summer before my senior year, ten years after we had left Budapest, he died of a heart attack at the age of forty-nine. It took me a long time to mourn for him, but that is another story. We gave up our apartment in Chicago and sold its meager furnishings. My mother and my little sister, who was nine years old, lived for a year in New York, then moved to Miami Beach to be near my uncles and aunt. Meanwhile, I spent a year in Paris after college (generously financed by Uncle Nick), then moved to Cambridge, Massachusetts to start graduate school at Harvard. Another displacement, another promotion.

I visited my mother once or twice a year: she treated me like a dignitary, parading me to family and friends. Rarely did a visit end without some outburst on my part. I had no patience with her; it was clear that we would never understand each other. I had adored her as a child in Budapest, but that time was very far away. A few years later, after I got married and became a mother too, there were no more outbursts. The gap between us, however, persisted.

It makes me feel sad and ashamed, with a different shame, not the shame I felt as a teenager, to realize how little I valued her. But there is anger there too. If I was incapable of feeling love for her—or of expressing love, which in a sense is the same thing—was it not her fault as well as mine? I tell myself that she was tactless, that she spoke too loudly, that she was interested only in the superficial signs of success.

Yet, others did love her. After almost twenty years of widowhood she married again, and her new husband doted on her. He was a retired dentist, Hungarian-Romanian, a widower—they got along well together, a real couple. When she became ill a few years later, he took care of her; when she died in 1988, aged almost eighty, he mourned her as if they had been together a lifetime. After her death, we kept hearing from people who had known her—she had been the belle of Lincoln Road, one old lady told us. She was fun to be with; she had a thousand friends.

My sister and I often talk about her now: she was impossible, yes, but she was brave and energetic too, and she had gone through a lot.

We inherited her photos and her few pieces of jewelry. I got the old photos from Hungary, many with inscriptions on the back. Among them was the picture of her wearing the silver pin, so elegant and beautiful. The pin also came to me, along with a delicate gold orchid pin she had acquired in America. I put that one in my jewelry box; the silver pin disappeared into a jumble of old trinkets in a drawer: an antique belt buckle given to me by a French friend many years ago, broken or unmatched earrings, watches that no longer ran. Devalued, like my mother in America? Yes, but not thrown out—lying dormant.

The gold orchid, when I wear it, often reminds me of my mother; but it is simply a pretty object, carrying no strong emotion. The silver pin evokes bruises and ambivalence, emotional knots difficult to untangle. When I dug it out of the drawer, it was nearly black with grime. I tried dipping it in jewelry cleaner, but it still remained dull and dark, so I took to it with silver polish and managed to get it to shine. It's quite pretty, as the jeweler said. I pinned it on a black jacket I wore a few weeks ago. I haven't worn it since then and don't know when I will again. But it has moved to the jewelry box on top of my dresser. I suppose that's progress, of a sort.

Illustration on page 66 by Myrel Chernick.

ANDREA LISS

The Body in Question

Rethinking Motherhood, Alterity and Desire

IN MY CONTINUOUS RESEARCH TOWARD thinking difference and desire other than markers of discrimination and inscriptions of unidirectional control, I turned to feminist philosopher Elizabeth Grosz's writing on ethics:

> In the work of French feminists, ethics is not opposed to politics but is a continuation of it within the domain of relations between self and other. Ethics need not imply a moral or normative code, or a series of abstract regulative principles. Rather, it is the working out or negotiation between an other (or others) seen as prior to and pre-given for the subject, and a subject. Ethics is a response to the recognition of the primacy of alterity over identity. Ethics, particularly in the work of Emmanuel Levinas, is that field defined by the other's need, the other's calling on the subject for a response. In this case, *the paradigm of an ethical relation is that of a mother's response to the needs or requirements of a child.*[1] [Emphasis added]

I knew that my attraction to Grosz's way of thinking, even in this short excerpt, would yield areas of touching between difference and desire. The strategic import of recognizing interpersonal relations as political investment. Making room for an other who would not be construed as so distant that there could be no points of convergence between self and other. Not confusing places of merging as sameness, respecting independent otherness. As I continued reading, my musing/theorizing came to a halt when I reached the point in Grosz's discussion where the mother is introduced. I was riveted by her representation, following Emmanuel Levinas, that the perfect exemplar of the ethical relationship is that of the mother's lack of selfhood ("the primacy of alterity over identity") and her complete giving to the child. Indeed, is this not a contemporary reworking of the all-too-pervasive legacy of the sacrificial (virgin) mother? My feminist-mother self felt betrayed. How disheartening to find, in a book titled *Sexual Subversions*, the figure of mother again, ad infinitum, at the selfless center bearing the burden of representation and singular responsibility. We can't blame Grosz, my microconversation with myselves continued, she's not speaking for herself. She's offering a concise recapitulation of Levinas's complex and alluring conception of self and other in an encounter where they might meet in the new space of alterity.[2] Yet, for all of Levinas's attempts to detour the self-righteousness embedded in much of Judeo-Christian ethics in order to reconfigure an expanded sense of self, he nonetheless falls into some central unquestioned biblical conventions. These conventions often occur in the instances when he weaves the figures of woman and mother into his writing.[3]

Feeling I had fairly well satisfied my unease with that portion of Grosz's passage, I wanted to move on. But I couldn't cut myself loose from it: "the paradigm of an ethical relation is that of a mother's response to the needs or requirements of *a child*." Wait a minute. There was something oddly impersonal in this description of the most perfect of inter-subjective ethical relations. Why didn't the passage read "her child" rather than "a child?" Was this distancing the author's perhaps unconscious fear of the child and/or her recognition of the impossibility of the mother in this paradigmatic relation?

It's 2:30 p.m. already. Naptime at the Song of Songs preschool. Miles is probably in luxurious sleep by now. I feel myself relax a bit. This is time I couldn't be with him anyway, so theoretically it doesn't have to be as productive as the hours when he is awake and out of the house. If only he could be transported here during naptime so we could be in each other's presence. I could continue to work, feel my love for him, but not have to attend to any of the caregiving. So I'm not the most ethical mother.

When Levinas was thinking about the ethical mother, he did not endow her to muse on childcare, economic, or professional concerns. But Marx and Darwin weren't thinking about their mothers at all. Freud thought about his perhaps in excess. Rather than being theoretically violated as the site of sensational lack as in Freud's conception, the Levinasian mother has the agency of caring, of not turning the other cheek. Caring and empathy, you (and I) might say, are the quintessential qualities traditionally coded as feminine, maternal. Who wants them? Let's give them up. But watch out: what we just gave away could become valued commodities and we'll be written out of the profits. An infinitely more difficult strategy whose benefits would be longer term, however, is to embrace just these qualities and not allow them to be kept solely in the private realm, assigned to their "proper place." Much more subversive is to embrace maternal giving and set it into motion in unexpected places rather than to passively-aggressively let it be stolen from us and allow ourselves to become men-women in a man's world. In other words, to grant oneself the gift of what is normally taken for granted.

At stake then is strategically negotiating between engrained codes of maternity and embracing the lived complexities of chosen motherhood. This process, as you can imagine, is hazardous double labor. There is no other body so cruelly and poignantly posed at the edges dividing the public and private realms. The issue may still be so silent, too, because of the uncertainties surrounding the issue of sacrifice related to women in a supposedly "post-feminist" culture. The dilemma becomes, indeed, how to speak of the difficulties and incomparable beauties of making space for another unknown person without having those variously inflected and complex experiences turned into clichés of what enduring motherhood is supposed to be. Such tyrannical moves occur in the propaganda where the diverse complexities are so flatly neutralized that the (feminist) mother finds part of herself being dumbly celebrated as the paradigm of domesticity and compliance to the limits of passivity in the (perverse) name of patriotism, especially if that public mother has stepped too far out of her assigned place. Remember Hillary Rodham Clinton reduced to participating in a chocolate-chip cookie bake-off with Barbara Bush? The (Im)Moral Majority's failed rhetoric is also embedded, however differently and unconsciously, in the minds of many feminists. There is the silent, sympathetic assumption that we will involuntarily lose part of our thinking, creative (male) minds when children are born from our all-too-female bodies.

How could I blame them for thinking this? During pregnancy and immediately afterwards, I had my own always-in-flux fears. My anxieties kept the body and mind intact; time is what I couldn't make sense of. "Will you be going back to work in three months?" asked one of my maternity nurses in the disembodied voice of an unemployment benefits officer. Little did she know that my life was about constantly thinking and working. Her foreign question was unwelcome and lodged itself in the private hospital room made public where my newborn child and I had come to know each other for only one day.

Then there is the false belief that these equally mindless creatures called infants will turn our heads to mush from our so-called idle hours of adoration or devour us by their own frighteningly relentless bodily needs. The hazards in approaching these half-truths are that, of course, these conditions exist, if only partially and temporarily. The taboo against representing motherhood again strikes deep because the real pleasures of caring for a new other and falling in love again differently are tyrannically conflated with essentialized, feminized qualities projected as implacable and designed to keep us assigned to our proper places. The "truth" is that we are constantly in motion; we are never only in one place. We work against allowing "mother" to slip into a place of nostalgia for the norm. The mind and body of the mother are constantly in labor.

I wonder if I am risking too much here, conjoining my voice as an art historian-critic with my newly acquired mother chords/cords? In a rare public forum on motherhood initiated by Mira Schor and Susan Bee in their *M/E/A/N/I/N/G* magazine (No. 12, November 1992), the editors posed a series of questions to a diverse group of women artists who are mothers. These included, "How has being a mother affected people's response or reaction to your artwork? How has it affected your career? Did you postpone starting your career or stop working when your children were young?" May Stevens chose not to respond to the questions the editors addressed to her. Here is what she offered as a counter response:

> How many artists are fathers? How has it affected their work, people's response to their work, their careers? Did Jeff Koons or Frank Stella postpone their careers in order to take their responsibilities as fathers seriously? Did Pace, Castelli, Sonnabend, or Mary Boone discriminate against Schnabel, Salle, or Marden because of fatherhood?
>
> ...I will be happy to discuss questions of motherhood after your journal seriously researches fatherhood among artists. In the present, when women bring up children alone and bear primary—often sole—responsibility, financial and emotional, for the next generation, it's fatherhood that needs looking at.[4]

Indeed, Stevens's warning call is absolutely necessary, lest public discussions of the dilemmas facing artist-mothers involuntarily shield the "prolific artist" father who so gratuitously moves between the public and private realms. But such a warning cannot be sent at the cost of silencing the mother, again. Indeed, as the editors wrote in their introduction to the forum, the "subject proved too painful for some artists who couldn't write responses. More than one artist wondered how we'd found out that she *had* a child, so separate had children been kept from art world life."[5] When I recently told a male academic colleague that I was writing an essay on motherhood and representation, he enthusiastically suggested that there must be a great deal of visual work on the subject. He said, "I would think that it would be natural." "What is 'natural' is the repression," I responded. It's about time the taboo was unleashed, for mother's sake. As Dena Shottenkirk so aptly put it in *M/E/A/N/I/N/G*: "Like morality, good manners, and a criminal record, motherhood has nothing to do with making art. Its presence neither improves one's ability, nor does it sap one's creativity like Nietzsche's worried model of having one's vital powers drained from sperm ejaculations. Giving birth does not automatically mean giving up."[6]

The "one's ability" and "one's creativity" in this section of Shottenkirk's account is strategically interpolated as both male and female. It is women, however, who give birth. And, as artist Joan Snyder put it, "The bottom line is that you don't have to be a mother or a daughter to be discriminated against in the art world ... you just have to be a woman."[7]

At stake in breaching this taboo and giving birth to a new provocation is recognizing that motherhood and women are passed over in the unacknowledged name of devalued labor, whether in procreation or artistic-thinking activity, within a patriarchal scheme crafted to inflate supposedly male qualities of rigor and singularly driven creativity. The uneven distribution of interest between woman and artist-thinker becomes all the more cruelly amortized in the case of mother as artist-thinker. "Mother" hovers as the uneasy subset to "woman" as well as silently operating as its unacknowledged frame. The devaluation of mother is always at once the devaluation of women. Conversely, and especially in relation to the current hateful debates and legal dogma against abortion, the degradation of women/woman is being forcibly exercised on her decision not to mother. "Mother" takes on an especially irregular symmetry to women/woman. Psychoanalytically construed, woman is always at a loss. The exception to her lesser condition is pregnancy, which gives her a provisional status of phallic proportions and privilege—another of Freud's dreams of plenitude. She immediately loses that privilege in the postpartum state. She is further insulted through the processes by which her children gain accession to "proper" or normal sexual coding. The young boy is traumatized by the difference in his and his mother's genitals; her gaping hole (we are inclined to write this abyss as a whole) signals primordial lack. He can proclaim what he has as distinct from hers and find clear-cut identification with the father. And with that, he can take a sigh of relief.

Have you ever tried to tell your young son that he has what his father has? I recently asked my three-year-old if he thought his genitals were like his daddy's. "Oh yucky, mommy," he most independently proclaimed, "daddy's are daddy's, and mine are mine." "Do you have balls, mommy?" he then asked. "No," I replied, "I have doors, and openings and other things inside." Miles looked at me thoughtfully, "Oh, that's good." Pause. "Can we make Jell-O now?"

According to the psychoanalytic scheme, the daughter's sense of identification is more marred, less distinct (we would write it as infused with oscillation, open-ended). Because the sign of "mature" sexual development in psychoanalytic terms is separation, the girl too must make her leave of the mother. But imagine her dilemma: she has what the mother has but must denounce it. This disavowal must not be too strong lest the young girl loses all identification with the mother and tries to accede toward male identity. She must not cast off the memory of her own tainted incompleteness, for it is her legacy to pass it on. The girl then becomes a mother and must undergo a triple debasement—her daughter's repudiation. So for the mother, Freud's deaccessioning of the feminine is a multiple site of violation. If woman is bodiless and the daughter is always the indistinct shadow of her mother, the mother (once a daughter) bears the impossible burden of being both the figure of invisibility and the embodiment of vulnerability, of exposed body. So the asymmetrical relation of mother to women/woman becomes even more acute. Between "woman" (the projection) and "women" (the deceitful ones who don't match up, who always inscribe their multiple selves onto the scene) there is forceful play. Ironically, "mother" has not been accorded an oscillating, de-referential term that acknowledges there is a real mother and that there are both grave and joyful differences between tyrannical expectations and lived experience. "(M)other" thus conflates the uneasy absence/presence of the mother's body in the non-space between palpable body and its impossible representation.[8]

Father's Day, 1989. I am ten moons pregnant and could give birth any minute. My brother is given a package of wildflowers to disseminate, although everyone's eyes are on me. So I take out the snapshots of a recent bike-riding jaunt, half forgetting/remembering that the roll also contains frames of my posed naked pregnantness. No one said anything until the photographs reached my husband's mother. "I didn't know you were such an exhibitionist!" she shrieked. I enjoyed her embarrassed surprise, for it seemed to be ever so coyly tinged with her own mischievous delight. So let the prepartum gazes be multiple. What I had been thinking about was making traces of pregnancy for myself and for my then-opaque child, far from the Demi Moore glamour on the cover of *Vanity Fair*.[9] Not to promenade my body, but to show her/him that there are no stigmata attached.

Susan Hiller documented the changes her body and her thinking underwent during pregnancy. In her photograph and text installation *Ten Months* (1977–79), she framed images of her expanding belly in a grid format. Strategically presented to ensure that the body would not be voyeuristically violated, the photographs distance the belly from its owner in images that nonetheless convey a lovely eroticism both estranged from and akin to medical illustrations. Serious and engaging artwork by mothers that acknowledges the monumental moments of pregnancy is crucial and rare. Astonishingly few are representations that bracket the differences between mother (the projection) and mothers (with child[ren]), living the conflation/complexities of their lives.[10] Mary Kelly's *Post-Partum Document*, which began in 1973, of course comes to mind.[11] Working both ironically within and outside the bounds/binds of psychoanalytic theory, Kelly's labor-and-time-intensive project meticulously establishes that the mother is anything but passive in the infant and young child's development. *Post-Partum Document* grants the mother an active writing and thinking position and an often preoccupied space within the Lacanian scheme of the child's Imaginary. The mother who meticulously measures her infant's intake of food, registers his excrement as traces, and, later, inscribes the parallel registers of their conceptual development is the artist-mother simultaneously claiming these mini-memorials as her own fetishes for exhibition. It is also the mother who, in terms clearly oppositional to patriarchy's incising of the romanticized mother, proclaims the mother and the child's in(ter)dependence while admitting her uncertain guilt around the notion of the "good mother." She thus inscribes the mother-child relationship both against and within the grain. Indeed, it is Kelly's very adherence to the psychoanalytic scheme, both in the timing and phrasing of the fetish/memorials and in her own writing within the book, that creates the necessary oscillation between psychoanalytic litany and how the mother-child/son relationship is played out in the everyday. In one particularly potent section of the *Post-Partum Document*, dealing with, as Kelly phrased it, "the mother's ambivalence about working outside the home" and the psychoanalytic scheme of separation anxiety, Kelly typed texts from her diary onto cut-up fragments of her son's comforter. At the mark of her son's two-and-a-half years, she wrote: "K's aggressiveness has resurfaced and made me feel anxious about going to work. I can't count the number of 'small wounds' I've got as a result of his throwing, kicking, biting etc.... I'm not the only object of his wrath but I'm probably the source. Maybe I should stay at home ... but we need the money."[12] When her son turned two years and seven months, she wrote again: "I'm really enjoying my present relationship with K., going out to lunch, to the park, shopping together. There're no potty problems and few tantrums. He's fulfilling my fantasy image of a son as little companion-lover."[13] It is both Kelly's poignant honesty toward and her rhetorical insistence on the intimacies of the mother-child relationship, among other factors, that have granted the *Post-Partum Document* so much attention.

Post-Partum Document was a crucial factor in British feminist debates of the 1970s centered around the uneasy status of representing women's bodies. In a long moment when women were reclaiming their bodies for themselves, and Laura Mulvey was establishing theoretical and practical links between Freudian looking and the male film spectator,[14] it was a strategic feminist move to eschew easily available mimetic representations of women's bodies. What I am of course bracketing here are the debates between female essentialism and a more analytic stance that posits bodies and identities as highly constructed and exploited entities. Strategic as these ways of thinking were in the 1970s, ways of representing that do not continue the patriarchal scheme that divides women's minds from our bodies and desires are crucial now. *Post-Partum Document*'s schematic and indexical objects were thus fashioned at the farthest remove from ethereal images of pregnant mothers surrounded in religiosity or from equally untenable romanticized representations of mothers in the aftermath of birth. So what sense can we make of the startling photograph of Mary Kelly seated with her son on her lap, the unspoken image which serves as the book's frontispiece? Her dark shirt (could it be crescent moons printed on it?) helps to highlight K's light-toned body and underwear. He stands out against her: his genitals are hardly contained within. She bends over looking down, while he resolutely holds a microphone in his hand and looks out with a determined, anchored gaze. Is this image included here as Kelly's way of breaching the taboo against mimetic representation, even against her own grain? Or is this phallic image present to remind us, before we move into the mother's assertions, that it is the boy who really reigns? No, let's be fair. It wasn't Kelly's fault that she had a boy. How differently we would read this photograph if a girl was couched in the mother's lap with that steadfast gaze? How different would the body of Kelly's *Post-Partum Document* be had her child been a girl?[15]

"Mommy," Miles said to me the way he does, inflecting this laden term with a healthy mix of wonder, curiosity and skepticism (my projections?), "Mommy, pee like me. Stand up and do it." Holding back my laughter, I tried not to say "I can't," but that I do it another way. He insisted, "No, do it like me." When I couldn't stall him any longer, he broke out in a scream and a torrent of tears such as I had never seen before. Then came the dreaded "I hate you." A few seconds later, calm. He embraces me to comfort him. "Mommy, I love you."

"Don't you think that risks reifying essentialism?" was the response one of my feminist colleagues gave me when I told her I was inviting into the classroom the facts, falsities, and experiences of being a mother. "No," I remember saying, "I am scheming on my 'mother' identity in order to bring out multiple, conflictive responses and encourage new ways of thinking." The conversation did not progress on those grounds and turned to more "objective" discussions of which feminist writers we were currently reading. What I would want to say, to continue the discussion, is that when only one student in my Feminist Issues class brings in an image of a mother to my call for images of working women, we have much more work to do. I would want to say that, indeed, this strategy does verge on provocative ways of acknowledging the body of woman/mother, those sensual and very sexy virgin spaces that must be conceived, that such conceptions help to breach the obdurate wall of fear that has so vehemently separated women's public and private lives. Call it essentialism if you like, but realize that such name-calling wrapped in binarism risks its own stultification. I would rather use my body as a site of knowledge than rhetorically give it up.

Writing on what she terms "essentialism with a difference," Rosi Braidotti asserts that:

> First and foremost in the revaluation of experience is the notion of the bodily self: the personal is not only the political, it is also the theoretical. In redefining the self as an embodied entity, affectivity and sexuality play a dominant role, particularly in relation to what makes a subject want to think: the desire to know. The "epistemo-philic" tension that makes the deployment of the knowing process possible is the first premise in the redefinition of "thinking as a feminist woman."[16]

The strategic move on Braidotti's part to affirm the sexed female "I" is not to be confused with a fantasized and ultimately patriarchal will toward exclusionary power. It is a provisional working politic that, it seems to me, would find an uneasy alliance with the essentialism of the 1960s and 1970s. In terms of visual representation, I am thinking particularly about Judy Chicago's *Birth Project*, begun in 1980 and published in book form in 1985, whose emphasis is so insistently focused on the physical/spiritual body of the universalized mother that the complexities of her material body in a politicized world are kept out of reach.[17] The 1990s' "essentialism with a difference" stands in closer relation with French feminism and *écriture féminine* and is careful not to pose itself in binary opposition with the history/culture dyad. As Braidotti thinks it:

> The "body" in question is the threshold of subjectivity: as such it is neither the sum of its organs—a fixed biological essence—nor the result of social conditioning—a historical entity. The "body" is rather to be thought of as the point of intersection, as the interface between the biological and the social, that is to say between the socio-political field of the microphysics of power and the subjective dimension.[18]

The political project in redefining "essentialism with a difference" is precisely to disengage the female "I" from its bindings, "defined as the dark continent, or of 'femininity' as the eternal masquerade," as Braidotti puts it.[19] "Far from being prescriptive in an essentialist-deterministic way," she writes, "it opens a field of possible 'becoming.'"[20]

To assert the sexed bodily "I" of the woman then becomes, indeed, a doubled and risky reinvestment in the body of mother. Claiming there is a body in the maternal subject might be, to some, stating the obvious. But in the face of this "natural body," this material presence, the patriarchal mode has manufactured the mother/woman into a site upon which it occupies feminine territory as mystery, artificiality, and emptiness. To reassert the sexed "I" of the mother engages her sexuality in a new field of becoming.

It is altogether fitting that Luce Irigaray's body of thinking would surface in any discussion about reinvesting the name of the mother. Merely coupling "essentialism" with Irigaray's own name in the same sentence enters the battlefields in the war over her particularly provocative inflection on the body of woman and women's bodies.[21] What I would like to highlight here is the special significance Irigaray gives to the body of woman and the doubled rhetorical insistence she accords the body of mother. Through her incisive and strategically "excessive" language, language rejoicing in women's bodily fluids and mindful openings, Irigaray renders psychoanalysis's feigned posturing an impostor. That is, male-inflected psychoanalytic theory tells us that we are being too literal if we read the phallus as solely biological and confined only to male member/ownership. It functions, after all, as a figure and a sign. But, let's remember, there is no corollary ambiguity when it comes to female members. Irigaray plays on this unbridgeable difference with a vengeance:

> Speculation whirls round faster and faster as it pierces, bores, drills into a volume that is supposed to be *solid* still.... Whipped along spinning, twirling faster and faster until matter shatters into pieces, crumbles into dust. Or into the substance of language? The matrix discourse? The mother's "body"? ...*The/a woman never closes up into a volume*.... But the woman and the mother are not mirrored in the same fashion. A double specularization in and between her/them is already in place. And more. For the sex of woman is not one.[22]

In rethinking the body of mother as a palpable, thinking space, I think back to the 1977 film by Laura Mulvey and Peter Wollen, *Riddles of the Sphinx*. Conceived within many of the debates out of which Mary Kelly's *Post-Partum Document* arose, this complex and lovely film reminds us, in our 1990s research for (im)possible representations of motherhood, that the issue is not necessarily about figuring mother as a paradigmatic body but endowing her with the space to look. Among many of its cinematic moves as well as the mother's economic and psychic transformations in the film, it is the camera's slow, sensuous caressing and often circular trajectories within the domestic/social spaces of the kitchen and the child's room that project a different guiding system for the gaze.

That the Lacanian gaze has more recently been construed as male is not only one (unfortunate mis)reading of Lacan but a giving-up of the very place where maternal touching can be reconfigured and differently insinuated. In his well-known essay "The mirror stage as formative of the function of the I as revealed in psychoanalytic experience," Lacan describes the mirror stage as the obscure border between the fragmented self and its imagined double, its "imago."[23] On one level, Lacan's conception of the mirror stage is based on child development: that infants from about six to eighteen months find pleasure, comfort, and amusement (Lacan's translated wording is "jubilant assumption") in viewing their specular image. The emphasis on the young child gazing into a mirror or at the mother's body is a highly appropriate image, steeped as it is in relations between vision and the body. It highlights the complex and patrolled intersections between the private and the public, the biographic and the collective, the psychic and the political. Indeed, the body is the stage on which these divisions leave their traces. It is especially significant that Lacan would place such weight on the image of two bodies facing each other in an asymmetrical relation. That is, the body of the infant/child not yet in full control of its motor faculties and the false fullness of its reflected image, either in a mirror or in the body of another/mother.

Lacan handles the difficulty of conceiving both the processes and the effects of the reflected/projected image of the physical body onto the psychic body through thinking it in the following manner: "the mirror-stage would seem to be the *threshold* of the visible world" [emphasis added].[24] Thus, the mirror stage is not simply the self's entrance into another, more stabilizing form, leaving the mother behind in the Imaginary for accession to the realm of language. Nor is the transformation of the child into the Symbolic a clear-cut division. A threshold is decidedly that place always bridging the next stage of entry. It is also the sill of the door, its buffer between inside and outside. The term "threshold" carries both a physiological and psychological significance, being the point at which an effect begins to be produced. If the threshold that the mother signifies is not easily crossed, it may well remain as a coherent trace of the splintery cushioning of the once unmarked self. Thus if the mother's body is coded at the site of specularization and assurance for the child, we know that the space of temporary intactness she holds for the child is maintained through her own touching and caressing, and the surveying gazes are reciprocal.

"Ethics ... is that field defined by the other's needs, the other's calling on the subject for a response. In this case, the paradigm of an ethical relation is that of a mother's response to the needs or requirements of a child": it has been two-and-a-half years since that passage, in the echo of Levinas, arrested me. It seemed an impossible burden for the mother (me, and many others) to bear. Even outside of the mother paradigm, it has been noted that Levinas's philosophy puts an enormous weight of ethicalness not only on the subject, but also on the other who is asked to call the subject to responsibility.[25] Yet the mother's responsibility no longer seems so formidable. In the Levinasian sense, it simply is. And one responds. Responding and giving to the child's utter otherness is, indeed, an act of sacrifice. Rather than construing the mother-child relation as an essentialized binding, the coupling can be embraced as yielding the fruits of reciprocal relations. The task now is to think of the mother-child paradigm in its material complexities and as a metaphor for new relations of alterity between sexes, races, and classes. In relation to the infamous Baby M case, feminist legal contract lawyer Patricia J. Williams juxtaposes her mixed ancestry with the legal ramifications of "likeness":

> A white woman giving totally to a black child; a black child totally and demandingly dependent for everything, for sustenance itself, from a white woman. The image of a white woman suckling a

> black child; the image of a black child sucking for its life from the bosom of a white woman. The utter interdependence of such an image; the selflessness, the merging it implies; the giving up of boundary; the encompassing of other within self; the unbounded generosity, the interconnectedness of such an image. Such a picture says that there is no difference; it places the hope of continuous generation, of immortality of the white self in a little black face.[26]

Embedded in the notion of sacrifice is the act of giving. This giving need not always devalue her/him by giving under unfavorable conditions, but may be construed as enhancing the giver through the offering. To attempt to represent the unrepresentable, shifting beauties of being a mother to a very specific child is also to acknowledge our historical inscription as gendered bodies while refusing boundaries and reinscribing desire. The more historically inscribed and arguably less desirable notion of sacrificing implies the giving up that verges on selflessness, on the mother's internal deaths. In one of Jacques Derrida's most crucial texts on mourning, he weaves a discussion of transfigured narcissism in which the self comes to understand its imprecise proximities with the grieved other. He was writing about the actual death of a friend.[27] I am thinking about this text in relation to the transfigured places of living alterity between mother and child:

> Memory and interiorization: since Freud, this is how the "normal" "work of mourning" is often described. It entails a movement in which an interiorizing idealization takes in itself or upon itself the body and voice of the other, the other's visage and person, ideally and quasi-literally devouring them. This mimetic interiorization is not fictive; it is the origin of fiction, of apocryphal figuration. It takes place in a body. Or rather, it makes a place for a body, a voice, and a soul which although "ours," did not exist and had no meaning before this possibility that one must begin by remembering, and whose trace must be followed.... We can only live this experience in the form of an aporia ... where the possible remains impossible. Where success fails. And where faithful interiorization bears the other and constitutes him in me (in us) at once living and dead. It makes the other part of us, between us—and then the other no longer quite seems to be the other, because we grieve for him and bear him in us, like an unborn child, like a future. And inversely, the failure succeeds;

> an aborted interiorization is at the same time a respect for the other as other, a sort of tender rejection, a movement of renunciation which leaves the other alone, outside, over there, in his death, outside of us.[28]

In the context of the mother-child schema, the first part of Derrida's text on mourning reads like the child projecting itself on and through the mother's body. The trace of the mother cannot be "successfully" contained, nor can the mother overpower the child. The mutual renunciations are tender rejections and acts of love. Be/coming different: outside of oneself, inside the other, in both places at once. Neither occupying nor dominating. To love without domination might then be a coming to understand that one cannot overwhelm, cannot completely inhabit, cannot "have" the other. To love without overtaking might then be an admission of distance, a recognition of sorrow. A little bit of figurative mourning. The geographies of self expanding. Succumbing as powerful abandon.

"Mommy, are you done writing about women?" In his tenderly demanding voice issuing forth with uncanny timing, Miles interrupts my reverie. I cross over the threshold between the mindful Imaginary and the maternal Symbolic, a space women/mothers have been crossing for an eternity, knowing that my work on both sides of the mirror will never be finished.

POSTSCRIPT

When I wrote this essay, I was in the midst of writing a book on rethinking how documentary photographs have been used to memorialize the victims of the European Holocaust during World War II.[29] I would think about mothers who became so debilitated by illness, war, or genocide that to mother went beyond the verb, was too painful for verbal or visual expression, challenging maternal representation. I also thought about children who were so sick they could not care for themselves, whose situations begged the depths of maternal care, no matter who painstakingly and lovingly gave it. My nightly ritual of caressing my then four-year-old son's cheek as he slept took on an urgency and profundity I could hardly bear. Even at such a young age, Miles's tenderness gave me a previously unknown sense of bodily and psychic solidity. My maternal self was in constant motion and transformation. It never ceases to be. How deeply dependent he was on my body and my love, a mutual love that over the years has become less bound to his physical needs and has ever-so-subtly and inextricably turned into my dependence on him, although not the life-sustaining kind. Our relationship is, indeed, interdependent. Yet naming it as such seems too fixed, too determined, too duly enmeshed. It is more undefined, open, part of the unconscious, like overlappings of the self with the intimate other where the mother's and the child's senses of being are constantly in flux. This more fluid and differently inflected sense of interdependence, this intersubjective alterity, recognizes the possibilities for mutual acknowledgements of needs and continuous unfolding of selves between the mother and the child. Yet it seems that I need him now more than he needs me. From the moment Miles was born, I knew our intimacies were already foreshadowing his own sense of self, time passing inexorably, his leaving.

Since the first publication of this essay in 1994 to its second appearance in 2004 and its gracious inclusion in this crucial book, it is still against the norm in the field of cultural theory and visual art writing for a feminist to proclaim herself a mother or a mother to name herself a feminist, and in so doing, allow the deepest textures of her maternal thoughts to collide and play with feminist thinking, psychoanalytic theory, popular culture, and the real life experiences of feminist mothers.[30]

"Andrea, you know we only take avant-garde projects." This remark represents the beginning of the stream of insults and injuries, some more covert than others, hurled at the mere idea of a book that challenged the cultural oppositions set up between motherhood and feminism. To even suggest that motherhood be loosened from its patriarchal bindings, even within the "avant-garde" milieux of publishing houses and exhibition venues, was not to be allowed. I am heartened that pioneering feminist artists whose early artwork brought maternal thinking to the artistic surface were represented in the recent international exhibition "WACK! Art and the Feminist Revolution."[31] It's about time, for mother's sake. These artists' works stand out to me like beacons.

I am a traveler on treacherous waters. I enter Miles's room. The quiet organization he is undertaking takes me over. This is a sure sign of his leaving. I have been watching for warning signs of this silent tsunami, waiting for it to strike. I am stranded before this surface of order and calm. There is no beacon of safety for me.

This is no longer figurative mourning. My son is leaving. Thank g-d he is healthy in body and soul, but his departure marks the end of an intimate ebb and flow that has developed between us over eighteen years. One way of stating it is that he will be "on his own," as if that is a valid aspiration, born as it is from patriarchal concepts of individuality and isolation. I cannot accept this codified concept of separation, the normality of "letting him go"—part Freudian (the mother is always left behind) and part capitalist realism (everything is trivialized and commodified). Separation, loss, and distance are painful, no matter how they are perversely normalized. Thinking of both of us, I have wondered for over a year now how I will cope with Miles's leaving, how I will mourn the impalpability of his presence. The perfect irony of completing my book *Feminist Art and the Maternal* the very week of his leaving marks the intricate alterities of our lives.[32] Thinking of our time together in his new haven and comforting me, Miles says, "We still have a week." *One week*. How does that stark number compare with the seemingly endless moments and days that wondrously wedded your infancy to your childhood to your young manhood?

The moment of your leaving. An unrepresentable moment that insists itself onto my psyche, resists physical location. An implacable distance fragments our words, our bodies. The water that bound us when I carried you now transformed into the miles of ocean that both separate and connect us. Still.

Notes

[1]Elizabeth Grosz, *Sexual Subversions: Three French Feminists* (Sydney: Allen and Unwin, 1989), xvii.

[2]For Grosz's reading of Levinas's notion of alterity through Luce Irigaray's ethics of sexual difference, see her Chapter 5 in the book cited above. For Luce Irigaray's reading of Levinas and the touch of the other, see her "Fecundity of the Caress," in *Face to Face with Levinas*, ed. Richard A. Cohen (Albany: State University of New York Press, 1986), 231-56. For Levinas's own writings, see especially his *Existence and Existents*, trans. Alphonso Lingis (The Hague: M. Nijhoff, 1978) and "Ethics and the Face," in *Totality and Infinity: An Essay on Exteriority*, trans. Alphonso Lingis (The Hague: M. Nijhoff, 1981).

[3]Jacques Derrida notes Levinas's ambiguity toward "woman's place" in "Choreographies," interview with Christie V. McDonald, *Diacritics* (Summer 1982): 72-73, note 5. It is interesting that Jacques Derrida, who himself weaves the figure of woman into some impossible projections (her "non-essence" within the fantasy of artificiality), would be so attentive to these slippages. For Derrida's use of the figure of woman, see especially the "Choreographies" interview as well as Gayatri Chakravorty Spivak, "Displacement and the Discourse of Woman," in *Displacement: Derrida and After*, ed. Mark Krupnick (Bloomington: Indiana University Press, 1983), 164-95 and her essay "Feminism and Deconstruction,

Again: Negotiating with Unacknowledged Masculinism," in *Between Feminism and Psychoanalysis*, ed. Teresa Brennan (London and New York: Routledge, 1989), 206-23.

[4]Susan Bee and Mira Schor, "Forum: On Motherhood, Art and Apple Pie." *M/E/A/N/I/N/G* 12 (1992): 40.

[5]Ibid., 3.

[6]Ibid., 34.

[7]Ibid., 37.

[8]The mother's in-between space of ever-presence and invisibility was again brought to the cultural surface when I was in search of the important and wonderful book *Narrating Mothers: Theorizing Maternal Subjectivities*, eds. Brenda O. Daly and Maureen T. Reddy (Knoxville: University of Tennessee Press, 1991). I first went to find it at a college bookstore whose critical studies section is especially good and whose buyer is very conscientious. When I queried him about why this particular reference was not ordered, he responded self-consciously, "I thought it was too specialized."

[9]Annie Leibovitz's photographs of a seven months pregnant Demi Moore were featured in *Vanity Fair*'s August 1991 issue. As cited in the magazine's October 1991 issue, in the United States alone ninety-five different television spots on the photographs reached 110 million viewers, sixty-four radio shows on 31 different stations were devoted to the subject, and more than 1,500 newspaper articles and editorial cartoons were generated. The movie star's nude appearance was also noticed in publication in the United Kingdom, Germany, Italy, Spain, Japan and South America. In a paper given by Susan Kandel on May 9, 1992, at the Whitney Museum's 15th Annual Symposium on American Art and Culture, whose theme was "Femininity and Masculinity: The Construction of Gender and the Transgression of Boundaries in 20th-Century American Art and Culture," the author noted that "while the self-righteous on the right lambasted the photos' flamboyant immodesty, the well-intentioned on the left hailed its progressiveness." In her paper, Kandel makes the crucial point that despite the photographs' insistence that sexuality and motherhood are not mutually exclusive, their feigned feminism "is fashioned out of a set of conventions peculiar to the little-known subgenre of pregnancy porn: belly displayed as if it were—to borrow from the pornographic lexicon—tits, ass or bush; and woman displayed as an expanded object, happily complicit both with her expansion and her objectification."

[10]A recent work is E. Ann Kaplan, *Motherhood and Representation: The Mother in Popular Culture and Melodrama* (London and New York: Routledge, 1992). Her discussion of projections of the mother in the films she treats is especially well situated between analysis of the psychoanalytic sphere and a sketching-out of the rapid changes in the cultural representation of mothers and fathers in the 1980s and 1990s. See also *Mothering: Essays in Feminist Theory*, ed. Joyce

Trebilcot (Savage, MD: Rowman & Littlefield, 1983).
[11]The installation was later formulated as a book, *Post-Partum Document* (London: Routledge & Kegan Paul, 1983).
[12]Ibid., 101.
[13]Ibid., 103.
[14]See Laura Mulvey's anticlassic essay "Visual Pleasure and Narrative Cinema," which originally appeared in *Screen* 16 (Autumn 1975): 6-18.
[15]How differently, indeed, Luce Irigaray reads and refashions the mother-child schema when the child is a girl. See especially "The Gesture in Psychoanalysis," trans. Elizabeth Guild in Brennan, ed., *Between Feminism and Psychoanalysis, op. cit.,* 127-38. In this essay, Irigaray is particularly concerned with the differences she discerns between the girl's gestures and the boy's game of *fort-da*, coined by Freud, in which the boy masters his mother's absence. The boy's game is one of throwing out a reel on a string and then drawing it closer again. The mother is made the object of the boy's play, as differentiated from the girl's gestures that attempt "to reproduce around her or inside herself a movement whose energy is circular, and which protects her from dereliction" (133).
[16]Rosi Braidotti, "The Politics of Ontological Difference," in Brennan, ed., *Between Feminism and Psychoanalysis, op. cit.,* 95.
[17]This comment is not meant to negate in any way the real effects the project created for the women who worked on it. The book's section on "Childbirth in America" and its discussion on the way midwives were maneuvered out of the profession are especially useful.
[18]Rosi Braidotti, "The Politics of Ontological Difference," in Brennan, ed., *Between Feminism and Psychoanalysis, op. cit.,* 97.
[19]Ibid., 103.
[20]Ibid., 102.
[21]Arleen B. Dallery's essay, "The Politics of Writing (The) Body: Écriture Féminine," in *Gender/Body/Knowledge: Feminist Reconstructions of Being and Knowing*, eds. Alison M. Jaggar and Susan R. Bordo (New Brunswick and London: Rutgers University Press, 1989), 52-67 is a particularly lucid and convincing argument for the political strategy of Irigaray's and Hélène Cixous's writing projects. Margaret Whitford, too, has been one of Irigaray's most steadfast interpreters. In her important essay "Rereading Irigaray," in Brenan, ed., *Between Feminism and Psychoanalysis, op. cit.,* 106-26, she acknowledges that there are indeed problems with the attempt to use the psychoanalytic conceptual framework to make cultural diagnoses. However, in unacknowledged alignment with Elizabeth Grosz's work on Irigaray, Whitford is in deep accord with Irigaray's project to give sexual difference an ethical and ontological, autonomous status.
[22]Luce Irigaray, *Speculum of the Other Woman*, trans. Gillian Gill (Ithaca, NY: Cornell University Press, 1985), 238-39.

[23]This English version appears in *Écrits: A Selection,* trans. Alan Sheridan (New York and London: W.W. Norton, 1977), 1-7. It was originally published in the *Revue française de psychanalyse*, no. 4 (October–December 1949): 449-55 and is a later reworked version of Lacan's 1936 essay "Le stade du miroir."
[24]Ibid., 3.
[25]See Alphonso Lingis's translator's introduction to Levinas's works cited above (n. 2).
[26]Patricia J. Williams, "On Being the Object of Property," *Signs* 14.1 (Autumn 1988): 15. Williams's poignant and powerful essay conjoins personal and rhetorically autobiographical voices with her knowledge of the law field to think the possibilities of rewriting personal property contracts. Such contracts might be flexible enough to respond to racial, class and gender inequalities as well as changing emotions and appreciations of the normally non-remunerated acts of loving and caring for the elderly.
[27]Jacques Derrida, *Mémoires for Paul de Man*, trans. Cecile Lindsay, Jonathan Culler, Eduardo Cadava and Peggy Kamuf (New York: Columbia University Press, 1986).
[28]Ibid., 33-34.
[29]*Trespassing through Shadows: Memory, Photography and the Holocaust* (Minneapolis: University of Minnesota Press, 1998).
[30]This essay was first published in *New Feminist Criticism: Art, Identity, Action*, ed. Joanna Frueh, Cassandra L. Langer and Arlene Raven (New York: HarperCollins, 1994), 80-96. It appeared in an edited form in *Maternal Metaphors*, exhibition catalogue, The Rochester Contemporary, April 30–May 23, 2004.
[31]This exhibition was on view at the Museum of Contemporary Art, Los Angeles, March 4–July 16, 2007.
[32]*Feminist Art and the Maternal* (Minneapolis: University of Minnesota Press, 2009).

II.

Maternal Metaphors I

Maternal Metaphors I

Curated by Myrel Chernick

IN THE MID-1990S, AS my video and installation work began to address aspects of maternal subjectivity and ambivalence, I felt isolated in the New York art world and became interested in connecting with artists who shared my interests and concerns. In 1997 I saw Mary Kelly's *Primapara*, created in 1973 during her son's infancy; the close-up, cropped photographs of the baby's face, creases of the ears, the nail clipper on the tiny fingers, were familiar yet unusual images in that they document the mother's experience of the child as she performs a quotidian ritual, constituting an intimate work that expresses the mother's desire. I was stimulated to create an exhibition that questioned, examined, explored and celebrated the passions and frustrations of artist/mothers.

I sought out work that criticized our cultural and social institutions rather than depicted the traditional mother/child dyad, and did not compromise my standards of quality, but encompassed what Susan Suleiman has called a "double allegiance," an allegiance to the contemporary and traditionally male avant-gardes, as well as a critique of dominant sexual ideologies.[1] I attended conferences on feminism and motherhood, met artists who led me to other artists, read journals and magazines, and attended exhibitions. It was not long before I began to locate the kind of artwork that interested me.

I detected certain themes that ran through much of the work that I saw: repetition in the form of multiple objects and series, materials that reflect the mother's potential for harm, and the oscillation in the desire to pictorially represent the mother's and the children's bodies. What these artists also have in common is their deep commitment to making art although they are aware of the difficulties inherent in that choice, as well as their commitment to pushing the boundaries of acceptability.

The exhibit included painting, sculpture, photography, installation and video; approaches to the topic that were humorous, critical, poignant and theoretical; and featured lesser-known as well as internationally famous artists. It was presented at the Rochester Contemporary Art Center in Rochester, New York, from April 30 to May 24, 2004, and included work by Monica Bock, Myrel Chernick, Renée Cox, Judy Gelles, Judy Glantzman, Rohesia Hamilton Metcalfe, Mary Kelly, Ellen McMahon, Gail Rebhan, Aura Rosenberg, Shelly Silver, Beth Warshafsky, Sarah Webb and Marion Wilson.

Note

[1]Susan Rubin Suleiman, "Introduction." *Subversive Intent: Gender, Politics and the Avant-Garde.* (Cambridge, MA: Harvard University Press, 1990), xvii.

Installation views, Rochester Contemporary 2004.
Top, clockwise from left: Judy Gelles, Monica Bock, Marion Wilson, Sarah Webb, Aura Rosenberg, Judy Glantzman, Renée Cox. Bottom: Sarah Webb, Marion Wilson, Judy Glantzman, Renée Cox, Myrel Chernick, Ellen McMahon.

Installation views, Rochester Contemporary 2004. Top: Mary Kelly, *Primapara.* Bottom, from left: Sarah Webb, Marion Wilson, Aura Rosenberg, Judy Glantzman.

Installation views, Rochester Contemporary 2004. Top: Sarah Webb, Aura Rosenberg.
Bottom: Judy Glantzman, Renée Cox.

Installation view, Rochester Contemporary 2004. Myrel Chernick.

ELLEN McMAHON

Suckled V, from series 1996–2004. Charcoal on Rives BFK, 20 × 13 inches.

This body of work, made while my children were young, is about the politics of intimacy and the tension between the desire to merge and the struggle to separate, which has always been central to my experience as a mother and a daughter. It is informed by my daily experience of mothering in relation to the social category of mother, constructed as natural and thus simultaneously romanticized and undervalued. I'm interested in expressing the pleasure, the humor, the ambivalence, and the resentment that are mixed up in my sense of powerless reponsibility and bonded to the prevailing discourse of maternal sacrifice.

We are staying at my mother's beach house for the month of August. Alice is fifteen and not really in the mood for the annual family vacation. One morning as everyone else is getting ready for the beach Alice pulls me aside and fixes me with her most urgent look. She has an idea but needs assistance to pull it off. I'm her best (and only) hope. "Mom, I want you to help me with something but you can't tell me that I can't do anything or ask a lot of questions." Okay, I say. "What kinds of writing can you do?" she asks. "Well, I can write in script, print in all caps or upper and lower case, and do this sort of formal all caps lettering with serifs." "Show me," she says. I write samples on a piece of paper and she decides my writing is good enough. We go to the upstairs bedroom, which is small, airless and humid. It must be 100 degrees. She brings some markers and a notebook of her writing and tells me where she wants each one of the words and phrases to go: "Life" and "death" on the bottoms of her feet; "Something poisonous delicious forbidden" on her lower back; "I was dying but inside her I lived" on her stomach. She takes various poses and art directs me as I take the pictures (four rolls of film for the next couple of hours). For moments I detach enough to be utterly absorbed in my job but most of the time I alternate between feeling like she's taken me hostage and feeling like I've invaded her privacy in some way that a 'good mother' would never do. Somewhere there is another feeling that makes my chest ache that she would trust me enough to have me help her like this. We take a break and I see our reflection in the mirror, me at the edge of my maternal capacity and her on top of the world. I am holding the camera so I take the shot. Later that evening before dinner she is leaning proudly on the kitchen counter scantily dressed still in her body writing. The rest of the family is unusually quiet. My mother raises an eyebrow, shakes her head, and bites her lip.

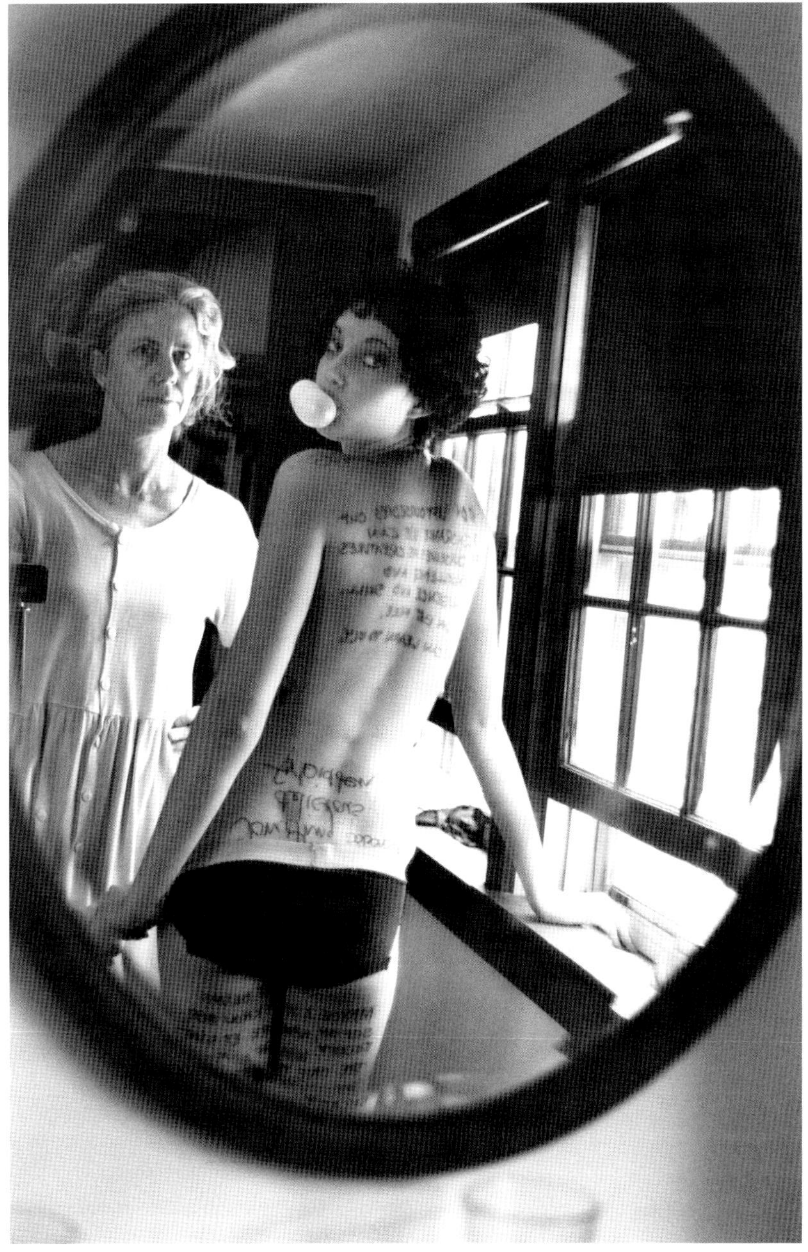

Alice's Idea, 2002. Gelatin silver print and text, 16 × 22.5 inches.

Suckled II, from series 1996–2004. Charcoal on Rives BFK, 20 × 13 inches.

MONICA BOCK

Maternal Exposure (don't forget the lunches), 1999–2000. Folded sheet lead, cast glycerin, hand-chalked wall text by Zofia Burr. Bags @ approx. 11 × 5 × 3 inches. Detail, left.

As an artist I'm interested in the life of the body. With my sculpture and installation, I reflect but also resist the loss to which bodies are subject. Of influence is the proximity in my experience of religious reliquaries and medical specimen cases, of ecstatic saints and flayed cadavers, of promised eternity and matter-of-fact death. I conflate sacred, scientific and domestic forms in work that is often based on castings of the body and of found objects. I use ephemeral substances such as salt and soap, as well as apparently durable materials such as porcelain and iron. My cross-disciplinary projects include photography, sound, performance and poetry. Thematically, my work has focused on the ordinary extremes of maternal life.

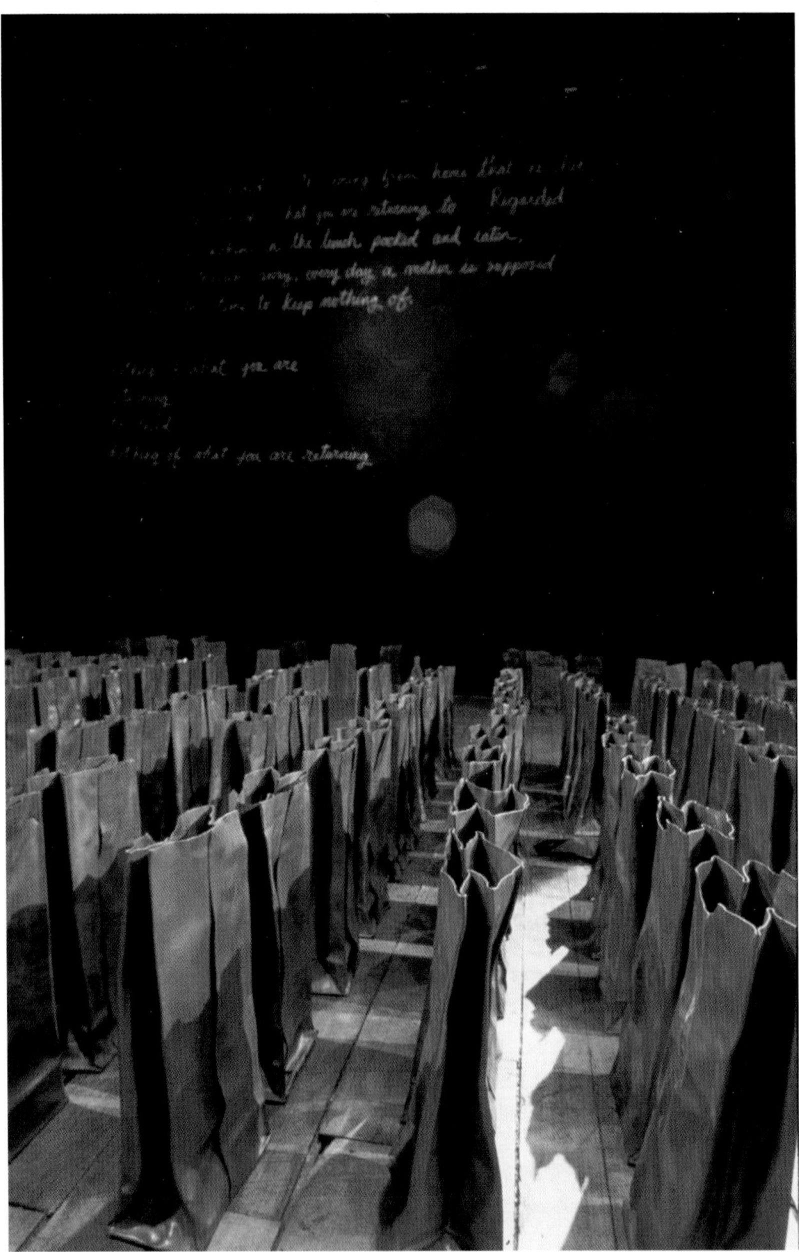

Maternal Exposure (don't forget the lunches), 1999–2000. Folded sheet lead, cast glycerin, hand-chalked wall text by Zofia Burr. Bags @ approx. 11 × 5 × 3 inches.

Sunday News (Daughter), 2001. Lead frame, newspaper clipping, antique doily, baby teeth. Frame: 1.75 × 1.375 inches.

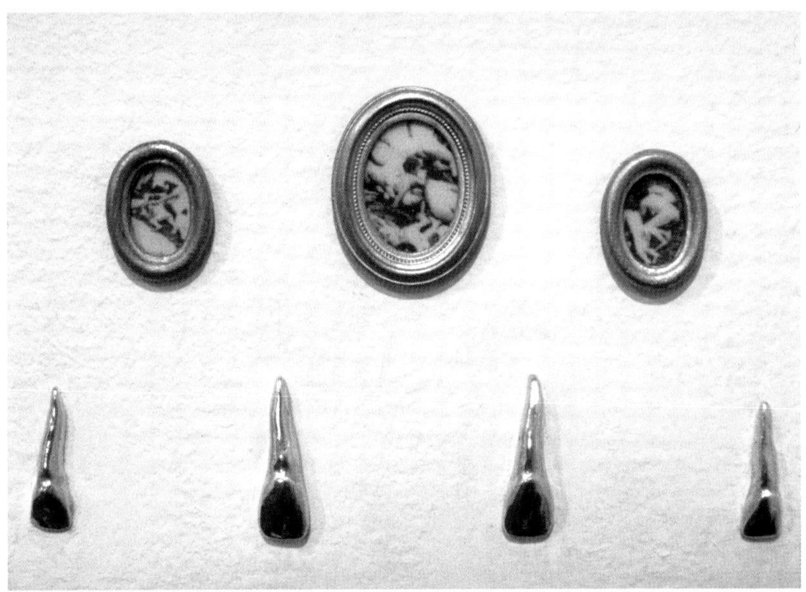

Sunday News (Mother), 2001 (detail). Lead frames, newspaper clipping, sterling silver, gold-capped molar. Installation 3 × 5 × .25 inches. Large frame: 1.375 × 1.125 inches.

RENÉE COX

Yo Mama's Last Supper, 1996 (detail). Digital photograph, dimensions variable.

Renée Cox has used her own body, both nude and clothed, to celebrate black womanhood and criticize a society she often views as racist and sexist. In her *Yo Mama* series, Cox depicts herself pregnant and postpartum, breastfeeding her child, holding her child, or relaxing in the nude at home. The photograph that created the most controversy was *Yo Mama's Last Supper.* It is a remake of Leonardo Da Vinci's *Last Supper* with a nude Cox sitting in for Jesus Christ, surrounded by black disciples and a white Judas. Mayor Rudolph Giuliani protested the photograph on the grounds of decency while Cox responded with a jibe at his own public infidelity.

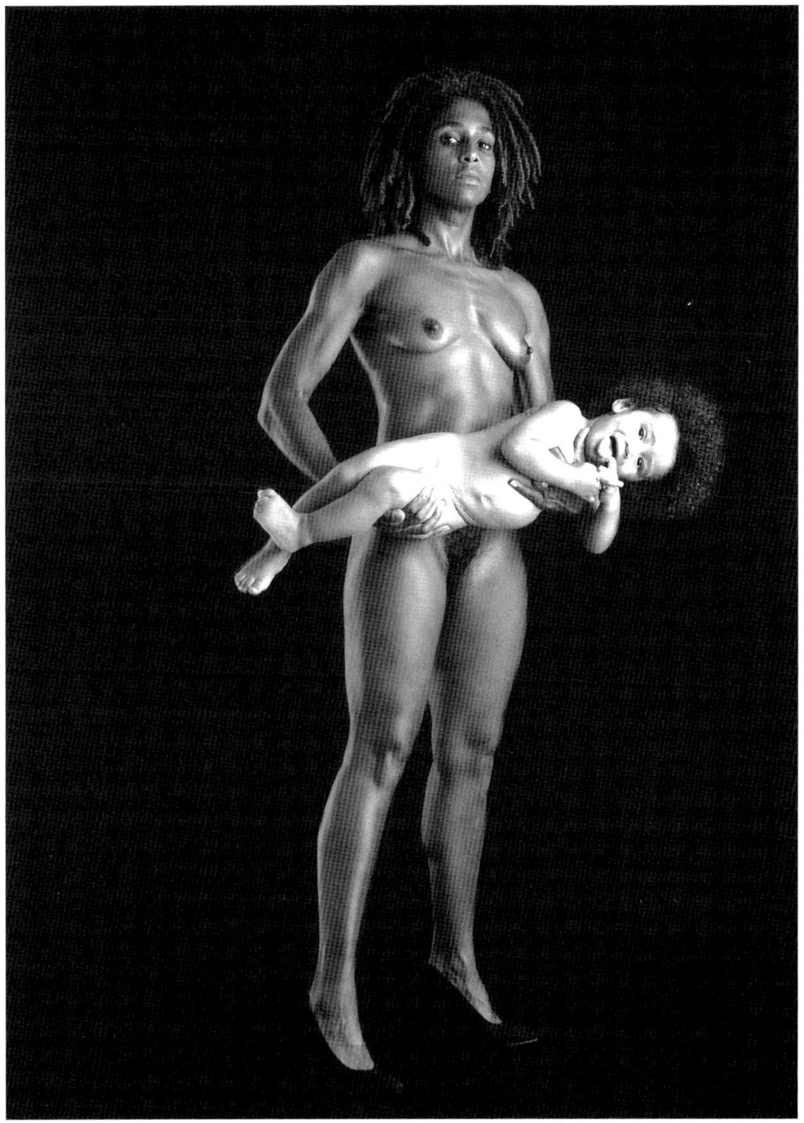

Yo Mama, 1993. Gelatin silver print, 80 × 49 inches.

Yo Mama the sequel, 1995. Gelatin silver print, 85 × 49 inches.

Yo Mama at home, 1993. Gelatin silver print, 48 × 48 inches.

JUDY GELLES

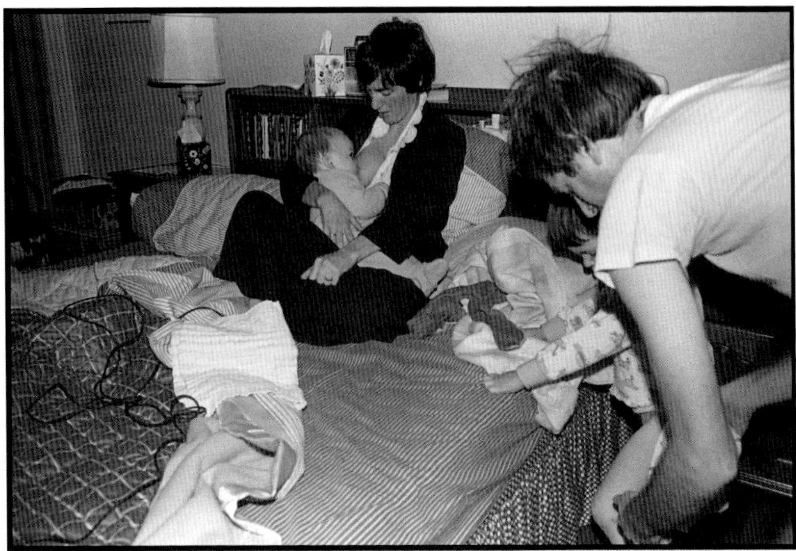

Oct 5, 1977
We were up all night again. David had an ear infection, and Jason kept waking up complaining that his foot hurt. It's been 3 1/2 years now since we've had a full nights sleep without interruptions.

Bedroom Oct. 5, 1977, reprinted 2004. Iris print, 20 × 24 inches.

I began in 1977. As a young mother of two sons, I was caught in the nexus of feminism, motherhood, finding a career and developing as an artist. I used autobiographical stories to depict subtle ways we were taught to be male and female in our culture. Text was used not to simply describe but to add another layer to the work. My intent was, and still is, to show that reality is not hard and simple but multi-leveled and fragile, that persons in complex societies tend to have multiple roles, and that there are discrepancies between appearances and reality.

In "Florida Portrait Series" I have photographed my family in the same fixed pose for over twenty-five years, commenting on the constancy and mutability of the photographic image and about growth, maturation, death and generations.

In "Family Ties: Three Generations," the passage of time is a thread running through the work; how things change, and how they stay the same. We all collect and keep things to stay connected to our past and to our families. Three generations of family artifacts have been paired to create a unique form of portraiture and provide social commentary on our lives. The diptychs offer new historical identities and help us think about the future.

Top: *Florida 1982.* Bottom: *Florida 2007.* Reprinted 2008. Iris prints, 7 × 7 inches.

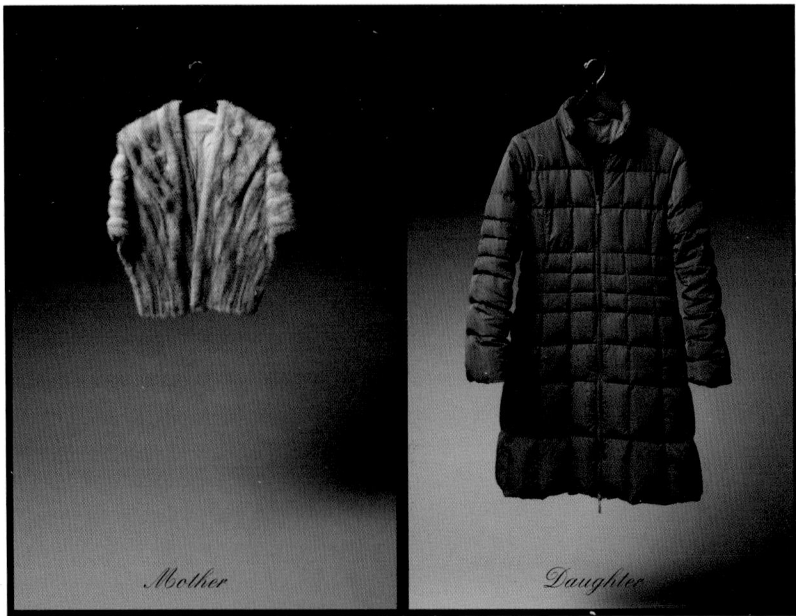

Top: *Horses 1955–1985.* Bottom: *Coats 1952–2002,* 2007.
Archival pigment print, 28 × 31 inches.

GAIL REBHAN

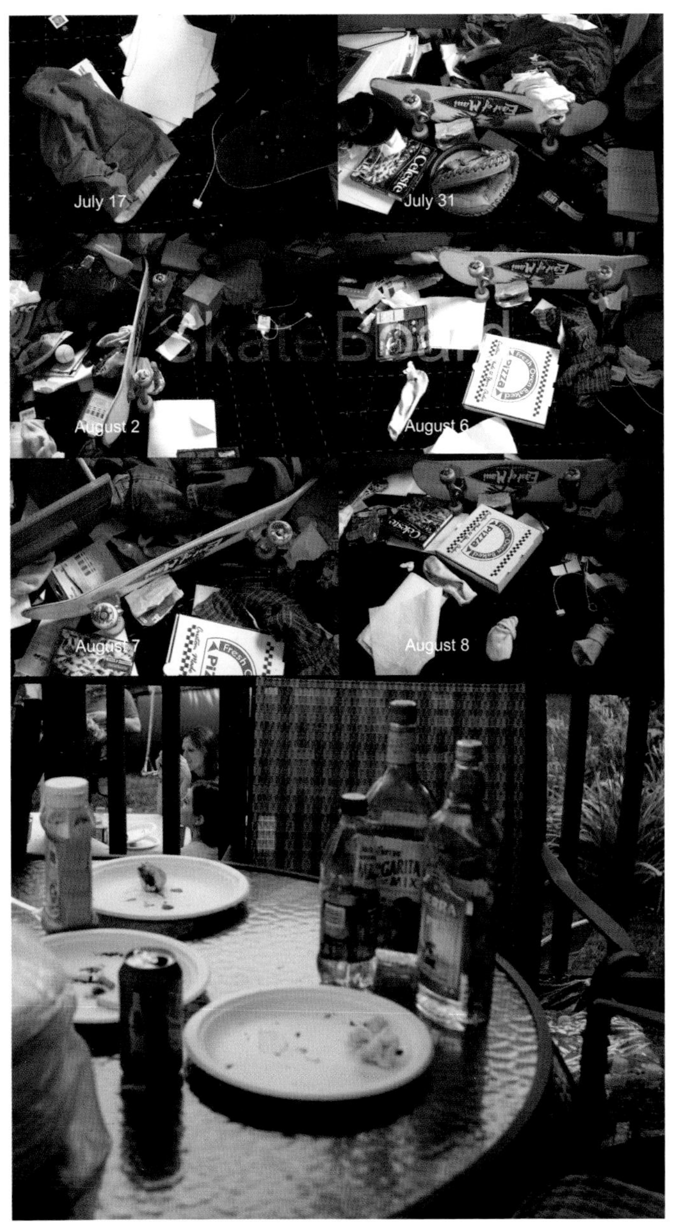

Above: From the artist's book, *Twenty-One* (page 5). Below: From the artist's book, *Twenty-One* (page 10). 8 × 9.5 inches. On demand printing by Blurb.com.

From the *Room* series (Keystone), 2007. Laminated Giclee print, 40 × 40 inches.

The focus of my work is family. I use my family (and myself) as typical representatives of quotidian, middle-class, American family life. I draw on my own experiences to create art that puts this into a social, cultural, and emotional context. In the early artwork, the act of mothering is overt, as I try to instill my values in my sons. As they grow older, that becomes harder as they engage in typical challenging behavior. The artwork reflects changing family dynamics. Through gentle humor and without didacticism, I examine inconsistencies, faults and problematic behavior as reflected in family life.

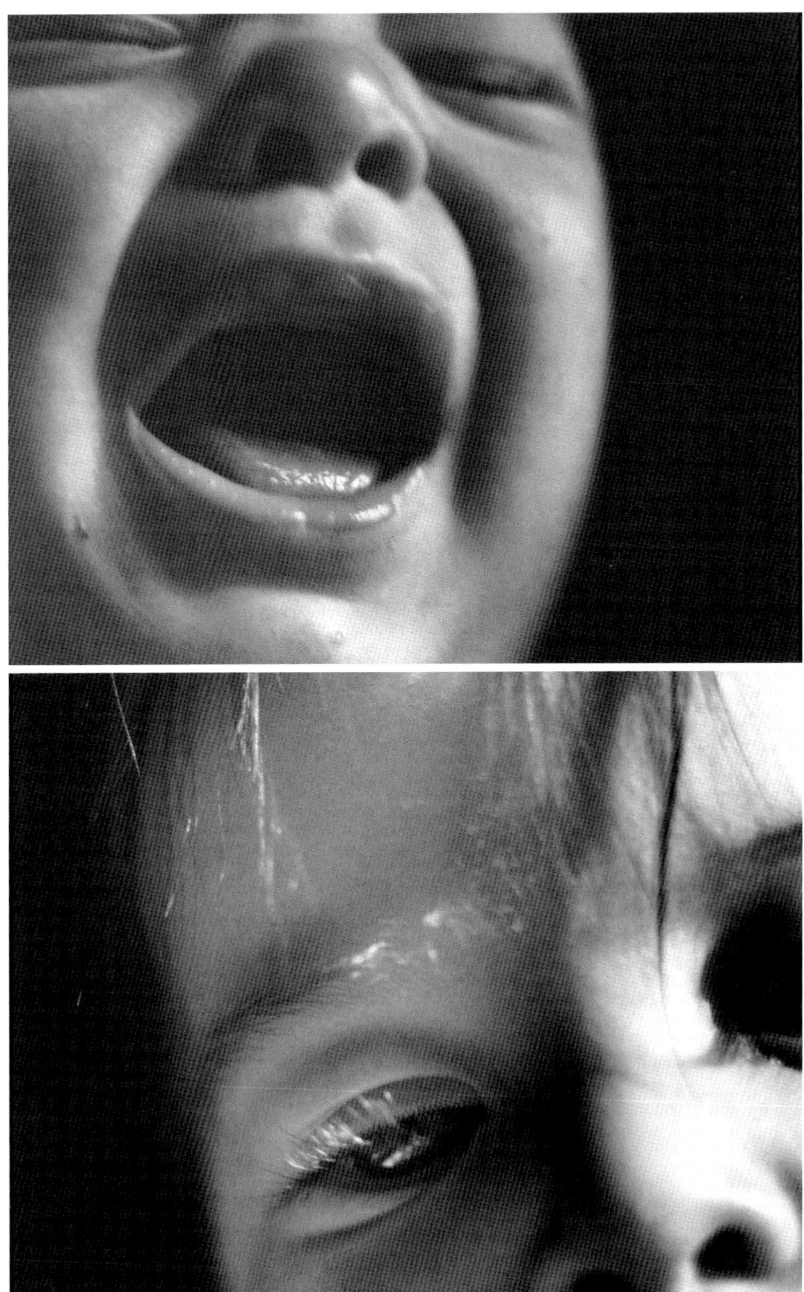

Above: *Baby 2.* Below: *Baby 3,* 1987–1988. Silver gelatin print, 16 × 20 inches.

MARION WILSON

Guns for Newborns, 1998. Cast bronze on steel base, each gun is 4 × 1 × 2 inches.

From 1995 to 2001 my work explored the connection between masculinity and aggression as it manifests itself in the activity of play, looking at the human personality from birth. Working in the permanent and historical medium of bronze, I created monuments and artifacts of war and masculinity while purposely critiquing and domesticating the medium by casting lace, blankets, bubble wrap and dolls to talk about feelings of ambivalence and flux. This body of work culminated in a solo installation called *Playing War* at Hallwalls Contemporary Arts Center in Buffalo in April 1999, where I reconstructed a medieval arms and armor room on the scale of a toddler while thinking about the subjective and interpretive nature of museum display. In the same way that the three marching baby soldiers are heroic in their efforts to walk and horrifying in being dressed for battle, the horses, chariot and helmets are ironic in their grandeur and vulnerability. My work is inspired by the experience of mother-as-witness as I raise my first son, schoolyard play, and violence towards children on the part of children, both real and imagined.

The newer digital prints and video, *and he was made flesh,* are created by virtually layering images of my sculptures with surgical photographs of interiors of the body, raising questions about reality and fantasy. *Playing War* links the ancient with the contemporary to create a weird world of corruption, fantasy and irony. It questions gender identity, pop culture and accepted codes of behavior that enlist young boys into an imaginary world of guns and warplay.

Above: *Blushing Yaksa*, 2003.
Right: *The Grand Thaumaturge,* 2003.
Bronze with patina, 24 × 8 × 8 inches.

Top: *Playing War* Video Still, 2000. 3 minutes long. Bottom: *Pistils vs. Stamens,* 1999–2002. Plaster dust, toy soldiers, colored lights, 10 × 12 feet.

AURA ROSENBERG

Mike Kelly / Carmen, 1996. C-print, 40 × 30 inches.

Dressing up, disguise and masquerade are all ways that children test the prospect of identity. My photo project *Who am I? What am I? Where am I?* is a collection of seventy portraits that uses this as its starting point. In each, I worked with a child and another artist. These works became three-way collaborations, based on play. While for children play is a way to learn, perhaps art offers adults a chance to play. In turn, artists are identified by their work. In these portraits, not only did the children get a different glimpse of themselves, but also many artists came away with a renewed sense of play. In this way, I ending up creating a social and artistic archive, something that now spans twelve years and the work of over eighty artists.

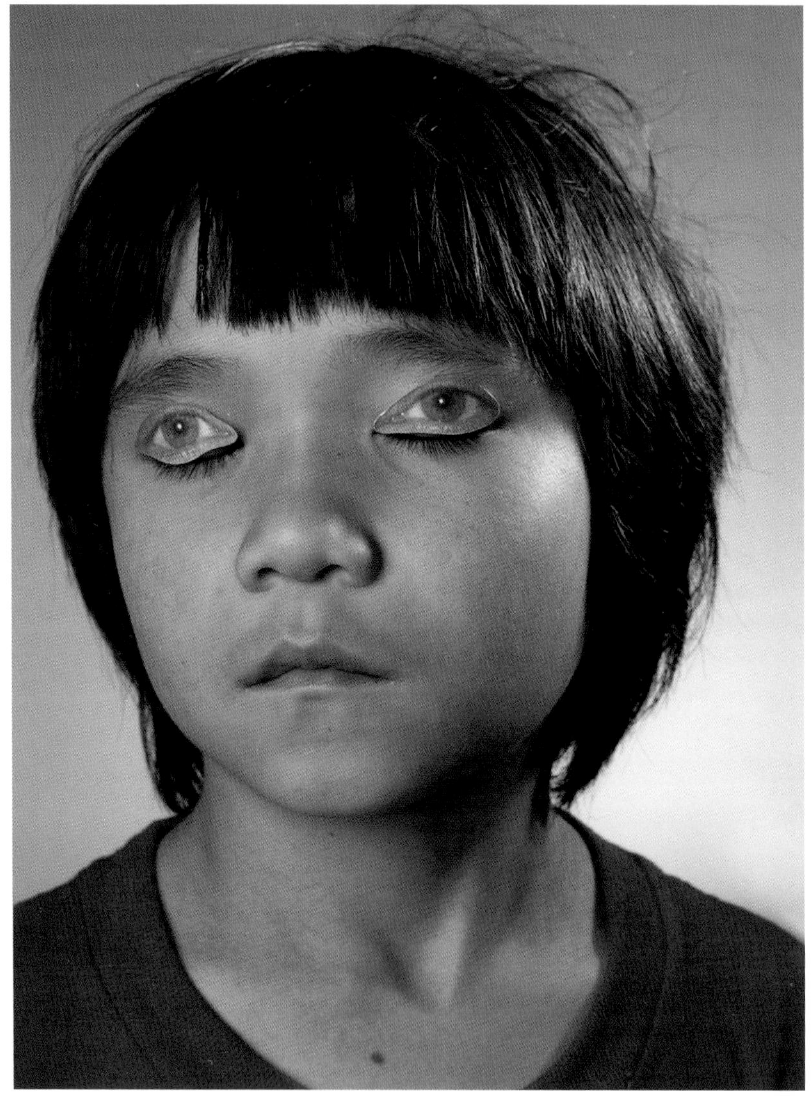

Fred Tomaselli / Desi, 2007. Archival Digital Inkjet print, 40 × 30 inches.

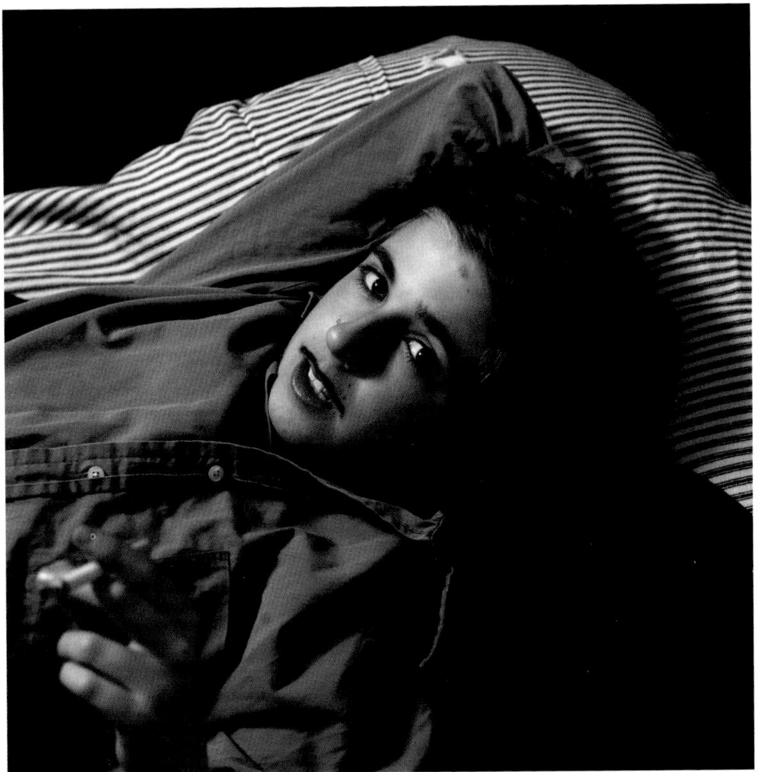

Moyra Davey / Barney, 2008. Archival Digital Inkjet print, 40 × 40 inches.

Matt Mullican / Lucy & Cosmo, 2007. Archival Digital Inkjet print, 30 × 40 inches.

JUDY GLANTZMAN

A Valentine for Lila, 2006. Oil on canvas, 80 × 70 inches.

The whimsical and dark characters that occupy my work come from my imagination. Through drawing, painting and sculpting, I concentrate on realizing these imaginary characters. My impulses reveal themselves to me without a preconceived plan, or time to second guess. Impulse allows me to bypass the literal to a reality that is perpetually changing, one form into the other, like the tenuous link to our past, our ancestors, and our humanity.

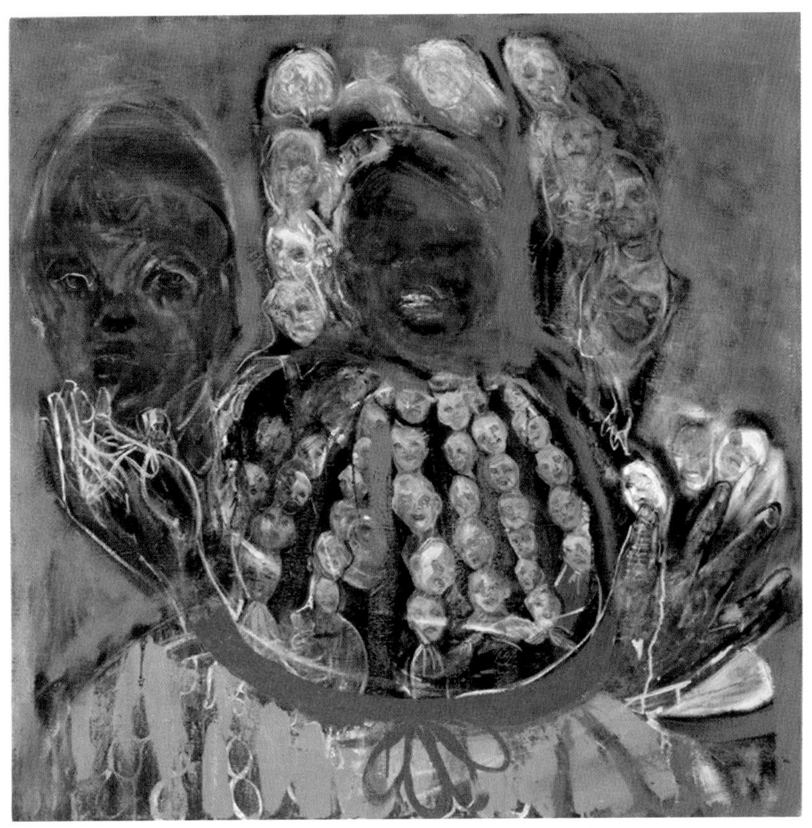

She Juggles, 2006. Oil on canvas, 36 × 36 inches.

Untitled, 1996.
Super Sculpey.
Top: 9 × 4 × 3 inches.
Bottom: 6.25 × 8 × 10 inches.

Untitled (Crown of Thorns), 2004. Oil on canvas, 80 × 70 inches.

III.

Contemporary Art and the Maternal

Articulating the Maternal Metaphor in Feminist Art

NANCY GERBER

"We Don't Talk About Mothers Here"

Seeking the Maternal in Holocaust Memoir and Art

My mother
she was hands, a face
They made our mothers strip in front of us

Here mothers are no longer mothers to their children.
—Charlotte Delbo[1]

Forced into cattle cars. Squeezed into squalid barracks.
Marched into showers raining with Zyklon B.
Thrown into mass graves.
Somewhere a child is crying. "Mutti!" "Maman!" "Mama!"
No one answers.

WHEN WE LISTEN FOR MOTHERS' voices of the Holocaust, there is silence. Mothers and young children were among the first groups of people systematically sent to the gas chambers: mothers, because they were reduced yet again to their traditional reproductive role, and children, because they were not strong enough to haul rocks, dig ditches or do other dirty work for the Reich.[2] The first-hand witnessing of the Holocaust is thus largely a witnessing by children who came to the camps as adolescents and survived.[3] Joan Ringelheim, one of the first scholars to study gender and the Holocaust, has written that mothers' experiences of pregnancy, birth, and death in the camps constitute a specific legacy of suffering. She notes that sexism left women especially vulnerable to abuse and exploitation, including rape and forced abortion.[4] Primo Levi, in the foreword to Liana Millu's memoir, *Smoke over Birkenau*, observed that the presence of the smoking crematoria chimneys, right in the middle of the women's camp at Auschwitz-Birkenau, was an undeniable, omnipresent reminder of the death of their children.[5]

This essay aims to recover the memory of lost mothers of the Holocaust through a study of the work of two of its daughters, Francine Christophe and Alice Lok Cahana. Although Christophe's legacy is written and Cahana's is visual, both women are concerned with similar themes: motherhood in extremis, the complexities and contradictions of maternal subjectivity, and the persistent desire for the mother's face. In addition, their work dislodges idealized expectations and assumptions about maternal passivity. We see mother as protector and advocate in Christophe's memoir, mother as spiritual anchor and artistic muse in Cahana's paintings. These two very different autobiographical projects invite a reconsideration of mothering outside familiar biological, familial, and social conventions, in a time and place where neither mothers nor children were seen as human beings.[6]

I draw on feminist critical theory to explain one of the powerful motivating forces in women's autobiographical work—to simultaneously recreate the lost or absent mother in order to recreate the self. This trajectory reminds us of the emotional power of the mother as an intrapsychic presence that endures well beyond the daughter's adolescence. Women's artistic responses to the Holocaust serve the dual purpose of reclaiming a seriously damaged and traumatized subjectivity while re-embodying the absent mother, in a thematics of reparenting.[7] The italicized passages that appear throughout, and at the opening and closing of this paper, inscribe my own artistic response to maternal experiences during the Holocaust, a response very much informed by my voice and experience as a mother.

Francine Christophe's memoir, *From a World Apart: A Little Girl in the Concentration Camps* (1967) is a first-person narrative written in the present tense in the voice of a child.[8] Francine Christophe is six years old in August 1939 when her story begins. The fairy tale beginning of the memoir, with its image of a happy family enjoying their holiday at the beach, is quickly shattered when Christophe's father is called to serve in the French army and taken prisoner of war when France surrenders to Germany. At home, French Jews are required to register their identities with the local *bureau de police* and Christophe's mother, Marcelle, obeys the order in spite of her non-Jewish sounding surname; she could have no way of knowing what horrors were in store for her as a consequence of her loyalty. By the time Marcelle decides to flee the family home in Paris for the Unoccupied Zone, it is too late. She and Francine are arrested at the border and deported first to prison and then to four different camps: Pithiviers, Beaune-la-Rolande, Drancy, and, eventually, Bergen-Belsen.

Francine started a journal of her wartime experiences in 1945, at the age of twelve, in order to document the horror she had witnessed. Her memoir, based on her post-war journal and written in 1967, was completed in just a few weeks, with memories revived by revisiting the scene of trauma. The childlike prose and voice of the memoir are shockingly juxtaposed against descriptions that are far from innocent, including narratives of beatings, suicide, and starvation. At the same time, the use of the present tense conveys the perspective and urgency of a child more effectively than a distanced retrospective past tense.

In the beginning of the memoir, Francine uses humor to underscore the feeling in Paris that this is a "*drôle de guerre*," a play on words meaning both a funny and phony war. Francine narrates a joke she has overheard that captures this spirit of *drôle de guerre*: "Two ladies are talking. 'Oh! My dear, I make an amazing chocolate cake.' 'Do give me the recipe.' 'Well, I don't use any chocolate, flour, eggs, sugar, or butter...' 'And is it good?' 'No!'"[9] Amusement rapidly gives way to terror as more and more arrests are made, property is confiscated, and Jews are forced to wear the yellow star. Posters appear in the *métro* and the streets portraying Jews with pointed chins, evil eyes, thick lips, hooked noses, clawed hands. Francine's family is not religious—they celebrate Christmas with a tree—and, through the internalization of these distorted images, she learns to see herself as monstrous: "I have learned that I am Jewish, that I am a monster, and that I must hide myself."[10]

Francine's insistence that a terrible mistake has been made, that she is French, not Jewish, occurs again and again. The yellow star becomes a sign of race when other signifiers such as surname and hair color fail. At the *Gare de l'Est* on the way to Bergen-Belsen, Francine says to Marcelle, "Oh Mother! How I wish I could tear this star off. I don't want people looking at me like that anymore. Make these people go away. I am not an animal."[11] The fragility of national identity and the arbitrariness of social constructions of race are underscored when Uncle Charles, Francine's grandmother's second husband, a Catholic who is a close friend of Pétain, goes to visit him to plead for the release of Marcelle and Francine. "This is about a mother and her child," he tells Pétain, invoking what he assumes will be regarded as an iconic relationship that transcends considerations of race. "Bah, Jews," says Pétain, and the two are not freed.[12]

Francine is a compassionate witness who is keenly attuned to other children and their suffering. At Drancy she writes,

> The herds of children filing by! Heads shaved, hollow cheeks, sometimes in rags, sometimes tied together with rope. Gener-

> ally children of Central European Jews, automatically separated from their parents.... We ask them their names, their ages, and they don't reply. Beaten dogs, stunned, they have forgotten everything.[13]

She identifies with these small prisoners, noticing that their arms are etched by scratch marks where their mothers gripped them as they were taken away. Animal metaphors resonate frequently as Francine struggles to retain her humanity while she is starving: "I'm turning into an animal who thinks only of its empty stomach."[14]

The blurring of the line between childhood and adulthood in the camps is another recurrent motif, because children in the camps are subjected to the same brutality as adults. Of Beaune-la-Rolande, Francine writes, "Since I no longer know what good times really are, I blossom, I skip ... and I take under my protection several children who have lost their parents." She says, "At Drancy I forgot my age. Very old, very young."[15] Francine's ability to nurture orphaned children enables her to emulate her mother, who is beloved by other prisoners for the kindnesses she shows them as barracks supervisor. Many send cards to Marcelle, write her poetry, and praise her kindness in a letter signed by sixty women. Francine is influenced by her mother's generosity, stamina, and resourcefulness. Marcelle's work as a nurse and supervisor takes her away from Francine during the day, and the little girl is left to fend for herself. We hear her anguish when Francine complains that she is only ten years old and wants her mother to herself.

In May 1944 mother and daughter are deported to Bergen-Belsen. Thus far, Marcelle and Francine have been shielded by the protections of the Geneva Convention because they are related to a prisoner of war, but at Belsen they lose their protected status. Upon arrival, mother and daughter try to sustain themselves and their creativity. Madame Christophe reads a children's book written by her husband to a group of youngsters. Francine befriends a Dutch girl in spite of the language barrier that divides them. She learns some Yiddish from an Eastern European woman. Yet these efforts soon fade in the overwhelming struggle to survive.

> *The stench of burning flesh. Dysentery, the draining of the bowels. Beatings. Typhus. So many lice that Francine's head must be shaved. Freezing outside during morning roll calls. Corpses everywhere. A constant hunger, so fierce the women fight each other for bread to give to their children. Francine's chest caves in, her bones stick out, and her stomach swells. In the barracks,*

a mother and daughter are being eaten alive by lice. A group of women try to rescue them, but it is too late, the mother dies. The women hear that in the men's camp, the prisoners eat one of their dead.

For Francine, the hunger and terror is so great she becomes angry at Marcelle. She reminds her mother every day she is hungry, so that Marcelle will not forget: "Mother, do you hear?" We do not hear the mother's voice in reply, for what is there to say? This is Bergen-Belsen: "Dead bodies lie in every corner. The crematorium chimney smokes all the time."[16] Francine imagines she will escape by climbing inside her mother's womb, the archetypal place of safety and protection.

How to survive? Marcelle trades some sugar in exchange for a yellow enamel basin that allows her and Francine to wash and relieve themselves in a place other than the barracks corner. Another survival strategy: the women imagine themselves eating croissants and drinking coffee in Paris, an example of Viktor Frankl's theory that the prisoners' capacity to imagine the past or the future helped keep hope alive.[17] A small miracle: a baby is born in the Belsen hospital and Marcelle goes to visit the mother, bringing her a special gift—a bit of chocolate she has saved. Such gestures, that nurture relationships and community, prevent the women from becoming *Musulman*, the term used in the camps to describe the walking dead—those who can no longer take care of themselves—who will soon be selected for the gas chambers.[18]

With the Russians advancing, Belsen is evacuated; prisoners are either shot or loaded on trains that are on their way to being blown up by explosives. Marcelle leaves her train to gather some grasses to eat and does not have the strength to return—another prisoner drags her aboard. Francine at first does not know her mother has boarded a different car and cries out that she cannot live without her mother, a *cri de coeur* telling her personal truth. The train, liberated by the Russians before it reaches its destination, a mined bridge, is abandoned, and, although Marcelle nearly dies of typhus in a Russian hospital, mother and daughter survive.

From a World Apart explores the hell of camp life through the eyes of a child who sees everything and forgets nothing. The conventional maternal role is expanded when the daughter becomes mother to her own mother. For example, Marcelle asks Francine whether she should trade her wedding band for more food for the two of them, and Francine tells her not to, saying Marcelle must keep the ring as a reminder of her marriage, an act of empathy and altruism unusual in someone so young.

Francine becomes a woman at the age of twelve, having learned the responsibilities of mothering at an age when most girls are worried about their appearance. Clearly, the mutuality between mother and daughter, where both nurture one another, is critical to their survival.

Alice Lok Cahana's work is on view at the Florida Holocaust Museum in St. Petersburg, where our family has gone to vacation. I go alone to the museum while everyone else is at the pool. On the first floor is a cattle car—not a replica but the thing itself used to transport people to the camps. Cahana's work is displayed on the second floor. I can scarcely concentrate because I am not sure whether the cries I hear come from the walls, or the cattle car—or me.

Emily Dickinson's poem, "My life closed twice before its close" serves as a metaphor for the Holocaust experiences of artist Alice Lok Cahana:

My life closed twice before its close;
    It yet remains to see
If Immortality unveil
    A third event to me,
So huge, so hopeless to conceive,
    As these that twice befell.
Parting is all we know of heaven,
    And all we need of hell.[19]

Deported from Sarvar, a village in Hungary, to Auschwitz at the age of fifteen, Cahana not only survived this first death sentence but also escaped a second: she was standing inside the gas chamber waiting for the gas when the *Sonderkommando* uprising began. Miraculously, she escaped with her life, an event she describes in Steven Spielberg's documentary *The Last Days*. Cahana lost her mother, two brothers, a cousin, and her grandfather in Auschwitz. Her sister survived the camp but died shortly after liberation, although Cahana did not know this and searched for her sister for fifty years.

A thematic of motherhood is central to Cahana's paintings and collages. In an interview in *The Last Days*, a book based on the documentary, she noted she was a mother to her youngest brother, Imi, who was five years old at the time of deportation.[20] Imi was sent to the gas chambers, along with her mother, grandfather, and brother Ocsi (age ten) upon arrival in Auschwitz. Thus, Cahana experienced her entry into Auschwitz as one of maternal loss. As a surrogate mother to her brother, Cahana was excruciatingly aware of the suffering of mothers in Auschwitz. She remembers approaching a Nazi guard, not knowing prisoners were not allowed to address the SS, and asking where her mother was. For her temerity she received a slap in the face, along with the response, "We don't talk about mothers here."[21] Later she approached a *kapo,* a prisoner who supervised other prisoners in return for favors and privileges from the Nazis, and asked again for her mother. The woman pointed to the smoke from the crematorium and replied, "There is your mother, and don't ask me this ever again."[22]

Cahana started writing about what she witnessed at Auschwitz shortly after the war ended. She had always wanted to be an artist. As a child, she used to sit in her father's factory and watch the workers weave sisal and fibers into rugs and baskets. In an interview with Barbara Rose, she describes the first piece of art she made, at a work camp called Guben, when she was asked to decorate the barracks for Christmas.[23] There were no pencils, no crayons, no paper—nothing except a broom for sweeping. Cahana says, "I decided we [children] should choreograph ourselves into a living candelabra and hold the pieces of the broom as part of this sculpture."[24] For her creativity she and the other children were awarded a prize, a small can of snails for each.

After liberation Cahana went to Sweden to recover. In 1959 she moved to Houston and studied at the University of Houston and then at Rice University, where she encountered the color field paintings of Rothko, Pollock, Motherwell, and Morris Louis. Her work as an abstractionist came to a halt during a visit to Sarvar in 1978, when she realized that no one remembered her mother or the vanished Jewish community. She began to paint about the Holocaust as a way of honoring her mother's memory and creating a memorial for those who had perished: "My art and my writing are my *Kaddish* (the prayer for the dead) for those who did not survive."[25]

Women often recreate their lost, absent, or damaged mothers through art. The painting, poem, book, or film embodies and restores that severed connection. I see this happening in my own work: the more my mother loses her voice to Alzheimer's, the more I write about her. I create her over and over, in multiple stories and guises. Which leads me to wonder: is art the mother?

Cahana grew up in an Orthodox home. Reinventing spirituality in Auschwitz, a place designed to destroy the human spirit, was Cahana's

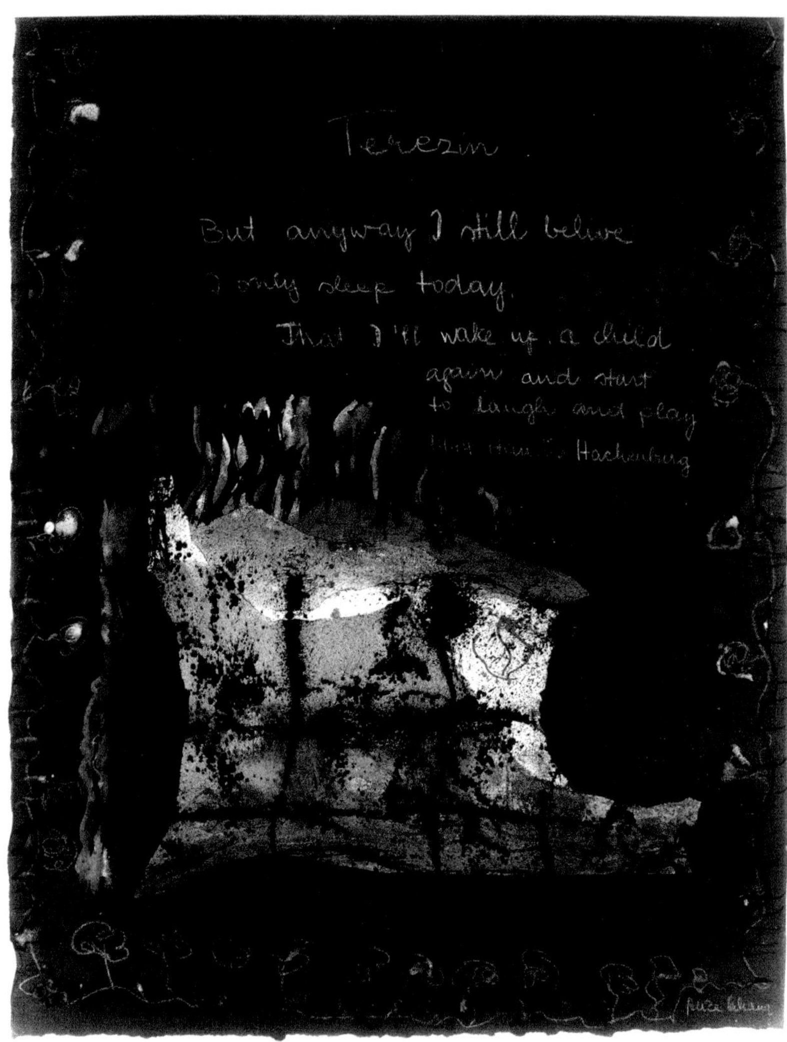

Alice Lok Cahana, *Children's Poem: I Still Believe,* 1978–79.
Mixed media on paper, 32 × 26 inches.

act of resistance, enabling her to keep hope alive and maintain a strong psychic connection to her dead mother. She and her sister Edith encouraged other prisoners to join in singing "Shalom Aleichem," the prayer welcoming the Sabbath, in the camp latrines. The two traded their bread rations for Sabbath candles. While such acts speak of a strong faith, they also memorialize the lost mother and nurture her memory, since lighting the candles and welcoming the Sabbath are a maternal obligation.

Many of Cahana's paintings are collages incorporating fragments from printed materials such as archival photographs, newspaper clippings, and Jewish texts such as the Passover *Haggadah*. The medium of collage, which relies on nonlinearity and fragmentation, seems especially appropriate to the telling of this story of loss and devastation. Too, the torn paper in collage evokes the renting of garments during *shiva,* the Jewish period of mourning. Some of the work is done in muted grays and blacks, colors of death and destruction. The persistent imagery of train tracks, a reminder that this was the only way into Auschwitz, compels viewers to imagine themselves as travelers on that apocalyptic journey. Other paintings use color in startling ways—slashes of red, bursts of gold and orange, markings of blue and green. While reds and yellows evoke the flames of the crematoria, the blues and greens are unexpected in their evocation of the natural world. Is Cahana reminding us of our competing desires for creativity and destruction, birth and death?

One of Cahana's most powerful works, *Pages from My Mother's Prayerbook* (1983) inscribes the tensions between creativity/birth and destruction/death in uncanny ways. At the very center of this collage is a page reproduced from Cahana's mother's prayerbook, which survived the war in her father's hands (her father had escaped deportation by hiding in Budapest, finding shelter in one of Raoul Wallenberg's "safe houses") and which her father gave to her after the war was over. The printed text is the mother's face, while the collage as a whole restores the mother's body. Luminescent teals and pinks are simultaneously beautiful and horrifying, reminding the viewer at first glance of abalone, and, on closer inspection, bruises or wounds. The paper has a crackled surface, evoking the delicacy and sacredness of the Torah scrolls printed on parchment and the shocking fragility of parched skin. The edges of this work are torn and burned, a reference to the rupture of families and the unspeakable burning of human bodies. The calligraphic marks may be read both as Hebrew letters or lives (lifelines) interrupted. In the upper left hand corner, two of these marks look like the letter "s," or SS.

Sabbath in Auschwitz (1985) refers to an eponymous poem written by Cahana after the war. In the poem, Cahana describes how she and her sister Edith used to whisper at night, imagining themselves arranging the table for Sabbath and lighting the candles. The painting is bordered like a tablecloth, in a field of soft greens and blues. Within that frame are shadowy, ghostlike images that evoke human hands, heads, and smoke. This blurring of the human form with non-human elements simultaneously attracts and repels the viewer. A similar response is evoked by Cahana's use of color, in which a background of opalescent teals and blues is highlighted by smears of red and strokes of black. Torn pages from the *Haggadah* provide a cultural and religious frame for Cahana's experience. In fact, as with *Pages from My Mother's Prayerbook,* Cahana's unconventional juxtaposition of the sacred and the secular, the historical and the familial, the beautiful and the horrifying, creates work that is simultaneously emotionally visceral and aesthetically powerful.

In "*Children's Poem: I Still Believe*," the devastating losses experienced by children are explored. The blackened paper is bordered by child-like relief drawings of flowers and trees that resemble barbed wire. In the center of the painting is an amber image that resembles a boot or perhaps a flame topped by ghostly apparitions. In relief above this image are lines from a poem called "Terezin" written by Hanus Hachenberg (the poem may be found in a collection of children's drawings and poetry from Theresienstadt, entitled *...I Never Saw Another Butterfly...*): "But anyway I still believe I only sleep today/That I'll wake up, a child again and start to laugh and play."[26] The painting, haunting in its representation of darkness and death through the voice of a child, is a visual expression of anguish.

Taken together, the written and visual testimonies of Christophe and Cahana are a starting point for a mapping of maternal texts. Their insistence on motherhood as dynamic rather than static, complex and contradictory rather than monolithic, active rather than passive, socially mediated rather than biologically determined, demands that we shift the figure of the mother from its altar of iconic beatitude to a place where the wishes and desires of mothers can be expressed, where their voices can be heard. The specificity of mothers' suffering during the Holocaust, of lives created and lost, situates them at the epicenter of this catastrophic story, demanding an account that is not forgotten.

At the gates of Auschwitz stands a little girl. In her hand is a crumpled piece of paper, a picture of her mother's face. The little girl is waiting for her mother. She will wait forever.

Notes

---

[1]Charlotte Delbo, *Auschwitz and After* (New Haven: Yale University Press, 1995), 55.
[2]Gisela Bok notes that the Nazis used women's childbearing abilities to achieve their racist goals: "The surest method of birth control is death, and Jewish women were targeted accordingly." Gisela Bok, "Racism and Sexism in Nazi Germany: Motherhood, Compulsory Sterilization, and the State," in *Different Voices: Women and the Holocaust,* Carol Rittner and John K. Roth, eds. (New York: Paragon House, 1993), 162.
[3]Accounts vary as to how old children needed to be to be deemed strong enough for physical labor. Liana Millu tells the story of an eight-year-old boy in Auschwitz who survived the selection and was put to work. Liana Millu, *Smoke Over Birkenau* fwd. Primo Levi, trans. Lynne Sharon Schwartz (Evanston, IL: Northwestern University Press, 1986).
[4]Joan Ringelheim, "Women and the Holocaust: A Reconsideration of Research," in *Different Voices*, 375.
[5]Primo Levi, "Foreword," *Smoke Over Birkenau*, 7.
[6]Barbara Rose notes the recurrence of floating numerals in Cahana's work, a reference to the reduction of a person to the number inscribed on prisoners' arms. Alice Lok Cahana, Barbara C. Gilbert, Barbara Rose, Alfred Gottschalk, Sybil Milton, *From ashes to the rainbow: a tribute to Raoul Wallenberg, works by Alice Lok Cahana* (Los Angeles: Hebrew Union College Skirball Museum, 1986).
[7]Rachel Blau DuPlessis describes re-parenting as an artistic collaboration between mother and daughter in which the daughter enters a more dominant art form in order to make prominent the work that both have achieved. Rachel Blau DuPlessis, *Writing Beyond the Ending: Narrative Strategies of Twentieth-Century Women Writers* (Bloomington: Indiana University Press, 1985), 94.
[8]Francine Christophe, *From A World Apart: A Little Girl in the Concentration Camps*, intro. Nathan Bracher, trans. Christine Burls, (Lincoln: University of Nebraska Press, 2000).
[9]Ibid., 35.
[10]Ibid.
[11]Ibid., 40.
[12]Ibid., 42.
[13]Ibid., 53.
[14]Ibid., 54.
[15]Ibid., 60.
[16]Ibid., 75.
[17]Viktor E. Frankl, *Man's Search for Meaning*. (Boston: Beacon Press, 2006).
[18]Myrna Goldenberg notes that often women's socialization skills in the home

helped them survive: "Women and girls found that this socialization, which included sewing and food preparation, provided avenues for survival that usually were unavailable to men and boys."Myrna Goldenberg, "Testimony, Narrative, and Nightmare: The Experiences of Jewish Women in the Holocaust." *Active Voices: Women in Jewish Culture.* Maurie Sacks, ed. (Urbana: University of Illinois Press, 1995), 95.

[19]Emily Dickinson, "My life closed twice before its close," was first published in Dickinson's posthumous third collection, *Poems by Emily Dickinson, third series*, 1896. The poem has been published in other anthologies under the name "Parting." The version of the poem used here was taken from Lilia Melani, "Emily Dickinson: Pain,"http://academic.brooklyn.cuny.edu/english/melani/cs6/closed.htm, accessed 1/07/11.

[20]Steven Spielberg and Survivors of the Shoah Visual History Foundation, *The Last Days.* (London: Weidenfeld & Nicolson, 1999), 60.

[21]Ibid., 67.

[22]Ibid., 69.

[23]Rose, *From Ashes to the Rainbow*, 61.

[24]Ibid.

[25]Ibid., 32.

[26]Hanus Hachenberg, "Terezin," in *...I Never Saw Another Butterfly...: Children's Drawings and Poems from Terezin Concentration Camp, 1942-1944*, ed. Hana Volavková, (New York: Schocken, 1994), 20.

MIGNON NIXON

Epilogue: *Spider*

> *Is it possible to reach the limits of primal repression, the point at which the symbolic character of human nature collapses into chaos? The analyst's heartfelt anguish is so clearly necessary, in the voyage to this estrangement, that few among us can tolerate it: few indeed are the analysts who possess enough of an ability to sublimate so they can "dive in" without "drowning."*[1]

TO DIVE IN WITHOUT DROWNING, to embark on the voyage to estrangement with the help of anguish and a heightened capacity for sublimation: this, according to Julia Kristeva, was Melanie Klein's gift, or ambition, "revealed in all its unbearable radicalism" in the institutional crisis of psychoanalysis in the 1940s.[2] For Klein was not alone: "women joined Melanie Klein in taking this risk en masse" (but "also counted among her most prudent adversaries"), plunging into the waves of an unconscious so inchoate it could only be described as chaos or abyss—or watching anxiously, reprovingly, from the shore.[3] The Oedipal scenario of patriarchy and psychoanalysis, in which men vie over a woman (whether mother or muse, disciple or daughter), was transformed into a contest between women over the corporeal fantasies of a child.

Louise Bourgeois was curious enough about the intellectual history of child analysis to consider professional training in the field in the early 1960s. Long before that, when she first turned to sculpture, the culture of child analysis helped shape her art. It is here in this shadow world of psychoanalysis that Bourgeois's work is theoretically founded. Especially in the sculpture she produced in the 1960s and early 1970s, Bourgeois seems to seek out "the limits of primal repression." Her roiling, viscous *Lairs* and *Soft Landscapes* test this limit in sculptural terms, even as her pointed return to the traditions of the sculptural medium in polished marbles and bronzes firmly demonstrates a countervailing "ability to sublimate." In effect, her work argues for the potential of sculpture to encompass the death drive: to enact destruction as an early and persistent trend, but one indissolubly linked to an equally primitive and tenacious tendency toward sublimation. For as Leo Bersani has observed, it is a singular feature of Klein's earliest theoretical writing that she attributes the capacity—even the instinct—for sublimation to the subject in the process of emergence, to the child.[4]

Klein, asserts Kristeva, "ripped off the veil of a culture based on the sacred conversation between mother and child, if not indeed on the Pietà itself."[5] Her risk was to reorient psychoanalysis toward the mother and the death drive *at once*. In the body of work she has produced over seventy years, Louise Bourgeois has pursued this negative trend in psychoanalysis—the death drive as an effect of the maternal-infantile relation—with an abiding determination comparable to Klein's. In this, she refutes an anxiety about the maternal body that has long haunted feminism, a fear Jane Gallop has described as the fantasy of "being trapped in some embarrassing, infantile, imaginary relation to the maternal body."[6] In Bourgeois's work, the imaginary maternal-infantile relation is instead the mother lode, a uniquely privileged site of theoretical and artistic investigation.

> *I was called Louise because Mother was a feminist and a socialist; her ideal was Louise Michel, the French Rosa Luxemburg.*[7]

Unspoken in the artist's story of her own naming is the compromise fashioned between Joséphine Fauriaux and her husband, Louis Bourgeois, whose favorite child, in being the namesake of Louise Michel, was also named for him. And so Louise Bourgeois's story begins with an act of naming that places her on the fault line between feminism and psychoanalysis, between her mother's feminist socialist politics and the patriarchal order of sexual difference that Jacques Lacan would famously describe, with special reference to French society of the time, as the Name of the Father.

Like her own mother, a restorer of antique tapestries, Bourgeois combined the work of parenting with that of her art. In this, her story also shares one feature with that of Melanie Klein, who raised three children while training, and then practicing, as a psychoanalyst. Both women developed a body of creative work that draws deeply on the dynamic of mothering children. It is even possible that Klein was a figure of transference for Bourgeois: that the figure of the "woman artist" Bourgeois embodies draws on an analogy with that of the "woman analyst" created by Klein. For if Klein's theories of the phantastic reality of the part-object and the death drive are useful in understanding Bourgeois's sculpture, it is not only because these theories became influential at a crucial moment in the development of her work—when the "father figures" of surrealism (and by extension psychoanalysis) seemed to demand rebuttal—or even because of the special explanatory power they hold in relation to Bourgeois's art. The neglected history that Kleinian theory makes it possible to summon—the history of child analysis and its interplay with feminism, the invention of the woman artist, and the emergence of art objects as part-objects—is also a history of transference, of the evolution of transference.

The test of any psychoanalytic theory—its interest, as François Roustang has observed—is that "it can be undone, first on a logical basis, and second on a fantasmatic level."[8] Surrealism showed that an artistic practice attempting to probe the unconscious is less inclined to confirm any psychoanalytic theory than to convulse it. By the time Bourgeois encountered surrealism in Paris in the mid-1930s, however, the movement had settled into a stable structure of masculine discipleship. Within the surrealist circles of Gradiva, as within the culture of Freudian psychoanalysis itself, the role of woman was to embody the unconscious, not to theorize it. For Klein, and later Bourgeois, to reconceive the unconscious theoretically or artistically therefore would mean undoing Freud—uncrowning the Oedipus complex—on a logical basis and on a phantasmatic level.

Bourgeois's art does this for surrealism, tracing phantasy to the part-object, to the mother, and *in* the death drive. But it also counters Klein, inventing maternal ambivalence as a psychic position of potential imaginative power. In this, Bourgeois's art extends the logic of Kleinian thought so far that another theoretical principle begins to emerge, that of the maternal death drive as the mother of ambivalence.

> *The material presence was there taking all that room and bothering me, bothering me by its aggressive presence. And somehow the idea of the mother came to me. This is the way my mother impressed me, as very powerful, very judging, and controlling the whole studio. And naturally this piece became my mother. At that point I had my subject. I was going to express what I felt toward her.... First of all I cut her head, and I slit her throat.... And after weeks and weeks of work, I thought, if this is the way I saw my mother, then she did not like me. How could she possibly like me if I treat her that way? At that point something*

Louise Bourgeois, *The She-Fox,* 1985. Marble and steel, 70.5 × 27 × 32 inches. Collection Museum of Contemporary Art, Chicago, Gift of Camille Oliver-Hoffmann. Photo: Peter Bellamy.

> *turned around. I couldn't live if I thought that she didn't like me. That fact that I had pushed her around, cut off her head, had nothing to do with it. What you do to a person has nothing to do with what you expect the person to feel toward you.... Now at the end I became very, very depressed, terribly, terribly, terribly depressed.*[9]

So Bourgeois recounts the process of making *The She-Fox* (1985), a black marble statue of a headless, multi-teated animal regally installed on a thick cushion of stone. The muscular haunches support a massive, canted upper body shorn of forelimbs and burdened with two pairs of swollen teats, spherical tumescent promontories rising toward a long vaginal slit in the elongated throat of the beast. Pocked with chisel marks, the stone's dark surface gleams at the throat where the pitted gash is laid. Surmounting the square solid neck is a polished block, planted firmly like a crown. At the foot of the statue, a miniature portrait is carved fetishlike into the hollow of the right haunch.[10]

Bourgeois's account of *The She-Fox* compares the aggressive presence of "the material" to a powerful maternal imago that commands the studio. Her description might be taken (might indeed have been adapted) from Melanie Klein's reports of the psychoanalytic play technique. For the role of the analyst, as Klein conceived it, was to provoke negative transference, or the transference of aggression, by constructing "total situations" in the analytic setting, where a complex of anxieties and phantasies could be played out.[11] (Remember Rita, the little girl who in the course of one session "blackened a piece of paper, tore it up, threw the scraps into a glass of water which she put to her mouth as if to drink from it, and said under her breath 'dead woman.'")[12]

In Klein's account, the beginnings of transference lie in the earliest months of life, in the vicissitudes of the drives. Transference therefore is not exclusively a displacement of sexual desire onto another, but a renewal of aggressive phantasy that targets, above all, the mother. "We can fully appreciate the interconnection between positive and negative transferences," she writes, "only if we explore the early interplay between love and hate, and the vicious circle of aggression, anxieties, feelings of guilt and increased aggression, as well as the various aspects of objects toward whom these conflicting emotions and anxieties are directed."[13]

In recent years, a sculpture closely related to *The She-Fox*, *Nature Study*, has often been installed at the entrance to exhibitions of Bourgeois's work. A similar figure can be seen in photographs of the artist's Brooklyn studio, its distinctive profile assuming a totemic clarity in the vast space of a former clothing factory. The centrality of these figures in Bourgeois's late work seems to declare an affiliation with the maternal imago as, in defiance of patriarchal convention, a figure that sustains ambivalence and aggression: not only an object of ambivalence or a figure produced with the help of ambivalence, but a figure in which the creative power of ambivalence is lodged.

> *When we think of the institution of motherhood, no symbolic architecture comes to mind, no visible embodiment of authority, power, or of potential or actual violence.*[14]

The emergence of the woman artist at the very moment when the death of the author was proclaimed has sometimes been interpreted as a theoretical regression, perpetuating the myth of the artist in another form. Bourgeois has countered this trend in a distinctly psychoanalytic way: by analyzing the transference. Since 1982, the moment of her designation as a feminist foremother, Bourgeois's sculpture has insistently returned to the mother—as a figure of anxiety and ambivalence.

Reclaiming ambivalence from the masculine Oedipal scene, Bourgeois's sculpture laces this emotion under the sway of the maternal-infantile relation, but also of the maternal subject. By Freud's account, ambivalence is passed from father to son, a gift with the help of which boys struggle to become men.[15] Klein counters that ambivalence is born of the infant's struggle with the maternal body; the baby's capacity to tolerate ambivalence is, for Klein, formative for both sexes. In Bourgeois's art, beginning with the *Personages*, her first sculptures, ambivalence is bound up with the mother, but not only as the archetypal object of ambivalence she is for Klein. In sculptures such as *Portrait of Jean-Louis*, *Dagger Child*, and *Tomb of a Young Person*, where aggressive cutting doubles as apotropaic protection against such aggression, maternal ambivalence arises as a psychical position (in Klein's sense of the term) in its own right. For if *Portrait of Jean-Louis* stands as a warning against maternal rage, it might also be a symbol of the phantasmatic potential of maternal ambivalence, an emotion that, as the feminist psychoanalyst Rozsika Parker has observed, even psychoanalysis has not dared to theorize.[16] Yet the maternal subject's heightened capacity for ambivalence—her ability not only to tolerate but to nurture this condition—is the very fulcrum of Bourgeois's art.

The iconic status of one figure in Bourgeois's late work, which she calls the *Spider*, declares the maternal imago as guardian of ambivalence

Louise Bourgeois, *Spider,* 1997. Steel, tapestry, wood, glass, fabric, rubber, silver, gold and bone, 177 × 262 × 204 inches. Private Collection, courtesy Cheim & Read, New York. Photo: Rafael Lobato.

and keeper of the death drive. Constructed on an architectural scale, the towering steel *Spiders*, balanced on tapered legs, recall the precarious stance of the *Personages.* With their spindly limbs and burden of egg sacs, the *Spiders* evoke in particular *Quarantania I* (1947-1953). There, a figure from Bourgeois's first sculpture exhibition, *Woman with Packages*, stands poised on the sharpened tip of a slender pole, encumbered by wooden batons, heavy appendages suggestive of maternal obligation. Like the legs of the *Spider*, a circle of so-called *Shuttle Women* leans in to buttress the figure. Commemorating the women weavers who operated the looms in the tapestry works supervised by Bourgeois's own mother in Aubusson, on the banks of the Bièvre, the *Shuttle Women* preserve a defensive distance between figure and viewer. A résumé of Bourgeois's sculptural production of the 1940s—the war years and her first decade as a sculptor and a mother—*Quarantania* is also testament to the formative role of maternal ambivalence in her art.

Harboring a cage festooned with artifacts of the past—animal bones, scent bottles, remnants of tapestry, a pocket watch, a mirror, a chair—*Spider* (1997) portrays the maternal imago as a presence at once protective and menacing, magnificent and monstrous. This figure summons early phantasies of the child in confrontation with the maternal body, a body littered with the enigmatic traces of past life, a bodily presence that is both refuge and cell. In this it shares a familial resemblance to *The She-Fox*, a figure that is at once object and emblem of aggression. The *Spider*, however, is also suggestive of maternal phantasies of ambivalence; phantasies in which creative and destructive trends converge in the shadowy realm (in exhibitions, the *Spider* is almost always dramatically lit) of maternal anxiety.

It was Adrienne Rich's *Of Woman Born* (1976), Jane Gallop has remarked, that brought maternal rage home to the feminist movement of the day.[17] Rich tells the story of an evening spent with "women poets, some of whom had children," talking of poetry "and also of infanticide." The poets confessed "our own murderous anger at our children."[18] For Rich, as for Gallop, maternal anger is a tragic symptom of patriarchal culture's "mind-body split," a violence in the symbolic order that fatally separates culture, history, and politics from "the realm of love and the body where mother carries, bears, and tends her children."[19] In Bourgeois's art, however, maternal anger is less a pathology of patriarchy—a social ill visited on mother—than a manifestation of ambivalence to which patriarchal culture is blind. If, then, for Rich the distortion of aggressive fantasy into murderous rage, even murder itself, is an effect of the cultural prohibition on women's, and especially mothers', ambivalence, Bourgeois's art bears out this claim. But with this caveat: that the maternal ambivalence to which patriarchy is oblivious is the very mother of ambivalence. Portraying this ambivalence through the maternal body, but also through its objects, Bourgeois suggests that the mother who carries, bears, and tends her child expecting to lodge it in "the realm of love" suffers phantasies of failure, abandonment, and destruction that may in turn rebound upon the child. In defense of them both, she nurtures her own ambivalence, and that of her child.

In extremis, maternal ambivalence assumes the guise of mother death, a figure of the death drive turned against death. The *Spider* encompasses the aggression of the other in its own monstrous phantasies of maternity. With its inconceivably slender, articulated limbs, engineered for speed, the *Spider* holds fast, awkwardly poised on pointed feet, crouched over its cage. At the center of the enclosure, under the egg basket, sits an old armchair, an ample lap to receive prisoner or charge, an imposing throne on which the maternal image might rest. Threaded with ambuigity, the *Spider's* nest holds the anxiety of aggression while holding it back.

> Je ne me fatiguerai jamais de la représenter.
> *I shall never tire of representing her.*[20]

Notes

[1]Julia Kristeva, *Melanie Klein*, trans. Ross Guberman (New York: Columbia University Press, 2001), pp. 211-212.

[2]Ibid., p. 211.

[3]Ibid., p. 212.

[4]Leon Bersani, "Death and Literary Authority: Marcel Proust and Melanie Klein," in Bersani, *The Culture of Redemption* (Cambridge: Harvard University Press, 1990).

[5]Kristeva, *Melanie Klein*, p. 212.

[6]Jane Gallop, "The Body Politic," in Gallop, *Thinking through the Body* (New York: Columbia University Press, 1988), p. 93.

[7]Quoted in Eleanor Munro, *Originals: American Women Artists* (New York: Simon and Schuster, 1979), p. 157.

[8]François Roustang, "On the Transmissibility of Analytic Theory," in Roustang, *Dire Mastery: Discipleship from Freud to Lacan* (1976), trans. Ned Lukacher (Washington: American Psychiatric Press, 1986), p. 59.

[9]Louise Bourgeois, taped interview with Jennifer Dalsimer, 4 September 1986 (Archives of American Art). Bourgeois offers a more detailed description of the piece in Jerry Gorovoy and Pandora Tabatabai Asbaghi, *Louise Bourgeois: Blue Days and Pink Days* (Milan: Fondazione Prada, 1997), p. 176.

[10]"Then under her haunches is a kind of nasty place, and there I placed myself. That is to say I put a statue that used to be called Fallen Woman." Bourgeois, quoted in Gorovoy and Tabatabai, *Louise Bourgeois: Blue Days and Pink Days,* p. 176.

[11]Melanie Klein, "The Origins of Transference" (1952), in *The Selected Melanie Klein*, ed. Juliet Mitchell (New York: Free Press, 1986), p. 209.

[12]I discuss Rita's case in relation to Femme couteau in chapter 6 of Mignon Nixon, *Fantastic Reality: Louise Bourgeois and a Story of Modern Ar*t, (Cambridge: MIT Press, 2005).

[13]Klein, "The Origins of Transference," p. 207.

[14]Adrienne Rich, *Of Women Born: Motherhood as Experience and Institution* (New York: Norton, 1976), p. 274.

[15]Sigmund Freud, "Some Reflections on Schoolboy Psychology," in *The Standard Edition of the Complete Psychological Works of Sigmund Freud,* ed. and trans. James Strachey (London: Hogarth Press, 1953–1964), vol. 13, p. 244. This text is discussed in chapter 1, Nixon, *Fantastic Reality.*
[16]Rozsika Parker, *Mother Love/Mother Hate: The Power of Maternal Ambivalence* (New York: Basic Books, 1995), p. 20. I discuss the relation of the *Personages* to maternal ambivalence in chapter 3, Nixon, *Fantastic Reality.*
[17]Gallop, *Thinking through the Body*, pp. 1–2.
[18]Rich, *Of Woman Born,* p. 24, as quoted in ibid., p. 1.
[19]Gallop, *Thinking through the Body*, p. 2.
[20]Louise Bourgeois, "Ode à ma mère" (Ode to My Mother), 1995, in Bourgeois, *Destruction of the Father/Reconstruction of the Father: Writings and Interviews 1923-1997*, ed. Marie-Laure Bernadac and Hans-Ulrich Obrist (London: Violette Editions, 1998), p. 321.

MICHELLE MORAVEC

Make Room for Mommy

Feminist Artists and My Maternal Musings

IN THE 1950S, FREUDIAN FEARS about "smother mothers" invaded the new medium of television. *Make Room For Daddy* (1953-1964), a sitcom starring Danny Thomas, focused on a comedian who struggled to balance family life and the entertainment business. The comedic aspects of this show derived from the reversal of roles created by Thomas' frequent absences from the home. Viewers in the 1950s would not have seen the humor in a show called *Make Room for Mommy* since in 1955 less than 25 percent of married women with children worked outside the home.[1] Fifty years later, however, this premise could be pitched, not as a comedy, but as a reality show about most women in the United States. Just over 70 percent of married mothers work outside the home, but few women find the situation funny. Survey after survey—and there are a seemingly endless number of studies—show that making room for mommy is a difficult challenge for most women.[2]

You can hardly turn on the TV, pick up a magazine, or read a blog without entering into some debate about motherhood. Motherhood is where the rubber of feminist theory hits the hard road of reality. While I'm heartened by all the attention motherhood is getting, the historian in me realizes that our society periodically voices anxiety about the role of mothers when women's status is undergoing profound shifts. That is perfectly understandable to me, since I am doing a fair bit of freaking out myself these days. After a decade of research and writing about motherhood, I had two children, in rather rapid succession, coinciding with my first tenure-track job.

Making room for the mommy in me has proved difficult, despite the serendipitous concurrence of my life and research. My fundamental understanding of myself—that I did not lose me when I gained my children—seems out of sync with the rest of society. I feel guilty that I never once considered quitting my job, an emotion fanned by the media, which seems to rejoice in publicizing surveys that reveal most women with children who work outside the home would quit their jobs in a second if they could. I know in part that I enjoy the luxury of guilt-free employment due to vagaries of my personal situation. I finished my education and found a job in my field, before I had children. I have a partner who is not only devoted to our children, but is also an academic and thus enjoys the same flexible schedule I have. (By *flexible* I mean the ability to work long hours into the night, rather than between the hours of 9 and 5.) We have made do so far, but at some cost. Missed meetings, class scheduling so as to avoid the use of daycare as long as possible, unavailability for evening or weekend events, the presence of children on campus—all have drawn negative comments. It seems even the most liberal of institutions, those of higher education, still are not prepared to make room for mommies (or daddies for that matter).

When I am not worrying that I might metaphorically disappear, I spend my time writing while wearing earplugs so that I'm not distracted by the sounds of my children. The very time for research is stolen from the seemingly endless cycle of domestic chores. I am like a demented hamster on a wheel, never getting anywhere but exhausting myself nonetheless. I know enough to know these years are so fleeting, that soon enough I'll have all the quiet and solitude that I crave, but I cannot put that on my tenure-and-reconstructing document. So every weekday morning I answer the same question: "Do you stay home or go to work today?" I pry my son's little hands off my neck as he begs to stay home with me and send him off to daycare so that I can write, in this case, ironically, about the difficulties combining motherhood and feminism.

I do my little bit to correct the record. (I am a historian after all.) During my life-as-literature search, I came upon Lauri Umansky's fine work, *Motherhood Reconceived: Feminism and the Legacies of the Sixties*, and my idea for a scholarly piece about motherhood began to emerge.[3] Umansky offered a valuable analysis of the role of motherhood in 1970s feminist rhetoric, but I wanted to show that what feminists *did* was as important as what they *said* about motherhood. I began thinking about a seventies feminist performance art group, Mother Art, about which I wrote my first published article. As a mother now, my relationship to the material felt different. My interest was piqued by the way the members of Mother Art constantly negotiated their own multi-faceted identities as feminists, as artists and as parents. As an historian, I appreciated the way members of Mother Art took what were all-too-often simplistic bumper-sticker-style feminist slogans and enacted them in public spaces to alter perceptions of motherhood. The mother

Mother Art Group Shot, 1976. Publicity photograph for the second *By Mothers* show.

in me understood their achievements were all the more remarkable for the barriers they had to overcome. Perhaps the best-known motto of the women's movement is "sisterhood is powerful." The familial metaphor imbedded in this mantra reveals a great deal about the movement itself. Young women framed their activism as part of the larger generational rebellion occurring in the 1960s. The mother-daughter relationship of staid 1950s families was left behind to forge bonds with sisters in the feminist movement, yet that left little room for feminists who were themselves also mothers.

That sad reality was made clear for the original members of Mother Art. The women met in the early 1970s at the Woman's Building in Los Angeles, California.[4] The Woman's Building was intended to provide a supportive community for women artists, but women with children often felt unwelcome. Suzanne Siegel, a founding member of Mother Art, remembered that dogs were allowed in individual artists' studios, but not children.[5] Laura Silagi, who also participated in Mother Art from its inception, recalled that one of the teachers at the Woman's Building, childless herself, blatantly stated that you could not be a mother and an artist. Gloria Hadjuk, another long-time member of the group, had expected to find support for herself as a single mother, but instead became disillusioned by the hostility she felt from some members of the organization.[6] Because there were so few women with children at the Woman's Building, the mothers gravitated towards each other, and in 1974 Mother Art emerged from their conversations about motherhood and feminist art.

In September of 1974 Mother Art created the *Rainbow Playground*, which literally made room for mothers and their children at the Woman's Building. Silagi explained that the *Rainbow Playground* was as much a political statement as it was a practical resource for mothers: "it was a way of asserting that the ideal of feminism needed to include childcare and a place for children, because children are part of society and women's lives and that you can't really divorce that fact from being a woman, being a feminist and being an artist."[7] Physical space for children took on added significance at a location like the Woman's Building, which existed because female artists felt excluded from male-dominated art institutions. Devoting a space for children alongside the "room of one's own" that initially inspired the Woman's Building was an important first, albeit symbolic, step in supporting artists who were mothers.

"The personal is political" is another well-worn catchphrase of the women's movement. Coined by radical feminists to indicate that intimate relationships are constructed by forces beyond our personal choices, "the personal is political" also reflected the issues that feminists saw as appropriate for a social movement to address. In the earliest years, these topics encompassed everything from the drudgery of housework to women's orgasms, but rarely extended to an analysis of motherhood. The members of Mother Art faced intertwining myths about motherhood and art that made it seem almost impossible to combine the two roles. Today the dominant discourse about women and work is framed in terms of balance, but in the 1970s the primary question for artists was far more fundamental. As Suzanne Siegel recalled, "in the early seventies some feminists considered being both a serious artist and mother to be in conflict." Mother Art challenged the notion that the roles of mother and artist were mutually exclusive. Once women cleared that hurdle, they still faced a tradition of male art history that limited depictions of mothers to the sentimental Madonna with child or the martyred mother of the *Pietà*. Instead, Mother Art argued that women's depiction of motherhood was appropriate content for serious art. Finally, Mother Art recognized the ambivalence many women felt about motherhood and argued that those feelings should be explored in women's art.

In 1975 and 1976, the members of Mother Art organized two exhibitions aptly titled *By Mothers*. On the most simplistic level, *By Mothers* illustrated that mothers made art. However, a month of workshops accompanied the exhibition to explore the various questions raised about combining motherhood and art. The topics of these workshops presaged feminist writing about motherhood that emerged over the next decades: analyzing depictions of the mother in mainstream art history, exploring women's experiences of motherhood, discussing how to combine motherhood with women's other roles, looking at mothering as a feminist activity, and of course, daycare.

The announcement for the second *By Mothers* show expressed the deeper intent of these exhibitions. Mother Art was committed "to taking the private, personal aspects of the traditional female experience of nurturing and making it the valid content for our public art."[8] Like the noted theorist Adrienne Rich, whose influential *Of Woman Born* was published the year of the second *By Mothers* show, the members of Mother Art recognized that this artwork would include negative as well as positive aspects of motherhood.[9] In their call for submission to *By Mothers*, Mother Art encouraged work that explored "the pain, anxiety, anger and guilt of mothers" in addition to "the delight, the strength, the care in nurturing."[10] While many of the pieces in *By Mothers* included images of mothers and children, always a popular subject for art, they differed dramatically from the sentimental portraits common to art history. In describing the images, Silagi characterized them as "grotesque, not sentimental ... ironic ... opposed to anything romanticized ... humorous, although some of them are very sweet." Suzanne Siegel produced a graphic piece that interwove statements about her role as a mother and as an artist. Gloria Hajduk created *Application for Prospective Mothers,* which de-romanticized motherhood by posing a series of thirty questions to prospective mothers as if they were applying for employment.[11]

Initially Mother Art focused on gaining greater visibility for mothers who were artists. In a second phase, the group began using the figure of the mother as trope through which to explore the devaluation of women's contributions to society. In 1977 Mother Art received funding from the California Arts Council for *Laundryworks*, a piece timed to a wash-and-dry cycle that was performed in laundromats.[12] In *Laundryworks*, the members of Mother Art entered the laundromat, put an item in to wash, strung a clothesline across the room and hung individual artworks from it.[13] While the task of cleaning clothes might be mundane, the members of Mother Art sought to alter perceptions of this experience. As Siegel recalled, "We were interested in the work women do in the home that is not acknowledged. We wanted to put that private activity into public space."[14] In order to create a dialogue, Mother Art created a pamphlet, published in English and Spanish, that they distributed to patrons during their performances.[15] The *Laundryworks* pamphlet posed twelve ques-

Laundryworks, 1977. Inside a performance of *Laundryworks.*

Laundryworks, 1977. Suzanne Siegel and her piece.

tions about the experience of doing laundry. Some questions pondered the more profound aspects of this everyday chore, such as "what in your life could the different cycles of a washing machine (soak-wash-rinse-spin-dry) be compared to?" Other questions were humorous, such as "when you look inside of a machine before putting in your clothes, what do you expect to find?" and "do you ever have the urge to put an obnoxious child through a short rinse cycle?" As Mother Art developed as a group, pieces like *Laundryworks* sought to broaden understanding about the role of mothers.

Laundryworks and Mother Art became a *cause célèbre* in 1978 during debates in Los Angeles over Proposition 13, a ballot proposition to reduce property taxes. The *Los Angeles Times* cited the funds given by the California Arts Council to Mother Art as an example of wasteful government spending.[16] Ronald Reagan, then working as a talk-show host between his stint as governor of California and his election to the presidency, derided *Laundryworks* as an effort to bring culture to housewives by staging plays in laundromats.[17] Members of Mother Art were angered particularly by the implication that women doing laundry did not deserve or need exposure to culture. The attack galvanized the group. While Mother Art's early artwork focused on making the personal political, Mother Art now became overtly political. In two performance pieces, *Mother Art Cleans Up the Banks* and *Mother Art Cleans Up City Hall* (1978), Mother Art attacked the sites they saw as the real locations of government waste.[18] Playing off "both a verbal and a visual pun about the role of women as purifiers and domestic sanitation workers of the work," Mother Art "cleaned" these sites with brooms, mops and dusters.[19]

Politics also drove Mother Art's next series of performances, which focused on abortion. The members of Mother Art feared that young women lacked an understanding of life before *Roe v. Wade*. *Not Even If It's You* (1981) explored the many situations in which women would find themselves unwillingly pregnant under illegalized abortion. The title of the piece neatly summarized the way Mother Art hoped to personalize the debate about abortion. Not even you, even if you think it justified, will be able to obtain an abortion if *Roe v. Wade* is overturned. Subsequent pieces on this theme, such as the *The Museum of Illegal Abortions* (1981), explored quite graphically the reality of illegal abortion by displaying the implements women had used in the past to induce abortion, while *Freedom of Choice* (1982) used the Statue of Liberty as an image of American freedom to make an ironic comment on the lack of freedom women would face if abortion became illegal.

Abortion Cabinet, 1981. Installation from the Museum of Illegal Abortions.

While a focus on abortion rights might seem odd for a group that initially formed around motherhood, Mother Art understood efforts to illegalize abortion as part of an effort to cast all women as mothers. Although Mother Art celebrated women's role as mothers and valued women's work as mothers, they never lapsed into an essentialist position that framed all women as potential mothers.

The last official Mother Art piece occurred in 1985.[20] *Dining Room Table* commemorated the founding in March of 1967 of Another Mother for Peace, an anti-war group, at the dining room table of Barbara Avedon.[21] Another Mother for Peace sought to end the war in Vietnam through a variety of strategies. The organization coined the slogan "war is unhealthy for children and other living things," organized a consumer boycott and worked to elect anti-war candidates. Deborah Krall, who joined Mother Art in 1980, explained "[w]e loved the idea of her [Avedon] working from her dining room table. Women could be powerful from within the home." The installation of *Dining Room Table*, which occurred in several venues, mixed images of domesticity, such as toys and coffee cups, with the tools of political activism, like a typewriter and letters to politicians. *Dining Room Table* summed up the themes Mother Art's work had addressed over the preceding decade, raising awareness of women as powerful people in society who are able to combine multiple roles, in this case motherhood and political activism.

If my life were a Mother Art piece it would be what I have come to think of as the Rollercoaster of Motherhood. A rollercoaster, not a modern, steel-framed amusement park version, but a rickety wooden one like those at a cut-rate carnival, that creaks round and round, as the mommy doll lurches first upward before a momentary pause and then a fall into speed-filled freedom. I ride that emotional rollercoaster of motherhood every day. At one moment I am exhilarated by a class that went particularly well or a key insight into a research project, and the next second I fall into the pit of guilt. On any given day, I'm pushed over the top by my fear that I am not a good enough—fill in one of the following—teacher/scholar/colleague/friend/wife/mother. At the same time I am angered that I worry so much about fulfilling the expectations and needs of others at the expense of myself. If I have learned anything from the members of Mother Art, or feminists of the 1970s in general, it is that I must exploit this contradiction, not avoid it. So I write articles like this one that allow me not only to function as a scholar, but also to muse about motherhood in a way that will hopefully be beneficial to other mothers.

Notes

[1]Prior to 1970, the labor force participation rates of never-married mothers with children were not published in reports by the United States Government. This data is derived from Sharon R. Cohany and Emy Sok, "Trends In Labor Force Participation of Married Mothers of Infants" *Monthly Labor Review Online* 130, no. 2 (February 2007) <http://www.bls.gov/opub/mlr/2007/02/art2full.pdf>
[2]For a recent review of some of these studies see Ruthanne Prioreschi, "Career Women Find Balancing Hard: Working Mothers Miss Out on Children's Growth" (May 2, 2007) <http://feminism.suite101.com/article.cfm/duality_of_womens_roles>, accessed May 24, 2007.
[3]Lauri Umansky, *Motherhood Reconceived: Feminism and the Legacies of the Sixties* (New York: New York University, 1996).
[4]Original members of the group included Christy Kruse, Helen Million, Laura Silagi, and Suzanne Siegel. The membership of the group fluctuated over the years. Only Siegel and Silagi remained in the group for its entire history. Gloria Hajduk, who joined the group in 1976, and Deborah Krall, who joined in 1980, remained active the longest. A history of the Woman's Building can be found on their website, www.womansbuilding.org.
[5]Suzanne Siegel, interviewed by the author, 2 October 1992, Woman's Building Oral History Collection, the Woman's Building. All quotations attributed to Suzanne Siegel are taken from this interview unless otherwise noted.
[6]Gloria Hajduk, personal correspondence with the author, circa July 2002.
[7]Laura Silagi, telephone interview with the author, 17 July 2002. All quotations attributed to Laura Silagi are taken from this interview unless otherwise noted.
[8]Mother Art, "Second By Mothers Show, July 17-August 14" (unpublished flyer).
[9]Adrienne Rich, *Of Woman Born: Motherhood as Experience and Institution* (New York: Norton, 1976).
[10]Mother Art, "Second By Mothers Show".
[11]Gloria Hadjuk, *Application for Potential Mothers* (unpublished pamphlet and artist's statement, c. 1976).
[12]By 1977, Mother Art was comprised of Suzanne Siegel, Laura Silagi, Helen Million-Ruby, Gloria Hajduk, and poet Velene Campbell. Information about *Laundryworks* is based in interviews with Siegel and Silagi as well as Dennis Hathaway, "Mother Art: Victim of California Carving Knife" *New World* 4 (1978): 21 and Jan Alexander-Leitz, "Laundromat as Art Gallery" *Ms.* (March 1979): 20.
[13]For example, Gloria Hajduk's piece played with the parallel notions between the wash cycle and life cycles. Suzanne Siegel created a Xerox series that transitioned from a clear image to one almost completely faded, equating colors fading in the

laundry and the invisibility of women's work. Helen Million, another founding member of the group, showed photographs of women doing laundry and of the actual items that each woman laundered. Laura Silagi created an ironic image of washing photos of water. Velene Campbell, who joined Mother Art in 1976, created random poems composed with words silk-screened onto pillowcases.

[14]"Revisiting Mother Art," *Crania* 11 (1998) <http://home.roadrunner.com/~lrsilagi/Crania/crania/issue11/motherart/motherartarticle.html>, accessed May 24, 2007.

[15]Mother Art, *Laundry Works* (unpublished pamphlet, c. 1977).

[16]W.B. Rodd, "Legislators Search for Ways to Cut Fat and Don't have Far to Look," *Los Angeles Times*, 12 June 1978.

[17]Ronald Reagan, "Waste," transcript of broadcast, KABC (29 November 1978). Files of Laura Silagi.

[18]Mother Art, "Mother Art Cleans Up ... The Banks ... City Hall," *High Performance* 1, no.32 (1978).

[19]"Mother Art Cleans Up..."

[20]Although the members of Mother Art officially stopped collaborating in 1986, Deborah Krall, Suzanne Siegel and Laura Silagi once again joined forces in 2000 for *Running Out of Time*, an installation piece that addressed the dichotomies of middle age.

[21]In 2003 this group was restarted to protest United States involvement in Iraq. For details of its history see "Another Mother for Peace" <http://www.anothermother.org/history.html>

MÓNICA MAYER

¡MADRES!

ON JUNE 23, 1983, MARIS BUSTAMANTE and I formed *Polvo de Gallina Negra (Black Hen's Dust)*, the first feminist art group in Mexico.

After leaving art school, Maris had been part of *El No-Grupo*, one of the most important artistic collectives in the seventies, and the first one to center its production exclusively on performance art. I, on the other hand, having studied at art school in Mexico and becoming involved in the women's movement, had recently returned from participating in the Feminist Art Program, a two-year course at the Woman's Building in Los Angeles.

By the 1980s, both Maris and I had participated in several collaborative projects with other women artists and were interested in forming a feminist art collective. We organized a meeting with many colleagues who had participated in these projects, to invite them to form a group. Except for photographer Herminia Dosal, who was part of the group for a while but left because she was not interested in performance art, none of the other women joined us, for all sorts of reasons such as "I won't be able to get a boyfriend if I am identified as a feminist" or "Collective work was part of the '70s."

The objectives of *Polvo de Gallina Negra* were (1) to analyze women's images in art and in the media, (2) to study and to promote the participation of women in art, and (3) to create images based on our experience as women in a patriarchal system, with a feminist perspective and with the goal of transforming the visual world in order to alter reality. To achieve this, our work would have to take whatever shape was necessary and we needed to reach large audiences. Our strategy was humor.

No one can say we weren't ambitious (or modest), but we also knew what we were up against, so we chose a name to reflect this. *Polvo de Gallina Negra* (Black Hen Powder) is a popular remedy against the evil

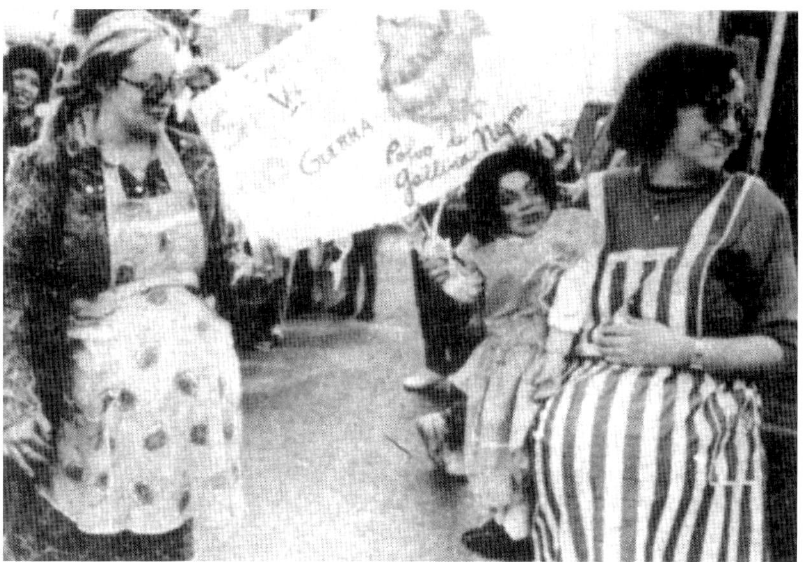

Manifestación: Performance during an abortion demonstration in Mexico City, 1991.
Maris Bustamente (left), Mónica Mayer (right).

eye. We believed that in this world it is difficult to be an artist, all the more so to be woman artist and it is almost impossible to be a feminist artist, so we selected a name that would protect us.

Our first event was the performance "*El Respeto al Derecho al Cuerpo Ajeno es la Paz.*" It took place during a demonstration against violence against women on October 7, 1983, at the Juárez Monument in Mexico City. It was based on the famous phrase of President Benito Juárez (1806-1872), known abroad as the Abraham Lincoln of Mexico, "Respect of the right of others is peace," which we changed to "Respect of the body of others is peace."

During the performance we prepared a potion to inflict the evil eye upon rapists. The ingredients were things such as: twelve dozen eyes and hearts of women who accept themselves as such, three tongues of women who don't become submissive even when they have been raped, thirty grams of powder of voices that demystify rape, a sprinkle of supportive legislators, etc., and it was distributed among the audience. The recipe was later published in several magazines and feminist appointment books and has been dramatized twice on television.

Polvo de Gallina's most ambitious project was *¡MADRES!*, which literally means "mothers," but is also an expression that can be loosely translated as "Holy shit!"

It happened between 1984 and 1987 and, as several of our pieces, it took very different shapes. At the time we defined these types of work as Visual Projects. In them we integrated life, art and politics and disregarded traditional definitions of art. We were particularly flexible about time. Thus, a project could be a tour of 30 performed lectures in the State of Mexico or something like *¡MADRES!*

The first thing we did as part of our in-depth research for *¡MADRES!* was to get pregnant. Naturally, we had the help of our husbands, who were both artists and as such understood our intentions perfectly.[1] Obviously, as feminists we had daughters, and our scientific accuracy was such that my daughter Yuruen and Maris' daughter Andrea were born only three months apart in 1985.

¡MADRES! was integrated by several sub-projects. I will try to describe them as best I can, but since a very important part of our work is playing with language, popular sayings and specific political situations in Mexico, I'm afraid some of it might be lost in translation.

Liberté, Egalité, Maternité: Polvo De Gallina Negra Ataca de Nuevo (Strikes Again)

For seven months (it was a premature birth), we mailed a total of seven art pieces on different aspects of motherhood to a list of 350 artists, feminists, friends and media.

Letter #1: *Mother's Day: Do You Know Where Your Mother Is?*

This letter included the *Polvo de Gallina Negra* formula to summon the Mother Archetype, which led the reader through a humorous guided fantasy in search of their own personal Mother Archetype, understood in the Jungian sense as "the self-portrait of an instinct." We claimed that true feminist art needed to break all chains, including those of thoughts and affections, conscious and unconscious.

Letter #2: *Brief History of Those Who Tried the Milk Before Buying the Cow*

I think the above title roughly translates the name of this letter, which was *Breve Historia de las que se Comieron la Torta Antes del Recreo,* a saying that applies to women who get pregnant before marriage. The letter had a page with texts on both sides. One had positive feelings on motherhood such as: "by having a daughter I recovered my mother" and the other, negative ones: "My only power is screwing my kids." Each phrase was attributed a color. The letter also included a plastic bag with confetti with these colors as a context for fragments of texts in which we pondered the fact that men had created the image of what we consider feminine and the impact of this on the images of Mother Archetype in different cultures.

Letter #3: *Epitaph*

On one side of the paper Maris drew silhouettes of animals through which you could see her face in mourning. It had a text that read: "My father is dead; like me, my children will say: my mother is dead." Mine had two layers. The first asked who the epitaph was for: "women who die giving birth or those who kill themselves because they didn't want to be a mother, or because they weren't able to become a mother, or those that kill their kids, or those that die from clandestine abortions, or lose their lives while saving their children...." Under the first layer was the image of my mother with a text about her suicide and a photograph of me and my young daughter hugging.

Letter #4: *On the Mystery of Conception or How to Stir Up Accumulated Sperm*

This letter celebrated the fact that we were the only group that believed in "*el parto por el arte*" ("birth for art's sake") instead of believing the more common "*el arte por el arte*" (art for art's sake"). The letter included the script for a performance we would undertake as soon as our work as mothers, housewives and teachers allowed us. The script was based on the story of the Virgin of Guadalupe, who first appeared to Juan Diego, an Aztec native in the fifteenth century. She asked him to pick some flowers, which he collected in his cape. When he notified the incredulous ecclesiastical authorities of her appearance, he was able to prove his story by opening the cape in which he carried the flowers and showing the image of the Virgin imprinted on it. In our performance we were supposed to appear with our backs to our audience, our hands on our breasts. As we turned slowly, the audience would see we were pregnant as we lifted our aprons like Juan Diego did his cape. As we let down our aprons, tons of hens, lizards, houses, pots, snakes, fingers, volcanoes, diapers, gold coins, flowers, children's scissors, corn, grapes, and two dreams would flow out.

In the end we asked the art recipients to share with us what they thought would be the best image on the apron of two pregnant feminist artists.

Letter #5: *Mother Wars: The Triumph*

This letter told the story of the pubic wars, where our descendants Mar-Is and Moni-Ka finally, in the year 5364, win the war we started against

Mother Wars, Letter #5 of the mail art series "Egalité, Liberté, Maternité, Polvo de Gallina Negra Ataca de Nuevo," which was part of ¡MADRES!

the Mother Archetype. We talked about a social process that went from Matriarchy, to Fratriarchy, to Patriarchy, to Childarchy.

Letter #6: *Beyond The A-Vanguard: Transmaternity*

This letter was dedicated to activist Rosario Ibarra, whose son was taken by the Government in the early seventies and never returned. Now a senator, she has fought bravely for decades against political repression.

In this letter we defined transmaternity as something that happens when motherhood takes us from the domestic realm to the political arena. We named Rosario Ibarra the highest representative of transmaternity.

Letter #7: *La muerte nos vale madres* (We don't give a shit about death)

The Mother Archetype. Life and death. No one ever received this letter, at least in their lifetime.

Letter To My Mother: A Competition

We organized a competition for anyone, regardless of nationality, age, sex, sexual preference, race, religion, class, education or occupation to write a letter with everything they always wanted to tell their mothers but were afraid to say. We received 70 submissions from all over the country. We had an award ceremony at the Carrillo Gil Museum on November 7, 1987. The winner of the best letter, Nahum B. Zenil, received an art work from my concurrent exhibition at the museum, and we raffled another work among all the participants, each of whom got a signed diploma for their participation.

Mother for a Day

¡MADRES! allowed us to understand that the basic problem of Patriarchy is the absent-father syndrome. We decided to "show men the true and only road to authentic fatherhood by granting them the possibility of becoming Mother for a Day."

Six men deserved this honor for their intelligence, charisma, leadership and good looks. One of them was anchorman Guillermo Ochoa, who invited us to his prime-time, internationally broadcast, high-rating news program, *Nuestro Mundo*, to give him his award.

Wearing our enormous paunches with aprons (which made us look very pregnant), we carried a ventriloquist's doll that sported an eye-patch like Catalina Creel's (the infamous mother in a very famous soap opera that was running in those days), which we used to teach us how to be bad mothers. We dressed Ochoa with his own apron, transforming him into a pregnant woman, and named him *Mother for a Day*. Ochoa joined in the fun and performed beautifully with us. He swallowed the pills we gave him to make him feel morning sickness and proudly wore his crown as queen of the home. The audience immediately responded: the men were deeply offended, but the women enjoyed it.

This performance has continued with a life of its own. Nine months after the show took place, someone from the audience called Ochoa's

¡MADRES! Performance during the TV program, *A Brazo Partido,* conducted by Marta de la Lama, Channel 13, in 1987, with the participation of Maris Bustamante, Mónica Mayer and our daughters, Yuruen Lerama and Andrea Valencia.

program to ask him whether he had given birth to a girl or boy. As time goes by, we find more and more young artists who tell us they remember seeing this performance as children. Some of them weren't even born yet when the program aired.

We continued *Mother for a Day* in our performance piece at the Carrillo Gil Museum discussed below. Several male friends had told us it was unfair that so few of them had been granted the privilege of being a mother, at least for a day, and so we generously decided to include them.

¡Madres! The Mythical Meeting Between the Sierra Madre Oriental and the Sierra Madre Occidental

This performance before an audience at the Carrillo Gil Museum on October 30, 1987, brought us together as the Venus of Turin and the Venus of Sombrerete in an effort to make two great mothers, the Sierra Madre Oriental and the Sierra Madre Occidental (the two main mountain ranges in Mexico), come together. Turin and Sombrerete were the streets we were living in. The invitation itself was a conceptual piece. It was a questionnaire to measure the real and unequivocal influence of motherhood. We asked things such as: Does motherhood teach you about life? Is it beautiful? Is it a pain in the ass? Is it an illness? A vocation? Is it mental?

During that performance, Maris and I signed a contract whereby if she died before me, I would spread her ashes in the Pino Suarez metro station (the most crowded one in Mexico City) at noon on a Friday or else, if I died first, she would spread mine at the Rotonda de los Hombres Ilustres, the place where famous men are buried, which at the time included no women. Today it is called the Illustrious Persons Monument, so we'll probably have to change our agreement. Life and death.

The Poems Are Also Pink?

As our friends got involved with the project, they started proposing their own activities. One of them was a poetry reading on motherhood. On October 23, 1987, at the Carrillo Gil Museum we had the privilege of having poets Carmen Boullosa, Patricia Vega, Magali Tercero, Enriqueta Ochoa, Angélica de Icaza and Perla Schwarts read their own work and Alma Sepúlveda read a selection of poetry by other women.

¡MADRES! On Television

We were invited to the television programs of Marta de la Lama and Patricia Berumen and combined the interview format with performance. By that time our daughters were about a year old, so we would take them with us to show how chaotic life can be with toddlers. I particularly remember Maris in one of those interviews, placing a fake tummy on her head and explaining that, just as Leonardo Da Vinci had said art was a mental thing, she claimed so was motherhood.

Novela Rosa O Me Agarró El Arquetipo

This was the title of the exhibition I had at the Carrillo Gil Museum in September 1987, which housed several of our events. I presented 14 series of mixed medias on different aspects of the Mother Archetype.

Our last performance was at the Universidad Autónoma Metropolitana. The main action of that performance was Maris sawing a plastic tummy off me. She didn't have to wear a paunch, because the performance took place the day before Neus, her second daughter, was born. She had enjoyed the experience of motherhood so much the first time around that she decided to close the project by repeating it.

During that performance, we decided to become a completely endogamous group and the only ones allowed in would be our direct descendants. Only our daughters or granddaughters would be entitled to become members of *Polvo de Gallina Negra!*

As time went by and a new generation of women and men started growing up accustomed to feminist ideas, somehow or other I began saying that all our children could be part of the group. Recently, Adán, my firstborn, heard me say this at a lecture and afterwards complained I had always said it was an all-girls club. I denied it vehemently. I couldn't believe I had ever been so sexist! I couldn't understand how, if I had always claimed that feminism concerned both men and women, I could have left my own son out! He went to the documents and, of course, proved me wrong. We have since amended the rule.

Note

[1]Maris was married to Rubén Valencia (México 1950–1990) until his death. He was also part of the *No-Grupo*. I am still married to Victor Lerma and since 1989 we have been collaborating on a long-term art project called *Pinto mi Raya*.

MARIA ASSUMPTA BASSAS VILA

S.O.S.

Searching for the Mother in the Family Album

SOME SPANISH AND ITALIAN WOMEN philosophers and historians who were involved in social and political movements during the nineteen seventies have realized that they were the most "anti-maternal" generation.[1] They not only rejected the "family of the father" where women, as Luce Irigaray describes, were exiled, but they also turned away from relationships with their mothers and many rejected biological maternity.[2] To the historical suppression of the mother, there was added what Milagros Rivera has pointed to, the severing of any dialogue between liberated women and their own individual mothers.[3] In her book *Mujeres en Relación: Feminismo 1970-2000,* Rivera wrote: "In the twentieth century, the ideology of liberation and emancipation, necessary for transforming extremely unjust social relationships born out of modern western imperialism and rampant industrialization, also swallowed up a daughter's relationship with her mother. It was a terrible loss."[4]

In fact, for those of us who have inherited and enjoyed the social conquests and models of female freedom from the 1970s, our relationship with our mothers remains an issue that causes us both conflict and confusion, often remaining concealed within the realm of intimate relationships. The legacy of the women's movement of the 1970s offered us a greater margin for making different decisions about family relationships and it was the key for the development of new family realities in western societies. However, we have also realized that our desires were not limited to political or social changes. We want to live and reframe our relationships using a different logic, what we like to call a "non-instrumental relationship." Feminist thought on sexual difference has brought into focus this key question for women and feminism, highlighting the importance of recovering and rethinking the relationship with our own personal mother as a political practice. To acknowledge our mother produces what we call a "*cut*" away from the patriarchal social paradigm (*un corte en el orden simbólico patriarcal*) and makes present the symbolic order of the mother in our life and in the world.[5]

In this text I have attempted to write about these "*cuts*" in works of the 1970s and 1990s that dealt with the family portrait through conceptual and post-conceptual approaches. The works discussed were produced by Fina Miralles, Eugènia Balcells and Cori Mercadé, three artists born in Catalonia (Spain) to whom I am grateful for the many conversations we have had through the years.

IN THE ABSENCE OF THE MOTHER, IN THE SHADOW OF THE ALBUM

Women's rebellion against "the family" at the end of the 1960s and in the 1970s in Spain emerged in a very particular context. On the one hand, "family discourses" were the key motifs of Franco's dictatorship and its particular politics of repression, which sought to control women and women's sexuality. "Homilies on the family" by the Catholic Church also played a key role in placing the nuclear family as the model, turning the heterosexual relationship into a moral issue and defining motherhood as women's destiny. Ideological and political control through "the family" didn't stop suddenly with Franco's death in 1975. These ideas have continued to model frames of life in successive generations, during the so-called period of democratic transition (1976–1980), and they survive today. At the same time, second-wave feminism and particularly the important intervention of women in movements advocating social change and a political transition to democracy also played an important role. For a large proportion of feminist women of that first generation, "the family" was the patriarchal institution par excellence from which women had to escape in order to create new ways of understanding sexual difference and relationships.

There is a generation of Catalan women artists that grew up at the end of Franco's last repressive period in power and who started their careers in the early 1970s. They were involved in local and international avant-garde scenes, both in and outside the country, and most worked with conceptual approaches and sought a new language for artistic production. Although the feminist movement did not have a direct impact on them, many have acknowledged in interviews that they took sexual difference into account in their projects and individual works.[6] In their production during the 1970s and early 1980s, alongside their interest in social questions, they also highlighted the "family issues" as a bridge between certain biographical and social questions and were well aware of their own relevance as political and symbolic subjects. These works are not well enough known in either Spanish or international conceptual histories and yet they could make an important contribution to rethinking the meaning of the personal as political. Analysis of these artists' works would modify and enlarge the current historical narratives on conceptual art in Catalonia, which has to date been characterized by a strong masculine social and political bias.

Matances (Slaughters, 1976–77) by Fina Miralles, born in Sabadell in 1950 and now living in Cadaqués, makes many critical statements on the family model inherited from the Franco era in Spain, at a mature moment in her conceptual body of work, which started in 1972, when she began exploring relationships between natural elements, her body, cultural representations and the uses of nature (1972–1974). In 1974, with *Images of the Zoo*, Miralles went deeper in her analysis of human relationships to concentrate on representations meant to manipulate persons and animals. *Matances* is the culmination of that line of research and is focused on the physical and psychological death produced by manipulative relationships. Alexandre Cirici, one of the few Catalan critics who have closely followed the development of conceptual art in Catalonia, wrote that it was an interesting "social" or rather "sociological" analysis of power relationships.

Matances is made up of a series of collages and photocompositions and was exhibited in 1977 at Barcelona's "G" Gallery, a pioneering venue for the presentation of conceptual and new art practices. On that occasion, the work also included an assemblage entitled *Diviértase matando (Have Fun Killing)* in which cutout silhouettes of a man-target were arranged and the viewer was invited to take a dart from the figure's male genitals and throw it at another to explode a small firework. The installation was completed by a video documentary consisting of a series of linked fragments showing: the process of slaughtering a pig, which had been a common practice amongst peasants in Catalonia; the to-and-fro movements of a dog shut in an apartment; and images of urban spaces and buildings from along the route the artist used to take as a girl from home to school. The gallery was filled with a strong smell of ether, which may have played a part in the work's powerful suggestion of dissection. There was also another object that required interaction with the visitor: a toy dog with a nodding head, very popular at the time, which was accompanied by a sound piece heard through headphones in which the definition of "dog" from the *Catalan Encyclopaedia* was translated into several languages. The collages and assemblages that formed the core of the work included newspaper photos documenting the brutal repression of the last years of the Franco regime and the rituals it staged. There were also a large number of pictures of animals, caged, wounded or dead. Some of these photographs had formed part of Miralles' earlier installation *Images of the Zoo,* while others were cutouts of reproductions of dead animals by the roadside, which the artist placed beside postcards from different places in Europe. The presence of violence and death was intensified by a bird's feather and a fox's skin added to two of the collages.

There were also several apparently more innocent images in those panels. I refer to those of a girl being dressed by a middle-aged woman. Those images came from an artwork that Miralles had produced earlier called *Standard* (1976). It was a performance work addressing the construction of the female body as an object of sexual use and commercial exchange. Slides of women from publicity and media alternated with images of a girl being dressed by a woman, step by step, as if she were a mother dressing the girl to go to school.

In *Matances*, we also find several disturbing photographs of a woman's head covered not only with a mantilla—the veil women had to wear to go to Catholic church during Franco's regime—but with a stocking, a sheet of plastic and other materials. These were pictures intended to make up a separate work called *Emmascarats* (*Masked Men*, 1976), which was never shown independently.

Collage compositions also included words and phrases like *Death*, *Justice*, *Fear*, *Wounded*, *Make your mark* or *Seeing is not being alive*, written graffiti-style with either pencil or spray paint. Beside these were maps of Spain, the symbol of Franco, the victor, reproductions of paintings like Goya's *Executions of the Second of May* and some of the many images of the crucifixion of Christ, as well as other drawings. These compositions were organized around a central motif in either three horizontal lines or two vertical ones on wide rectangular pieces of cardboard.

As I said in the introduction, the family had become a space of ideological discourse in Spain during Franco's regime. Miralles' images of the artist and her family from her private album share the same space with images of women from newspapers and magazines. Across these images, we see women performing rituals that they had to learn in school, in compulsory social service, in the church and in other different educational institutions. We have to remember that there was an explicit "doctrine" on femininity in Franco's Spain. There was a written doctrine on what a spouse was, what it meant to be a wife, on appropriate relationships between couples, on sexual relations, on relationships with your own sex and on sexuality. It is also important to note that public representations of women from Franco's regime were visually constructed to reproduce this transmission of ideological values. For example, many images show

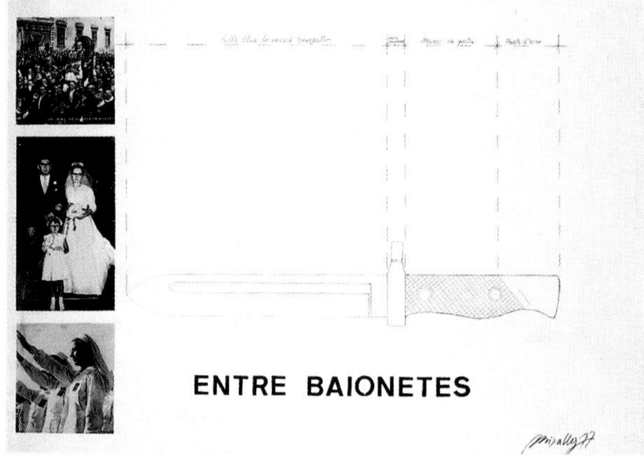

Fina Miralles, from the series *Matances*, 1977. Photographic collages 51.5 cm × 66.5 cm.

Top: *España (Spain)*, Right: *Entre baionetes (In between bayonets)*.

Fina Miralles, *Images of the Zoo*, 1974. Installation, dimensions variable.

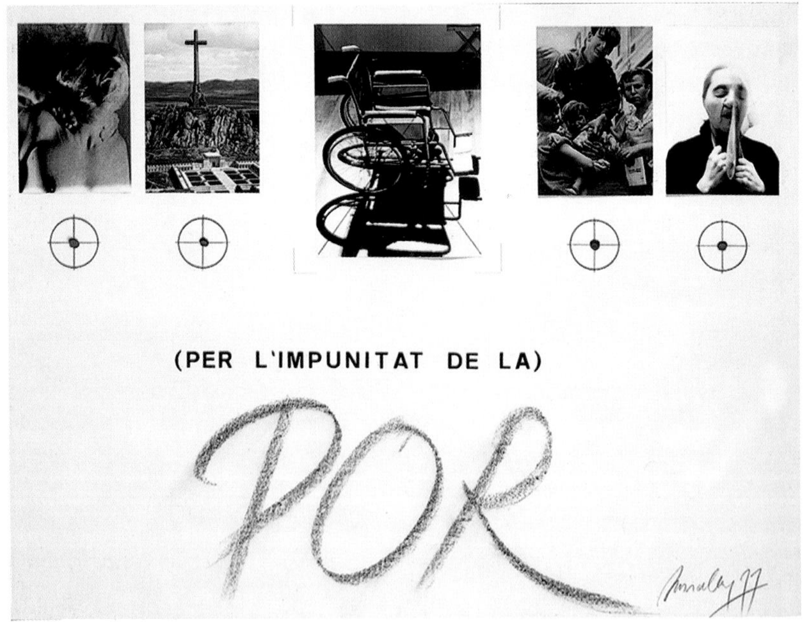

Fina Miralles, from the series *Matances*, 1977. Photographic collages 51.5 cm × 66.5 cm. Top: *Veure-hi no és estar viu (To see is not to be alive)*, 1976. Bottom: *Per l'impunitat de la por (For the impunity of fear)*, 1977.

women dressed only in white and whiteness became a metaphor of purity, of "the healthy against the unhealthy," in a situation in which the unhealthy people were those who had lost the war: the communists, anarchists, or leftists. Women were often represented in the media wearing uniforms. The uniform became a metaphor of service to the homeland, to their husband, to their sons, to their men. Their open smile combined with a gaze into the darkness suggested how women should always be ready to work happily for the ideals of the fascist society. The Spanish writer Carmen Martín Gaite has offered a detailed study of these correspondences in *Usos amorosos de la postguerra española* (Amorous Customs in Post-War Spain, 1987).[7]

Beyond this ideology and its systems of indoctrination, the family photographs included in *Matances* have also led me to explore the private nature of family life as it occurred and evolved amongst bourgeois Catalan families in that period. It has been difficult to find historical and social research on these family relationships. However, many novels by women authors of that period focused on those experiences.[8] In my interviews with Fina Miralles and other women artists of the same generation who were from a similar social class, they have told me that they experienced family life as a context in which violence occurred at many different levels: in silences, in an absence of communication, in the distance between parents and their children, in an authoritarian education, in abuses of power and sexual mistreatment. The "pictures" of the family are not represented in any direct way in their work. However, I have noticed that in *Matances* the family photographs, particularly those in which we see the artist as a baby or as a young girl, are often positioned as objects or targets for different levels of violence. In this sense, we could also understand *Matances* as a between-the-lines reading of the family album in-so-far as the violence that the artist documents in the public sphere also suggests the latent violence in the family sphere.

Matances is not only about entwining the public and the private sphere in its analysis of the social—if it is true that it makes visible different kinds of power relationships and the violence that is lived and inherited by Miralles' generation in post-Franco Spain—but it is also, for me, a raw and bloody exposition of the logic of violence on which the system of relationships is structured in the patriarchal symbolic order. Miralles' mother appears in one of the family photographs with her children as if this was the only safe space in the midst of many images of physical and psychological violence. With her mother's visual presence perhaps Miralles is pointing to the possibility of non-manipulative (instrumental) relationships. However, the shadow of the "family of the father" is omnipresent in this work and the artist's relationship to her mother is here unreadable at a symbolic level. It is interesting to note that her desire to reconstruct her relationship to her mother played a very important role in much of Miralles' later work, after she stopped producing conceptual work and began unfolding painting into space and then producing paintings which deal with different levels of visual reality.

Beginning in the 1950s, Hollywood was a major manufacturer of new family stereotypes that were propagated for political purposes. During various periods of "opening up" during the Franco regime in the 1960s and early 1970s, these American representations of the family joined those produced in Spain. Eugènia Balcells, an artist who also belongs to the generation of conceptual artists in Catalonia, created several works that explore and record the reception and dissemination of these models in the cinema, advertising, photo-novels and the mass communication media in general.[9] In her installation *Re-prise* (1976–77), in her book and exhibition *Fin* (*The End*, 1978), and her film *Boy Meets Girl* (1978), the artist accumulates film stills and other cutouts of pictures from magazines and photo-novels. She orders and projects them in accordance with the basic structure of the film industry's standard screenplays: the beginnings of films, the key images of the female lead and the male lead, how boy meets girl, first kisses, engagement scenes, happy endings and so on. The end result offers us an "X-ray" of the patterns between woman and man, of different relationships between couples, of love and happy families. In a nutshell, she appropriates and repeats the type of relationships that were produced and reproduced ad nauseam by the narratives of the commercial cinema and means of communication. As always happens in Balcells' work, the simplicity of the script not only reveals the caricatural nature of these models but also finally "cleans" our perception, and therefore unleashes the potential pictures have to evoke, intertwine and multiply into much more fertile stories. For example, at the end of *Boy Meets Girl*, the random meetings of feminine and masculine images finish up pairing off boys with girls, girls with girls, close-ups with full-body pictures, and so on, provoking interesting displacements, surprises and changes of perspective that would be at the origin of new creative forms for conceiving the narration of human relationships.

IN THE SHELTER OF THE FAMILY ALBUM: RECOVERING THE "GRANDMOTHER" AND THE "SISTER"

Whereas Balcells was mainly concerned with media images in many of her works, there is one piece from the 1970s in which the artist explores images more directly related to her own private life. I am referring to the film *Album* (1976–78), which she made on her return to Barcelona after a long period living in the United States, where she had completed her training and experienced the "buzz" of the 1970s New York art scene. In *Album*, she films, from the first page to the last, her grandmother's album of postcards that Balcells often used to look at as a child.

The album of postcards is a characteristic version of or complement to the family album, especially at a time when the postcard still performed a function that would later be served by travel photography. In this way, the postcard album became the receptacle of personal recollections where the postcard is the "souvenir" of a journey, but also, like the letter, it is the object that displays something of the subtle and elusive world of personal relationships, some of which, especially for women, did not have space in the most stereotyped representations of the "official relations" recorded in the family album.

Album is mainly a documentary on one object but it underlines the interest albums have as objects in themselves. Once opened, the contents of the pages are gradually impregnated with a deliberately literary and romantic tone: postcards of different European cities, of spas frequented by the wealthy bourgeoisie, the calligraphy of the grandmother's handwriting, the signature and the messages written in the margins. These pictures are accompanied by a background recording of the music of Richard Strauss and the voice of Balcells' grandmother, Eugènia Gorina, reading some of the fragments of the postcards. The camera films from a fixed, static viewpoint, clearly establishing the presence of an observing eye, while the magic of the album unfolds before the viewer like a magic spell. The film invites us to unveil the potential of a living relationship with objects and images, but it also reconstructs the artist's relationship with her grandmother and thus exhibits a link that reveals a female genealogy within the family.

In another work, *Album portàtil* (*Portable Album*, 1991), a performance staged by Balcells in the Tartessos bookshop in Barcelona, she presented another female genealogy, a "portrait of a second family" by both men and women artists through the ages, designed to visualize their personal and cultural references. In the case of women, in view of their "exile" within the typical patriarchal family, this difference in emphasis has a special significance. The work consists of an overcoat with plastic pockets containing postcards of pictures of different women: film stars, intellectuals, writers, historical women, scientists and others less well known. Swathed and at the same time armored in this second skin, Balcells strolled naturally and proudly through the main hall of the bookshop.

I relate this work to an important number of works that begin in the 1970s with the aim of representing and naming a female creative genealogy, in order to understand women's historical role as producers of culture and claiming their legacies, the legacy of half of humanity, made invisible by the patriarchal culture. Two well-known examples are Judy Chicago's emblematic *Dinner Party* (1974–79) and Mary Beth Edelson's *Some Living American Women Artists/Last Supper* (1972). These works explicitly highlight both the exclusion of women from the tradition and the symbolic and political importance of these relationships of recognition among women themselves. Relationships between women show us the existence of relationships in history that are not structured around "fathers." Although feminism often invoked "sisterhood" as a model for this genealogy, where family relationships are constructed through women's relationships, the concept of "sister" has been heavily contested within feminism because it did not give enough importance to what we now call the "disparity" between women, which doesn't mean differences (of social class, sexuality, race) but a relationship with a personal mother as a point of departure for a new genealogy. However, since this important moment in feminism, relationships between women have always been fundamental for women as a means to create new political practices. We are more and more aware that our freedom originates when we create and work out relationships with women from what we have called relationships of "affidamento" and/or "female authority."[10] Female authority displaces relationships from the sphere of power to reframe them as a means of validating confidence.

BUT WHAT HAPPENED WITH "MY MOTHER"?

A few years ago I read *The Symbolic Order of the Mother* (1991), in which Luisa Muraro, an Italian philosopher at the University of Verona, describes her own process of recovering a dialogue with her mother, which transformed her philosophical practice. The maternal symbolic order is not a metaphorical or symbolic representation of the mother understood in the abstract as a generative principle, but the practice of what she establishes and what she gives us when we acknowledge her in the real origin of our life and as the first teacher of language that helps us to give names to things. Chiara Zamboni, a thinker of the female philosophical community *Diótima*, has written:[11] "In entering the world, we receive from our mother the gifts of life and language. These two gifts cannot be separated: in entering the world we are born into language."[12] The link with the mother is simultaneously biological and symbolic. It instigates

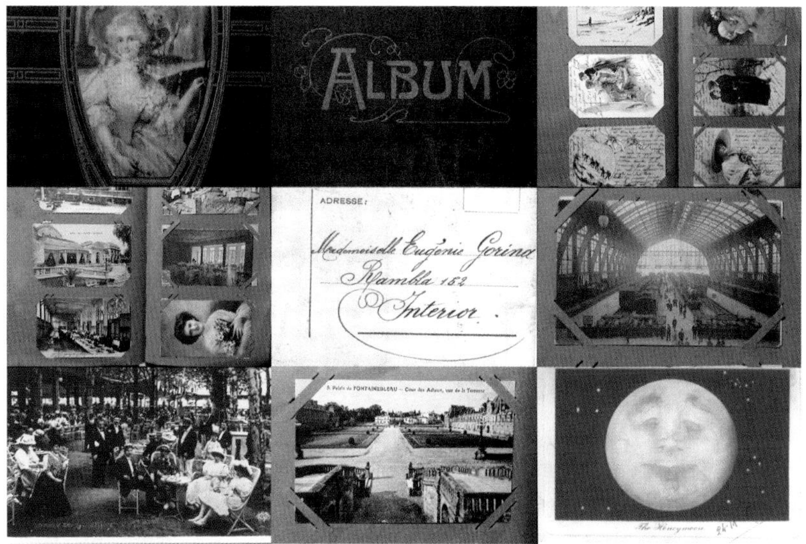

Eugènia Balcells, *Album*, Super 8 (1976) 20' / 16mm (1978) 11'. Color, magnetic sound.

Eugènia Balcells, *Album portàtil,* 1993. Object (special coat made with transparent flexible plastic sewn with nylon thread, 66 postcards).

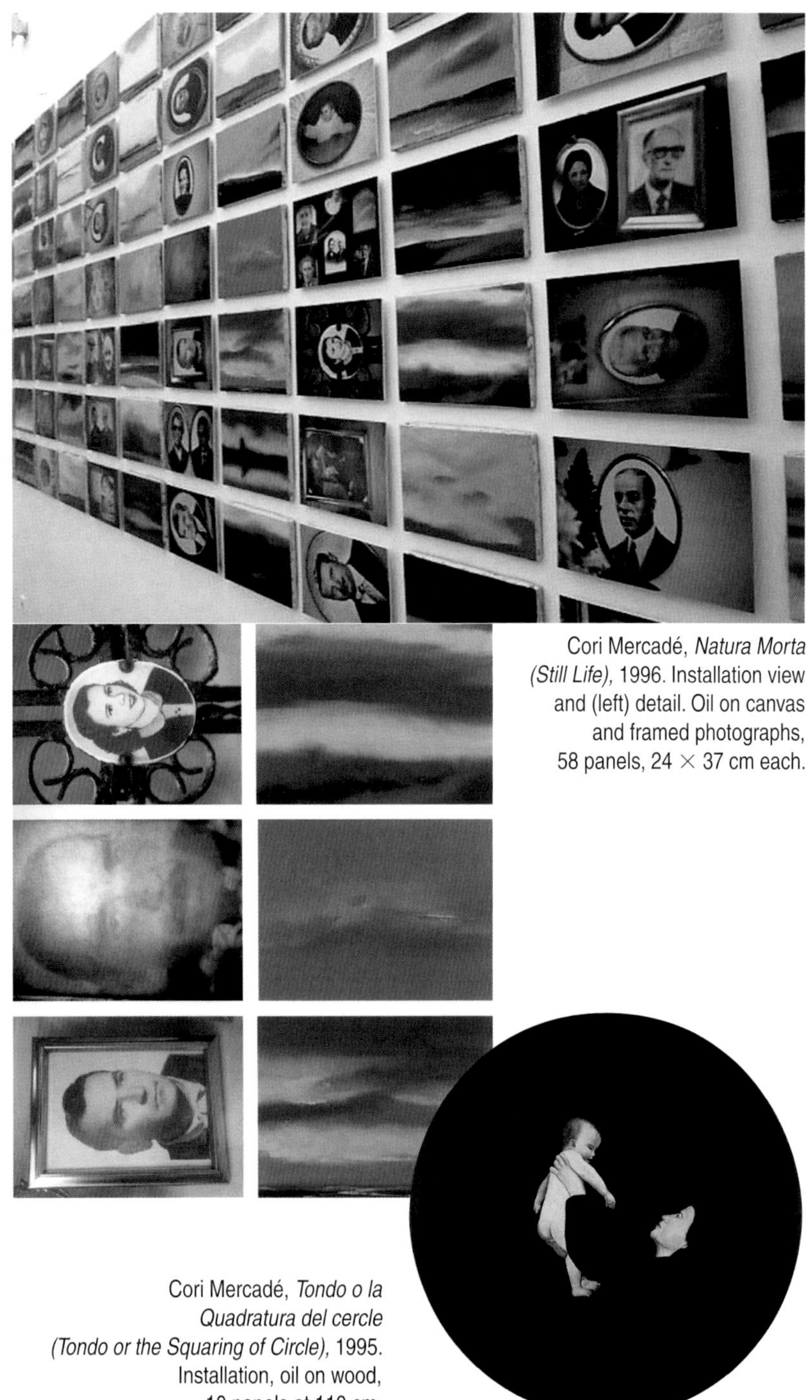

Cori Mercadé, *Natura Morta (Still Life),* 1996. Installation view and (left) detail. Oil on canvas and framed photographs, 58 panels, 24 × 37 cm each.

Cori Mercadé, *Tondo o la Quadratura del cercle (Tondo or the Squaring of Circle),* 1995. Installation, oil on wood, 10 panels at 110 cm.

a principle of a non-instrumental relationship that cuts across the often conflictual and loving relationships that exist in each particular case, but does not push these difficulties aside. It also goes beyond the variables that have existed in the mother-son or the mother-daughter relationship as seen from the perspective of social relationships and places in question the central thesis of interpretations from psychoanalysis.

Luisa Muraro called the "maternal symbolic order" the practice of relationships that maintain the significance of this maternal origin and recreate the principle of relationship that is established with the mother.[13] This principle is not a moral order, nor does it represent a duty. As Zamboni explains, it can be understood through the logic of the relationship that arises when, for example, we receive a gift: we do not feel obliged to give anything in return because the transaction is not an exchange, but we feel linked to the person who has given it to us, and if we want to maintain the relationship on the same lines "we have to express our gratitude or give something."[14] Recreating the dialogue with the mother is thus as important for women as for men, because it represents a restitution of the mother in the human genealogy and in particular the possibility of recovering the dialogue, as Milagros Rivera wrote, "on the foundations of life and human coexistence."[15]

Balcells' *Album portàtil* differs from the American proposals of the 1970s I have cited because she does not point to a patriarchal referent (like the *Last Supper*) to evoke the symbolic but to her own female body and what we can consider an "ornament": the coat or dress that shows it off. A number of women writers and thinkers have studied the interesting and controversial relationship between the ornament and the female body in the West over the centuries. Milagros Rivera interestingly concludes her contribution to this debate by highlighting the relationship between ornament and the maternal symbolic order: "the feminine ornament is a language that dialogues with the origin of the female body and its root in the world, with its source of strength in life; a language that expresses admiration and love for the maternal work. It forms part, therefore, of the symbolic of the mother, a mother who has given life and has also taught us, her daughters, to speak—so that when we were little girls we did not feel 'naked.' (That is to say, she has guaranteed, during the early infancy of each and every one of us, the order of the world, the coincidence between words and things.) This taste for self-adornment is a feminine inheritance that reminds us that it is she—the mother—who is the creator of the body, the vessel and image of human existence."[16]

At first view, Cori Mercadé's work *Natura Morta* (*Still Life*, 1996) seems to deal with themes far removed from what could be the celebration of the maternal and its gifts. The subject of this work is death, memory and the relationship between the "time of painting" and the "time of mourning" as the artist defines them. However, as I will attempt to show, to acknowledge the mother as an origin of life and the fundament of culture and therefore civilization does not mean to deal necessarily with images of the maternal body.

Cori Mercadé, born in Barcelona and trained at the School of Fine Arts at the University of Barcelona, is one of the few Catalan women artists who have worked continually on family portraits and family life issues in a post-conceptual language of painting. Works like *Tondo o la quadratura del cercle* (*Tondo or the Squaring of the Circle*, 1995) on the cultural construction of the representation of maternity, or *Compte enrera* (*Countdown*, 1997), a series of 52 gynaecological and obstetric instruments painted in oil day by day during the final period of her last pregnancy, demonstrate her approach. The latter work alludes to On Kawara and includes a circular painting representing "paternity." In *Sang i caritat* (*Blood and Charity*, 2001) she explored one of the classical virtues which was habitually represented as a matron with two children. Starting out from painting, Cori Mercadé's work customarily explores what happens between the lines, for instance between displacement through painting, photography and video. Her project proposes an increased consciousness of the processes of perception and comprehension that we habitually perform automatically. With this in mind I read the frequent displacements in the work as movements towards a symbolic order of the mother.

Natura Morta begins to unfold as a kind of album of absences. We see photographic portraits of dead people next to oil paintings on landscape themes. Photography and painting (portrait-landscape) unfold in an ordered manner on the wall where they are displayed together, recreating overall a new, serene chromatic landscape before the viewer's eyes.

The photographs are taken by the artist at cemeteries from the photos that are placed at gravestones. What leads the artist to "appropriate" these particular pictures? What relationship does she establish with each picture, and through them with the people that are shown there who she does not and has never known? Is there morbidity or indecency in this gesture that seems to intrude into such a private ritual? Who or what is the landscape for?

Mercadé's work tells us nothing about the people or their histories beyond what the pictures themselves show us. The portraits from seemingly private family albums are displaced in these public spaces. Mercadé has observed these photographs in her frequent walks through cemeteries and her work grows out of a particular and specific relationship that she establishes with their faces. She often does not know their names. The relationship begins when she selects a number of particular portraits from among the many she has seen and continues with her attentive, prolonged and particular observation of each picture in her studio. This observation is primarily an analysis of the picture, but it does not reject an emotional relationship with it nor with the person it represents; at the same time, it does not allow the picture to intervene by superimposing upon it a content that would shift our attention away from its qualities as an image.

The relationship she seeks rests on how to maintain an intersubjective dialogue, not a monologue, with the image, but it is the picture that provides the framework for this, each with its own guidelines. Starting from the range of colours and other features she observes in each portrait, Mercadé paints an oil landscape by hand. Each photo is thus accompanied by a painting and each portrait has a landscape beside it. These landscapes lie between figuration and abstraction, naturalism and symbolism. They are images that condense something of the singularity of the initial image, a singularity that has been filtered through the artist like a sediment left after decantation.

This process of creating distance from the portrait seems to entail the dissolution of an original sense, but paradoxically it makes it clearer than ever. Each landscape seems to be a commemoration of the singular deceased person, and further still it seems to exist and to be there to honour the nature of a singular relationship between the artist and her subject. The painting, or rather what the artist calls "the time of the painting," also gradually unfolds the time spent relating to that image and to the person whom the image represents. Portraits in cemeteries are signs that revive the physical memory of a relationship, the singularity of a face with regard to the abstract and the unknown that death represents in western lay culture.

Situated, then, in "the time of the painting," each unit (photographic portrait/oil landscape) seems to be a decomposition of the classic approach of background against figure, which painting up to and after Cubism has debated, as well as between reality and representation, knowledge and language. On the one hand, each photograph is a "still life," a symbolic object in the framework of the landscape. Mercadé knows and is interested in the history of the genre, specifically how the "still life" signals themes of reflection on life and death, on pleasure and morality. The objects are symbolic and mark a contemplative *tempus* for the painting. They define it as a space where looking means searching for the meaning of materiality, of the body and of life itself. On the other hand, the landscapes overtly recall the tradition of German Romanticism, that is, a painting that is also made up of reflections on finitude and infinitude and the understanding of being in relationship with nature. The landscapes that accompany the photographs in this work by Mercadé are inhabited by no one, but situated beside the portraits, they also become a kind of horizon where the anonymous face seems to take root and become more concrete, closer and somehow more accessible to the viewer.

There is something in this work by Mercadé that makes me think of the figure of Antigone as portrayed by María Zambrano. The Spanish philosopher transforms the ending of Sophocles' tragedy in two powerful texts: "The Delirium of Antigone" (1948) and "The Tomb of Antigone" (1967).[17] Antigone, immured alive, speaks to the protagonists of the tragedy from her tomb and watches the knots of her social and family history coming undone.[18] For Zambrano the tomb is the "space and time" where awareness of her innermost feelings symbolically germinates, and what emerges as transcending this experience "is only visible at certain moments, at others it is not seen and it is never seen in full." Through Zambrano's words I have understood that Antigone does not appeal to any authority when she decides to bury her brother Polyneices and disobey the laws of the city dictated by the tyrant Creon. Antigone is imbued with the authority given to her by the recognition of her maternal origin. The burial of her brother and the dedication of a funeral rite continue the task of care and respect for the body and for life. Like Antigone's, Mercadé's work is also a gesture of gratitude and love for the work of the mother; it is a practice of the maternal symbolic order.

This is a rewritten version of an article published in Album. Family Pictures in Art *(exhibition catalogue. Girona: Museum of Art in Girona, 6 November 2004–17 February 2005). First published in* n.paradoxa: international feminist art journal, *volume 15, January 2005.*

Notes

[1]María Milagros Rivera Garretas, *Mujeres en Relación. Feminismo 1970-2000* (Barcelona: Icaria, 2001).

[2]Luce Irigaray, *Sexes and Genealogies* (New York: Columbia University Press, 1993).

[3]Victoria Sau, *El vacio de la maternidad. Madre no hay más que ninguna* (Barce-

lona: Icaria, 1995). This short book was very important for me when I began to study feminism in our country, because it offers explanations on the invisibility of a feminine legacy. Its goal is to present evidence of the disappearance or, as the author calls it, "the phagocytation" of the mother in language and in the two traditions that largely make up Western culture: the Judaeo-Christian and the Greco-Roman.

[4]Rivera, *Mujeres en Relación. Feminismo 1970-2000*, 19.

[5]See Luisa Muraro, *El orden simbólico de la madre* (Madrid: horas y Horas, 1991).

[6]Interviews were made by the author with Fina Miralles, Àngels Ribé, Silvia Gubern, Eulàlia Grau and Eugènia Balcells.

[7]See Carmen Martin Gaite, *Usos amorosos de la postguerra española* (Barcelona: Anagrama, 1987). More recently, the Catalan writer Maria Mercè Roca wrote monologues from interviews that she made with women of the same generation from different social and cultural backgrounds on issues of family and sexuality. See Roca, *El món era a fora. L'educació sentimental de las dones catalanes durant el franquisme (The World was Outside: The Sentimental Education of Catalan Women during the Franco Years*, 2001), which shows how women created different ways of negotiating with those "feminine" roles inside and outside the family and with the "doctrine" on women made by fascists so they were able to find ways to live on their own terms.

[8]For instance, Esther Tusquets, *Correspondencia Privada* (Barcelona: Anagrama, 2001).

[9]See the artist's website: www.eugeniabalcells.com

[10]Duoda, "Les relacions d'autoritat i la libertat" in Duoda, *Revista d'Estudis Feministes* (Center of Women's Studies of the University of Barcelona), no. 7 (Barcelona: University of Barcelona, 1994).

[11]Diótima, *Traer al mundo el mundo. Objeto y objetividad a la luz de la diferencia sexual* (Barcelona: Icaria, 1996), 225-252.

[12]Chiara Zamboni, "La vía simbólica en la relación materna y el cortejo de las imágenes del 'yo' in Duoda, *Revista d'Estudis Feministes* (Center of Women's Studies of the University of Barcelona), no. 19 (Barcelona: University of Barcelona, 2000): 89.

[13]Luisa Muraro, *El orden simbólico de la madre* (Madrid: horas y Horas, 1991).

[14]Chiara Zamboni, "La vía simbólica en la relación materna y el cortejo de las imágenes del 'yo' in Duoda, *Revista d'Estudis Feministes*.

[15]Rivera, *Mujeres en Relación. Feminismo 1970-2000* (Barcelona: Icaria, 2001).

[16]María Milagros Rivera Garretas, *El cuerpo indispensable. Significados del cuerpo del mujer* (Madrid: horas y Horas, 1996), 67-68.

[17]María Zambrano, "The Delirium of Antigone" (1948) and "The Tomb of Antigone" (1967) in *Senderos. Los intelectuales en el drama de España. La tumba de Antigona.* (Barcelona: Anthropos, 1986), 201-265.
[18]Elena Laurenzi, *María Zambrano. Nacer por si misma* (Madrid: horas y Horas, 1995), 55-76.

BARBARA T. SMITH

The Coffins

Xerox Books

I KNEW DEEP INSIDE THAT my marriage was in trouble.

Despite years of therapy, spiritual breakthroughs and learning to pursue my own work as an artist, I knew an irrevocable schism had occurred that our marriage could not sustain.

Divorce was not a part of my plan, personality, or upbringing. I simply could not face it. I had made a vow and under no circumstances could I revoke it.

But another part of me could feel the promise was gone. That part was like a somnambulant sleepwalker who carried out the artworks that followed as if in a dream.

I had recently traipsed over to Gemini GEL, the internationally famous lithography studio, to present my idea for a print I hoped I could make there. I was naïve. I was told that it was not possible because I had no dealer, it was very expensive and I was basically unknown. Besides, Joseph Albers was currently printing there. It was a shocking comeuppance and I was miffed. I reasoned that lithographs were a 19th-century print medium. This was the 20th century. The print medium of our time was the business machine.

Historically, printmaking has evolved in each era from the mass media of the times. It has been used as an inexpensive way to communicate with the masses, in many cases to people who cannot read. In the hands of artists the medium becomes an art form. Witness Daumier with newsprint and lithography.

But now in my view lithography was obsolete (not the least of this idea was due to the fact that I had just been spurned).

I resolved at once to find out which of the business machines was technically the most advanced and researched various copy machines, e.g. 3M, ditto, and blueprints. I found Xerox to be the only one which was entirely new.

Xerox would print an image of 2-D or 3-D objects when placed on the glass plate by an *electronic charge* that configures the *toner* in the exact pattern of the material to be copied. The toner is made of tiny beads of *plastic* that become *charged* as the *light* scans the glass plate. The paper is then passed beneath a heating unit where the toner slightly melts (is *scintered*) into the paper and forms a permanent bond. This was completely new. The ink is neither pressed into the paper by force as with etching and engraving (intaglio) nor spread or stamped onto the paper like lithos, or serigraphs or wood blocks (planar). It is *semi-melted* into the paper.

I was thrilled and leased a big (914) Xerox machine that was put into my dining room. It immediately took over my life. While I had developed preconceived ideas of what I would do, the thing itself was so full of potential and options that I worked every day. I did not get around to my initial plans until a few days before I gave the 914 back. I could not seem to stop. I printed word texts with imagery. I replicated all manner of objects. I made visual stories, and stacks that in specially designed plastic bases became small sculptures. I made series that became large framed pieces. I wrote in lipstick on the glass, and I made images of my body, face, and hands, which became forerunners of my body-oriented performance work. I could not stop.

I began to have heaps of assorted prints all over my dining room and no clear idea of what they were or how to present them.

There was a deep undertone in some of the groups of prints. I had engaged Jerry McMillan, an artist photographer whose studio was near mine, to photograph my children for this project. Somehow I knew the photos would be part of this work. I then used these images in many different ways. A certain set were even dye-cut with four different types of circular holes.

As I made this work, especially the work with my children's images, I was gripped by a state of deepest grief, which I could not even acknowledge. What was it about my children that exacted such a price?

Soon I had even more piles of printed paper and realized they were books. Books are physical artworks that have to be held to be seen, which is an action, rather than mere passive viewing. They are intimate and personally engaging as art.

Once I found the bookbinder I could work with, I had to design my covers. I already knew what they would be. They were coffins. I could hardly bear it. The covers were all black, and except for the book with the children all bore a common logo on the cover. It was a circle with a cross within it embossed in silver in the center of each cover.

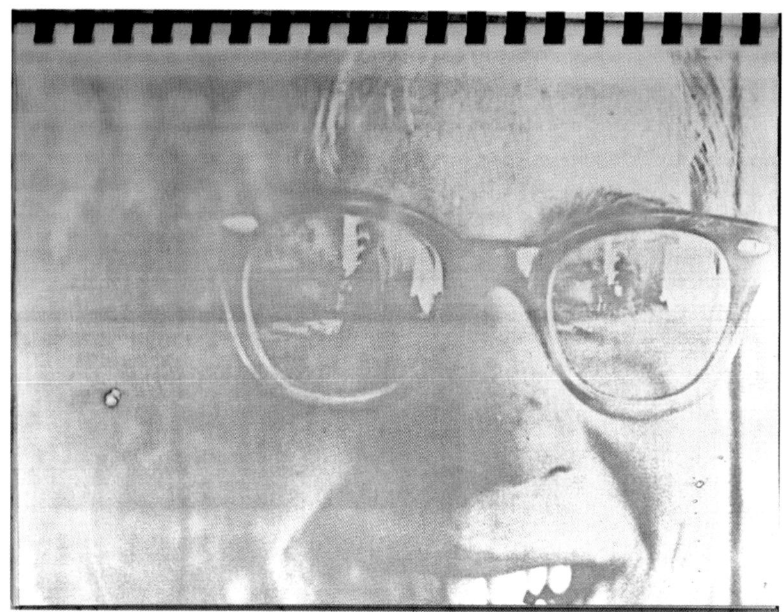

Bond, 1966. Xerox book, 12 × 8 inches.

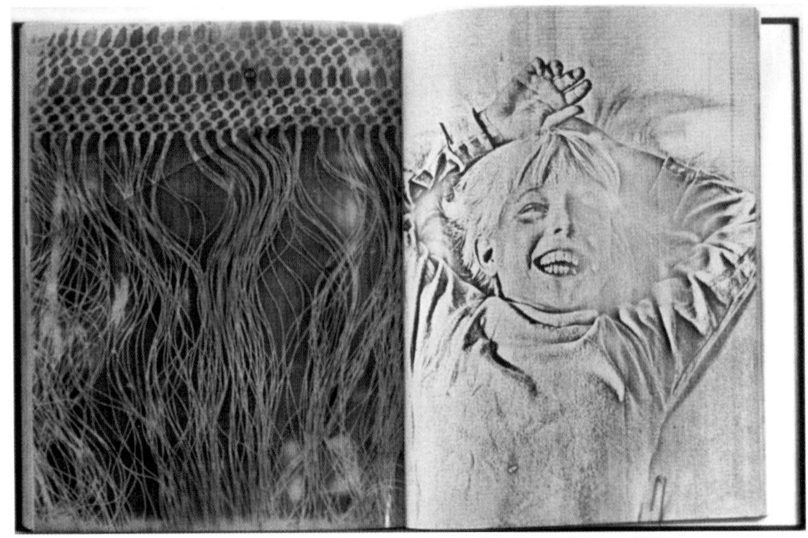

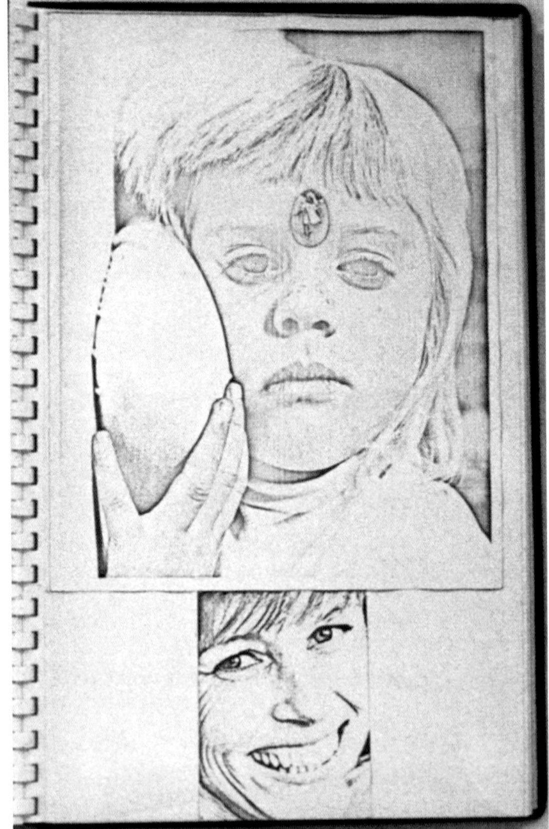

Bond, 1966. Xerox book, 12 × 8 inches.

To me this represented that point in space and time when you reach an impasse that leaves no options. It is like a death sentence of impossibility.

Everyone hits these places from time to time. They are completely intractable and life only goes on by giving up. That is where I was.

It could not be put in words. What could not be said is in the artworks, the books. I was going to lose my family. It would never be the same. These books were coffins and memorials at once.

The cover of the book with my children was somewhat different because it makes such a beautiful pun on the issue of paper and pain and my kids and life itself. On this cover the word BOND is embossed in silver. My children, Richard, Julie, and Katie, are bonded to me and to each other. Maybe that is all that endures now. All the rest ARE coffins.

The strange thing is that the idea I had for a print at Gemini back then was that of a gravestone, a print of a stone made on a stone with a flower pressed between them.

I did not actually get a divorce until 1968. It took that long and was as if it was a dream that was happening despite me.

Note:
These were some of the first Xerox artworks ever made. Now, of course, the computer is *the* dominant machine. All the works are black and white; no color existed at the time. But I did find all sorts of colored papers, vellum, and acetate, etc., on which to work.

JENNIE KLEIN

Visualizing Maternity in Contemporary Art

Race, Culture, Class

IN "THE LONELIEST BIRTHDAY GIRL," Monique Truong recalls her desire for a birthday cake that was just like the ones that her classmates brought to school on their birthdays. A Vietnamese refugee newly resettled in a tiny town in North Carolina, Truong wanted nothing more than to fit in with the rest of her elementary school classmates, who mercilessly picked on her because she looked and acted different. The mothers of her classmates sent in cakes made from boxes and canned frosting. On Truong's birthday, her mother also brought in a cake. Much to Truong's horror, her beautiful mother, raised with the tradition of French *patisserie*, showed up with a three-tiered, elegantly decorated cake that had nothing in common with the routine Betty Crocker cakes that her classmates shared. Only in retrospect did it dawn on Truong how difficult it must have been for her mother, a political refugee in a tiny town in the American south, to make this improbable cake for her child. Truong concludes that "normal life, with its celebrations, its photographs, and its cakes and candles, had to begin again sometime."[1]

Right up until the formulaic ending, Truong's story, published in the pages of *Parents* Magazine, is compelling. In the past several years, mainstream magazines such as *Parenting*, *Parents*, and *Good Housekeeping* have included stories that reflect the changing demographics of America. Truong's story, which narrates her mother's experience of estrangement from the foreign culture in which she found herself, rewrites the 1970s to include an alternative image of mothering that was premised upon difference rather than sameness. Truong reads her mother's cake as representing the resumption of normal life. But what is normal? And how could life in a small southern town in the U.S. ever compare to life in Vietnam? Rather than suggesting the resumption of normal life, the *patisserie* cake becomes a subtle act of rebellion, an assertion of difference that reads more like an act of creative resistance than an attempt to fit in with the other box-cake-making mothers. The *patisserie* cake, itself a product of French Colonialism in Southeast Asia, is transformed into a gesture of anti-assimilation.

In "The Loneliest Birthday Girl," this gesture of anti-assimilation is one that is narrated by the daughter rather than the mother. From *The Jazz Singer* (1927, starring Al Jolson), whose Jewish immigrant mother did her best to keep Jolson from becoming a jazz singer, to Amy Tan's *The Joy Luck Club* (1989, made into a movie in 1993 starring Ming Na) about immigrant Chinese mothers, the trope of the immigrant mother caught between the old country with its traditional ways and the new country with its modern ways has been trotted out with some regularity. These immigrant mothers seldom speak from a position of authority or even from any position at all. As Katrina Irving has argued in her book *Immigrant Mothers: Narratives of Race and Maternity, 1890–1925*, "enshrouded always within an extremely prevalent sociological analysis that stressed the difficulties many immigrant women in particular had adapting to American culture, the nurturing immigrant mother emerges as diffident within her family and unacquainted, or uninformed, by the broader social arena."[2] Indeed, even today, language, cultural, and class barriers make it difficult for the immigrant to fit into a foreign community of mothers. Pranee Liamputtong has pointed out in her study of immigrant Thai mothers living in Australia, that many of the women that she interviewed stayed home with their children and had limited access to the outside world due to modest education levels and poor command of the English language. As a result, motherhood is even more important to these women, who focus their energy on their children.[3]

This essay is about the work of artists who, like Truong's mother, are outsiders looking in, mothers who experience maternity from the edges of mainstream American culture. Unlike Truong's mother, whose identity is constructed by her (assimilated) daughter, these artists aggressively take control of their representation and presentation as mothers. Two of these artists—Patricia Cué and Youngbok Hong—are immigrants themselves. Gail Rebhan is the descendent of a Jewish family that immigrated to the United States from Europe. Myrel Chernick, the only artist included here whose work is not autobiographical, becomes the "voice" for a woman whose social class precluded her membership in the motherhood club. For these artists there is no resolution that results in the resumption of "normal" life. Images of mothers, most of them archetypal or stereotypical, are ubiquitous in popular culture and art history. What is missing is the representation of the lived experience of being a mother from the vantage point of the outsider. What does it mean to be a mother from the wrong class, wrong religion, or wrong race? bell hooks has argued that the margin can be a site of radical possibility and resistance.[4] How can representation best capture the contradictions between iconic and ideological representations of motherhood and the actual experience? This is probably the most pressing question for the artists whose work is considered here. What unites these artists is their desire to tell stories and give voice to experiences at the margins of motherhood.

Youngbok Hong, *What She Carries,* 2002. Interactive computer piece.

YOUNGBOK HONG, *WHAT SHE CARRIES* (2002)

Many years ago Trinh T. Minh-Ha wrote that a fine story "neither wraps itself in a cloud of oratorical precautions, nor cocoons itself in realist illusions that make language the simple medium of thought.... S/he who speaks, speaks *to* the tale as s/he begins telling and retelling it. S/he does not speak *about* it."[5] Born in Korea and currently living in the United States, Youngbok Hong, like Monique Truong's mother, has had to live between two cultures, two languages, and two identities. In *What She Carries,* an interactive computer piece from 2002, Hong tells the non-linear story of her mother's visit from Seoul for the birth of her baby, a girl. Throughout the piece, a combination of short videos and text, the meaning of the title changes and shifts, as Hong deconstructs the idea of what it means to "carry" something. "Truth," Trinh writes, "is both a construct and beyond it; the balance is played out as the narrator interrogates the truthfulness of the tale and provides multiple answers."[6] *Who* is carrying something? *What* is she carrying? What does it mean to *carry*? Hong's piece, activated by the viewer who must click on the mouse in order to advance to the next frame, travels through various truths and stories. The first "she" is Hong's mother, who comes from Seoul to visit Hong and her husband in Chicago. Hong's mother carries condiments—seaweed, hot pepper flour, sauces—that she has been preparing all her life in Seoul. "She" is also Hong, who carries a name other than that of her husband or her mother and who carries her baby girl. And "she" is Hong's daughter, who "carries" the expectations of American femininity (pink everywhere for the baby shower) and a name that is different than the one carried by Hong.

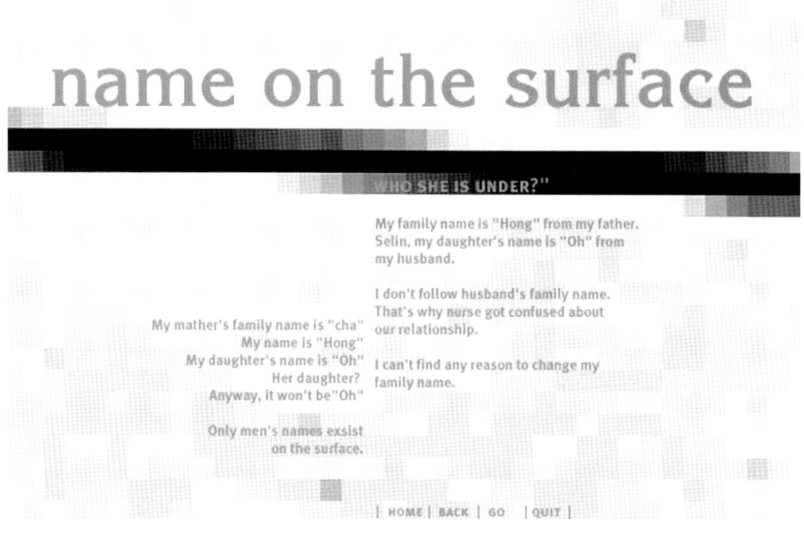

Youngbok Hong, *What She Carries.*

Particularly compelling is the way in which the web-based format of *What She Carries* uses an overlapping narrative. Upon opening the piece, the viewer has three choices in the form of three small circles. Each circle leads to a different story. The menu at the bottom of the Web page allows the viewer to navigate through the site differently each time. These non-sequential stories are a reflection of Hong's oblique relationship with Korean and American culture.

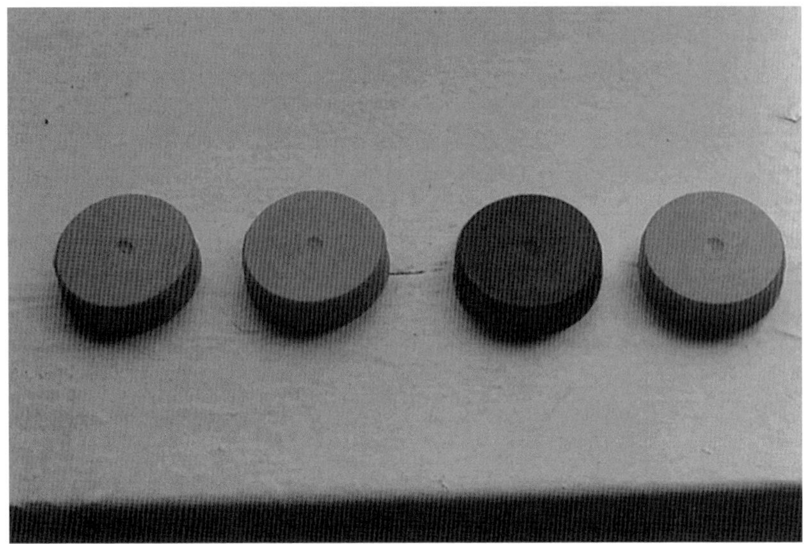

Youngbok Hong, *What She Carries.*

Although raised and educated in Korea, Hong pursued an MFA in Chicago and presently teaches graphic design in the American Midwest. Hong's story, spoken and written in her second language, reflects her distance from the culture of her mother; her mother's importation of Korean condiments in her suitcase and her aversion to letting her son-in-law see her smoke seem foreign to Hong. At the same time, Hong is not entirely comfortable with her adopted American culture. The pink things that proliferate around the birth of her daughter—pink balloons, pink clothes, and pink blankets—are bewildering to Hong, who is still familiar with Korean customs associated with the birth of the baby. Hong foregrounds her discomfort with American culture by making a conscious choice to use her English—grammatical mistakes, misspellings, and all. For Hong, there is no "normal" resolution of the cultural contradictions that inform her experience of motherhood.

PATRICIA CUÉ, *BUNDLE OF JOY* (2004)

Like Youngbok Hong, Patricia Cué has grappled with what it means to be a mother in a culture that is foreign to her own. Raised in Mexico and presently living in the U.S., Cué found herself taken aback when she had her first child at the age of 39 while living and working in Ohio. *Bundle of Joy*, the book that Cué made about her experience as a new mother,

Patricia Cué, *Bundle of Joy*, Abycedium Press, 2004. Portfolio bound book, 15 folios, 7.5 × 15 inches. Letterpress, laser prints and machine stitching on Arches paper.

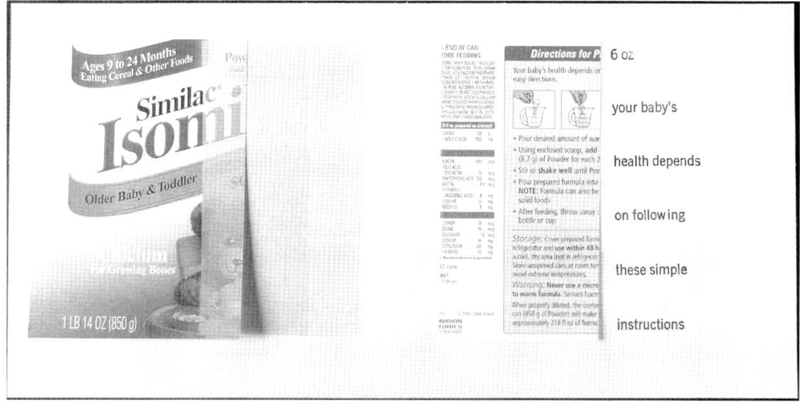

Patricia Cué, *Bundle of Joy*.

expresses both the intense absorption that Cué felt with her daughter and her ambivalence towards being a mother. Constructed with a sewing machine on Arches paper and a diaper cloth, *Bundle of Joy* is comprised of fifteen pages wrapped in diaper cloth and encased inside a four-flap portfolio with ties and cloth spine. The book is meant to represent her daughter Julia. As her starting point, Cué used a box of keepsake items that she had collected from the first year of Julia's life. A graphic designer who had done commercial work prior to moving to Ohio, Cué was interested in the difference between the marketing of babyhood in the U.S. and Mexico. She was particularly struck by the degree that the mother is required to monitor her child in the United States, something that is wholly absent in Mexico, with its more laissez-faire attitude towards childrearing. *Bundle of Joy* addresses the ambivalence Cué felt as she tried to raise a Mexican child in the Midwest. Several of the pages include instructions that Cué had taken from popular magazines and formula labels: on the page with the Similac label, Cué writes "6 oz Your baby's health depends on following these simple instructions." Other pages include feeding charts, diaper changing charts, and notations that indicate Cué's worry that she is not doing something right. "Did I feed her in too flat a position? Did I bounce her too much? Did I eat chilies and garlic?"

Andrea Liss has suggested that "the feminist mother" still "loves, forgives and sacrifices for her child(ren), but not at the expense of losing herself. It is not a matter of '*balancing motherhood and work*,' as the medial culture likes to insidiously simplify matters.... It is the feminist mother's admission that ambiguity is often the norm."[7] Almost 30 years after the publication of Jane Lazarre's *The Mother Knot*, Cué, in spite of very different circumstances from those of Lazarre (a well-established career, a salaried position, excellent daycare), struggled with the same ambivalence towards caring for her baby, losing her identity, and failing to measure up to the image of the perfect mother perpetrated in the media.[8] "I think the messages marketed to us as mothers create a lot of guilt," Cué told Susan Wittstock. "I'm hoping this will maybe speak to somebody out there who, even though it was a wonderful experience, felt isolated and exhausted and bored at times. I'm just not sure that women are allowed to feel those things."[9] Enthralled with the tiny human be-

Patricia Cué, *Bundle of Joy*.

ing that she had created, Cué was simultaneously overwhelmed by the bleak winter landscape and her lack of contact with the outside world. One of the last pages of *Bundle of Joy* shows the view from Cué's living room—trees stark and leafless, the ground covered with snow. "Bush might bomb Iraq," the text informs us, followed by "She smiled today. She smiled today. She smiled today." With this page, Cué turns the old adage that the smile of a baby trumps all on its head by lamenting the fact that Julia's first smile has narrowed her world to the point where she does not care if Bush bombs Iraq.

Cué is both a feminist mother *and* a Mexican mother. Feminist literature on mothering and motherhood has been predominantly about middle-class women. When mothers whose identity falls outside of those parameters are written about, it is generally in relationship to cultural, ethnic and class oppression. In anthologies such as *Mothering: Ideology, Experience, and Agency* (Routledge, 1994) or *Mother Troubles* (Beacon Press, 1999), the Latina women are domestic workers, battered women, or illegal Mexican immigrants.[10] Cué, an immigrant by choice whose "Diasporas" have been occasioned by nothing more urgent than employment opportunities, stands in contradistinction to her compatriots. *Bundle of Joy* is an important document not only because it acknowledges, and even embraces, maternal ambivalence, but because it expands upon our knowledge of what it means to be a Mexican immigrant and mother. It is a book written and constructed from a Mexican perspective that belies the stereotype of the oppressed Latina mother that is still so prevalent in contemporary North American culture. Absent are the indigenous colors, Aztec symbols and Marxist rhetoric that we have come to associate with a certain kind of "Mexicanidad" in the visual arts. Nevertheless, it is a book that speaks to a different paradigm of maternity, one in which the trappings of American maternity have become foreign.

GAIL REBHAN, *MOTHER-SON TALK* (1996), *DIVERSITY* (2000), *FAMILY SHIELD* (2003)

Unlike Cué and Hong, Gail Rebhan is the grandchild of European Jewish immigrants rather than an immigrant herself. Having been born and raised in America, Rebhan is no stranger to the relentlessly homogenizing consumer culture of this country. Like Cué, Rebhan's work challenges the implicit assumptions of America's consumerist society. Rebhan's challenge is more direct however. Possessed of a biting wit and sly ironic humor, Rebhan uses found objects in her photographs and

When my older son was about three or four years old I realized that everything he was learning about Judaism was negative.

The things we don't do.

We don't celebrate Christmas.

We don't celebrate Easter.

My husband and I decided we needed to start observing the Jewish holidays and rituals more frequently. After the silent prayer at our first Friday night Shabbat service, my son told me he prayed that he could celebrate Christmas.

From *Mother-Son Talk.* 1996. Offset artist's book, 7 × 9 inches.

artist's books that narrate her uphill battle to teach her secular children what it means to be Jewish. Rebhan's artist's book *Mother-Son Talk* uses found images along with text to narrate Rebhan's frustrations with imparting Jewish feminist values to two boys enthralled with popular culture. Next to an image of a plastic Santa Claus and toy Torah scroll, Rebhan writes:

> When my older son was about three or four years old I realized that everything he was learning about Judaism was negative. The things we don't do: We don't celebrate Christmas. We don't celebrate Easter. My husband and I decided we needed to start observing the Jewish holidays and rituals more frequently. After the silent prayer at our first Friday night Shabbat service, my son told me he prayed that he could celebrate Christmas.[11]

A few pages later, Rebhan's son tells his mother that he wants to marry someone blonde—or maybe a Jewish girl provided that she is pretty like his mother. By the age of 15, Rebhan's son Jackson has apparently embraced a life of teenage consumption, as evidenced by Rebhan's "portrait" *Jackson—Age 15* (2003), an assemblage of found objects that includes a dirty sock, CDs, candy wrappers, and Coke cans. Rebhan's

Family Shield, 2003. Giclee print, 19 × 19 inches.

portrait of her son, whose detritus marks him as a "typical" American male, stands in stark contrast to her photographic portrait of her family tree, *Family Shield*.

Rebhan assembled images of her family and archival family photographs of the Kachor family (spelled several different ways) surrounding a large menorah/family tree. The one sepia-toned image of Rebhan's immigrant family is layered behind the menorah. A small section in the right hand corner is cut away to reveal a photograph of Rebhan's son, dressed as a pirate. The Statue of Liberty in the top right corner is juxtaposed with images of Rebhan's family from the 1950s, post-immigration. *Family Shield* insists that Rebhan's sons acknowledge their Jewish identity. Images of her two sons playing baseball, roller-blading, visiting Disneyland, and participating in their bar mitzvahs are interspersed with two older photographs of Rebhan's immigrant grandparents and her relatives.

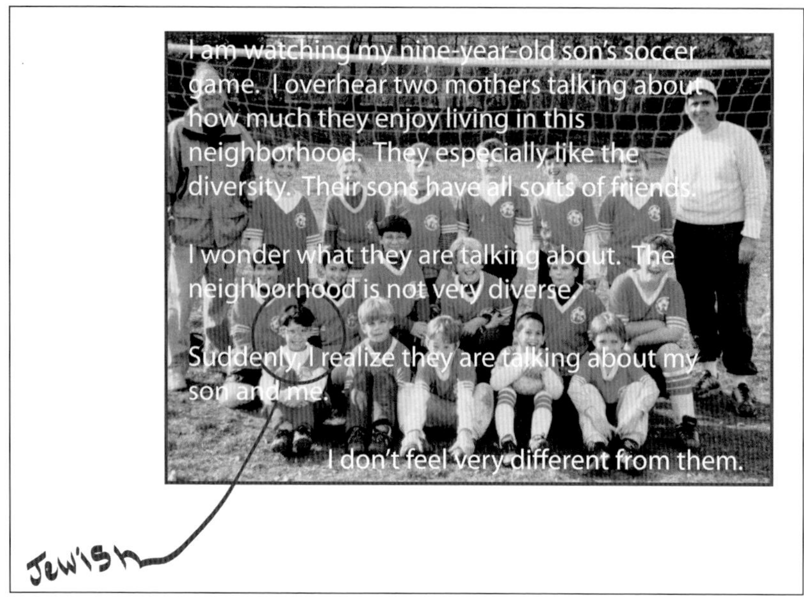

Diversity, 1997. Giclee print, 8.5 × 11 inches.

Growing up in the Washington DC area, both of Rebhan's sons experienced the quintessential American childhood, including team sports. In *Diversity*, Rebhan layered the following text over a picture taken of her son's soccer team.

> I am watching my nine-year-old son's soccer game. I overhear two mothers talking about how much they enjoy living in this neighborhood. They especially like the diversity. Their sons have all sorts of friends. I wonder what they are talking about. The neighborhood is not very diverse. Suddenly, I realize they are talking about my son and me. I don't feel very different from them.

In fact, Rebhan's son is completely interchangeable with all of the other boys on the team. Rebhan has helpfully written the word Jewish and drawn a line to her son's face, which she circled. Rebhan's experience mothering two sons in the late twentieth century appears on the surface to be fairly typical of the institution of mothering in North America. She is a soccer mom, she works, she cleans up after her very messy children, and she is able to laugh about the whole thing. Nevertheless, as the text in *Diversity* suggests, to be Jewish is to be still considered not quite white and therefore different. In Rebhan's case, the "diversity" that the other mothers congratulate themselves on attaining is more humorous than anything else. Many years and miles removed from the pogroms and concentration camps of Hitler's Germany, the well-intentioned anti-Semitism of Rebhan's neighbors makes them unwitting buffoons, the butt of the laughter issuing from gallery goers encountering Rebhan's work for the first time.

Rebhan's ironic labeling of her son as "Jewish" causes the viewer to try and find "Jewish" traits in her son's face, traits that would not seem evident in the absence of the label. *Diversity* thus raises the ugly specter of eugenics, the pseudo-science developed by Sir Francis Galton in 1883 based on the idea that it was a moral imperative to improve humanity by encouraging the best and most able to breed. From there, it was a short step to encouraging the less fit not to breed. In Nazi Germany, eugenic science went hand-in-hand with anti-Semitism and the ultimate extermination of millions of people. American eugenics, which flourished during the first three decades of the twentieth century, did not result (fortunately) in the mass extermination of any group of people. It did fuel instances of enforced sterilization and discrimination against those perceived to be less "fit"—initially the poor immigrants that crowded the cities of America. Although the science of eugenics has been largely discredited, its specter still looms large over contemporary notions of motherhood and childrearing, which are as class-based in the early twenty-first century as they were in the early twentieth century. Mothers can now be blamed for both rearing their children incorrectly *and* passing on bad genetic material.[12]

MYREL CHERNICK, *ON THE TABLE* (1996-2007)

"The idealized Good Mother," Sara Ruddick has argued, "is accompanied in fear and fantasy by the Bad Mother.... The Really Bad Mother's evils are specific, avoidable, and worse than her own."[13] As demonstrated by the philosophical and legal articles included in the anthology *Mother Troubles*, the ideological and social construction of the bad mother is based on race and, more significantly, class. "Bad" mothers are mothers who take drugs during their pregnancy, refuse prenatal care, accept welfare, and allow their children to be abused at the hands of their boyfriends. It almost goes without saying that "bad" mothers often contend with poverty and discrimination. There are many instances of bad mothering in America, but the cases that get attention are when white, middle-class women such as Susan Smith and Andrea Yates kill their children for no

On the Table, 1996. Table, chairs, television sets and videotapes.

On the Table, 1996.

apparent reason. While race and ethnic identity are frequently discussed in relationship to maternal ideology, the issue of class is less often considered. And yet the debate around good and bad mothers is one that is often colored by perception about social class and middle-class behavior.

Murderous mothers are one thing. The territory of bad mother—and blighted child—is more nebulous. Very often, the blighted child—and the bad mother—are seen as a result of socio-economic circumstances. The mother's class background precludes her from understanding how to interact properly with her child and influences her to make terrible mistakes.

In the video installation *On the Table*, Myrel Chernick takes on the myth of the bad working-class mother as constructed by popular culture and in the media. *On the Table* is comprised of an old yellow Formica table and chairs with two very old television sets placed on top. One television set shows women sitting at that table while narrating incidents about their mothers. These incidents range from bizarre—one mother uses a blackhead remover on her daughter's chin but refuses to acknowledge that she has a bad case of acne—to terribly poignant—another mother who was forced to drop out of college takes her daughter to the University of Toronto and tells her that she will love it there. These stories of motherhood serve to unpack the ideological construction of mothers and motherhood as white, middle class, and self-sacrificing. The women seated at this table—itself a nostalgic evocation of a childhood from the fifties, sixties, and sometimes seventies—are of all different classes, races, ages, and sexual preferences. What they bring to the table is not so much a universal narrative of motherhood as a commonality of having mothers—as well as the implicit knowledge that the definition of motherhood depends on a number of social factors.

The other television set, a black and white portable from the sixties, alternates among images of Chernick and her family having breakfast on Mother's Day at the Formica table, a series of "headless" women carefully setting and clearing the same table, and a straightforward presentation of the story of Alice Crimmins, who was convicted for murdering her children in the mid-seventies. A lovely young woman who was "a former cocktail waitress," Crimmins denied that she had murdered her children right up until her conviction. Paroled five years later, she could be found yachting off the coast of New York with her husband, a former prison guard, in a ship named after her murdered daughter. The inclusion of Alice Crimmins' case, read against the more moderate descriptions of motherly intervention, calls into question the construction of the bad—as opposed to good—mother. Alice Crimmins supposedly dated many men after the breakup of her marriage and was apparently out with one of her boyfriends just before the children were murdered. Newspaper accounts of the Crimmins case emphasized Alice's appearance, clothing, former (and brief) profession as a cocktail waitress, and numerous boyfriends. Even today, the issue of Crimmins' guilt or innocence remains unresolved. What was at stake, as Chernick's video makes clear, is Crimmins' transgression of the norms of the institution of motherhood. Crimmins' membership in the proletariat class is confirmed by both her choice of profession and the media's focus on her sexuality. The fact that Crimmins' children were murdered is almost beside the point. Crimmins was guilty, regardless of whether she did or did not murder her children.

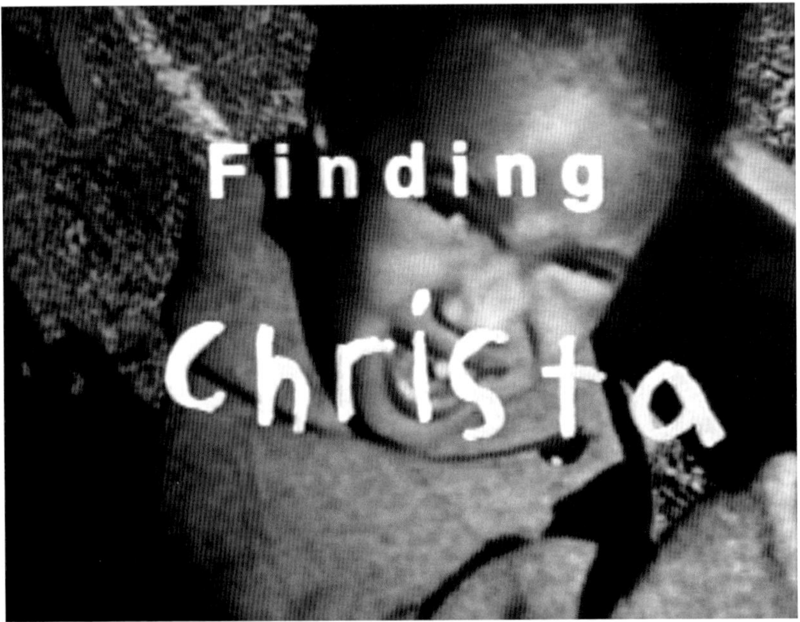

Camille Billops and James Hatch, *Finding Christa*, 1991.

CAMILLE BILLOPS AND JAMES HATCH, *FINDING CHRISTA* (1991)

What is worse, the mother who murders her children or the mother who gives her child up for adoption? *Finding Christa*, a film made by the artist/filmmaker Camille Billops and her husband, college professor James Hatch, is a disturbing film that plays on the conceit of the black, middle-class family and the ideal black mother. The film tells the story of Billops' reunion with her daughter Christa Victoria, whom she gave up for adoption at age four. The film, shot in 16 mm, opens with a shot of Christa shortly before she was given up for adoption while a voice-over from the adult Christa asked plaintively why her mother had left her at the children's home. The film then segues to a re-enactment of a conversation between Billops and her friend Coreen Simpson, in which Billops tells Simpson that the adult Christa has contacted her. Billops tells her friend that she isn't sorry that she gave Christa up, noting that she wanted something better for herself and for Christa.

Finding Christa then returns to Los Angeles in the years before Billops, a single mother who was becoming increasingly desperate, decided to give up Christa for adoption. The Los Angeles period is recreated through family films, old photographs, and interviews. Valerie Smith has pointed out that these photographs and movies seemingly recreate the joy of the middle-class family life that Billops enjoyed in the late fifties, a joy that is undercut by the interviews and by Billops herself.[14] Billops, when she meets Christa, as she does slightly later in the film, clearly has a lot of difficulty connecting with Christa, trying to force her at one point towards the end of the movie to look at family photographs while Christa speaks with her adoptive mother on the phone. The testimony of Billops' relatives suggests that they would have taken Christa and raised her themselves. Billops' cousin Bertha goes so far as to suggest that Billops

Film still: *Finding Christa,* 1991.

gave up Christa in order to pursue her career and travel with Hatch to Egypt. Slightly later in the film Billops suggests otherwise, pointing out that her family wasn't willing to care for Christa as they claim they were, and that she had little choice but to give Christa up.

Finding Christa is an extraordinary film, in part because Billops' portrayal of herself as an ambivalent mother is so unflinchingly honest. In fact, Christa probably *was* better off without her mother, the pain of the initial separation notwithstanding. In the second section of the movie, "Where Were You Christa?" it turns out that Christa was adopted by a loving family. This second section focuses on Christa's adoptive mother, Margaret Leibig. Leibig, a singer who encourages Christa's love of music, is in many ways the archetypal African American mother—warm, loving, and self-sacrificing in comparison to Billops' distant mother. *Finding Christa* is a documentary, albeit an unusual example of the genre that was made almost eight years after the initial reunion. Because of its resemblance to films that purport to give the viewer a "true" and unedited narrative, *Finding Christa* has elicited more negativity than any of Billops' other films.[15] And yet, as Janet K. Cutler has argued, *Finding Christa* in fact poses a challenge to the hegemonic Hollywood depiction of African American maternity as eternally self-sacrificing. The film ends somewhat ambiguously—Christa is still torn between her biological mother and her adoptive mother, and Billops does not suddenly become warm and cuddly. As Cutler argues, "*Finding Christa* challenges the idea that women should be more responsible than men for child-rearing—even if it means raising a child alone or largely delegating childcare to extended family members."[16]

CONCLUSION

By way of conclusion, I would like to return to Truong's silent mother, who must have suffered terribly as she watched her daughter struggle to fit into the American South. Truong recalled that "In the fall of 1975, I came along and provided these students with something new, an entirely revised idea of what it meant not to fit in. They rewarded me for introducing them to multiculturalism with a daily barrage of name-calling, with most of the epithets being generic and inaccurate."[17] Much has changed since 1975, when it was still acceptable to make fun of somebody because of their race, religion, or appearance. Nevertheless, there is still a long way to go before there is parity in the media representation of the institution of motherhood. Feminists and feminist artists, as Andrea Liss has demonstrated, have been reluctant to embrace motherhood and the figure of the mother because of their need to "distance themselves from all that was culturally coded as passive, weak and irrational, sometimes repudiating their own mothers."[18] Until we do so, however, the gains realized by women in the second-wave feminist movement will not be fully realized.

Notes

[1]Monique Truong, "The Loneliest Birthday Girl," *Parents* (May 2007): 98.
[2]Katrina Irving, *Immigrant Mothers: Narratives of Race and Maternity, 1890-1925* (Illinois: University of Illinois Press, 2000), 15.
[3]Pranee Liamputtong, "Motherhood and the Challenge of Immigrant Mothers: A Personal Reflection," *Families in Society: The Journal of Contemporary Human Services* 82.2 (2000): 197.
[4]bell hooks, "marginality as a site of resistance," *Out There: Marginalization and Contemporary Cultures*, eds. Russell Ferguson, Martha Gever, Trihn T. Minh-Ha, and Cornel West (New York: The New Museum of Contemporary Art, and Cambridge, MA: MIT Press, 1990), 337.
[5]Trinh T. Minh-Ha, *When the Moon Waxes Red* (New York and London: Routledge, 1991), 12.
[6]Ibid.
[7]Andrea Liss, "Maternal Rites: Feminist Strategies," *n.paradoxa* 14 (2004): 25.
[8]Jane Lazarre, *The Mother Knot*, intro. Sara Ruddick (Boston: Beacon Press, 1976, 1986). Lazarre's book was the first to explore the ambivalence that many educated women felt in the face of institutionalized motherhood.
[9]Susan Wittstock, "Tiny Muses," *Perspectives* (Spring/Summer 2005): 28.
[10]Evelyn Nakano Glenn, Grace Chang, and Linda Rennie Forcey, eds., *Mothering: Ideology, Experience, and Agency* (New York and London: Routledge, 1994); Julia E. Hanigsberg and Sara Ruddick, eds. *Mother Troubles: Rethinking Contemporary Maternal Dilemmas* (Boston: Beacon Press, 1999).
[11]Gail Rebhan, *Mother-Son Talk: A dialogue between a mother and her young sons* (Rochester, NY: Visual Studies Workshop, 1996), 26.
[12]Most of my information on the Eugenics movement was taken from the web site *Image Archive on the American Eugenics Movement* <http://www.eugenicsarchive.org/eugenics> viewed 11/12/09.
[13]Sara Ruddick, "Talking about Mothers," originally published in *Maternal Thinking: Toward a Politics of Peace* (1989), reprinted in Moyra Davey, ed., *Mother Reader* (New York: Seven Stories Press, 2001), 190.
[14]Valerie Smith, "Photography, Narrative, and Ideology in *Suzanne Suzanne* and

Finding Christa by Camille Billops and James V. Hatch," in Marianne Hirsch, ed., *The Familial Gaze* (Hanover, NH: University Press of New England, 1999), 94.
[15]Janet K. Cutler, "Don't Say Mammy," in Heather Addison, Mary Kate Goodwin-Kelly, and Elaine Roth, eds., *Motherhood Misconceived* (Albany: State University of New York Press, 2009), 222.
[16]Ibid.
[17]Truong, "The Loneliest Birthday Girl," 98.
[18]Liss, "Maternal Rites," 25.

MARGARET MORGAN

Home Truths

> [W]ith the question of the importance of telling the truth, knowing who is able to tell the truth, and knowing why we should tell the truth, we have the roots of what we would call the "critical" tradition in the West.[1]

DEMOCRACY HAS ALWAYS NEEDED CRITICS. In his seminar "Discourse and Truth" Foucault examined the concept of the *parrhesiastes*, from the ancient Greek—the one who speaks truth to power. To summarize, these critics shall be honorable and dutiful. They shall speak frankly and fully. They shall speak that which they sincerely believe to be true. The proof of their sincerity should lie in the fact that they speak to the powerful without consideration of the consequences for themselves should they incur the wrath of those to whom they speak or should they incriminate themselves. Artists have often served the role of the *parrhesiastes*, and in this essay I discuss two contemporary artists who perform that critical function. Before examining the work of Catherine Opie and Andrea Bowers, it is important to consider the social and political contexts from which their projects have sprung.

The administration of George W. Bush did not honor the *parrhesiastes*. Instead they punished critics. Rather than take difficult questions from the press corps, they handpicked reporters and scripted press conferences. Rather than listening to dissenting opinions from within the White House, they chose to keep counsel only with those whose opinions matched their own. Rather than looking for evidence to establish fact, they chose "facts" that confirmed pre-existing conclusions. Potential enemy nations were attacked; possible enemy operatives were imprisoned without trial. Wiretapping and torture were condoned. Each of these contributed to a collective repression of free speech.

Simultaneously, family values were invoked to appease the religious right of the Republican Party and/or to distract from more pressing issues like war, federal debt and governmental deception. Thus, women's reproductive rights came under threat, federal funding was prohibited for international health-care providers who even so much as mentioned abortion, and moms on welfare were required to work one third more hours before receiving assistance. Meanwhile George W. Bush embodied an easy populism exemplified by his impish grin and rolled-up sleeves, his simple homespun attitudes, and his boyish pleasure in recreational sports. In Kenneth Frampton's presageful words of more than twenty years earlier, "[T]he primary goal of Populism is to function as a *communicative or instrumental sign.*"[2] Thus the image of George Bush functioned as a sign of the 'average Joe' in lieu of policies and programs to support ordinary people. In short, the political climate in which artists Opie and Bowers found themselves suppressed dissent, invoked family values while decimating families, and paraded a populist president while undermining the populous.

During this period, the art market was booming. Auction houses were experiencing price scales never before known, art museums were building global franchises around fleets of buildings by internationally renowned architects, many more artists' incomes were skyrocketing, international biennials became the playgrounds of the rich and their cohorts. Although critical artistic practice always coexists with the commercial art market, during such periods it is overshadowed by the extraordinary flows of capital through the art world. In the first decade of the twenty-first century, the look and feel of money dominated.

It is in the confluence of these phenomena—the suppression of dissent, a rigid construction of family, the booming of the art market—that I wish to examine two bodies of work from the period, one by Catherine Opie and the other by Andrea Bowers. Each artist can be aligned with the kind of critical tradition described by Foucault at the beginning of this essay. Each body of work critically engages contemporary understandings of family and motherhood—"motherhood," that most easily instrumentalized of signs. As a subject for artistic expression, the last time motherhood was highly valued was during the Renaissance and that of course in an idealized form. Making *critical* art about mothering under the specific political and economic forces outlined above is none other than the work of the *parrhesiastes*.

"So you see, the *parrhesiastes* is someone who takes a risk."[3]

By risk, I mean nothing so extreme as incarceration or death. But certainly, the political climate at large and the economic forces specific to the art world were not conducive to speaking truthfully about mothering.

Such a topic was neither fashionable nor remunerative at the time these artists made their work. Even five years later, much of the work of which I will speak has not been acquired, though arguably it is all of major significance. Yet Opie and Bowers both chose to take that risk because truth-telling compelled them to do so.

Though different in form and content, Bowers and Opie both foreground the politics of motherhood, Opie by documenting the present, Bowers by retrieving the past. Opie photographs the life of her own family, her neighborhood, and home. Bowers documents families of another era by drawing meticulous reproductions of newspaper clippings and letters from people seeking abortion some half a decade before its legalization in 1973 under the landmark U.S. Supreme Court case, *Roe v. Wade.* Catherine Opie and Andrea Bowers depict private life as both an elegy for the promise of an earlier era and a fight back: in their work, we see motherhood in all its possibilities and this motherhood is powerful, its image not your average *Madonna and Child.*

CATHERINE OPIE: NOT YOUR AVERAGE MADONNA

A red acanthus-leafed drape enfolds the background. Before the drape sits a mother, her oblique gaze rapt with care upon the child cradled in her arms, who, in returning her gaze, brings full circle the powerful unity that is the maternal dyad. The child is a silver-haired boy, a Baroque angel, a curl of body, fetal in position though obviously a budding two-year-old, molded into the pliant corporeality of his mother, the pellucid flesh of the suckling child a study in the modulation of color and light akin to Boucher. The image, however, is not a painting, but a photograph, a self-portrait of Catherine Opie, *Self Portrait / Nursing* (2004). Her flesh is forty-ish, middle aging, scarred and tattooed in sado-masochistic ritual, delicately filigreed with pale pink ridges, lines, swirls, traces of words, curlicues of scarification. We see sagging breasts, puckered aureole; freckles; a sun-stained diamond of neck-flesh merging into what was once of the same chromatic hue and luminosity as that of the boy who is obviously her son: all this bears an unequivocally local tenor. As much as the image invokes a sixteenth-century Madonna or an eighteenth-century portrait painting and as much as each element—the folds of fabric and skin, the concentrated gaze, the baby toes tucked into a motherly upper arm, the coloration of the whole—brings with it rich and what might be understood as universal associations—the stuff of art history and religious iconography—the image is naught if not confounding of these conventions. With each registration, comes its deconstruction: universality/ specificity; purity/

partiality; fecundity/ middle age; gentle mother/butch dyke. Centuries and moments of association swirl and jump and connect and disconnect and reconnect again in rapid circulations: it is the image that blinks before you, the viewer, in a surfeit of stops and starts, simultaneously making sense and nonsense of your witness. It is a nuanced and masterful piece of motherhood indeed. And in this it reminds me of Kenneth Frampton's Critical Regionalism, of local culture and universal civilization: in its courage and liberty, its shamelessness of spirit and its economy of means, the image is the late-born child of an aging modernity. In its specificity, it is something else again: if Frampton was interested in ways in which local architecture could resist a modernization that was reducible to a communicative or instrumental sign, Opie's maternal self-portrait offers a universal sign—motherhood—inflected by a set of powerfully resistant counter-signs, a kind of "regional specificity," if you like, that makes the image extraordinarily affirming of the maternal bond, fulsome in all its complexity, yet extremely resistant to easy instrumentalization.

Catherine Opie has been documenting domestic life—queer, complex, multifaceted, across race, class and country—for about two decades. The oeuvre has always run counter to prevailing hegemonies about gender, sexuality and community. On occasion, as part of this oeuvre, Opie has taken self-portraits, of which *Self Portrait / Nursing* is an example. During the administration of G. W. Bush, Opie's practice became explicitly critical of the prevailing political culture and her self-portraiture became extended into an entire series, documenting the life of the self in terms social, political, intellectual, psychological. In *In and Around Home* (2004-5), as the body of work is known, Opie has extended the single self-portrait into an at-times vitriolic but always insightful critique of the dominant political culture. At first glance the aesthetic seems to take a back seat to the driving force of documentation: the laudable desire to scream, to chant, to make visible a politic and to make sense of the real effects of politics in people's lives. Yet this would be too narrow a reading of the work: indeed in this series Opie deploys a very knowing use of the anti-aesthetics of Robert Frank, Lee Friedlander, Helen Levitt and other mid-twentieth-century American photographers, thereby invoking, *ipso facto*, an American sensibility while insisting on the historical specificities of the time and place *she* occupies, the local tenor of this most American of bodies of work. There is an apparent passivity verging on the abject in which, for example, dark interiors set against bright windows are not magically lit from within with fill-flash. Instead of marveling at the photographer's technical bravura (as we do in her *Self Portrait / Nursing*), the viewer is left to ponder their lack of knowledge, what has been

Catherine Opie, *Self Portrait / Nursing,* 2004. C-print, 40 × 32 inches. Courtesy of Regen Projects, Los Angeles. Edition of 8.

Catherine Opie, *Christmas West Adams,* 2004. C-print, 16 × 20 inches.
Edition of 5.

absented from their view, what can hardly be seen. One such image, *Christmas West Adams* (2004), is fully two-thirds in darkness, but this under-exposure becomes a literalization of profound political omissions: just outside the window, in full daylight, a rainbow flag hangs from the front eave of the house, upon which are the words, "SAY NO to the Bush Agenda"—but the letters as the viewer of the photograph sees them are in reverse. For the flag is seen from behind, as if we are standing in the space that would be the house's darkened interior, facing the street from the point of view of the flag's advocate (and referent), from the position of the one who says the 'no' the flag declares to the world beyond the lush vegetation of the front garden. We see through multiple registers of social space: home, replete with a Christmas tree invisible in the darkness but for its colored lights in the foreground (and the cue for the photograph's title); in the middle ground, a liminal space upon which to project an idea, with which to connect to community—the space of the rainbow flag and beyond that, the verdant plantings, like a kid's picture book slice-of-paradise; then, the space of the street, low fences, cars parked, houses in rows. We register these spaces, on a continuum from private to public and back again, from the point of view of an anti-Bush rainbow coalition. The viewer does not simply observe this homely protest: the viewer occupies its subject position. So it is the viewer who is given only partial access to, a tantalizing suggestion of, the family festivities, the family life, in the foreground but who is required to see literally from the point of view of that family. In this the viewer's position is radicalized: neither comfortable voyeur, the old scopic privilege conventionally reserved for masculinity, nor privileged intimate: the viewer has been invited in but not fully so—for this home, though seen up close and personal, is, literally and symbolically, barely visible.

Taken within a short radius of the artist's domicile, the series *In and Around Home* documents a multitude of subject positions and registers of being, knowing and ways of having agency, all of which articulate malleable yet durable connections: from local protests to parades to graduation celebrations to murals to memorial shrines to protest banners (and their tagging by graffitists) to handmade signs painted on the exterior of a local store to film crews and television journalists as they construct the evening news, to the still interior of a single, local polling booth. *In and Around Home* is a vivid portrait, in microcosm, of democracy at work: contested, constructed, registered as joyous, angry, disputed, celebratory, by people standing together, partying together, marching together, being together and being alone, and the traces of their writing, drawing, speaking, engaging, lively and in all fractious contestation connected to a belief in the right to voice opinion, the right to exist. As different as the specifics of the depicted subject positions might be, Opie's photographs speak to this commonality, to this shared, messy, noisy coexistence.

Consider, for example, the triptych, *In Protest to Sex Offenders 2005; Homecoming USC 2004; M.L.K. Parade 2005* (2004-05). As the title describes, there are three scenes. Each event takes place on the street. Each relies on a critical mass of people for its existence. The first is a group of mostly black figures, adults and children, protesting the concentration of a significant number of sex offenders in a local halfway house, an angry man sporting a bullhorn anchoring the left of the composition, the oblique late-afternoon light unifying the whole. Next is a scene of a USC homecoming party of mostly white, mostly male figures, three beards and a pro-Bush T-shirt prominent in the middle ground, a blanket's stripe on the lower right echoing the diagonal shaft of sunset on the lower right of the first image. In each of these two scenes are figures standing with folded arms, and signage on either placards or T-shirts that seem to serve as much as barriers as markers. The third is a scene of mostly standing figures, mostly black and female, at a Martin Luther King Day celebration. The figures' looks are askew, their glances sideways across the picture plane, attention diverted to action taking place outside our view. As such, the images recall nineteenth-century paintings like Renoir's *Le Moulin de la Galette* (1876), in which casually posed figures occupy the pictorial space and reach beyond it, their truncated forms suggesting the extension of activity beyond the frame, this a fragment of a much larger whole, a "painting" of modern life in West Adams, Los Angeles. And in the center of each of these compositions is a woman, face turned to the side, looking askance—a pregnant woman in a pink singlet, a woman in red sitting quietly amused, a woman in pink hiding her face—the still centers of dynamic scenes. "Mothering" is not foregrounded in this piece but neither is it sentimentalized nor sequestered away. Women and children are always there. Mothering is implicitly part of the political life of the culture, literally linked through color and form. In two of the scenes, the color red dominates, in the clothes worn and in signage, and in a beer can in the foreground. Pink links one of these two with the third of the trio as do the crowds themselves, taking the middle-ground of all three images and together forming a continuous undulating line, a wave of humanity, albeit one that never floats unanchored and drifting into vague and sentimental humanism but rather is always insistently attached—to cultures and events as different socio-politically as they are similar in form and place. While the documentary function of the work is overt and the images so content-laden as to make the formal aspects seem merely incidental, these arrangements of shapes and lines and colors are anything but passive. In Opie's work meaning is situated in and through the logic of form and in this it imbricates form and content, those once-upon-a-time separate spheres of modernism.

FORM AND MALCONTENT

The series *In and Around Home* embeds its politics in the very stuff of its formal language. Its overt political content is registered not only by the images themselves but in the difference between photographic media employed: the documentary images, some of which I have described above, take the form of C-prints. These are accompanied by Polaroid photographs of TV news broadcasts and talking heads. The C-prints function indexically while the Polaroids document the manufacture of politics as media spectacle. Sometimes in groupings of as many as nine, they are redolent with images of the war in Iraq, domestic political storms in teacups, the gesticulations of politicians and pundits at home and abroad. Together the two types of photograph make vivid the contradictions between grass-roots reality and the gloss of political rhetoric. Thus the viewer connects a rather blank image of a polling booth in Los Angeles, empty, poorly lit, full of unmarked ballots, with what one can think of as its complement, the TV image of the purple-stained fingers of an enfranchised population in Iraq. In another photograph we see a news anchor filmed in the neighborhood with the attendant cameras and crews as she constructs the evening news. Its complement?—the Polaroids of sensational and vacuous newscasts. In yet another coupling we look to a newspaper lying folded on a front porch step. When we read its headline, that Bush's doctrine is to "spread liberty," we glean through the television images of the presidential visage with its artificial smile that this "liberty" is like margarine: easy to spread but of dubious content.

If "*art no longer wants to respond to the excess of commodities and signs but to a lack of connections*"[4]—and here I quote Jacques Rancière—Catherine Opie's work at once documents and, in the documenting, enhances the very connections that are lamented lost: the social bonds at work in the contestation of democracy, the right to freedom of expression, the right to assembly and, in the most profound ontology, the right to be. In this, Opie's work positions the public sphere and the private, the political and the domestic, on a continuum: individual agency is a family matter and family is a feminist issue and being queer is being normal: and mothering is at the center of it all.

ANDREA BOWERS: CIRCA 1968

Being and subjectivity are ostensibly at the root of the debates around abortion rights and family values still contested in the United States. Where does subjectivity begin? Where does it end? Who speaks or acts for whom? Since the advent of the oral contraceptive pill, American women have experienced the promise and entitlement of having children, or not, at the time of their choice. Generations of feminists and progressive leaders have fought to privilege the subjectivity of the woman over the theoretical subjectivity of the fetus and, since 1973, women have had the right to abort a pregnancy unwanted for whatever reason: *abortion without apology*. Yet the anti-abortion movement has made up a lot of ground since then and women of child-bearing age seem more complacent about the eroding of rights that might have a direct impact on their lives. Enter Andrea Bowers and her exhibition entitled *Nothing is Neutral*. Shown at REDCAT, Los Angeles, in 2006, it is a tribute to pro-choice feminist activism and the individual women who have pioneered it. Working from papers found in the archives of the Society for Humane Abortion and the Association to Appeal Abortion Laws, Bowers' tribute takes the form of an installation of drawings, wallpaper, video, and books. A series of meticulous, lovingly detailed pencil drawings reproduce letters dated circa 1968 that were addressed to the Association to Repeal Abortion Laws. The original letters were written for women and girls seeking abortions when abortion was still illegal. Some were written by the women themselves, others by their families, husbands, fathers and boyfriends. Bowers' suite of drawings, collectively entitled *Wall of Letters: Necessary Reminders from the Past for a Future of Choice* (2005), has the feel of a shrine of remembrance, the solemnity of a war memorial. Each drawing is spare in form but extremely studied in articulation as it precisely iterates the written word down to the very physical being of each letter: the weight of the typed character on the page, the press of a pen, the scratchy eccentricity of the handwritten word. The drawings are exacting, photorealist one could say, and as such they are indeed "reminders of the past," both historically and aesthetically speaking.

The formal concerns of a branch of Pop painting (photorealism) and the specific histories of women leading up to the legalization of abortion are not usually invoked simultaneously, yet they occurred within the same historical period. In Bowers' *Nothing is Neutral*, nothing, not even a painting technique, is outside the social and historical forces of its time. Though the period is circa 1968, Bowers focuses not upon the grand revolutions and student riots of the era but the rather less spectacular revolution of

Andrea Bowers, *Nothing is Neutral,* 2006. Installation view, Gallery at REDCAT, Los Angeles. Photo: Scott Groller.

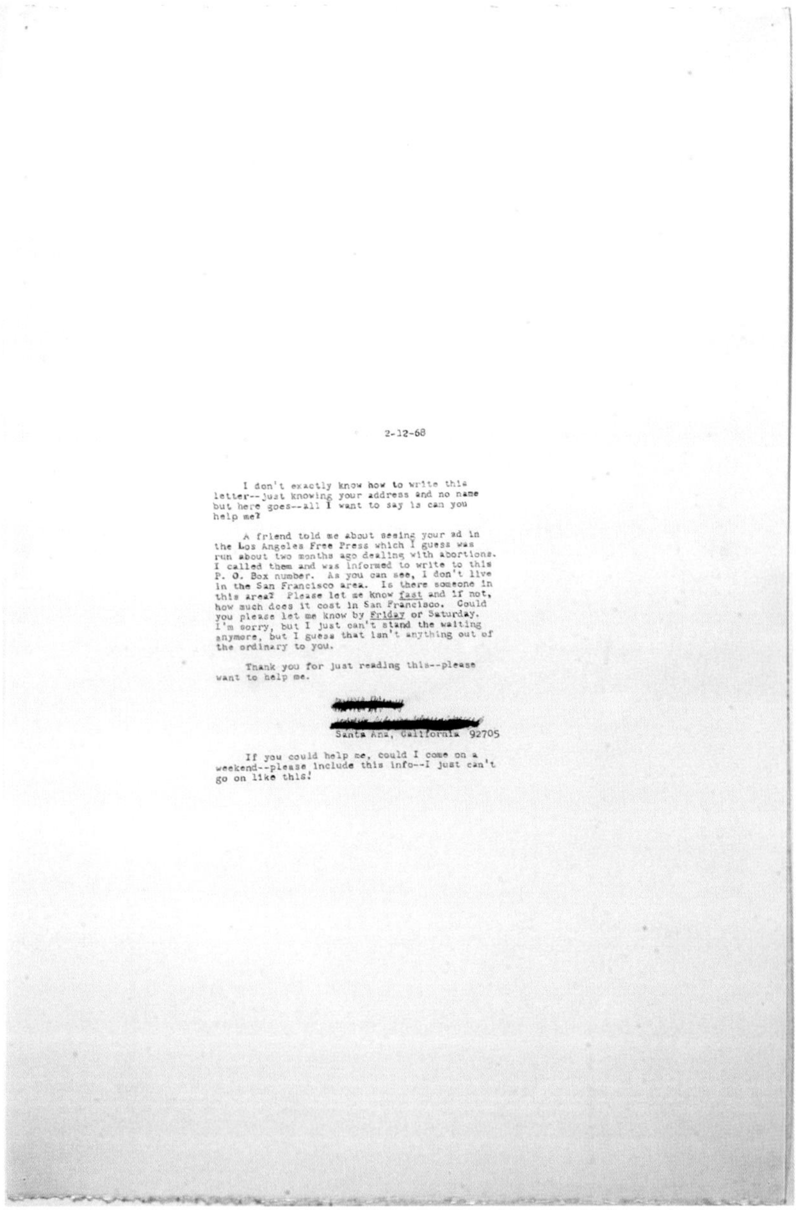

2-12-68

I don't exactly know how to write this letter--just knowing your address and no name but here goes--all I want to say is can you help me?

A friend told me about seeing your ad in the Los Angeles Free Press which I guess was run about two months ago dealing with abortions. I called them and was informed to write to this P. O. Box number. As you can see, I don't live in the San Francisco area. Is there someone in this area? Please let me know <u>fast</u> and if not, how much does it cost in San Francisco. Could you please let me know by <u>Friday</u> or Saturday. I'm sorry, but I just can't stand the waiting anymore, but I guess that isn't anything out of the ordinary to you.

Thank you for just reading this--please want to help me.

Santa Ana, California 92705

If you could help me, could I come on a weekend--please include this info--I just can't go on like this!

Andrea Bowers, *Wall of Letters: Necessary Reminders from the Past for a Future of Choice, #4,* 2006. Pencil on paper, 15 × 22.25 inches paper size.
Courtesy of Susanne Vielmetter Los Angeles Projects. Photo: Gene Ogami.

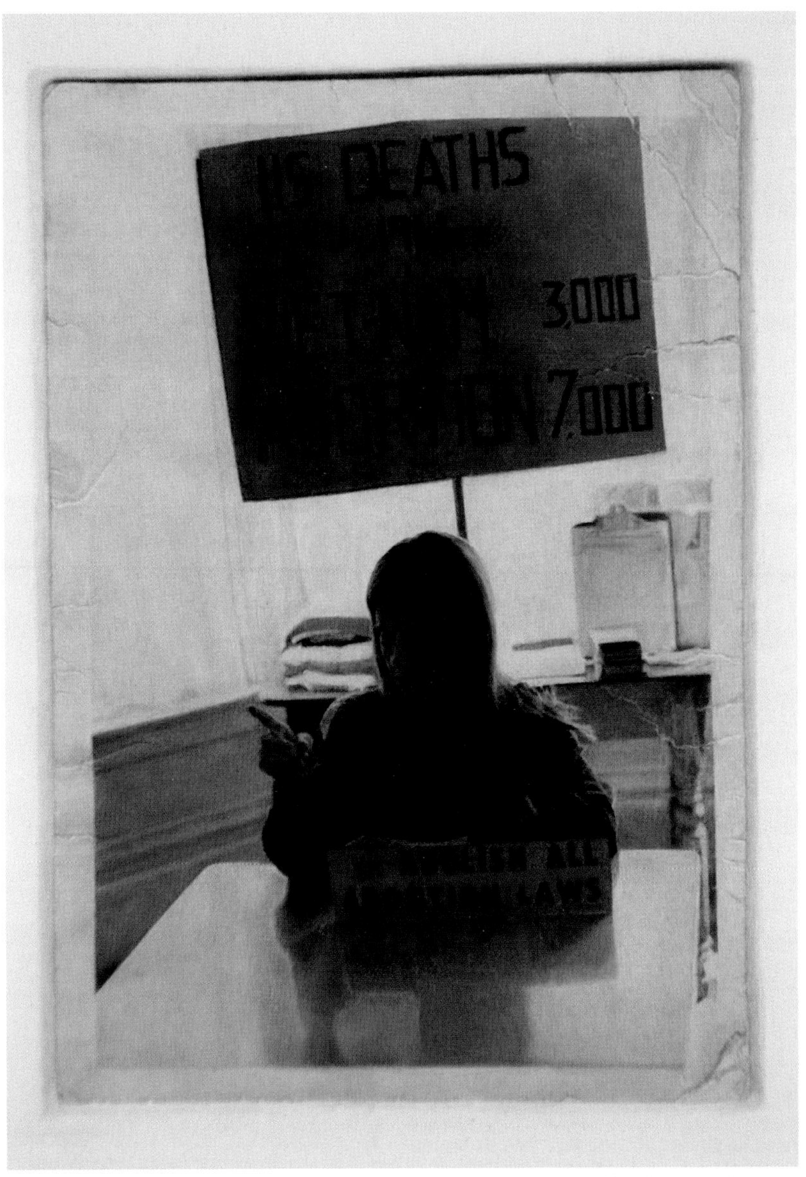

Andrea Bowers, *Young Abortion Rights Activist, San Francisco Bay Area, 1966, (Photo lent from the Archives of Patricia Maginnis),* 2005. Colored pencil on paper 15 × 38.25 inches paper size, 52.5 × 40.75 inches frame size. Courtesy of Susanne Vielmetter Los Angeles Projects. Photo: Joshua White.

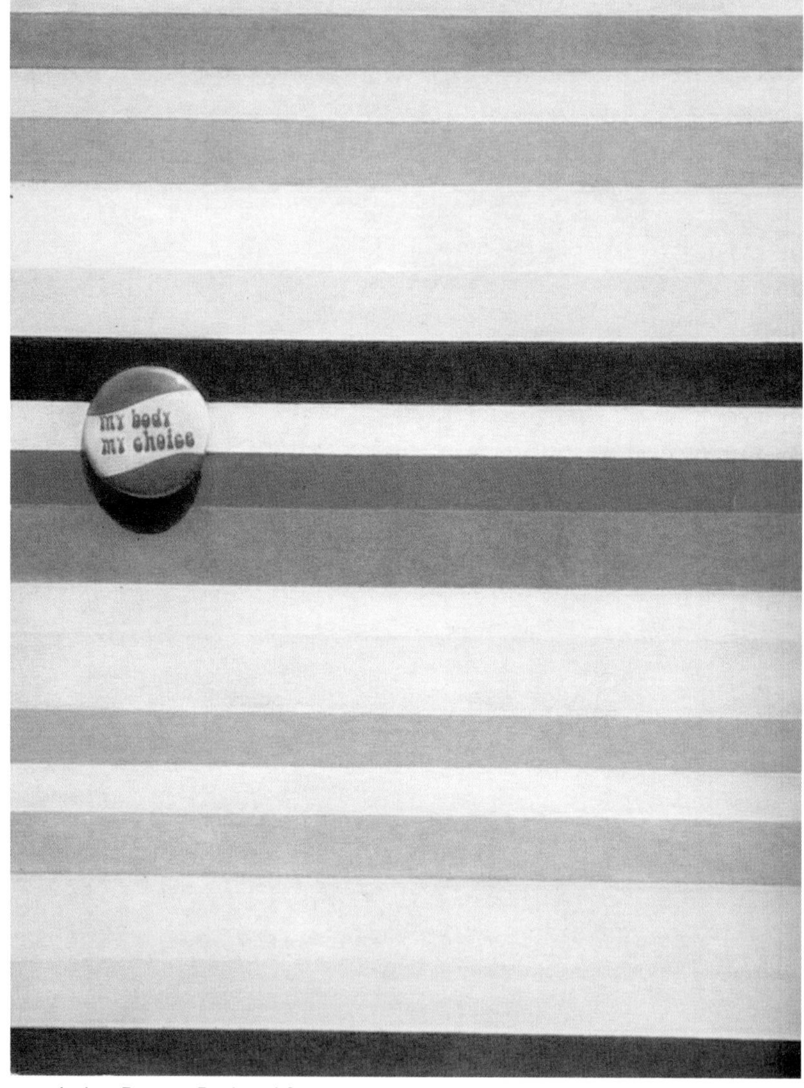

Andrea Bowers, *Design of Choice (My Body My Choice with Stripes)* (detail), 2005.
Colored pencil on paper, 13.875 × 10.375 inches.

family values and domestic choice, sheet by mimeographed sheet, small town by small town. Analogously, Bowers' photorealism is very different from photorealist paintings of the 1960s. In a painting by Richard Estes, for example, one encounters a kind of Pop optimism, a celebration of the vernacular world of spectacular capital. Shop fronts and objects for sale are frozen and splintered in a dazzling array of reflections and mirrors and reflections of mirrors, all surface and shine and disorientation, so that the viewer may never be certain of their witness, except for the fact that the viewer witnesses an impressive bravura, a *tour de force* of technical achievement on the part of the artist. In historical photorealism, the flash of the artist's skill subsumes the overt content of the painting, and that content's connection to life. Content is secondary, a vehicle to display painterly technique. Bowers' use of hyperrealism has none of the showy bluster of such historical forebears.[5] Certainly we are impressed with her technical bravura, her ability to emulate a photograph, yet, as with Catherine Opie, it is impossible to separate that formal technique, however brilliant, from its subject. The artist's hand is subsumed by the content of the material depicted in what must be a meditative process indeed, a tender and modest testimony to these extraordinary responses to desperate times.

Wall of Letters #4, as a drawing, is a remarkable facsimile of a typed letter, the words of which float on a white surface in a simple milk-white frame. The letter, though dated 2-12-68, without addressee and with the sender's name obliterated, still has a tone of urgency. At the level of overt content, the author implores the addressee several times in the missive, "Please want to help me," the word "please" recurring four times in the brief. At a subliminal level, the very typography reiterates this distress. In the original, many of the individual characters' "holes," or "counters" to use the typographical term, are filled in with ink as if the typewriter's ribbon overflowed its bounds, like blood or desire, like a body's holes overwhelmed and overflowing, or clogged and drowning as much as the person whose fingers punched the keys. Across the form of the characters, word to word with each keystroke, we note a subtle undulation of color, the fading in and out of ink, a darker impress here, a lighter one there, like breathing, in and out, in and out. We notice the physicality of the original *because* it is reproduced by Bowers' hand, the copy allowing the viewer more fully to know the source.

Many of the letters have a sense of sometimes barely contained ignominy as the authors anxiously seek to establish the reasonableness of their requests, which of course brings to mind how much their reason was already under suspicion and how much things have indeed changed for women since then. "Due to circumstances," "my doctor has informed me," "fully aware of my responsibilities," the authors write, arguing, deferring, apologizing, begging for what is as one woman put it, "a 5 minute operation." The verisimilitude of Bowers' handmade drawings of these pleas for drastic measures, the close observation of each detail of the physicality of the text, returns the originals' attempt at objectivity to the intimate realm, even while the content of the written words takes us from the personal right back to the political, from the past right back to the present. As the viewer peers into the page to examine Bowers' technique, the viewer becomes all the more aware of these things. Thus, rather than the content serving the technique, it is Bowers' drawing that *brings home* the overt content to us, her technique in service to that end.

As with Catherine Opie's work, technical bravura is as much at the service of the content as it is a quality in and of itself, marking out the formal and the political on a continuum with each other. The first paragraph of letter #*4* contains a plea, "Can you help me?" The drawing of the letter functions in reply by positioning the original in a place *to help us*. For in copying the original, stroke by tiny stroke, and making an image of this cry for help, the letter helps us remember lest we forget all there is to lose. There is a humility in the respectfulness with which Bowers copies these forty-year-old missives, as if in penance for ignorance, as if by copying each indentation of ink on paper, she might herself begin to comprehend and reveal for her audience the enormous difficulties women experienced negotiating their reproductive lives pre *Roe v. Wade*. And in a political culture in which that decision has been increasingly contested (and legally tested), the revelation comes none too soon.

There is another aspect to the use of hyperrealism at work in Bowers' project. What is documented in her realism is as much about the reproduction of the original as the original itself. Thus the drawings reproduce the quality of a typewriter or a photocopy or a mimeograph or a battered old photograph, its edges all turned, a last physical relic of events past. If a photograph is an event's index, then Bowers' drawing of a photograph speaks to how very fragile an index it may be. Consider *Young Abortion Rights Activist, San Francisco Bay Area, 1966 (Photo Lent from the Archives of Patricia Maginnis)* (2005). The image, drawn in colored pencil, sits in the middle of a pristine sheet of paper. It is a drawing of a small color photograph, tones faded, yellows dropping out, surface mottled, edges rubbed and frayed. The photograph casts a slight *trompe l'oeil* shadow on the page. It is an old photograph that, we are told in the title of the drawing, is from an archive. What was photographed all those decades ago was a young woman holding a sign and gesticulating.

Her finger is pointing. Her sign reads, "Abolish all abortion laws." We know the era because behind her is a larger banner that declares: "U.S. Deaths 1966, Vietnam 3000, Abortion 7,000." As with Catherine Opie's documents of protest banners, there is built-in a complex registration of history and the recording of history and the history of recordings of history. Bowers' viewer learns some old facts, or remembers them, but then she may also learn how very fleeting those memories may be and how easily overturned those monumental historical changes.

In Bowers' installation, *Nothing is Neutral, Wall of Letters* was juxtaposed with *Letter to the Army of Three Displayed*, which consisted of two entire walls papered floor to ceiling with decorative gift-wrapping papers and still more letters photocopied from the archive. Totaling some 316 sheets, each 24 inches high by 18 inches wide, the effect was to multiply the sense of urgency of the discreet and solemn individual drawings of the *Wall of Letters*. Like a giant quilt, or the ghost of feminist wallpapers past,[6] *Displayed* overwhelms the viewer with its repetitions and its patterning, its variety and its color, and brings home the enormity and banality of these tragic narratives. Some of the wrapping papers are also reproduced as drawings, a series entitled *Design of Choice*. These drawings on first sight seem like a trivial surfeit, a purely decorative display—until one notices that the images contain renderings of activist pins discreetly placed over areas of matching color. Again, the decorative and the political, the formal and the social, form and content in modernist parlance, are on a continuum, never one without the other.

A video entitled *Letters to an Army of Three* (2005), consisting of readings of the texts of the letters that Bowers has so tenderly rendered in *Wall of Drawings*, played on a monitor suspended from the gallery's ceiling. In the video, each letter is read aloud, the reader sitting awkwardly upon a stool before a closed curtain. It is as if the readers are compelled to complete their task but cannot help reacting to the content of the letters. They squirm. We hear the quiver of their enunciation, the timbre of their voice making palpable their reactions. They pause, sometimes for many seconds. The gender, age, ethnicity and perhaps class of the sitters vary widely. They are not necessarily actors. The figures sit in front of changing decorative curtains and beside each is a changing arrangement of flowers. We never see the ground beneath their feet and the scene is always swathed in a dim half-light. Each reading is very individual and yet it is all the same, all of a piece. It is simultaneously local and universal. There is neither beginning nor end to the video, no narrative arc, only the cumulative fragments of these real stories reenacted. The video is paced by each changing text, reader, curtain and vase of flowers, each fading in, fading out, again rather like a slow but insistent breathing. The floral arrangements are highly formal and deployed to punctuate the readings, their placement shifting as the shot fades from reader with flowers to flowers alone to reader with flowers. As with the *Wall of Letters*, the piece has an elegiac quality, a memorial function and the flowers become almost funereal. Whose funeral, one might wonder? What happened to those whose voices are being resuscitated? What of liberty? Choice? What of the centuries of association between women, domesticity and the artful display of flowers? Each bowl of flowers, beautifully arranged, makes of the scene a tableau, a still life, meaning to be gleaned from the shadows of the tableau like a painting from the Northern Renaissance. For as with a traditional still life, the tableau may be deciphered: *still life*: we are still here, still alive and the "pro-life" position is really *nature morte*.

As someone who came of age in the 1980s, half a generation after *Roe v. Wade*, Bowers is a self-confessed apolitical non-activist, who has only relatively recently come to believe in "the power of the people," in the ability of ordinary folks' social activism to change public policy. Perhaps because her realization is only recent, her conviction is full of wonderment and awe at the courage of activists whose historic work she brings to light: those such as the Army of Three and A.R.A.L. (Association to Repeal Abortion Laws and predecessor to the still-extant NARAL). We learn from reading the *Wall of Letters* about the Army of Three, whose steadfast criticality and clear-sighted understanding of the dangers of illegal abortion and practical advice for women needing abortions were so important to changing laws and attitudes about women's reproductive rights in the United States. We learn from the installation and from the catalogue that the Army of Three was Patricia Maginnis, Rowena Gurner and Lana Phelan. In the decade preceding the legalization of abortion, these three women worked tirelessly to disseminate information about safe abortions, the old-fashioned way, long before the internet, by traveling around the United States, distributing leaflets and speaking to women in union halls, meeting rooms and private homes. Their mimeographed information included the names of abortion providers as far afield as Mexico and Japan and detailed descriptions of how to terminate a pregnancy oneself.

INDIRECT ACTION

As representations in an art gallery and not in themselves direct action, Bowers builds into the work the political limits of her practice when compared to the activism she documents, the very busy work of distributing information about safe abortion while women were still dying by the thousands in botched backyard jobs. As if to reiterate that it is the Army of Three, to whom the letters were addressed, that is the radical heart of her project, Bowers signals the relative modesty of her contribution through a number of cues: she makes the ephemera of activism the subject of her artwork; in video, she *stages* readings of the letters; in drawings, she reproduces the letters as images and depicts activist buttons pinned to patterned papers; all the while the artist points to the work's status as surfeit, as reconstruction, as decoration, a subtle acknowledgment that the work reifies activism rather than embodies it. Yet Bowers' project is an honorable one, for what remains engaging about it is its memorial status, as if to remind us that the gallery persists as a place for the possibility of social exchange: the sharing of information and the potential activation of political consciousness—something the religious right has known at least since Jesse Helms.[7] For Bowers' work allows for rational communication: people stand around *reading* the drawings of the letters. The work's commemorative aspect, the authenticity of its source material, the sincerity of its author—these are qualities that speak to the urgency of the current situation while acknowledging the artist's historical remove from the source material—*I have placed vintage activist pins onto a decorative ground. They function as valuable sentiment and they are also part of a legacy.* Mea culpa, *I acknowledge I have no direct experience of these historical events, only second- and third-hand access. Yet I must still tell all of you who may have forgotten or who may never have known.* We understand Bowers' reconstruction of a specific historical moment as a self-conscious act that does not claim to be the activism it documents. Nor does it sensationalize its subject matter or seek to produce in the viewer an abject reaction to explicit depictions of, for example, the results of backyard abortions. To do so would be to put Bowers' practice on the side of the anti-abortion movement with its vivid depictions of purported fetal distress and so on. Instead Bowers seeks the viewer's active engagement with studied and utterly respectful depictions of the relics of activisms past and she donates 10 percent of her sales to Planned Parenthood and other pro-choice organizations for the sake of the future. Like the newly converted, she is zealous and her zeal is contagious: in a culture disillusioned with truth, Bowers' meticulous renderings ring true. Like Frampton's critical regionalism, it is the very specificity, the precision of the renderings of precise historical fact that draws us in and which makes us believe in the veracity of the narrative. If we are skeptical of what is presented to us as fact, our eyes widen as we peer into the "reproduction of fact" and the fact of reproduction: the artist's *and our own*.

THE PERSONAL IS (STILL) POLITICAL

The work of Catherine Opie and Andrea Bowers functions as *consciousness raising* or perhaps as loci for consciousness raising, which is to say that they prompt discussion, opinion and perhaps redress, their audiences metaphorically sharing experiences as if in a circle and understanding the political patterns that underpin individual experience. To see the work is to want to talk about it and through it. In this neither they nor their audience is mute or passive. Rather they wear their politics and their persuasions on their sleeves. *Without apology*. In this they take up the Jesse Helmses of the world, ironically the very conservatives who most understand the power and potential of art, the power as Foucault put it of "the 'critical' tradition in the West." This is their truth and truth their value.

Opie and Bowers speak to the truths of mothering and not-mothering on a continuum, they document the present via the past, they situate family values in the center of political and aesthetic discourse, they refuse to place content and form in a hierarchy of value, nor indeed mothering and not-mothering, each instead addressing the other. Opie and Bowers situate the politics of the maternal at the very center of political life, motherhood functioning in all its specificity as a counter to the rhetorical spin of the simplifications of its contemporary milieu. The personal is still political but if feminism from the seventies was largely from the point of view of the daughter, and here Mary Kelly's *Post-Partum Document (1972–78)* is exceptional, it is high time for the voice of the mother—no, for lots of voices of lots and lots of mothers, loud and strong, and talking back and taking over the discourse: Bowers and Opie offer such powerful voices, the urgently needed *parrhesiastes*.

—Margaret Morgan 2007

Coda: I am happy to say that after the 43rd administration came the 44th and with it the promise of a White House that eagerly looks to the *parrhesiastes*. The incoming Obama administration itself promises a return to truth-telling and a restoration of democratic principles decimated under Bush 43. It also promises an arts policy that supports art and art education as crucial parts of our democratic life. However, the right to privacy and human dignity are yet to be restored and the centrality of mothering to our political well-being yet to be recognized, so I am glad to be reminded by the examples of Opie and Bowers of the one role of the artist that is most important now: the role of truth-teller.

—Margaret Morgan, January 2009

Notes

[1]Michel Foucault, *Fearless Speech*, ed. Joseph Pearson (Los Angeles: Semiotext(e)/ Foreign Agents, 2001), 5.

[2]Kenneth Frampton, "Prospects for a Critical Regionalism'" in *Theorizing a New Agenda for Architecture*, ed. Kate Nesbit (New York: Princeton Architectural Press, 1996), 471.

[3]Foucault, *Fearless*, 16.

[4]Jacques Rancière, "Problems and Transformations in Critical Art (2004)," in *Participation,* ed. Claire Bishop (London: Whitechapel, 2006), 90.

[5]Certainly Bowers' project has a link to her feminist photorealist predecessors such as Audrey Flack, whose work also placed equal value on content and technique.

[6]I refer to Charlotte Perkins Gilman, "The Yellow Wallpaper," 1892.

[7]In 1989 Jesse Helms, former five-term Republican Senator from North Carolina, 1973-2003, widely known for his racist and homophobic attitudes, spearheaded major cuts to the National Endowment for the Arts, bans on funding art deemed offensive or depicting sexual or excretory activities, and the end of grants to individual artists entirely—policies from which the NEA, as of 2008, has never recovered.

JANE GALLOP / PHOTOS BY DICK BLAU

Observations of a Mother

PHOTOGRAPHY, ACCORDING TO ROLAND BARTHES, can be considered from three possible points of view. First, of course, is the photographer's point of view. At the beginning of *Camera Lucida*, his book on photography, Barthes tells us that he "could not join the troupe of those (the majority) who deal with Photography-according-to-the-Photographer" because he does not take pictures.[1] While for many this would not in fact pose a major obstacle to adopting such a perspective, Barthes is committed to grounding his study in his own subjective experience. Thus he restricts himself to the two remaining standpoints: that of the person photographed and that of the person who looks at photos.

Barthes's next chapter, entitled "He Who Is Photographed," talks about how he feels when being photographed and when looking at pictures of himself. The following chapter, "The *SPECTATOR*," turns to the third perspective. And the rest of the book, forty-two more chapters, never departs from that third perspective.

With this preponderance of "the spectator," the single chapter devoted to the photographed subject becomes no more than a fleeting memory. I want here to pick up the position *Camera Lucida* briefly assumes and then drops. If, according to Barthes, photography is most often treated from the photographer's point of view, almost all the rest of the writing on photography is surely from the perspective of what he calls the "spectator," whether the latter be art historian, critic, or amateur. Formal discourse on photography is rarely from the standpoint of the photographed subject. Although all three points of view are, for Barthes, subjective, there may be something about the second point of view that is most troublingly personal, anecdotal, self-concerned. It may be the position from which it is most difficult to claim valid general insights. Perhaps that is why Barthes—who is, to be sure, darlingly subjective in this book—drops it like a hot potato.

Later, in the second half of the book, long after he is comfortably ensconced in his role as spectator, Barthes definitively if subjectively locates the essence of photography in one specific picture: "Something like an essence of the Photograph floated in this particular picture. I therefore decided to 'derive' all Photography from the only photograph which assuredly existed for me" (73). That singular photo is a picture of Barthes's mother. Given the exemplary status of this picture, we might say that in *Camera Lucida* the quintessential photographed subject is the mother.

Barthes would resist my last phrase—not "the mother," but rather "my mother," he would say. And he does say that quite emphatically in the text: "[nor] would I reduce my mother to the Mother.... In the Mother, there was a radiant, irreducible core: my mother.... To the Mother-as-Good, she had added that grace of being an individual soul" (74-75). If I don't here respect Barthes's otherwise quite moving insistence on his mother's singularity, it is because in examining the photographed subject in *Camera Lucida*, I am struck by its similarity to the position of the mother or, as Barthes would say, "the Mother."

Back in the only chapter where Barthes inhabits the position of "He Who Is Photographed," he writes: "the Photograph represents that very subtle moment when ... I am neither subject nor object but a subject who feels he is becoming an object" (14). In the course of the book, "He Who Is Photographed" becomes "She Who Is Photographed"; the son flees this position and attaches it definitively to his mother. Upon rereading Barthes's description of the experience of being photographed, I notice that it might also describe the experience of being a mother ("I am a subject who feels she is becoming an object").

I want to pick up the perspective Barthes drops, to pick it up where he has dropped it, in the mother's lap. I want to pick it up as the mother's perspective, and try to inhabit it for a while. I'd like to write about photography from the standpoint of the photographed mother.

In *Camera Lucida*, that position is characteristically silent: not only is his mother dead at the time of the book's writing, but, he tells us, "during the whole of our life together, she never made a single 'observation'" (69). The mother is defined in this book precisely as never doing that which the author does—observe and comment. In fact, the very paragraph in which Barthes praises his mother for refraining from ever making "observations" begins with the words "I observed," to refer to what he saw when he looked at her in the photograph.[2] He observes; she does not: she is observed.

Barthes's mother, the subject of the quintessential photograph, makes no comment. Barthes himself begins to speak of his experience of being photographed and then changes the subject. If the position of the photographed subject seems to lead to silence in this book, it is surely because it is a position where the subject feels himself becoming an object. Unlike a subject, an object does not speak. I can't help thinking that the experience of the subject's becoming an object fits all too well with the movement in the book by which '*He* Who Is Photographed" becomes "She," offering an example of the classic gendering of subject and object.

This classic gendering comes with the standard Freudian package. *Camera Lucida* has occasion to quote Freud on the Mother (40), and, although Barthes's use of psychoanalysis is typically delicate and unsystematic, the book still jibes with the usual psychoanalytic view of the family, in which the subject is the son and the object the mother. And so I find in *Camera Lucida* the predictable but nonetheless troubling scenario by which the man saves his subjectivity, his voice, by palming off the risk of becoming an object onto the mother.

Predictable is indeed the word for it: since I am both a psychoanalytic and a feminist critic, it is all too predictable that I should produce such a reading. If that were all there was to my reading of *Camera Lucida*, it would certainly not be worth doing here. Although I have been disrespectful in reducing his finely sketched mother to the Mother, I want to stop now and pay my respects to Barthes, to assume my debt to this book, and to reveal why I'm talking about it here, at the beginning of this essay.

My suggestion that Barthes abandons an uncomfortable position should be placed in the context of my admiration for *Camera Lucida*'s considerable daring, for its presumption that his subjective experience counts as knowledge for others. That he might shy away from one of the strands of that experience is of niggling concern when compared to the path he opens up for those of us who, like Barthes, would presume that our subjective experience—particularly our subjective experience of photography—might also count as knowledge.

If I begin here with a reading of *Camera Lucida*, it is, to be sure, in order to make myself more comfortable. It allows me to begin by showing you my professional persona, the feminist and psychoanalytic critic, the reader of Roland Barthes, the very sort of person authorized to make observations in a book published by a university press. But my reading of Barthes is also a way of deferring, offsetting, hedging the writing I have committed myself to here. I have contracted to write here not as a reader of Barthes, not as a professor of theory, but as a photographed mother. And—whereas doing a reading of Barthes makes it easy to write, words and ideas fairly tumbling onto the screen—the thought of publishing a text about photographs of me and my children threatens to reduce me to silence.

It is no wonder that I turn to *Camera Lucida*. I've written on Barthes's book before, the only other time I wrote about photography. That piece appeared in a book with a photograph on its cover, a photograph of a birth.[3] The mother in the birth photograph could certainly be seen as a subject becoming an object: while her body looms large in the photo, she has no head; in fact everyone in the picture has a head (nurse, baby, doctor) except the mother. While her head is missing, there is a head attached to her body, her son's (the picture was taken at the moment his head emerged from the "birth canal"). I spoke about this photograph in that book, but I did not mention that I was the mother in the picture. Rather than speak as the photographed subject, like Barthes I made observations from the spectator's point of view.

Since it's already been published, I'm not reproducing that photo here. I would like instead to show you another photograph of the subject becoming a mother, one that even more dramatically portrays the mother as object. I suppose I could say that this is a picture of me, but that doesn't feel right. I would be more comfortable saying it's a picture of my belly, which makes it more a picture of something attached to me. I'm eight months pregnant, at my monthly obstetrical check-up, where I've gone with Dick Blau, the father, who took this picture, as he did the one on the book cover, and as he did all the photographs I will discuss here.

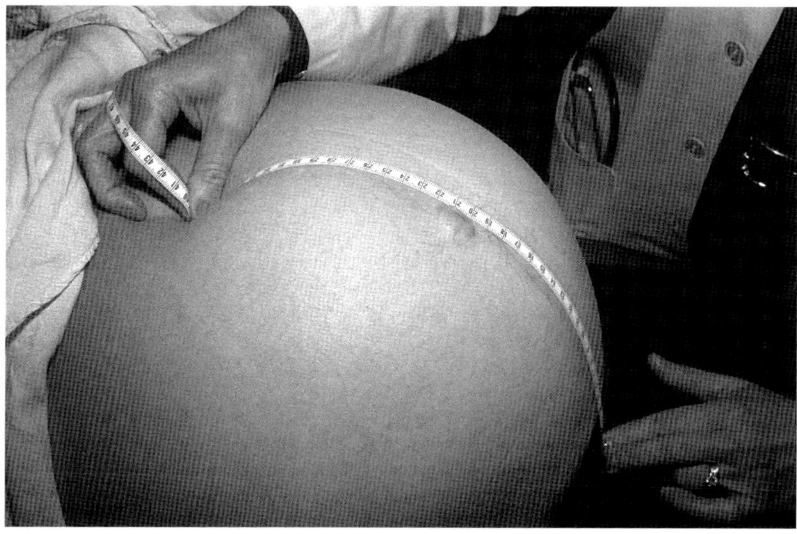

Dick Blau, 1995.

I take this picture as the very emblem of the mother becoming an object because of the measuring tape, because of the way we think of numbers as the very measure of "objectivity." Since I've already invoked the feminist critique of the objectification of women (in my reading of *Camera Lucida* above), and since I'm talking about being turned into an object, you might think that I'm complaining here about being objectified. So I want to make it clear that I'm not complaining. In fact, I'm bragging.

I like to call this photo "The Prize Watermelon." I imagine the viewer impressed by my belly's size; I imagine it being measured at the county fair; when I show you this photograph, I'm proudly displaying the big belly I grew.

My caption for the photograph suggests a relation to my body somehow like a farmer's relation to her prized produce. This is a way of embracing my objectification, not simply becoming an object, but rather doubling into subject and object: I am at once the farmer and her watermelon. Putting my "fruitfulness" on display, I am, in short, proud to be a mother.

The desire to be a mother (which I would here distinguish from the desire to have a child) might be precisely the wish to become this sort of impressive object: the sort of object that, according to psychoanalysis, our mothers once were for us. While such fantasies are common, they seem better left unspoken. Like Barthes, we prefer to admire the silent mother. To speak one's pleasure in being taken for that magical object called Mother is to display an unsightly narcissism, a narcissism which may be inevitable when the photographed mother speaks.

Narcissism is indeed the word for it. The photographed subject speaks from a position that is literally narcissistic, the position of someone looking at an image of herself. I see now why Barthes might have fled that position. To remain too long, to be too interested in one's own image, is to fall into the trap of Narcissus.

When Barthes does briefly discuss photographs of himself, he complains that he never likes them. I imagine this is the most common sort of observation made by the photographed subject: She is most likely to say "I don't like that picture of me." While this is undoubtedly a resistance to objectification (that object is not me), it might also be a strategy to evade Narcissus's fate. We gaze at our image and insistently reject it, refusing to love it.

While this might get us out of the classic position of Narcissus, it leaves us with a common form of vanity. In his chapter on "He Who Is Photographed" Barthes writes: "What I want ... is that my image ...

should always coincide with my (profound) 'self'" (12). We reject our images because we would so love to see our "self";[4] our rejection of our images actually manifests our love for our self.

Barthes's complaint goes on to specify that his image and his self "never coincide" because the image is "heavy" while his self is "light."[5] Barthes's writing, whatever the topic, quite consistently privileges the light over the heavy, and here as elsewhere the pair of terms carries a range of symbolic and figurative meanings.[6] But when he uses these terms to reject his photographic image, their concrete sense comes to mind. For all its theoretical subtlety, his complaint thus recalls one of the more common themes of vanity[7] and prompts me to show you a photograph I had decided not to include, an otherwise wonderful picture, though I don't like how heavy I look in it.

Dick Blau, 1991.

A few years ago Dick showed this photograph in Europe and came home to report that a psychoanalyst had found its Oedipal resonances disturbing. I liked the idea of shocking a psychoanalyst, but a month or so later as Dick was preparing to exhibit this same picture here in Milwaukee, I realized that I too was disturbed by the photo. While I did not mind people knowing that my son and I lie around naked together, I didn't exactly like the idea of neighbors and colleagues seeing my unduly large belly. In this one, no tape measure and no pride; I'm not pregnant.

My feelings about this photograph contrast neatly with my exhibitionist pleasure in "The Prize Watermelon": whereas the tumescent belly fills me with pride, I feel shame in displaying one that is soft and flaccid. In the first picture, my belly sticks up; in the second, my breasts hang down. Such corporeal ups and downs are not without relation to the light and the heavy—the light rises, the heavy sinks. I'm struck by the phallic dimensions of my pride and shame. While my narcissism delights in the image of me as phallic mother, my vanity shrinks from the sight of my fallen flesh.

The photograph that shames me has given us serious and repeated pause. Dick and I keep finding ourselves unable to decide whether to show it—no other photo has caused us this kind of trouble. Throughout our conversations about it, we have not been disagreeing with one another; rather we have both been of two minds about what to do. The issues are always the same: both of us really like this photograph as statement and composition, but neither of us likes how heavy I look in it. Three years ago when Dick was preparing to exhibit locally, we had several such discussions, going back and forth about what to do. Finally we decided that not to show this unflattering image betrayed the spirit of naked honesty that is one of our family values; so we showed it.

Nevertheless, just last week we had the same discussion about whether or not to include it in this essay. And we seemed to reach a decision not to show it. We reasoned that, whereas an exhibit was ephemeral, once the photo was published it would be in a sense permanently on display—and that seemed like just too much exposure.

What clinched my decision not to publish this picture was imagining my parents' horror at seeing it, at seeing me expose myself that way, in public. (Since I now seem to have decided to publish it, I hope my parents never find this essay.) The thought of my parents as spectators suggests the peculiar way in which this is a "family photograph." A conventional family photograph is precisely the sort of thing one would send to relatives who live out of town: grandparents would want a photo of their daughter and grandson. They would want it not only to look at it themselves, but to show their friends, to show off. The family photograph conventionally traffics in bragging and pride.

The photo of Max and me on the couch is not the sort of thing grandparents show their friends, and thus not a conventional family photo. But my vision of parental shame reveals that this photograph still functions within the realm of the family. Family photos are in fact all about showing, about taking the privacy of family life and exhibiting it to a public gaze (if only to friends and relatives). The family photo is intended to induce pride by showing a private life for public admiration, but the family photo can also produce shame by exhibiting privates that shouldn't be seen in public.

Although I seem to have decided to publish this picture, I'd like to focus on the repeated difficulty of that decision. I take the repetition as a sign that my problem with this photograph—whatever fantasies I might have of bold decisiveness—is just not going to go away. And I wonder if what troubles me about this photo may not, after all, be related to what troubled the psychoanalyst.

When the psychoanalyst saw this picture of a son and mother lying naked together, he thought about the Oedipus complex. The Oedipus complex makes the mother's body taboo, prohibits our finding it desirable; the taboo makes us uncomfortable with the mother's nakedness, introduces an element of disgust into our viewing of that body. Perhaps my objection to the picture seems different because I am viewing from the perspective of the photographed mother; I experience the disgust at that naked body as my own shame. But I'm struck by how the foci of that shame (the large, soft belly and breasts) are the very parts of the body most connoted maternal. Is this body undesirable because, looking too maternal, it elicits the Oedipal taboo?

While I don't want to discount this Oedipal reading of my shame, I also must confess that for me it makes the photo less, not more, disturbing. Interpreting the body's excesses as generically maternal tempers the shame I feel about the specificity of that body as my own. Barthes insisted that we not reduce his mother to the Mother. Although earlier I chose to make theoretical hay by not respecting his insistence, I want here to return to his caution because I see how my theorizing is not only reductive but defensive. Contemplating a photo of his mother, Barthes observes that, beyond the Mother, his mother "had added that grace of being an individual soul." I must likewise admit here that to the generic problem of seeing the Mother naked, this photograph adds the shame of my individual body, its particular weight.

Reducing my body to that of the Mother makes it easier for me to bear its heaviness. Barthes, on the other hand, finds the Mother a heavy, crude concept, which his particular mother lightens by "adding grace." *Camera Lucida* tells the story of how Barthes looked through and rejected a slew of pictures of his mother until he finally found the one photograph which for him exemplified both her and photography. Only one of the photographs could coincide with her self, her individual soul. And that was a picture of her as a little girl.

"Starting from her latest image ... I arrived ... at the image of a child: I stare intensely at the Sovereign Good of childhood, of the mother, of the mother-as-child" (71). To the Mother, this image adds the grace and lightness of the child. In a way, the picture of Max and me on the couch does the same thing. But rather than the mother-as-child, here we see the mother-and-child, the child's lightness juxtaposed with the mother's heaviness. As I look at this photo, I find myself sharing Barthes's preference for lightness, experiencing the difference between these two bodies as my lack, thanks perhaps to an aesthetic that reinforces the sense that more is less.

What disturbs me in this spectacle of a mother's body and a child's body naked together is not, *pace* the psychoanalyst, the possibility of incest. When I see those bodies together, framed by the symmetries of the windows, mirroring each other in the similarity of their position, that mirroring makes comparison and contrast inevitable. And I suffer from the comparison.

The insistent symmetry of this photograph creates the expectation of balance between the two bodies and produces an uncomfortable awareness of their difference. My sense of shame at looking so different from Max here perhaps explains why another photograph of the two of us, one where we look strikingly similar, gives me so much pleasure.

In this picture, we are no longer so indecently exposed. While the living room photo is suffused with the light of the outside world, its large windows open, the bathroom's single window is dark and closed. Here in the most private part of the home, nakedness returns to its proper place, not only because nakedness belongs in the bathroom rather than in the relatively public space of the living room, but because now only the child is naked. Conventional family photos show naked children, not naked parents, and the classic place for the naked child is the bathtub.

The two photos frame us quite differently. While Max and I are together on the black couch, he is alone in the white bathtub. In the bath photo, Max and I are balanced in opposite corners of the frame: my head in the upper left, his in the lower right. The symmetries of this composition do not demand equivalence between our two bodies but benefit instead from our relative sizes. Rather than face each other, Max and I face the same way. Our bodies seem not disproportionate but literally in proportion: he reproduces me in miniature.

A friend of mine calls this "the picture where Max and Jane have the same face."[8] While on the couch the bodies shock and their difference unsettles, here in the bathroom it's the faces. Their similarity is positively uncanny.

"In a certain photograph," writes Barthes, "I have my father's sister's 'mug.'"[9] This sentence is *Camera Lucida*'s only mention of a photo of

Dick Blau, 1990.

Barthes outside the chapter "He Who Is Photographed." It appears in a chapter called "Lineage," in the middle of a passage that proposes that "the Photograph sometimes makes appear ... a genetic feature.... The Photograph gives a little truth ... the truth of lineage" (103).

Earlier in the book, Barthes says he does not want to write about the institution of the family (74): "Lineage" deals with the family not as institution, but as something genetic, bodily, biological. And this animal sense of family echoes in the word Barthes uses for the face he shares with his aunt. "Mug" here translates the French "*museau*," which is slang for human face but more commonly and literally means "muzzle" or "snout," the front part of certain animals' heads. Barthes's muzzle reminds me that our household name for the picture of Max and me in the bathroom is "The Wolf Family."

Our pet title for the photo picks up on the striking family resemblance between Max and me. If, as my friend says, Max and I have the same face, it's not only because we look alike but also because we're making the same face. With two such similar faces making the same expression, the expression itself seems to be a genetic feature, its hostility an instinctual response.

While the genetic resemblance makes this unquestionably an image of family, this is not an orthodox family photo. Although suspicion and hostility are frequently experienced in families, they are not usually represented in family photographs. The subjects here are too unsociable for a proper family image and seem to resist, or at least resent, being photographed.

The idea of a "wolf family" suggests that here the family is not domesticated but rather captured by the photographic gaze. The mother and child look like unwilling subjects of display, resentful of the photograph's trespass into this private space. Our look says, "Get out of here."

Lying on the couch, the mother and child expose too much for a polite family photograph; here we are too protective of our privacy. Although our bodies are conventionally decent in this picture, our faces suggest something was not meant to be seen. If family photography makes the private public and sociable, this picture sees that as an intrusion.

The intrusion begins with the photographer; he is the object of our hostile gaze. While here the photographer is literally the father, the "wolf family" views him as an outsider, not a member of the pack. And Max's striking appearance as my reproduction in miniature even suggests the father's genetic irrelevance.

In most families, the father is the photographer. Not usually in the pictures, the father-photographer stands outside the image of the family. He is not simply outside the image but its master: the father-photographer directs the family picture, framing and composing the mother and children.

As a father photographing his family, Dick has assumed this role. Because his family photographs are his artwork, the role is exacerbated. In taking photographs of his family life intended for exhibition, publication, and even sale, he raises the public-private stakes implicit in all family photography. Making images of his family for public displays, Dick places himself between family and world, representing both the family to the world and the intrusion of the world into the family. This is a pretty damn conventional role for a father to play.

All the players in the bath photo—father, mother, child—are in our most traditional places. But in portraying the mother and child's resentment of the father, this is hardly a conventional family picture. With its combination of traditional roles and hostile resistance, "The Wolf Family" could be said to expose the patriarchal relations underpinning polite family photography.

The subjects' hostility may also suggest another equally conventional if not so photogenic dynamic. The father-photographer has entered a space of mother-son intimacy and that intrusion is resented: "Go away so we can be alone together." Perhaps that psychoanalyst was right to worry about Max and me.

If I've come close to concurring with the psychoanalyst, it may be because up till now I haven't been speaking from my experience as subject; I've been reading this photograph as a spectator instead. I'm beginning to see how easy it is to slip into that position. Let me now speak as the photographed mother.

While as a spectator I find myself producing feminist and psychoanalytic readings, as the mother I see in this picture the texture of our home life. The photograph was taken on a Sunday evening during Max's weekly bath. I'm usually the one giving him his bath, and often, when Dick's finished the dishes, he appears in the bathroom, camera in hand. I am generally glad to see him arrive with his camera, always hoping for another beautiful picture of my son, but sometimes I do get annoyed if he gets in the way as I'm washing Max's hair. I don't remember the actual moment of this picture, or why I regarded Dick with such hostility. Just recently he and I were talking about the photograph because I thought I would include it here, and I voiced my puzzlement at Max's and my expression: "Were we angry at you that evening?" Dick laughed: "I made you two look at me that way." He explained that he opened the bathroom door and commanded us to look at him, knowing that a command would produce in both of us the same immediate, instinctive response—momentary but dramatic hostility. Dick used to be a theater director, and he knows how to get what he wants from actors. By sounding like a patriarch, he produced a tableau of resentment from the subjects of patriarchal authority. The response was so fleeting, I never even knew I'd participated in a drama.

"I imagine," writes Barthes, "that the essential gesture of the [photographer] is to surprise something or someone … revealing what was so well hidden that the actor himself was unaware or unconscious of it" (32). The word "actor" here suggests Barthes shares Dick's understanding of the affinity between photographer and theater director.

If Barthes had said "the person" rather than "the actor," this revelation of something "unconscious" would lead to a psychoanalytic version of truth, to the kind of Oedipal reading with which I briefly flirted. When we read that something "well hidden" has been revealed, we tend to take this as the very sign of truth, but Barthes's word "actor" implies that what is revealed is not a personal truth, but something the person lends her body to portray.

Which doesn't mean it isn't true, but that it is true the way theater can be true: resonant human truths are portrayed even though the actors are conventionally "lying," that is, speaking in character rather than as themselves. The patriarchal melodrama in the bath photo does not reveal some personal truth about Max and me but is rather a piece of theater we have enacted all unawares. Although as a spectator I can appreciate the truth of this drama, it is not part of my experience as a subject.

Family photographs are normally taken to represent the particular family. But Dick didn't shoot "The Wolf Family" solely for that reason. Seeing the bathroom as a set and us as a theater troupe, he stages an archetypal family. Not a conventional family portrait, "The Wolf Family" instead portrays the conventional family.

Dick's theatrical sense of the family probably has something to do with his having grown up in the theater: his mother is an actress, his father a director. But *Camera Lucida*'s use of the word "actor" to describe the photographed subject, as well as its consistent use of "spectator" to name the photo's viewer, means that Dick's theatrical sense of photography is not simply idiosyncratic. At the very least it suggests a congruence between Dick and Barthes, who tells us in his autobiography that "the Theater" is "[a]t the crossroads of [his] entire *oeuvre*," that "spectacle is the universal category" in which he sees the world.[10]

Dick has always said that his photography derives from his work in theater, but I never understood what he meant by this until I brought Barthes's description of the photographer to bear on Dick's photography. That *Camera Lucida* should help me appreciate Dick's perspective is ironic. Dick does not like this book; he is offended by its dismissal of the photographer's point of view. As a matter of fact, it occurs to me that I may have chosen to approach Dick's photos with Barthes's book in hand precisely because of this resistance to the photographer's point of view.

At the beginning of *Camera Lucida,* Barthes proclaims his independence from "the troupe who deal with Photography-according-to-the-Photographer" (10). But ten chapters later he makes an exception to that rule: "I imagine (this is all I can do, since I am not a photographer) that the essential gesture of the [photographer] is to surprise something or someone (through the little hole of the camera), and that this gesture is therefore perfect when it is performed unbeknownst to the subject being photographed" (32).

Unlike Barthes, I don't have to imagine the photographer's gesture. Another photograph of Max and me actually shows Dick taking our picture, thanks to a mirror. In this photo neither Max nor I manifest any awareness of Dick, who is behind us, his one visible eye shut, the other presumably looking through his Leica which is focused on us.

This picture seems to reflect the structure of the classic family photograph. By including his image, Dick lets us see the father-photographer, the figure conventionally left outside the frame, observing unobserved. The viewer can see him here looking at the subjects who aren't looking at him.

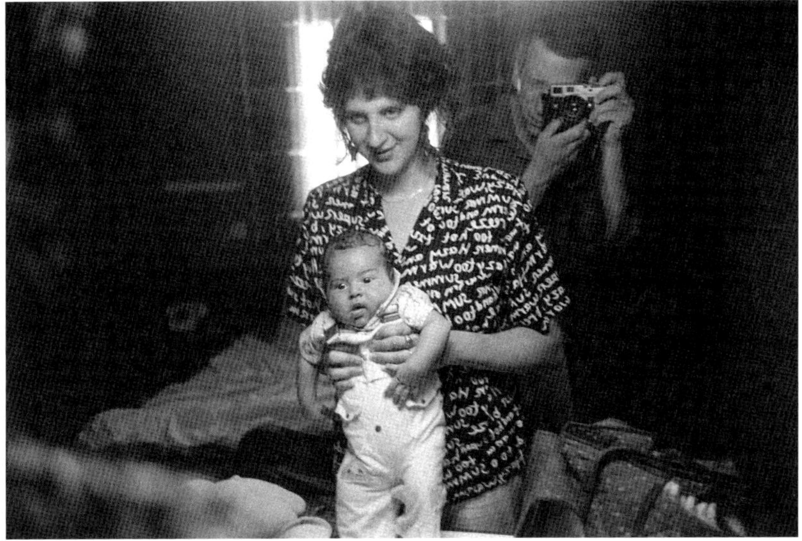

Dick Blau, 1986.

Once again, we are all three in our most traditional places. The baby narcissistically contemplates his own image; the mother holds and supports her son, gazing admiringly at his image; the father is at a distance, capturing mother and child with his technology but not touching us, not interacting with us. The entire little family is centered on the baby's image, mother and father both helping construct that image in their typically differing ways.

Although I'm not sure how much I like seeing myself as the conventional mother here, I really like the shirt I'm wearing. As frivolous as it might seem, I connect the writing on my shirt with Dick's sporting a camera. Not just Mom and Dad here, we both display the means of our expression, the symbols of our respective trades: this photo includes not only the father-photographer but also the mother-writer. While no one else may be able to read the shirt this way, I like to think it says that the woman in this 1986 photo is not just the baby's proud mother but also the author of a book on Jacques Lacan, which came out a few months before Max did.

Perhaps that explains why I see this photograph as a dramatization of Lacan's "Mirror Stage."[11] "The Mirror Stage" is about the moment in which the baby meets his image. Lacan specifies that the baby looking at himself in the mirror cannot yet stand on his own, but is standing with the help of "some support, human or artificial." The support makes possible an image that is more mature, more together, more erect than the baby really is. In this photo, Max is two-and-a-half months old; it would be nearly a year until he could stand on his own. In this photo, I play the quintessential supporting role for his false and narcissistically pleasing image of self.

As it turns out, Barthes too associates Lacan's "Mirror Stage" with a family photograph. In his autobiography, underneath a photo of a woman holding a baby, Barthes has placed the caption "The mirror stage: 'you are that.'"[12] The baby is presumably Barthes, the woman his mother; their gazes are aimed in the same direction. The caption implies that, like Max and me, Barthes and his mother are both looking at the baby's mirror image.

The caption further suggests that the mother is saying "you are that," thus teaching the baby to recognize his image as himself.[13] This gently reinterprets Lacan's formulation, giving the mother a leading role in the historic moment when the baby takes his image for himself. Because Baby Barthes in the photo is not pretending to stand, not producing an image that pretends to more than he can really accomplish, the moment does not carry the Lacanian sense of the image's tragic falsity and the mother's role seems innocuous enough.

Looking back at Max and me in the mirror, I see myself like Barthes's mother taking the active role. But Max *is* "standing," and my activity does not seem so innocent. Lacan locates the onset of the mirror stage at around six months of age, when a baby first wants to be seen standing. Here, more than three months ahead of schedule, it must have been my idea to stand him up. In this picture I can see myself as the worst sort of pushy mirror-stage mother.

Barthes's use of "the mirror stage" shows us the mother in a scene usually imaged as a solo performance. A closer look would discern yet another presence, beyond the mother-child dyad. This third presence appears in the sentence that "The Mirror Stage" uses to introduce its description of the infant confronting his image: "This event," writes Lacan, "has often made me reflect upon the startling spectacle of the infant in front of the mirror."[14] The third figure—the one who views the spectacle, finds it "startling," and "reflects upon" it—is Lacan himself, whose reflection has brought us "The Mirror Stage," his most famous theoretical contribution.

Dick's mirror photo shows something like the "spectacle" Lacan "often reflects upon." But this mirror image also includes the gaze that reflects upon the spectacle. When I imagine that this photo represents Lacan's "Mirror Stage," I like to think that Dick's inclusion of himself as part of the image somehow reveals Lacan's theoretical gaze, bringing the third player in the drama to the stage, allowing us to see the shadowy figure who observes the well-lit image of baby and supporting mother. And this strikes me as a more complete picture of the system that supports the baby's image.

Reading the photo as a further elaboration of the mirror stage depends upon seeing the father-photographer as somehow analogous with the psychoanalytic theorist. I find this analogy enormously seductive, whispering a grand theorization that would connect the mirror stage to both family photography and the Oedipal triangle. I start to fantasize myself as the author of the great psychoanalytic theory of images, which would explain how the image of the self is constructed in the family. But as soon as I try to work it out, the fantasy fades and my writing grinds to a halt.

Perhaps there is a less grandiose, more idiosyncratic explanation for why I see the father's place in this photo as Lacan's place. Years ago I wrote a book about French feminism and psychoanalysis in which I staged the relation between the two in Oedipal terms, casting Lacan in the role of the father. At the time I was not a mother and the Oedipal relation I was interested in was not the classic one that's been dogging me here, but the daughter's version. I was writing that book at the moment I met Dick. One day, looking at his photographs, I found this picture I thought would be perfect for the cover of the book I planned to call *The Daughter's Seduction*.

That's Dick's daughter in the foreground, the very image of girl beauty and innocence, lost in her contemplation of a few wisps of grass. Like the mirror stage photo, this one has a foreground and a background, and like Max and me in the mirror, Anna seems oblivious to what is behind her. Once again the background contains an image of the father. On the ground, in a posture that seems somehow reminiscent of lovers, are a father and a daughter—Dick's best friend Jake, and Jake's daughter Laura, Anna's best friend. I see this romantic background as the unconscious, dreamlike in its softer focus and gorgeous light. The daughter, innocent in the foreground, seems unaware of the Oedipal scene behind her.

Although there are no mirrors, here, Dick has found another way to include the father in the image. In place of the mirror, he has a stand-in—a figure identified with himself, both as his best friend and as the father of a daughter. The relation between the background father-and-daughter could be said to mirror the relation between the unseen father-photographer and his daughter. The inclusion of the father in the image allows the photo to dramatize and gloss the erotic exchange that appears in its more conven-

Dick Blau, 1978.

tional form in the foreground, where the father-photographer focuses our gaze on his daughter's delectable skin, sensuous hair, and pouty lips.

The image in the foreground belongs to a large and over-familiar genre: fathers' adoring photos of their daughters' innocent beauty. The background stages the unconscious of the genre. Juxtaposing the manifest and the latent, this photograph both reproduces that genre and reflects upon the taboo eros that underlies it.

While my relation to this picture was not familial, it was immediate and intense: I had professional designs upon it. I thought it the very image of "the daughter's seduction," with its different levels echoing the ambiguities and psychoanalytic resonances of the writing I was doing. I wanted it for my book's cover and asked Dick if I could use it. At first he liked the idea, but a couple of days later he told me that, as much as he regretted it, he couldn't let me use the photo. What stopped him was the thought of Anna.

Not the girl in the image, taken a few years before our conversation, but the girl in his life. Anna and I hadn't yet met, and he was afraid she might not like gracing the cover of a book called *The Daughter's Seduction*. As much as he wanted us to publish together, he wanted more to avoid anything that might make Anna resent me. The photographer wanted to publish this picture; the father cared more about his daughter's feelings.

The father won out. Which suggests that, however much these photos are Dick's artistic work, they are also still very much family photographs.

Not simply because they are images of family members, but because they never can be completely outside the family. Family photography is not just about how the family looks in the pictures; it's also about how the pictures look in the family. And as great as Anna would have looked on the cover of my book, the fact of her appearance there might not have looked so good to her.

Like all the photographs I've discussed here, this one portrays people Dick loves while at the same time catching those loved ones in poses that convey classic family dramas. When I asked to put this picture on the book cover, I wasn't thinking about his family and its actual dramas, about Anna's real relation to her father; I only saw this picture as an eloquent portrayal of the generic daughter's Oedipus complex.

My theoretical gaze also sees *Camera Lucida* as perfectly Oedipal. Like the psychoanalyst viewing Max and me on the couch, I feel mildly and agreeably scandalized when I read in that book that Barthes lived with his mother his whole life (75). But in the very same chapter that contains this confession, I notice he insists that while such a theoretical understanding can explain the "generality," "the Mother," it misses *his* mother, the individual being he loved: "it is because she was who she was that I lived with her" (75).

In a startling move, Barthes does not show us the photograph of his mother that he makes central to the book, the picture that for him captures both the essence of the woman he loved all his life and the theoretical essence of the photography. "I cannot reproduce the Winter Garden Photograph," baldly asserts Barthes (73) about the photograph he devotes pages to describing and analyzing, thereby adding to his analysis an absolute insistence in its, and her, singularity. While the book's lengthy discussion of this photograph in fact makes theory by seeing generalities in the picture, Barthes's refusal to show it resists its reduction to those generalities: "no more than I would reduce my family to the Family, would I reduce my mother to the Mother"(74).

The theoretical designs I had on Dick's picture of Anna correspond to the relation Barthes's reader would have to the picture of his mother. Back then, Dick's photos were for me only portraits of "the Family," not of "my family." Now I no longer have the luxury of forgetting the particular family, and I find my responses as a reader don't jibe that well with my responses as a mother. The reader sees the generic drama of family; the mother thinks of the individuals.

In drafting this essay, I have experienced the split between mother and critic most acutely when choosing which photographs to write about. In the hope of creating a text that would be valued professionally, I have

Dick Blau, 1997.

made my pictorial choices based on theoretical and writerly demands. But as a mother this leaves me with a problem.

I haven't shown you my daughter. She was the seed in "The Prize Watermelon," but now she's a girl out in the world, a wonderful girl who hasn't yet remarked that I have pictures of only her big brother on the walls of my study, none of her. I'm hoping to get some of her up before she notices.

Since I'm even prouder of her than I was of my protruding belly, it would give me pleasure to show her to you. But what really compels me to do so is imagining her reading this some day. How could I explain to her that I sacrificed her for compositional unity? As I was writing this essay, I kept trying to find a way to get from the themes of this text to a picture of her; I never did. So, although it may be bad form, before I go, I gotta show you my Ruby.

Notes

[1]Roland Barthes, *Camera Lucida: Reflections on Photography*, trans. Richard Howard (New York: Hill & Wang, 1981), 9-10.

[2]Roland Barthes, *La Chambre Claire: Note sur la photographie* (Paris: Gallimard Seuil, 1980), 107-109. The original French has the verb "observer," an exact

cognate of our English verb "observe" to match the later "observation" (in both languages). The English translator has obscured the resonance by translating the initial verb as "I studied."

[3]Jane Gallop, "The Prick of the Object," in *Thinking Through the Body* (New York: Columbia University Press, 1988), 149-160.

[4]Barthes's French word "moi" could also be given the more psychoanalytic translation "ego," *Chambre Claire*, 26.

[5]In the context of photography, it must be noted that the French word he uses, "léger," unlike its English translation, does not mean the opposite of dark but only the opposite of heavy (*Camera Lucida*, 12; *Chambre Claire*, 27).

[6]"Heavy," for example, is in this passage linked to "motionless" and the ideological; "light" to dispersion and the "zero degree."

[7]This is, to be sure, a theme for Barthes as well. In his autobiography, he places this caption above a photograph of himself as a young boy: "Sudden mutation of the body: changing (or appearing to change) from slender to plump. Ever since, perpetual struggle with this body to return it to its essential slenderness"—*Roland Barthes by Roland Barthes,* Roland Barthes, trans. Richard Howard (Berkeley: University of California Press, 1994), 30.

[8]Lynne Joyrich, various personal conversations.

[9]*Camera Lucida*, 103; *Chambre claire*, 161, translation modified.

[10]Barthes, *Roland Barthes*, 177.

[11]Jacques Lacan, "The mirror stage as formative of the function of the I as revealed in psychoanalytic experience," in *Ecrits: A Selection*, trans. Alan Sheridan (New York: Norton, 1977), 1-7.

[12]*Roland Barthes par Roland Barthes* (Paris: Seuil, 1975), 25; translation, 20; translation modified. The phrase in quotation marks (originally "Tu es cela") can be found in Lacan's "Mirror Stage," where it also appears in quotation marks (*Ecrits*, 7).

[13]In *Camera Lucida*, Barthes dislikes his image because it doesn't correspond with his "self." Here, in a book published five years earlier, we see his mother imposing the equation of self and image upon him. It is probably worth noting that between the writing of the two books, Barthes's mother had died.

[14]Lacan, "The mirror stage as formative of the function of the I as revealed in psychoanalytic experience," 1.

IV.

Maternal Metaphors II, Doublebind

Maternal Metaphors II

Curated by Myrel Chernick and Jennie Klein

JENNIE KLEIN AND MYREL CHERNICK became co-curators when Klein, who wrote the essay for the original *Maternal Metaphors* catalog, proposed the exhibition to the Art Gallery at Ohio University. The first incarnation of *Maternal Metaphors* at the Rochester Contemporary consisted of artists residing and working in the United States. In order to address an increased diversity of maternal perspectives, *Maternal Metaphors II* included an expanded group as well as an international roster of artists. Patricia Cué (Mexico), Youngbok Hong (Korea), Denise Ferris (Australia), Margaret Morgan (Australia), and Signe Theill (curator of *Doublebind,* Germany) approach motherhood through the lens of their different cultural experiences.

As with the first *Maternal Metaphors*, we included work in a variety of mediums, including painting, drawing, photography, video, sculpture, and installation. This exhibition also included artists' books as well as a web-based piece by Youngbok Hong. The artists—Camille Billops, Monica Bock and Zofia Burr, Myrel Chernick, Patricia Cué, Denise Ferris, Cheri Gaulke and Sue Maberry, Judy Gelles, Judy Glantzman, Heather Gray, Rohesia Hamilton Metcalfe, Youngbok Hong, Mary Kelly, Ellen McMahon, Margaret Morgan, Gail Rebhan, Aura Rosenberg, Shelly Silver, Barbara T. Smith, Signe Theill, Beth Warshafsky, Sarah Webb and Marion Wilson—have questioned and continue to question what it means to be a mother. Some have challenged the representation of motherhood as an institution that is primarily white, middle-class, young, and heterosexual. Others have explored their relationships with their own mothers, relationships that changed after they had children themselves. And two of the artists have made work about voluntary or involuntary loss of custody because they were not "good enough" mothers.

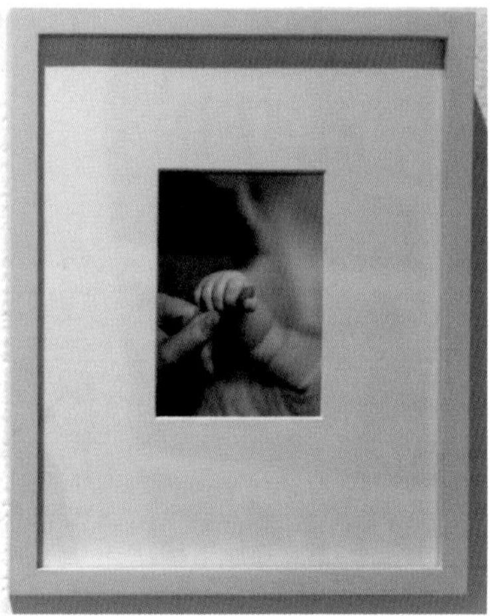

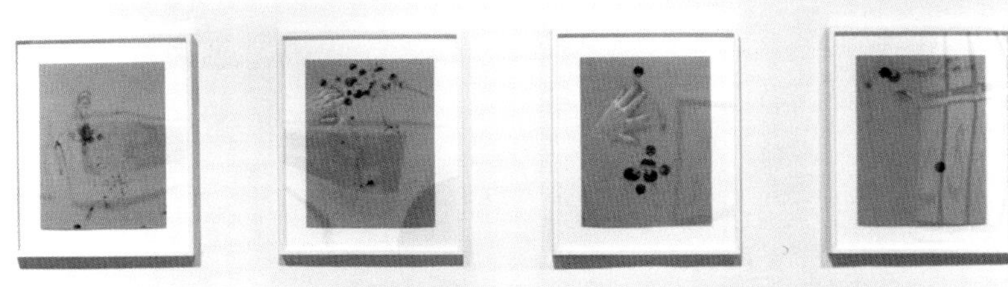

Installation views, Ohio University Art Gallery, 2006. Facing page, top, front to back: Monica Bock, Sarah Webb, Judy Glantzman. Center: Judy Glantzman, Sarah Webb. Bottom: Mary Kelly. This page, top: Barbara T. Smith, Cheri Gaulke and Sue Maberry. Center: Sarah Webb. Bottom: Margaret Morgan.

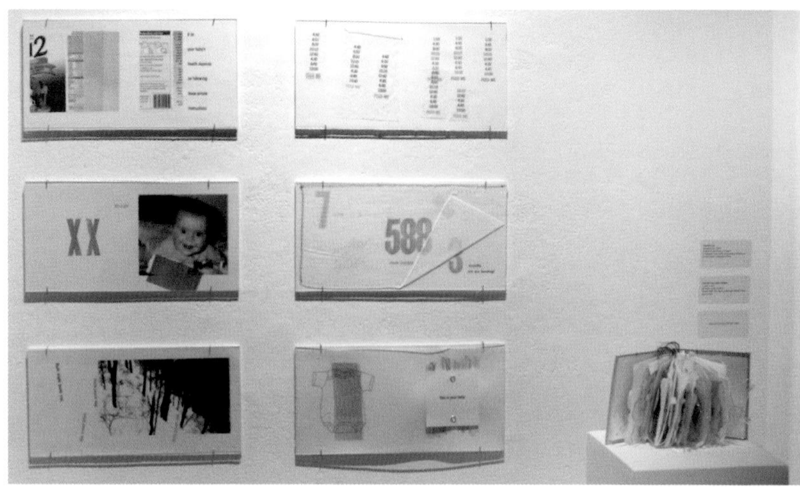

Installation views, Trisolini Gallery, Ohio University Art Gallery, 2006.
Top: Patricia Cué.
Center: Myrel Chernick.
Bottom: Youngbok Hong, Cheri Gaulke and Sue Maberry.

DENISE FERRIS

Untitled, from series *Vestment*, 2005. Casein on Arches, 112 × 79 centimeters.

My prints are made from milk and poison. Articulating the maternal, these photographs come into existence because of a chemical coexistence. Though the milk appears visible, the poison is hidden, suspended in the blended emulsion. Exposed to sunlight, the emulsion forms a hardened

colloid, each substance trapped inside the other, inseparable. A milky odour emanates from the print's hardened surface. I developed this "language of casein," milk prints, to convey duality and ambiguity, loss and maternal pleasure, assertion and transgression, and significantly, ambivalence and resistance. The toxin and the milk metaphorically suggest the emotional conflicts of mothering. Interrogating the emotional geography of mothering, these works picture the unacknowledged burden of carework as well as mothering's state of permanence.

Opposite page, this page top and bottom: *Untitled*, details of work from series *Home Decorum*, 2003. Casein on BFK, entire print size 79 × 56 centimeters.

PATRICIA CUÉ

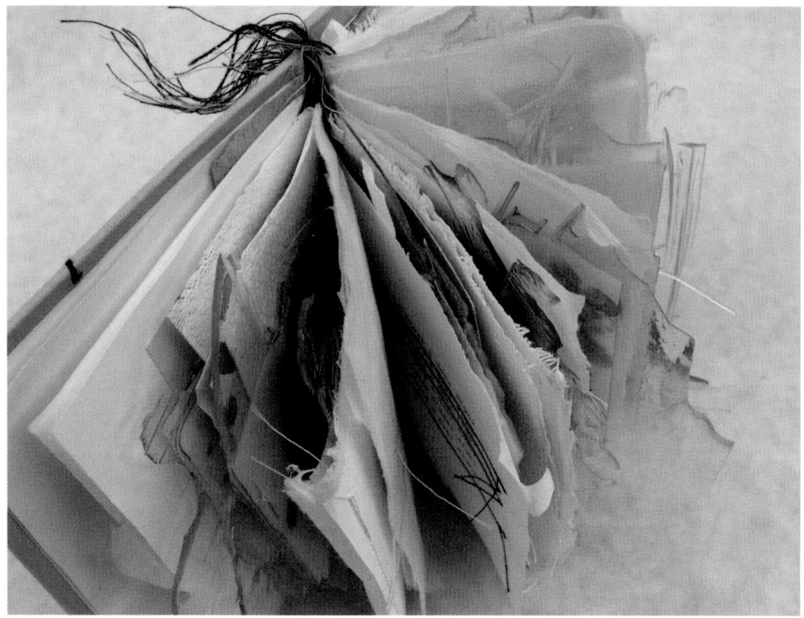

I need, I want (detail), 2007. 42 folios. Coptic binding. Cozo paper, acrylic resin, sewing thread, fabric, laser prints, milk caps and diaper cloth, 6 × 5 inches.

Through my work I record the rituals and the events that define my interactions with my daughter. The experimental book format is a space where I can record and represent past experiences using the remains of our everyday routines. My aim is to provide a material testimony free of sentimentality and clichéd notions of "motherly love."

For me, American culture has been a substitute for the potential wisdom and advice of all the women who are not in my life. It has also, at times, surreptitiously undermined my intuition. Reacting to these influences, my work questions the ideals of motherhood prescribed by the popular media, and the supposedly selfless mission of idealism and martyrdom that motherhood is often charactierized as. My aim is an honest and candid account of my personal experience, a journey tinted with ecstasy as well as exhaustion and boredom. I strive to convey the chaos of living with a toddler, and also to depict the fantastic reinvention of our mundane reality using fairies, plastic pets, and princesses.

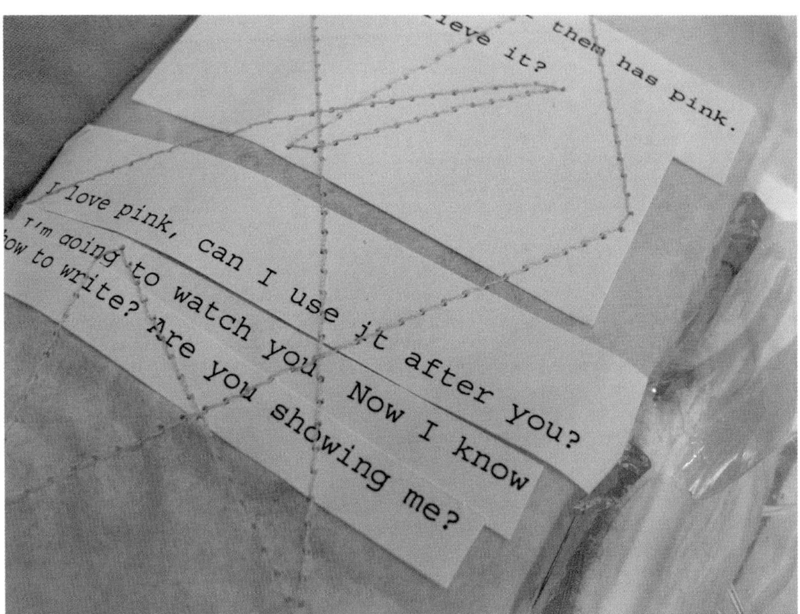

Top and bottom: *I need, I want* (detail), 2007. 42 folios. Coptic binding. Cozo paper, acrylic resin, sewing thread, fabric, laser prints, milk caps and diaper cloth, 6 × 5 inches.

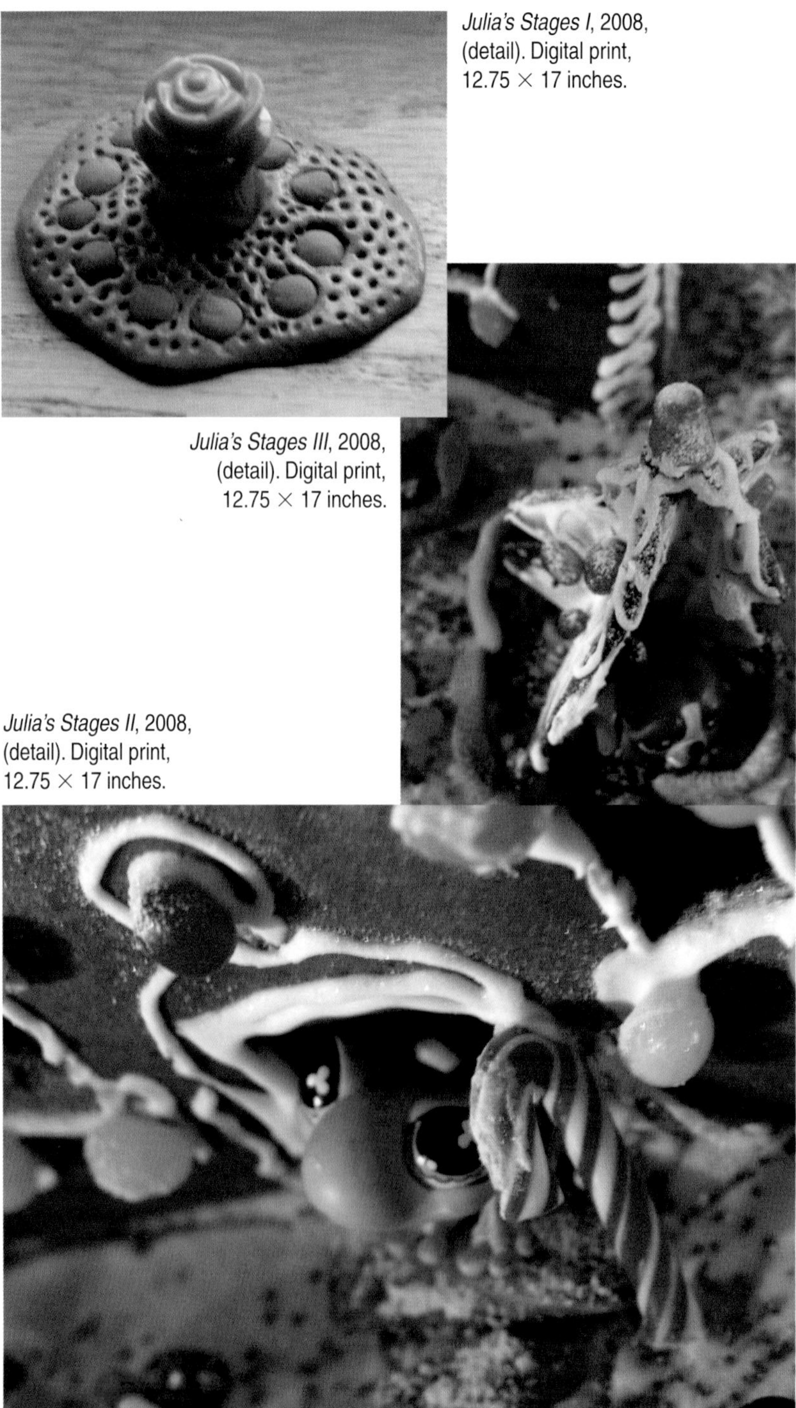

Julia's Stages I, 2008, (detail). Digital print, 12.75 × 17 inches.

Julia's Stages III, 2008, (detail). Digital print, 12.75 × 17 inches.

Julia's Stages II, 2008, (detail). Digital print, 12.75 × 17 inches.

HEATHER GRAY

Dysfunctional Antics of a Happy Housewife, 2004. Black and white photograph, 12.5 × 8.5 inches.

Cocktail Hour, 2004. Black and white photograph, 12.5 × 8.5 inches.

My content is driven by my personal experience as a woman, mother and housewife. I use it to incorporate and process the several obstacles, emotions and changes and loss of self-identity that have arisen in my daily life of mothering. My work explores the themes of identity and gender and the discrepancies between prescribed social roles and private realities. I'm interested in the impact of media and how media images shape and control behavior. My work engages with the myriad ways in which women and the body are depicted by the mass media through powerful images that represent notions of beauty, consumerism and the role of women in society.

Top: *Wonderbread (Age 4),* 2008. Digital photograph, 18 × 12 inches.
Bottom: *Untitled,* 2008. Digital photograph, 18 × 12 inches.

Top: *Offerings at the Crossroads,* 2005. Artists' book, edition of 100, 3.5 × 12 × 1 inches. Bottom two images: *Sea of Time,* 1993. Single-channel color videotape, 12 minutes.

Being lesbian mothers and creating family informed by our feminist values are important parts of our lives that we have chronicled through video, artists' books and installations.

Mark began dying of AIDS *long before I began trying to conceive, both of us racing against the inevitability of time....* So begins the video *Sea of Time* and our journey into motherhood. We were trying to get pregnant through artificial insemination while our best male friend, Mark, was fighting for his life. With Mark and his partner, we two couples traveled to Bali—considered by its people to be the navel of the world and where all life began. The lush visuals of Bali form the backdrop for *Sea of Time,* which is part travelogue, part metaphoric journey between birth and death.

Later we re-crafted the video's text for an artists' book called *Offerings at the Crossroads.* Nestled within a pouch made from Balinese sarongs, the book resembles a traditional palm-leaf book. Indonesian teak covers are held together by a central red cord which passes through the center of its pages. The imagery includes Balinese scenes and the lovely textures and colors of woven, batiked and dyed fabrics that were scanned on a flatbed scanner. The title references the woven offerings that Balinese women place at crossroads as a gift to appease the spirits.

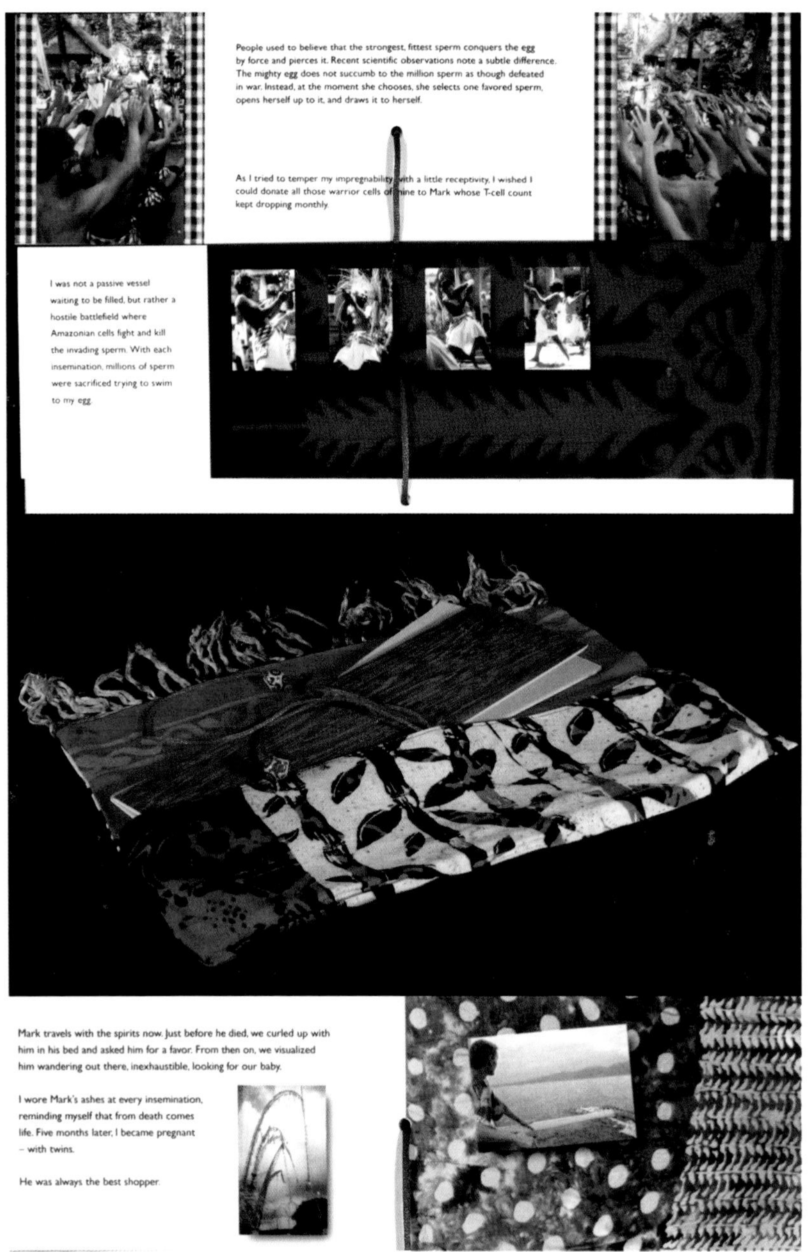

People used to believe that the strongest, fittest sperm conquers the egg by force and pierces it. Recent scientific observations note a subtle difference. The mighty egg does not succumb to the million sperm as though defeated in war. Instead, at the moment she chooses, she selects one favored sperm, opens herself up to it, and draws it to herself.
As I tried to temper my impregnability with a little receptivity, I wished I could donate all those warrior cells of mine to Mark whose T-cell count kept dropping monthly.
I was not a passive vessel waiting to be filled, but rather a hostile battlefield where Amazonian cells fight and kill the invading sperm. With each insemination, millions of sperm were sacrificed trying to swim to my egg.
Mark travels with the spirits now. Just before he died, we curled up with him in his bed and asked him for a favor. From then on, we visualized him wandering out there, inexhaustible, looking for our baby.
I wore Mark's ashes at every insemination, reminding myself that from death comes life. Five months later, I became pregnant – with twins.
He was always the best shopper.

Details of *Offerings at the Crossroads*, 2005.

Sears portraits of Cheri Gaulke, Sue Maberry, Marka and Xochi Maberry-Gaulke from mixed-media installations *Thicker Than Blood: Portrait of Our Lesbian Family,* 1992, *Families Next Door*, 1995, and artists' book, *Marriage Matters.*

A number of years ago, we began creating installations with Sears portraits—to invert this middle-American tradition and question what and who defines family. These installation artworks were titled *Thicker than Blood: Portrait of Our Lesbian Family* and *Families Next Door.* Creating the portraits results in an artwork, but we also see the process as a conceptual performance.

More recently, in response to intensifying debates over the freedom to marry, we invited ten lesbian and gay couples to go to Sears and have their portraits taken. These family portraits

Marriage Matters, 2005. Artists' book, edition of 50, 10 × 8.5 × 1 inches.

were accompanied by personal stories and the story of our own almost 30-year relationship in the artists' book, *Marriage Matters.* The pages were color laser printed on iridescent paper in shades of purple, lavender, white and peach with a silk ribbon closure. The accordion spine allows the book's covers to open back and be held with the silk ribbon. With the alternating vertical and horizontal pages splayed open, the book's shape resembles a two-tiered wedding cake. The text tells our story of making a home, from first vacuum, to pets, to life with twin daughters and our family of choice.

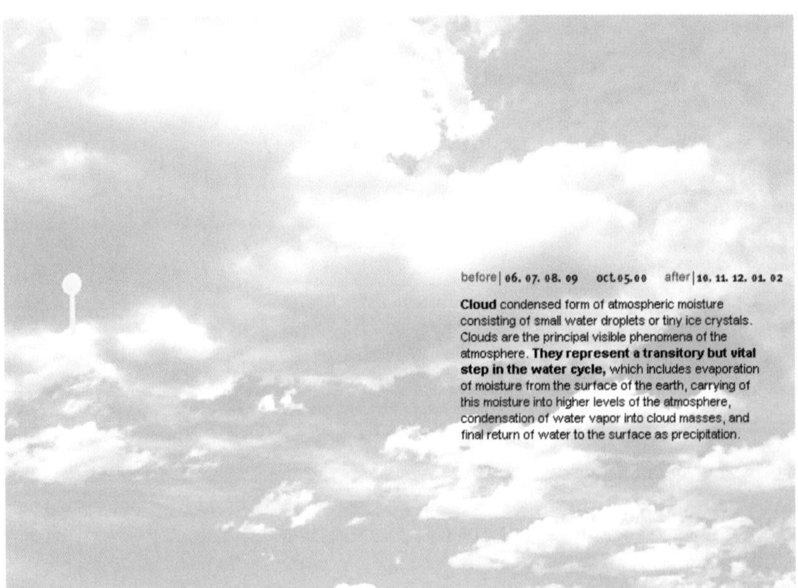

The Condensed is comprised of 54 digital images of formula cans and excerpts from Hong's diary. The final work has been presented as interactive media and installation.

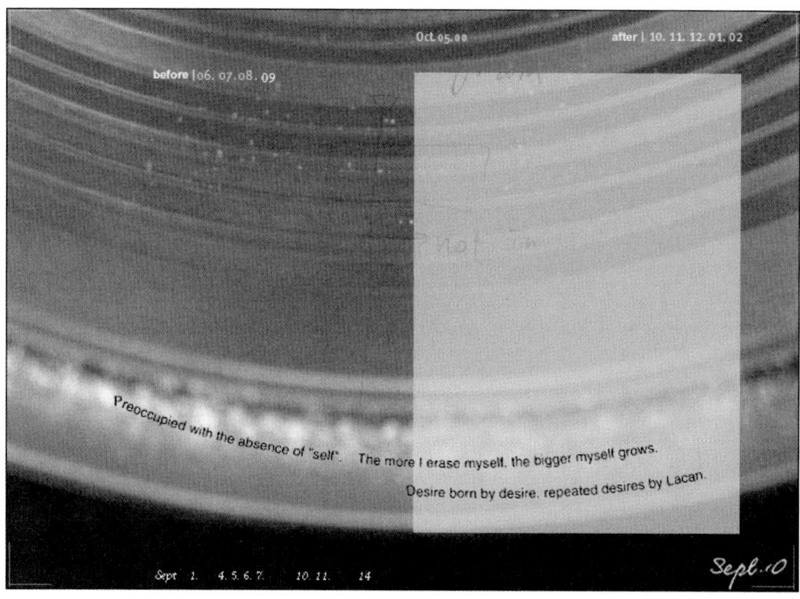

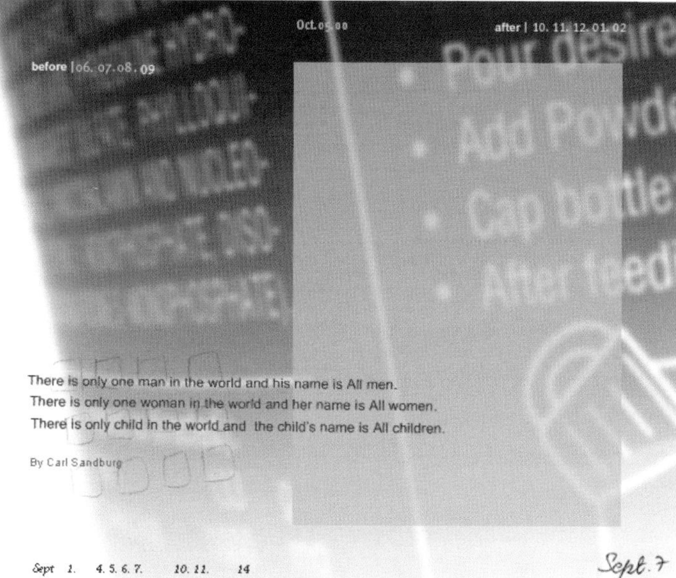

According to Lacan (*The Four Fundamental Concepts of Psychoanalysis*, The Seminar of Jacques Lacan, Book XI), selfhood begins in the womb. *The Condensed* is a story about the relationship between selfhood and motherhood.

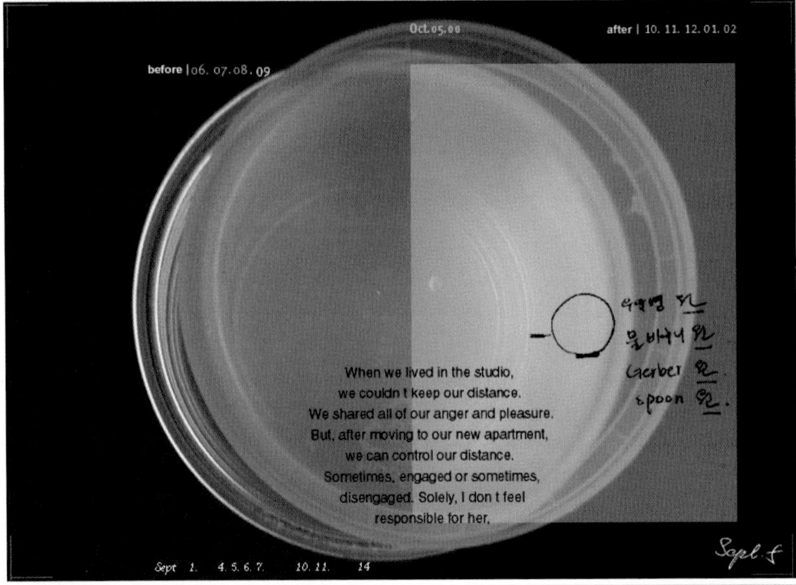

For a certain period of time, I collected everything my daughter used. Specifically, the formula can after bottle-feeding meant something to me beyond the aluminum can itself. It was an extension of my daughter in terms of growth. The collected formula cans competed for the limited space in my small studio with my thesis materials. The volume of the space occupied by the formula cans was an indicator of my anxiety over my future. Examining my engagement with my daughter and observing the flow of my thoughts, I found that my selfhood had transformed into something new in relation to motherhood. Condensation is the metaphor that explains the quality and the nature of my selfhood transformation.

Doublebind. kunst. kinder. karriere

Curated by Signe Theill

I STARTED WORKING ON *Doublebind: Art/Children/Career* in 2001. At the time I had a six-year-old son and a daughter who was almost twelve. My husband had just completed his second degree and was still unemployed. I had two computer graphic design jobs at two different television stations that almost equalled full-time work. I also had a studio and a career as an artist. After having taken some time off to have children, I was beginning a successful "comeback." I was part of several exhibitions and received a grant in 2000 to study abroad in Australia. It was all too much, and I was absolutely exhausted.

Right after my stay abroad, it became apparent to me how different my working methods were from the other scholarship winners, one of whom had no children, the other with a young child. To stay on top of things, I had to organize my time very carefully and use time-management strategies. This is in opposition to the rhythm of art, where one spends a great deal of time dealing with and thinking about the work. At the same time, I found Australia much more child-friendly and woman-friendly than Germany. For me, a special experience was viewing an exhibition in Sydney about the role of women in the conquest of Australia.

Once back from Australia I started thinking about my situation. Three words came up: art, children, and career. I began reflecting on artists who were in the same situation as I. I first looked at and questioned artists in my immediate environment, including colleagues at my studio and artists who were in my circle of acquaintances. I immediately received positive feedback, with many of my acquaintances feeling that an exhibition on art, children, and career was urgently needed. Other artists that I came into contact with via my professors were also supportive of the idea. I needed time for reflection, and time is money, so I decided to make a project out of it in order to apply for funding.

I designed a three-part project consisting of an exhibition, a film and video program, and a book that included interviews with the artists. The first grant application was rejected. However, I received so much positive feedback from the artists I planned to include that I pressed on. I decided to expand the project to include artists/mothers who began working in the 1970s like Valie Export and Ulrike Rosenbach. In my research I discovered the work of Mary Kelly, which inspired me to expand the exhibition to include artists from outside of Germany. With an expanded list of 27 artists from different generations and countries, I was finally successful in being awarded a grant to realize the project.

I used the following criteria to select the artists. The artists had to have children themselves. Their role as mothers had to be reflected in their artwork. Along with the existing work, I was given the option of including the work of ten much older artists—50-90 years old. From these choices came the actual process of selection.

I selected the work for the show based on social situations in which mothers—and not just the artists in this exhibition—come into contact with each other when their children go to school (Susanne Stövhase), from the growing importance that one's own parents take on when one becomes a parent (Eva Bertram), through coming to grips with military service, as in Tina Baras's work *Strange Comrades*. Seemingly coinciding with the beginning of the war in Iraq, the work depicts the artist confronting the death of her own son, the son who went to war.

I was particularly interested in interviewing the artists. In these interviews, I asked them about their personal circumstances, where they were in their career when they gave birth, if their career had suffered as a result, and if the birth of their child was responsible for more rather than less productivity as an artist. I asked if they saw a difference in the work of women artists with children and women artists without children. What had changed after the birth of their child? Did they incorporate their children into their artwork? And finally, why was it that the earlier generation of women artists/mothers had not been more concerned with the relationship between art, children, and career?

The resulting twenty-one interviews are very different from one another. Together they form a veritable universe of ways to manage the problems faced by artists who are trying to have a career, make art, and be mothers. An extreme position was to hide the children from the art world altogether, as did Rune Mields. Keeping your children from the art world is mentioned even in the context of Mary Kelly. As Lucy Lippard noted, Mary Kelly was the first woman in the art world who let it be known that she had a child. The rest of them kept it hidden.[1] At the other extreme is motherhood as a shared social experience. Ulrike Rosenberg brought her young daughter with her to the university. "They all had children—Beuys, Richter, Imi Knoebel-Anatol (a student of Beuys)—and they would watch my daughter for me." Decades later this particular situation no longer exists. According to Rosenberg, "I miss it that my students, who would once bring their children along with them to class, now view having children as a purely private matter."

In the 1980s the feminist movement had a slogan "the personal is political." In this sense I would like *Doublebind: Art/Children/Career* to be an appeal for changes to be made for women, children, and careers.

I was often asked about the difference between being a woman artist and a woman in a normal profession. Do women artists have a particularly hard time? Well, on the one hand women artists do have an advantage,

Exhibition View, Künstlerhaus Bethanien, 2003. In the back: work by Käthe Kruse.

because they have time to reflect on their situation. On the other hand, art is probably the field with the strongest bias against motherhood, because it still subscribes to the patriarchal notion of the art work as "child" and the artist as Creator. In the art world, the male creator competes with the woman who gives birth. It is not uncommon to hear observations in the art world about how a woman can no longer be an artist once she has had a child, or that women have had children because they are unable to make any more art. It is rare that women can no longer make art, although it is true that women artists are worse off economically than their male counterparts. One cannot live by the maxim advocated by artist Marcel Duchamp: "At a certain point, I understood that life need not be burdened with too much weight, with too many duties, usually called a wife, children, a country house, a car.... The artist today is free to die of hunger. He should have no social obligations. If he marries or has children he will soon sacrifice himself.... One person alone, who doesn't need to be fed, is easier than three or four. An artist must be an egoist. He must be completely blind to all other living things—he must be egocentric in the broadest sense."[2]

No, women artists/mothers take responsibility for their children and look for a way to survive professionally. In the debate in Germany regarding "uncertain professions," women artists have taken the leading position in two ways. First, they are always accustomed to dealing with uncertain job prospects and are therefore portrayed as role-models. Second, women artists and women stand on the frontlines of change. *Doublebind: Art/Children/Career* is therefore an homage to women in general, to their courage, their imagination, and their talent for organization.

Notes

[1]Lucy Lippard, Foreword *to Post-Partum Document,* by Mary Kelly (London: Routledge & Kegan Paul, 1983), xi-xiv.

[2]Marcel Duchamp, *Ready-Made. 180 Aussprüche aus Interviews mit Marcel Duchamp,* ed. Serge Stauffer (Zurich: Regenbogen, 1973).

Exhibition View.

Children's Program, Tyyne Claudia Pollmann, Künstlerhaus Bethanien, 2003.

Interference, Installation, Ute Weiss Leder, 2003.

Top: Judith Samen, *Lehrbild der Fauna*, 1998. C-print and watercolor, pencil on paper, framed, 150 × 150 cm. Collection Stelzner, Essen. Bottom: Twin Gabriel, *Think Tank Sixties*, 2004. Photography/Performance.

Top and bottom: Tina Bara, from the series *Fremde Kameraden, St. Martin, Jennersdorf, Oberdrosen*, 2003. C-print, each 70 × 90 centimeters, framed.

V.

Finding the Maternal in the Visual Field

Practice, Narratives, Images

DANIELLE ABRAMS

On Mommas and Mothers

Quadroon, 1998

Janie Bell

Artist's Note:
Janie Bell is a character I perform who is based on my father's mother. Janie died when my father was six and her life story has remained a secret. I wrote this script based on a short interview I conducted with Janie's sister, Margaret. My father has a few memories about his mother. There is also a great deal of conjecture that comes from what my family won't ever say about Janie.

Talking head sitting on a park bench
Yes, here I am, I'm Janie Bell
They say I ain't got much to say but I'm not a sayin kind of woman
I've always been here but when you're out here it's up to your babies then to come and find you
I like it out here, it's real quiet and I get to watch, finally I get to watch
No, not with a wantin or scornful kind of eye
That's all over for me
But I get the time to really sit and study things and watch em grow and live and grow and get old and die
Everybody's dead now
That's what my sister Margaret keeps sayin, she's 79 but she's still my baby sister
We come from Ashland — Ashland, Virginia
Where the sunshine was hot and the moonshine was good
That's what my uncle made — he was a big bootlegger and real friendly towards white folks
A sunshine jam they called it that bootleggin mix he made

Oooooo, it was a nasty kind of firewater
My mother, Mama Landonia Jackson, she was so light she looked like a white lady
Might've been that sunshine jam that my Stepdaddy was drinkin when he set my house and my Mama on fire

A spot
A spot on your lung
A spot that holds you in your babies' minds
All that fire and death down in Ashland brought me up North like my brother Big Eddie
There were six others besides him — there was me and Eddie, Price, Robert, Leroy, Daniel, William, and Margaret
Hell, once we all came up North we'd have a good old time out there in Flushin'
Flushin' was where Momma lived, out there in the country
Momma was Margaret's old man Walter's mother
Flushin' ain't no country no more, not with all them people and shops and cars and railways
But back then, back then, I knew that'd be a good place to raise my babies
Cause there was land and lots and rivers and creeks and porches and places for my children to run free
Cause babies — Babies gotta run free

Up at Momma's we'd play cards and laugh and dance and drink our liquor
And Momma, so many times, Momma wanted to throw us out the house but with all them complexions and colors from high yellow to coconut to almond joy
I knew that this is how we kept the family together
And I knew that this was why Momma never closed the door on us
Never on my babies either
See I had to move myself up to Harlem
Up there I was a workin woman and I had to let my babies go
I put my Dolores with Momma and I put my littlest, Ronnie, with my brother Price
I kept my middle one, Eddie, with me
Little Eddie, he could entertain himself
Drawin, runnin the fire escapes, messin in the streets, and I knew that he was a watcher

See I'd come home late at night and there'd be my Eddie, up on that fire escape watchin out for me
I knew he liked it up there cause he was learnin all about the world, and sometimes you just can't teach your babies right from wrong in the big city
Sometimes they gotta learn it from watchin with their own set of eyes

Y'see things are real fast by y'all right now
Ain't got no time to tell a little tale, have a little party, or maybe even be sweet on each other a bit
When I left Ashland, I was gonna find me some sweets, and I found Richard
Richard Hershey, and he was sweet on me
Took me dancing and to the 'pollo
He turned me into a party girl in the big-time city
I might've been doin things that they think a Mama shouldn't be doin, but Mama needs some lovin too
'specially after longin so much to love everybody who was gone
And I loved my children, and I knew we had family who'd grow em up and love em too
Cause y'see I got sick
Pneumonia they called it, and then it turned into a spot on my lung
Little Eddie, he didn't know what was goin on with his Mama
All layed up in the bed like that, he must've thought I had one of them party-night hangovers
But they took me away from my Eddie, back and forth to the hospital, and then they put me out on Welfare Island
Quarantined me so I wouldn't make my babies sick

I didn't know that my Eddie was sleepin couch to couch back then, up in the mornin at dark with my brother Big Eddie who worked at the slaughterhouse and then off to a couch at Inez's house —
"Aunt Inez's" house
They'd feed my Eddie slaughterhouse bologna and then take him to come and see me on the weekends
I'd tell my Eddie to go outside that hospital and play on that ride they had outside, so I could watch him
I'd watch my Eddie run and jump on that spinnin ride and all that life he had in him, I felt like he was puttin the last breath back in me
He was my life force
Runnin with them other kids whose Mamas was dyin too

And watchin him run and jump on that spinnin ride I felt like he was spinnin that spot on my lung clean
He was keepin me alive
But somethin about when Mama and baby start switchin places like that and baby starts keepin Mama alive I think it's time then for Mama to go
And I could see my sister Margaret lovin my babies and my babies' children and grandchildren
And always havin a little something for them down the road —
An Avon, a $20 bill, or a cooked-up dinner of black-eye peas
I thought of Margaret and I thought of Momma and I knew my Eddie would be just fine
So I took my last breaths from watchin my Eddie run and jump on that spinnin ride and we took the train up to Harlem and we went up to the park, that Mount Morris Park, and we sat under that great big bell they had there
And I told my Eddie that his Mama was dyin
And I told my Eddie to be good, to be good for the sake of his Mama
And we said goodbye, me and my Eddie
And I knew, I knew I'd always hold a spot in my babies' minds

Pigeon Co-op or How I learned to respect my Mama

He had a pigeon coop on top of a roof. He'd wrap chicken drippings in a mesh from tangerines and hang it from the chicken-wire walls of the pigeons' home. He was inside of that coop, watching from the outside, like the time he saw his mother through the toy mailbox. He looked into the form-fitting hexagon through the width of the box's insides, and there on the other side was his mother, wearing the same nightgown/robe set she wore in the hospital. She looked so beautiful and peaceful and loving, like she wasn't sick at all, and like she had a million dollars banked under the bedsprings. He woke up crying, and laughing at himself for crying, and he brought me to tears with grief over his unbelievable loss. The loss of one's mother needs to be accompanied by tears shed from two.

He was raised by a new mother: Momma, Mrs. Flowers, Molly Flowers, Mom, Great. Great worked hard ironing shirts in the cleaners, and left the child-rearing to Aunt Liz. Liz... "she was kind of a sadist," he says. She whipped him with a cat-o'-nine tails, and told him, "Turn around so I can beat your penis." Great raised nine children and moved them from house to house when she couldn't pay the rent. No matter what happened, she always kept a roof over those babies' heads. Some of them houses used to be where the Bland Housing Project is now. I went to nursery school at the Bland, got beat up on a school bus at the Bland, had a babysitter in an apartment up at the Bland, and later I bought my reefer over at the Bland.

But when my Dad lived with Great they were over on Farrington Street. On the other side of Flushing. She cooked on Sunday and they ate for the week. Aunt Liz had a West Indian boyfriend so she'd make Jamaican dishes. Rice and peas and chop meat in curry. Joseph was his name and they'd drink and fight in the staircase. Great would come out of her bed mumbling about that Black bastard with her broom. I wonder if Aunt Liz wanted to beat Joseph's penis.

There's a picture of everyone sitting in front of a Christmas tree. Chew, who looks like his boy Chuckie, and Uncle Walter and everyone who looks dressed for the Cotton Club but is dead behind the eyes. My Aunt is there, and she's young and beautiful and wears her dress just right. In her arms she holds her white baby doll. "Cecilia," she could call that doll and hang it from the tree. My Dad with his skinny knees is not in the picture. He might be in the bed crying. I go into the picture and I am looking for my father. I don't hear nothing because nobody is talking and everything is deafened, like the conversation is over and has been for a long time. Nobody is looking at me to find out what Eddie's daughter turned out like but I can't stop looking at them. So much so that I forget what I came here for ... to pet my father on his lamb's wool head with my index finger. Because I'm in the living room I cannot find the bedroom and the apartment ends at the picture's edge. I can sit with my young Aunt on the rug in front of the tree and be in the picture, or I can leave.

I remember being at Great's house when I was about six or seven. I'd never go over there alone like my cousins because I was scared ... scared of Great's voice. My mother's parents were old but they didn't talk like that, with a strain from their throats on their words. Great talked like that because she spent a lifetime smoking half-Kent Cigarettes. Smoke half, put it in the ashtray, and smoke the other half later. That way you don't get cancer. Great was yimmering and yammering about how my father don't bring me over to see her and I was trying to climb in his shirt, climb into his heart. I didn't want to put my feet on Great's linoleum. I wanted him to carry me. I knew my cousins weren't like this. They went over to spend the weekend with Great for a treat. That would be like throwing me into a hole with no end. How would anyone find me? And would they ever come back to pick me up? My cousins didn't have no contact with their white grandparents, and like me, they didn't find white voices the most comforting sounds in the world.

"Playland" the sign spells, and its guts are rotted out. It's part of the old midway that I used to walk on when my feet were in too-tight jellies filled with scratchy, glassy-ass sand. Coney Island was a scary place. The horrors from its Haunted House bled out onto the streets. Mom would never take me there alone without my father. Not like the tough, tattooed, rope-chained, short-short-wearing, brown-skinned, bruised single mothers I see with strollers there now. These mothers in their 110-pound frames could flay the skin off of a 200-pound man. Don't mess with their babies or their tall boys. They're rough on their kids, once their kids start to walk. They make everybody look at their mothering methods on the subway. At the Park Slope station, a progressive train full of organically fed parents look at these mothers with their disapproving glances.

My father thinks that my mother saved him from marrying one of these types of women. It's true. My mother would never take the train, only her Oldsmobile, to the beach. You would never catch her wheeling no stroller along the train platform, or carrying it up and down the subway stairs.

My mother's body isn't much bigger than these women, but her size is massive. My mother hasn't seen a frail day in her life. The thought that someday she might astonishes me. She wasn't raised being smacked on the subways, only punished through mental anguish. She wouldn't smack me on the trains in front of those disapproving eyes. Only in the Oldsmobile, from front seat to back seat, or behind the doors of our apartment, and it never really happened if you ask her about it now. I'll tell you one thing though. Those mothers on the subway would never say they never smacked their babies. That's why they smack their babies right in front of your face. Their babies should thank them for that beating. That's how they learned respect.

Weddings, weddings

My mother has to cut our conversation short to click over to the other line so she can talk to my grandmother about Lee's granddaughter's wedding
I can hear the questions: What was her dress like? Oh, off the shoulders? Did they have a sushi bar? Oh, so it was buffet style? They had a DJ?
Yesterday as I was about to read my mother some of my writing she had to take a call from my godmother so she could hear about Tina's son's wedding which took place the night before
So they were still so ungracious? Did they have a sushi bar?
She hangs up with my godmother
She ignores my treasure chest of my words
to tell me what a bitch that Tina's son's new bride is and how Tina's son didn't even go around to the tables at the wedding
He was just hanging out with his friends getting drunk all night
And at the shower
The bride was also so ungracious, she just opened the gifts and had no expression
My mother only uses words like gracious when she talks about weddings, showers, or ceremonies where there are expensive cash gifts and lots of photos being taken
I look at the piano in my mother's living room where she has all the family photos in frames
All the pictures of me are from when I had long hair, lipstick, and could have potentially been a gracious or ungracious bride
I have to remind my mother that my laptop is open and that I am ready to read to her
Sometimes I wonder about my mother's love for Black people
Is it deeply rooted, down in her core?
Like the way Jews and Blacks are supposed to bond, in a way that transcends language, derived from centuries past
From the dust, from the bones, from the skull and the spine of the earth
I mean she wasn't raised around Black people
Not in the post-war housing development where she was raised
Made for Jewish veterans who survived American wars
They showed no bitterness, only patriotism for their country
My mother reminded Richard Dreyfuss that they were both from the same housing development when she saw him perform a few years

ago in Sag Harbor
"He was impressed," she says
Yesterday my mother and me watched *The Color Purple*
And when Celia reconciled with her sister after half of their lifetime had already passed, I thought I was going to cry my guts out
I began to wonder about my tears and my own estranged relationship with my sister of color, and when we would meet and see each other in a field of tall grass
I also listened for my mother's tears
Did she feel as deeply about this moment as I did?
I listened for her breaths
Were they short and gaspy like my own?
In this endless scene on a tv screen of Celia being hugged by her son, then her daughter, then her son's wife, and finally her sister
"Momma," they all said
My throat was in my teeth and it hurt
So much to think about amidst the tears
I was tearing on my insides
Just as I was about to give up on my mother and take an empowered step in not caring whether she saw and heard me crying and witnessing my vulnerability even if she herself wasn't sad
She passed me a Kleenex after pulling one for herself

Quadroon, 1998, 4-channel video installation, courtesy of the artist.
Detail: Janie Bell, Butch in the Kitchen, Dew Drop Lady, Dee.

MYREL CHERNICK

The Studio Visit

CAROLINE PICKED UP HER WATCH from the dresser in the bedroom and strapped it onto her wrist. It was tight, the buckle slightly digging into her skin. She looked up at the clock on the kitchen wall. I'll have more time if I pace myself by the watch. I'll keep it on for now, even though it will leave a mark. The visit was scheduled for eleven, which left plenty of time for Caroline to be ready early and for the curator to call and mention casually that she was running late. Or she could say that something had come up and she needed to reschedule. She could even cancel outright without any excuses or apologies. It had happened before.

She looked up at the clock on the kitchen wall.

Already anticipating the tension of the next two hours, Caroline glanced into the studio at her newest work. She could barely make out the paper cutouts, which moved almost imperceptibly in the unlit room. She had a lot to do to get these pieces ready: when functioning they required complete darkness, as well as all the electricity in the loft. She checked the lights repeatedly and obsessively before each visit, worried that they would blur and shift and the bulbs blow at the last minute.

It was important for her to determine the final order of the viewing now. She didn't need any surprises. The sculptural work used so many different lights that her tiny studio really heated up. During winter mornings or late afternoons she could stand it for about twenty minutes, but by the middle of a sunny day even that was too long. If she showed another piece first she had to move equipment and cords around, with the curator standing there in the dark. When Caroline was already nervous this process could be very awkward.

The sun was streaming through the back windows this morning.

She could almost smile now as she remembered the worst studio visit ever. The woman, who was scheduled to arrive at eleven, had called at ten and said she had needed to make an unexpected visit to her holistic doctor in Connecticut. She couldn't possibly be there before one, she said. Was that all right? Of course, Caroline had replied, straining to prevent the sweetness in her voice from developing a rancorous edge. Of course, come whenever you like. (I have nothing better to do than wait for you all day.) That visit had been a disaster. The curator, who got there even later than her original estimation, was tired and distracted from her trip to Connecticut and whatever ailment was preoccupying her, while Caroline was anxious and edgy from the long wait. She was previewing a new projected slide piece that depended on carefully choreographed movements when the equipment went haywire. She could still feel her hands trembling as they jammed the buttons on the projector, bumbling through the explanation while the timing was completely off. "Keep me informed of your subsequent projects," were the curator's parting words. "Thanks so much for accommodating me." Of course they had never seen each other again. But that was a long time ago. After that visit Caroline changed her attitude. She convinced herself not to have any expectations, as hard as that was. And yet a friend who thought highly of Caroline's work recommended today's curator, who had rescheduled only once with plenty of notice. She also lived in the neighborhood, which made her less threatening in some ways. Maybe they had passed each other on the street. There was a lot at stake for Caroline here though, as she showed her new work for the first time.

She collected the dirty breakfast dishes, straightening and arranging the kitchen as she moved around the loft. She regularly offered coffee or tea to her visitors but was relieved when they preferred water after the long climb up four flights of stairs. She placed a cup near the stove and set the water glass on the counter next to the door. The sun was streaming through the back windows this morning, reflecting off the building across the airshaft, and highlighting the filthiness of the glass. The windows, impossible to clean even if Caroline had the time or the inclination, were streaked and pitted, but produced unusual shadows that she had often photographed. As she moved around the brightly lit space she calculated how long she had lived and worked here. It was usually one of the first questions she was asked. More than twenty years now, she would answer, almost surprising herself. When she moved in she was a young artist with the world at her fingertips, the neighborhood was expanding and galleries were opening right and left. She was thrilled and excited with the possibilities that existed for her then. Her work was formal and grand, and she created ethereal installations of light and paper and projected words that filled the entire loft. When her husband moved in he needed a place to work too, and then the children took up space as they grew, so her studio shrank in size. Still she was lucky even to have a studio here. Almost all of the artists as well as the galleries had been forced out by the high rents. Without the loft law to protect her she would be gone too, and despite the filth and congestion of the streets below she couldn't imagine living anywhere else at this point. Most of the buildings on her block had been sold for huge sums of money, and there were dollar signs in her landlord's eyes. He was civil, even pleasant with her when she dropped off the rent in his office on the second floor, but he had never put a penny into improvements and she knew he regretted this building full of ungrateful tenants.

Caroline walked back to the kitchen table with the cup of the coffee she had just prepared. She brushed off a few crumbs left over from the children's breakfast and sat down. In case she doesn't have much time I'd better start with the most recent work, although we'll have to move around quite a bit. After sitting there for a few minutes, she glanced at her watch and, seeing that it was nine thirty, got up and walked toward the bedroom door. She had always disliked this trajectory through the bedroom to her studio. She spent a lot of time cleaning—the bed needed to be made, papers arranged, clothes put away—and she would have preferred to display less of her private life. Although her work since the birth of her children incorporated aspects of domesticity, it did not include the quality of the bed linen or her embarrassingly chaotic personal space. When she sensed her visitors lingering in front of the family photos or the window with its view of lower Manhattan, she regretted never having cut that door through the living room wall directly into her studio. Of course the issue arose only at times like this. Once the stranger left she never thought about it.

The extension cords reminded her of orange snakes.

She cleared a space on the studio table for her coffee cup, then knelt down on the floor to disentangle the extension cords that reminded her of orange snakes. She had photographed them in that state. Now she brought them out into the common room, so they could be plugged into separate circuits. When she first worked on the light pieces they were all plugged into the same line and were constantly tripping the switch. She would be on the verge of achieving the effect she was looking for when she would hear a sudden popping sound, followed by silence and pitch darkness. So she had devised her system of extension cords. For the first time in a while she was working with projected light, these new pieces referring back to her earlier, large-scale installations, and as she worked out the kinks she remembered hours spent locating and connecting ancient electrical circuits in old buildings. She had been showing regularly then, and every installation was an adventure and a challenge.

After she plugged in the cords Caroline came back to the studio and turned on the power strips, one by one. Her pulse quickened as she pressed the last switch. She closed the door and stepped back, surveying the altered space. As her eyes adjusted to the darkness and the fans kicked in, the pieces began to move slowly, randomly. She could still marvel at the dense and layered three-dimensional shapes that resulted from the light passing over and through these paper cutouts, dangling from the ceiling with nylon fishing line, invisible in the darkness. The light fused into the forms, edges shimmering, while the dense black shadows, dancing, sliced through the surface of the wall. The projected words, suggested by her current ambivalence toward her adolescent children, were fractured and fragmented with the desultory movement of the cutouts. When her children were small Caroline assuaged her guilt from abandoning them for the selfish pleasure of making art by including them in the work. They complied eagerly with her requests while she videotaped them, inventing rituals and performing gleefully for the camera. Now it was more complicated. She resented their demands on her time, the arguments and accusations, the defiant stares. And yet she dreaded the day, not so far in the future, when they would be leaving home. She escaped into the studio to maintain her equilibrium. She had always loved the look of projected text, the visual

evocation expanding the significance of the carefully chosen words. Each slight shift of the paper created a new shape, with new angles and layers and meanings. There was just enough light to decipher the short texts she had so painstakingly hand lettered onto the wall. She half recited, half read in a soft voice, each phrase evoking an image or a memory:

"She had a fleeting vision of small bodies in motion" had been the impetus for the idea of the cutouts as windows or barriers. She could see the children passing her by, growing, separating, and leaving, in a continuous process that began at the moment of birth. She had often taped them at their games, from a distance, marveling at the inventiveness of their continuous play, sometimes wondering at her need to record it all, to get it down on tape, to have something concrete to hold onto.

Another phrase, "she listened for the sound of his footsteps on the stairs," brought back a recent afternoon spent worrying about her son Sam. He had been coming home late from school without calling to let her know. As the hours passed her concentration dissipated and she gave up trying to work. When he finally showed up, cool and nonchalant, with an excuse he'd been rehearsing along the way, she was too exhausted and relieved to dwell on her lost studio time. She wanted to hug him and scream at him simultaneously. But she held back. If she yelled at him would it make him even more defiant? She wondered what he did and where he was during those missing hours, questioning how much she knew about him these days. He had grown up quickly this year, going to parties and hanging out on weekends with his new friends. She moved on to "Suspicion: days of silence and regret, of brooding anger, questions unanswered," and her voice trailed off, thoughts drifting to an acrimonious exchange earlier in the morning. Her daughter had stormed out of the house, yet again, without saying goodbye. Simone, from the time she was tiny, had an almost preternatural sense of Caroline's emotional state, and often chose to act out during those times when she was

under the most pressure. Her most recent crime consisted of ignoring one of Simone's rambling complaints about her English teacher's ludicrous assignments and unfair grading practices, a minor offense in Caroline's eyes, but which precipitated a "you care more about your art than you do about me," and the slamming of the door. Today she let Simone go without following her into the hallway for a last-minute reconciliation, hoping the long subway ride would calm her down. Caroline knew she would suffer for it later, and was prepared to make amends, but for now she pushed away the guilt and turned to the door of the studio where a thin ray of sunshine penetrated from the bedroom on the other side. She opened it wide, turned off the surge protectors and checked her watch. Ten o'clock. Sally hasn't called yet, so there's a good chance she's on her way.

She walked back through the bedroom to the living room, pausing to straighten the books in the pile by the bed, removing a pair of shoes from the doorway, glancing again at the clock as she passed. The tension was mounting as the hour approached, and Caroline used these simple tasks to maintain her calm exterior. She closed the door that led to the children's room, then stopped to look at a wall of photographs. When she first started working on these pictures she hadn't intended for them to accompany the three-dimensional work, but she was happy with the way they complemented each other. The longer texts accompanying the photos, short episodes she recorded during bouts of insomnia, described incidents of material lives, momentary impressions and revelations. Her children were testing her, with the stirrings of adolescence, to see if she could be trusted. She had always loved to watch them as they negotiated their days. The texts were obliquely related to the images, leaving room for speculation and mystery. She had photographed the paper cutouts—the results were abstract enough to function as compositions of light and dark with edges of color—and paired them with other shots of light and shadow she took on the fly, keeping her camera loaded and ready. Her friends seemed to appreciate the relationship between the stories, brief glimpses and memories, and the abstract shapes, but she hadn't shown them to a curator yet.

In the bedroom Caroline stared briefly into the mirror at her face, picking out the newest wrinkles, wondering if she should wear her customary red lipstick, then took a pair of black pants and tunic from the closet and laid them carefully on the bed. Her artist's outfit had been much bolder in her youth, when she sported a shaved head and tight skirts and dressed in bright colors. With the weight she had gained in middle age she wouldn't wear anything like that now. Besides, she liked the elegance and the slim lines of the black clothing. And she wanted the emphasis to be on the work. She turned around and looked at the clock again. Almost ten thirty. It was really time to get moving. Not that anyone had ever been early, but she couldn't take any chances. She hurried to get her bathrobe from the closet, stumbling over the extension cords in her way. Exactly why I warn people to be careful, she admonished herself. Robe in hand, she ran to the bathroom, threw off her clothes and got into the shower. As she relaxed under the running water, she fantasized the perfect visit. "What great work, of course we'd love to give you a one-person show, I'll call you next week to talk about the details...."

The loud jangling of the buzzer startled her. How could this be? How long have I been standing here? It couldn't possibly be eleven o'clock already. Caroline quickly turned off the water, threw on her robe and ran to pick up.

"Hello..."

"Hi, this is Sally, I know I'm a little early, but I thought you wouldn't mind."

"Of course, no problem. I'll buzz you in; it's the fourth floor. The elevator doesn't work so you have to walk."

She panicked. There she was, after all her careful preparations, standing in the middle of the room, undressed and dripping wet, with, depending on the physical condition of the woman coming up the stairs, anywhere from two to five minutes to dry herself off, get dressed, and greet her at the door.

At any other time the situation might have seemed comical, even to Caroline. Now she turned around so quickly, flung herself almost, toward the bedroom with such intensity that she barely kept her balance on the wet floor, slippery with the water dripping off her body. She reached out to the wall to steady herself and, with that sickening sensation of knowing what is going to happen but being powerless to do anything about it, knocked over the water glass that she had set so carefully on the counter. As she stood there in disbelief, the glass flew, crashed, and shattered into a million pieces that lay there, sparkling where the sunlight reached them, mocking her.

She sprang for the bedroom, threw on the clothes that, thankfully, she had laid out on the bed, and ran back to the living room. She bent down to pick up the largest piece of glass in her path and opened the door. Sally Carmichael was leaning against the railing, looking rather bewildered.

"Hi, I'm Caroline, sorry to keep you waiting, I had a little accident."

"I'm Sally. I thought I must have the wrong floor." She held out her hand.

A million pieces lay there, sparkling where the sunlight reached them, mocking her.

Caroline transferred the piece of broken glass to her left hand, put it behind her back and held out her right.

"Come in. But be careful. There's glass everywhere."

Sally stepped gingerly into the room, and Caroline guided her away from the mess toward the sofa.

"Please sit here for one minute while I clean this up. Then I'll explain everything."

As she reached for the broom Caroline noticed her left hand was bleeding. She was oblivious to the pain until she dropped the piece of glass in the garbage and awkwardly swept the rest of the debris into a pile near the wall. She set down the broom and, reaching furtively for a roll of toilet paper on the shelf by the closet she knelt down and wrapped a thick wad around her hand.

She stood up and tentatively approached the woman on the couch, keeping her left hand behind her back. Sally looked back at her inquisitively.

She wasn't young, thank goodness, she was at least as old as Caroline, maybe older, and she wasn't fashionably dressed. Her jeans and sweater were casual and her shoulder length hair was streaked with grey. She didn't appear to be wearing any makeup, and wasn't beautiful either. Caroline, who lately felt older than almost everyone else in the art world, was relieved. Sally worked at a mid-sized museum outside of the city that had a good reputation and a decent budget. Caroline tried to explain:

"I was a little late getting into the shower. When you buzzed I stumbled and broke this glass...."

Sally stared back at her, impervious. "I have another appointment. Let's look at the work."

She seemed brusque at that moment and as Caroline stood there with her hand behind her back, hair damp and uncombed, clothes somewhat disheveled, she wondered what Sally was thinking. Just another crazy, unprepared artist. Caroline hadn't planned it this way at all. What had happened to her carefully orchestrated sequence?

"Come with me."

She led Sally through the bedroom into the studio, closed the door and quickly turned on the power strips. Fortunately none of the lights had shifted since the earlier run-through, and as the room lit up she felt the same palpable excitement, despite the pain in her hand that she tried hard to ignore. She turned her attention to Sally, who was moving slowly and gradually through the space, focusing intently on each piece and then pausing to read the text on the wall. The expression on her face had softened to a half-smile. Caroline took it as a good sign.

When Sally came back to the center Caroline moved closer and began to describe her history and the genesis of this installation. She mentioned a few of her earlier pieces, her life with her twins and their involvement with her work. Maybe it was the condition of her hand but she loosened up and talked about the ethereal beauty of light and shadow and the pain of separation that she wanted to embody here.

She worried about going on too long but Sally listened closely, watching her with interest. With more of a smile on her face she commented on the many layers and changing forms that she observed in the work and asked a few technical questions. Then she talked about her own son who had gone to high school nearby and was now a college student, and they compared notes. She mentioned how difficult it was when he left home, and Caroline felt grateful for the years she had left. She was also appreciative of the unexpected connection. These visits were always about so much more than the art, and the maternal link was unusual.

She kept her hand behind her, shifting it occasionally to relieve the throbbing, glancing at Sally to see if she noticed, and was careful to have her go first when they moved out into the daylight to look at the photographs. Nothing had changed in the room since they left it and Caroline was careful to steer Sally away from the bits of glass in their way. They spent some time reading and discussing the texts and images. Sally focused on some of the details in the pictures, the lights and darks, and asked thoughtful questions about the implied stories.

She said she particularly enjoyed the shadows reflected across walls and through windows and the shot of the children walking away into the distance, which reminded her of an incident with her young son, who had once been lost in a similar setting. Caroline was beginning to relax when Sally glanced at her watch, turned toward the door and announced, "time to go."

Caroline had planned to offer her some catalogues and other documentation but was reluctant to reveal her hastily bandaged hand. She let Sally retrieve her coat and bag from the sofa and noticed how she stepped gingerly while she followed her to the door.

She was about to mouth her customary closing remark but Sally spoke first.

"This was an unusual visit. Perhaps I seemed rushed but I found the work stimulating and original. My colleagues will be contacting you in the near future. We're working on a new project that I think you'll find interesting.... Good-bye. And take care of that hand." She smiled and moved over to the stairs.

"Good-bye. And thanks for coming. I'm sorry about the chaos."

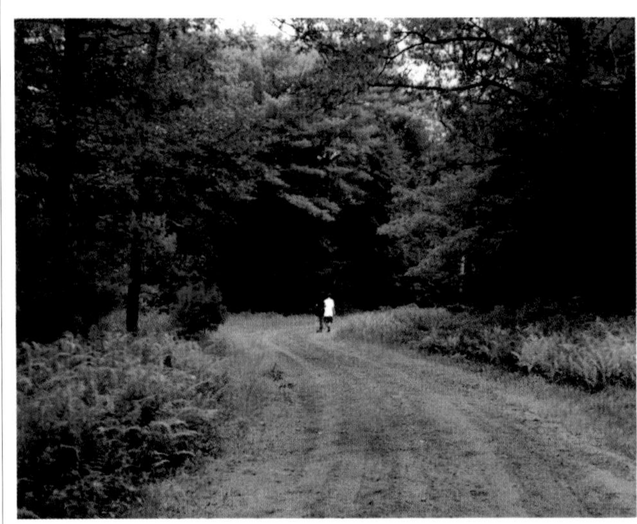

They were almost gone now, mere specks in the distance. A flick of the wrist, a toss of the head, out of sight, out of mind...

She was gone. Caroline stood motionless in the doorway until the footsteps grew fainter and she heard the building door slam. She shut and locked the door to the loft and looked up again at the clock on the kitchen wall. It was just a little past noon, but the morning seemed far away. She felt suddenly exhausted and weak, and the throbbing in her hand grew stronger as she brought it out from behind her back. Blood was seeping through the top layer of the now sodden and sticky wad of toilet paper. The pile of glass shards lay in the corner while other smaller pieces sparkled here and there on the floor where the sunlight hit them. They beckoned to her, waiting to be photographed, but then, cradling her damaged hand, and carefully circumnavigating the stray fragments of glass, she made her way carefully towards the broom in the corner.

TIME PASSES

The top drawer had been her mother's. That same dresser now sat in the corner of her own bedroom, dark and massive, its size and bulk overwhelming the tiny space. It had been carted around North America in the years since its creation, and the nicks and scars remained. Built in North Carolina, transported to Winnipeg by her uncle's furniture company, given to her parents as a wedding present in 1939, it traveled with them to Minneapolis, to Kansas, and back east to New Jersey, where it remained during the years of her childhood and young adulthood. After a few years in her loft in New York City when the house was sold, up four flights of stairs and down, it landed here, in the small country cabin. The family had little history, few roots, no heirlooms, and this veneered construction hardly qualified, but it was all she had. It had been full of her mother's lingerie, that top drawer, secret, feminine objects. Did the mother anticipate the daughter's curiosity, the longing, the sifting through the objects in the drawer, the fingering of the soft fabrics, the thrill and anticipation in the search for answers? It's hard to say now, so many years later, as the subject was never discussed.

mother

mother

mother

mother

mother

mothe

motherles

oday, January 26, 2006. I am sitting in the hospital
m with my mother who broke her hip yesterday.
is muttering and moaning incessantly, speaking
idly without inflection or enunciation, pausing
ely, words tumbling over each other. On an impulse
gin to write down what she is saying in my note-
k. She is reaching into the last vestiges of her memory.
ounds like some eerie stream of consciousness
ry and I am fascinated as I strain to keep up.
calls my name often and seems to have some sense
y presence. myrel I want her to come may I come
ause it's so wonderful may I go over here to see
. I don't want to die now are you going to let me
you? Please let me do that I want to go home to my
her I have to tell her. may I come over with another
nd who's good please tell me you're going to let
go once where's Jack why isn't he here? I have to
him at night will you you darling you're wonder-
so wonderful please let me go I want to go can
can you help me I want to die will you let me
a second of silence I want to die I have to go you're
derful you look so lovely may I come darling just
you there coming down you have one yes you do I
to see you you look so beautiful come I'll take you
inner please let me please let me you're wonderful
you let me come here I want to see you you look
tiful please leave me I'm dying can you leave me
n't take much I want to go now please come I want
t to come down and see everybody myrel can I come
I'll have dinner let me go oh it's beautiful I'll die
se let me go what's the name of the place I'm going
myrel please let me go and you look so beautiful
ses fast and it's good I can't stand it let me go
re going to let me help you you're wonderful
el are you going to let me come now may I come
may I come now OK good wonderful OK I'm
y to come my glasses are in my yours are beautiful
to come to my house OK wonderful I love to see
please OK I want to get this OK myrel will you let
work it would you let me do it it's very hard is
going to come I'm going to die good wonderful I'll
you home you're wonderful beautiful is it all
that that's a nice place I like that color let her see
ake sure that's the nicest thing to give them what
ant I see them they're lovely fine you're wonder-
she's doing it nicely did Jack go too fast he did
o fast I'll use the book and I'll help him it's
ll right I want you to come here because you're so
derful over here just one thing I want to die I don't
to die I want you to come myrel I want to die
I want you to come you don't have those they're
tiful myrel do you have those beautiful ones let
o there I'm gonna die let me go please oh it's

T I M E

PASSES

10/26, trip to Boston: The sky is almost dark now. I spent nine hours on a bus to visit him for three. He sat across from me in the Indian restaurant and talked a blue streak. I was happy to hear his voice, to listen to him speak with excitement about his plans. I miss the daily give-and-take of the family living and interacting together. This is my life with him now, these little snippets of conversation, an occasional phone call late in the evening, when he is going strong and my lights are out. It is so much easier to concentrate when he is here, facing me across the table, while I revel in his youth and contagious excitement. Of course I'm a bit wary and apprehensive as I remind myself of his pattern of preliminary enthusiasm and subsequent regrets, and he tells me I sport a look of dismay. I'm upset by his description of my expression, as I must betray my anxiety. Yet he seems so large and solid to me today, head and shoulders ensconced deep in his hooded sweatshirt. He thinks quickly and speaks even more so, and I relish his exuberance. Here is my child, grown-up. He walks me to the T stop, three steps ahead of me, miss him already

SHE STUMBLES OUT OF THE BEDROOM HALF ASLEEP, REACHING FOR HER GLASSES AND THEN FOCUSING ON THE TABLE STREWN WITH DIRTY DISHES, DRIED FOOD AND RICE KERNELS FROM LAST NIGHT'S DINNER. SHE PICKS UP YESTERDAY'S NEWSPAPER, HALF READ, PUTS IT ON THE RECYCLING PILE, COMES BACK AND GATHERS UP THE DISHES, STACKING AS MANY AS SHE CAN HANDLE, AND SETS THEM IN THE SINK WITH A LOUD CLANK. SHE PUTS THE NAPKINS IN THEIR NAPKIN HOLDERS AND MOVES THEM TO THE BUTCHER BLOCK. SHE PICKS UP A CHOPSTICK OFF THE FLOOR AND THROWS IT INTO THE SINK, MOVING BACK AND FORTH AND AROUND THE TABLE, ATTEMPTING TO BE EFFICIENT WITH HER STEPS. SHE PUTS A POTHOLDER AWAY, TAKES *THE ILLUSTRATED SHERLOCK HOLMES* TO T'S DESK ALONG WITH A CRUMPLED PAIR OF S'S PANTS SHE FINDS DRAPED OVER A CHAIR, WHICH SHE DEPOSITS ON HIS BED ALONG THE WAY. SHE PUTS ANOTHER POTHOLDER IN ITS PLACE AND SETS THE BOTTLE OF TAMARI SAUCE IN THE REFRIGERATOR, MOVES THE HALF-EMPTY BOWL OF STRAWBERRIES TO THE BUTCHER BLOCK, PICKS UP HER SET OF PENCILS, MOVES IT TO THE STACK OF PAPERS SHE IS COPYING FROM, PUTS THE PORTABLE PHONE BACK IN ITS CRADLE, THROWS THE METROPOLITAN MUSEUM OF ART PLAN INTO THE PAPER RECYCLING BIN AND THE EMPTY PLASTIC WATER BOTTLE INTO THE OTHER BIN IN ONE TRIP. SHE TAKES S'S EXERCISE BAND OFF THE CHAIR AND DUMPS IT ON HIS BED, SETS DOWN T'S GLASSES ON TOP OF THE SHERLOCK HOLMES BOOK. SHE SETS THE WATER PITCHER IN THE SINK AND TURNS ON THE WATER TO FILL IT UP, GOES BACK TO THE TABLE, PICKS UP A DEAD LEAF FROM THE FLOWERS THE FRENCH GUEST BROUGHT, MOVES BACK TO THE SINK, TURNS OFF THE WATER, REACHES UNDERNEATH THE PILE OF DISHES FOR THE SPONGE, WETS IT UNDER THE FAUCET AND WRINGS IT OUT, BRINGS IT BACK TO THE TABLE. THE FOOD IS ENCRUSTED AND IT TAKES SOME HEAVY SCRUBBING TO LOOSEN IT. SHE FINISHES SCRUBBING, TAKES THE SPONGE BACK TO THE SINK, RETURNS TO THE TABLE, ORGANIZES THE CHAIRS AROUND IT, BENDS DOWN TO PICK UP A FORK, A RANDOM PIECE OF PAPER, DEPOSITS ONE IN THE SINK AND THE OTHER IN THE GARBAGE, THEN HEADS FOR THE BROOM.

I CAN RUN. I'M QUITE A GOOD RUNNER, ACTUALLY. MY RED RUNNING SHOES ARE SLEEK, WITH PINK STRIPES ON THE SIDES. MY DAUGHTER DOESN'T LIKE THAT COLOR COMBINATION, BUT I MUST NOT BE THE ONLY ONE WHO DOES BECAUSE, AFTER ALL, SOMEONE MANUFACTURED THEM. AFTER I PUT ON THE SHOES I ATTACH THE LITTLE WINGS TO MY ANKLES. THEY'RE QUITE SMALL, THE FEATHERS SILKY WHITE AND INVISIBLE. NO ONE KNOWS WHAT MAKES ME GO SO FAST AND GLIDE SO SMOOTHLY, BARELY MOVING MY LEGS. I COVER A LOT OF DISTANCE THIS WAY. LET'S SEE, IF I LEAVE AROUND MIDNIGHT I'LL BE WEST OF PENNSYLVANIA BY DAWN. I WON'T STAY THERE THOUGH. I'LL GO EVEN FARTHER, SO THEY CAN'T TRACK ME DOWN. OF COURSE THEY MIGHT NOT EVEN TRY, ALTHOUGH THAT THOUGHT MAKES ME SHUDDER. I'LL SET MYSELF UP ONCE I GET THERE, IN A LITTLE TOWN IN NEBRASKA, ONE I DROVE THROUGH ONCE, WITH BRIGHT GREEN HILLS, CLEAR SKIES AND SHARP SHADOWS. THE CLOUDS ARE ENDLESS, WHITE AND COTTONY, AND THE TOWN IS NOT SO UGLY. AS A MATTER OF FACT THE MAIN STREET IS QUITE CHARMING. I'LL SHOW UP JUST LIKE THAT, I'LL WALK INTO THE LUNCHEONETTE, CARRYING MY SUITCASE. I'VE ALWAYS INTENDED TO BRING MY GRANDFATHER'S STRAW SUITCASE. IT'S SMALL AND FIRM, WITH A LATCH THAT SNAPS SHUT, AND STILL IN GOOD SHAPE DESPITE ITS AGE. I HAVEN'T BROUGHT MUCH, A FEW CHANGES OF UNDERWEAR, A NIGHTGOWN, MY TOOTHBRUSH AND THE NOTEBOOKS. BUT I CAN ALWAYS GO TO WALMART. I BET THERE'S ONE ON THE OTHER SIDE OF THE HILL. I WALK INTO THE LUNCHEONETTE AND ASK ABOUT THE APARTMENT FOR RENT SIGN IN THE WINDOW. I'M GUIDED TO A MAN SITTING AT THE COUNTER. HE'S THE PERFECT GRIZZLY OLD FARMER, WHO HAPPENS TO CONVENIENTLY OWN THE BUILDING. I SIT DOWN NEXT TO HIM AT THE COUNTER. COFFEE, I SAY, MILK AND SUGAR, LOTS OF SUGAR. HE LIKES THAT, FOR SOME REASON. HE LAUGHS, A LOW THROATY GUFFAW. I MOVE IN THAT SAME DAY. THE PLACE NEEDS PAINTING BUT AS THERE'S NO PAINT STORE IN TOWN, I TAKE A FEW DAYS TO SCRUB IT DOWN. IT DOESN'T LOOK SO BAD WHEN I'M FINISHED. I GET A JOB IN THE LUNCHEONETTE, OF COURSE. IT'S ALL PART OF THE PLAN. I FALL SOMEWHAT EASILY INTO MY NEW LIFE. NO ONE KNOWS WHO I AM, OR WHERE I'M FROM, AND THEY DON'T ASK. I'M NOT SUCH A GOOD WAITRESS AT FIRST. BUT AS THE LUNCHEONETTE IS NEVER CROWDED, I HAVE TIME TO PRACTICE, AND BEFORE LONG I CAN BALANCE TWO OR THREE PLATES AT A TIME. IT'S QUITE AN ACCOMPLISHMENT, IF I DO SAY SO MYSELF. ***TIME PASSES.*** HOW MUCH TIME REALLY? IT'S HARD TO SAY, IT COULD BE A FEW MONTHS, OR YEARS. LOOKING BACK, IT SEEMS FOREVER, ALTHOUGH I DON'T FEEL MUCH OLDER. I'M SURROUNDED BY THE SILENCE I CREATED. IT *IS* WHAT I WANTED. AN ENDING? COULD IT BE POSSIBLE THAT SOMEONE WHO KNOWS ME WALKS INTO THE LUNCHEONETTE? A PHONE CALL? HAVE THEY TRACKED ME DOWN? OR IS IT MY OWN LONGING? DOES A WOMAN, A MOTHER, REALLY LEAVE THIS WAY? BECAUSE WHEN SHE LEAVES THEM BEHIND, ARE THEY NOT STILL ALWAYS WITH HER? I BEND DOWN AND PUT ON MY RUNNING SHOES. THEY'RE BLUE, MUCH SIMPLER THAN MY OLD ONES, NO STRIPE. I TIE ON THE WINGS. ALTHOUGH THEY HAVEN'T BEEN USED SINCE I CAME HERE, THEY'RE INTACT. THEY KNOW WHAT TO DO. THE WIND WHISTLES IN MY EARS AS I MOVE SWIFTLY ALONG. I MEAN TO GO WEST BUT SOMEHOW I AM COMING BACK WHERE I STARTED. I AM HIGHER THAN I WAS BEFORE AND CAN SEE MORE OF THE LANDSCAPE, GREAT VISTAS STRETCHING OUT BEFORE ME. THE EAST COAST IS REALLY BEAUTIFUL FROM THIS HEIGHT. WHAT IF THEY SLAM THE DOOR IN MY FACE? WELL OF COURSE I CAN RUN. I'M A GOOD RUNNER, ACTUALLY. ALTHOUGH I'VE NEVER RUN THE MARATHON. IT JUST FEELS THAT WAY.

Domesticity into art

Since my daughter was very young she has been fascinated with napkins and dish towels. First, she learned to place them on the floor and smooth them, eliminating every last wrinkle. From age one till twenty months or so she played a game of conceptual order and disorder. As soon as she learned to say the word "napin" she wanted them all; all the napkins and dish towels were spread out, smoothed and arranged around the house in spontaneous configurations, some bespeaking order, others chaos. We tiptoed carefully in order not to disturb the designs. As she grew, the napkins took on additional functions. She became interested in folding them. "Corner to corner," I told her. They were both beds and covers for dolls and animals.

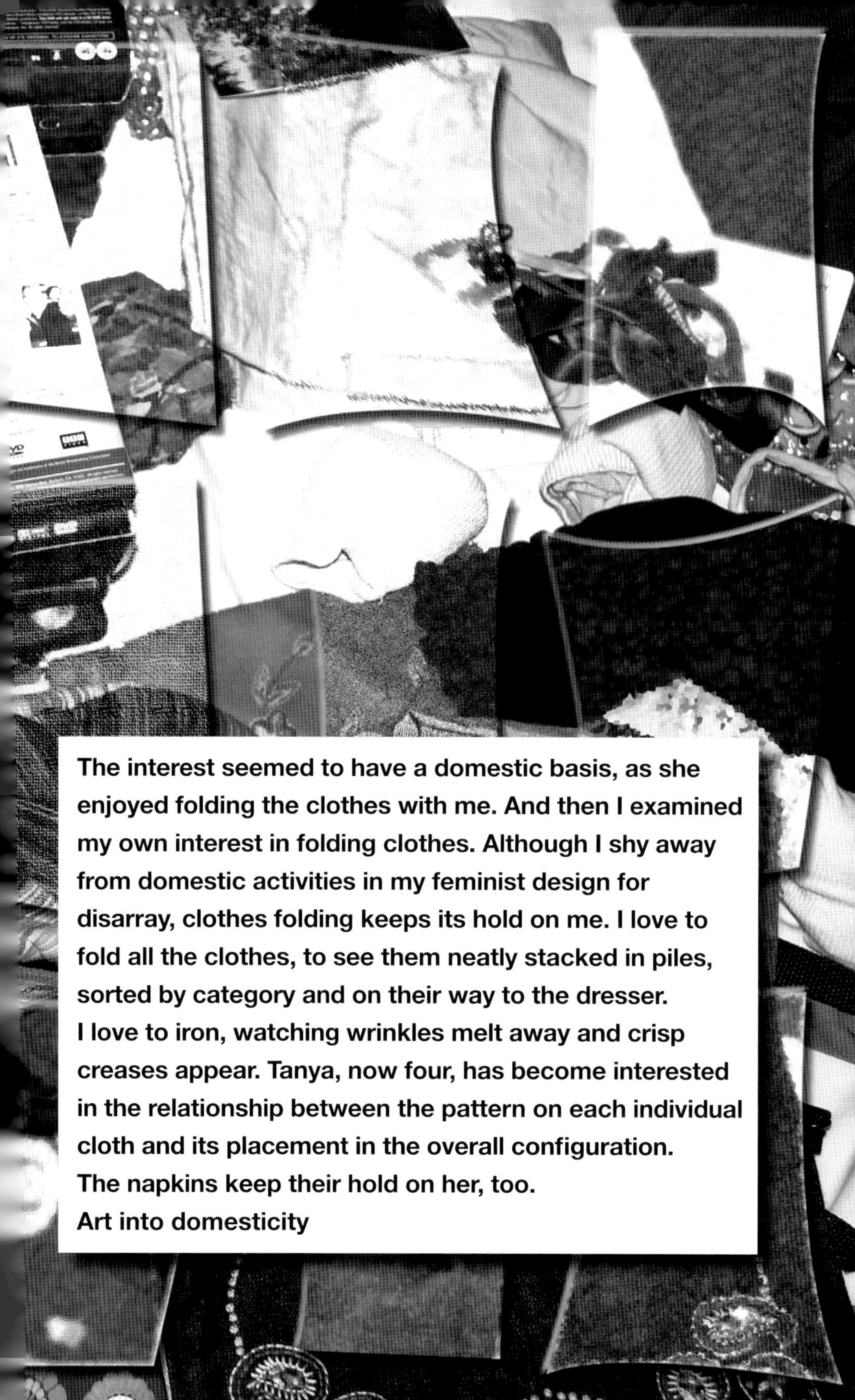

The interest seemed to have a domestic basis, as she enjoyed folding the clothes with me. And then I examined my own interest in folding clothes. Although I shy away from domestic activities in my feminist design for disarray, clothes folding keeps its hold on me. I love to fold all the clothes, to see them neatly stacked in piles, sorted by category and on their way to the dresser.
I love to iron, watching wrinkles melt away and crisp creases appear. Tanya, now four, has become interested in the relationship between the pattern on each individual cloth and its placement in the overall configuration.
The napkins keep their hold on her, too.
Art into domesticity

TIME PASSES

MYREL CHERNICK, 2006

ELLEN McMAHON

Art Between Us

WHEN MY DAUGHTER ALICE WAS seventeen she was assigned a series of narrative images for her high school photography class. She cast me as Medea, the mythic child murderer, applied scary makeup to my face and teased my hair into a terrible tangle. She painted herself and her twelve-year-old sister Della with red watercolor—little trickles of blood from their eyes and mouths. In one of the photographs I'm holding Della dead in my arms like the Pietà. For another shot Alice used a tripod and cable release so she could show me tenderly tucking both of them into bed, dead. She told me my expression should be serene and calm because she wanted to bring out the beauty of the scene. She made black and white prints in the darkroom at school and then began to experiment with the color processor. She made an oversized print of one of the images of Della, dead in my arms, in lurid tones of red and yellow and gave it to her for Christmas.

Years later Della still displays it proudly on her bedroom wall. It seems to represent their solidarity, the way they suffer living as children under the unfair rule of parents, me in particular. Alice submitted slides of these images to apply for a scholarship from the university where I teach. As a member of the scholarship committee, I sat in a darkened room with my colleagues when suddenly I appeared larger than life on the screen, holding my dead and bloody children in my arms.

* * *

When Alice was born I was a professional designer with ambitions to be an artist. Five years later, pregnant with my second child, I was hired in a tenure-track teaching position without the terminal degree necessary to be tenured. So I enrolled in a low-residency MFA in Visual Art and spent a few years teaching full time, raising young children, being a graduate student, traveling to lecture and exhibit my work and eventually was tenured.

My MFA exhibition was about the pressures of my daily life and my ambivalence toward motherhood. It consisted of oversized photographic self-portraits, my head wrapped in baby undershirts, covered with projections of my daughters' writing and drawing. The photographs were printed on vellum and hung from the ceiling a foot or so from the wall. Large vinyl letters on the wall behind them told stories of my power struggles with Della as a formidable toddler.

My husband and I went into considerable debt furthering my education, so after I was tenured I moved out of my large studio and started making artist books in my office at the university. They were small, economical to produce, easy to transport and conducive to combining text and images.

* * *

Alice showed early signs of artistic inclination in her focus and serious approach to making things. I have a photograph of her at five years old ceremoniously sticking a small ball of mud onto the spikey leaf of a desert Agave plant in our front yard. Another more distant shot shows that she has adorned the sharp spike at the end of every one of the 40 or 50 leaves on the plant with a mud ball or Palo Verde bean.

When she was nine I had to stop bringing her to my studio because of her fascination with my materials and the ferocity of her artistic vision. Within an hour of her arrival, I'd find myself dashing around mixing her plaster, finding her wood, wire, wax, ribbon, sticks, glue, paper, ink or a certain color or type of paint.

Alice was interested in everything, companionable and sweet during her preadolescent years. She was compassionate and patient even through her younger sister Della's hours of tantrums. Her extreme shyness was the only thing that seemed to trouble her. Alice was eleven when I had my MFA exhibition. She spent a long time contemplating the work and asked, "How come your art is always about Della and never about me?"

I told her I made art about things that trouble me and maybe when she's a teenager it will be about her. The first part is true, but I said the second part playfully because I didn't think it would happen.

* * *

A few years later, when Alice was fifteen and entering high school she had transformed herself into a walking work of art, her shyness seeming to flip into theatrical flamboyance. She withdrew behind a mask of makeup, plucked her eyebrows down to tiny fine arches, and dyed her hair maroon. She wore thrift shop clothes that she cut up and tacked back together Frankenstein-style with crooked hand-sewn seams of silver thread. She drew big black stars with permanent markers on both of her arms and shredded her stockings into tangled black webs. She produced a series of photographic self-portraits taken late at night in her room. In them she plays an array of glamorous and often tragic characters in chaotic apocalyptic settings. In one she is covered in glitter—or is it dirt—looking over her shoulder into a broken mirror. In another she is wide-eyed, staring in terror into the camera with thick black stripes painted across her mouth and eyes.

One morning when I woke her up for school, she opened her door covered from head to foot in downy multicolored feathers that she had rubber-cemented all over her face and body the night before. After the photo shoot in the wee hours of the morning she was so tired she just curled up in her feathers and fell asleep. She was a dazzling sight but the rubber cement jar she left open all night in her room necessitated yet another motherly lecture about the hazards of art materials. Like all my advice it fell on deaf ears, maybe more so that day because of her rubber-cement headache.

Later in the semester her art teacher invited her to exhibit some of her work in a display case at the public library. The vertical case was three feet wide, three feet deep and seven feet high with three glass shelves. The work had to be there in a week and I'm sure Alice's teacher thought she would submit something she'd done in the class. But Alice thought about the situation for a few days then asked if I'd buy her forty pounds of clay. She collected some big branches from the craggy desert mesquite tree in our front yard and for the next four days and nights sat on her bedroom floor, producing three anatomically accurate clay figures, in graduated sizes, using only her own body for reference. For the largest one, which was almost life-sized, she used my aluminum mixing bowl as an armature. The figure is on her knees, bowing forward with her forehead on the ground. A fan of two-foot-long black branches juts out of her spinal column. The next one down in size is sitting cross-legged with her back arched way back with a mass of tangled branches thrusting out of her abdomen. The smallest figure has her head thrown back, branches projecting out of her mouth in a frozen scream.

It took the whole family to transport the sculptures, still wet, downtown to the library in cardboard boxes. They were impossibly fragile because they were unfired. When I mentioned this to Alice she said it was part of the concept to have the figures crumble under the pressure of the branches as the clay dried in the library case. These sculptures expressed what Alice couldn't put into words. She was crumbling under the pressure of her life at fifteen.

Later, I discovered she had also started secretly cutting herself.

***

A few months later, as I was leaving the house for yoga class, I noticed the light on in the bathroom. It seemed too early for either of the kids to be awake. I went up to the partially closed door to say I was leaving. I heard a faint "don't go" and opened the door to find Alice lying on the floor curled around the toilet. In a barely audible voice she said, "I need you to take me to the hospital. I'm sick. I've taken a lot of Tylenol."

I called 911 and heard the siren before I even hung up the phone. I didn't realize the gravity of our emergency. I didn't know how deadly Tylenol could be. The first response was a fire truck. One of the medics knelt down by Alice and asked, "Were you trying to kill yourself?" She looked startled and confused and said no. Later she explained she had just stayed up late making an oil painting on the inside of her door, gotten a really bad headache and taken a handful of Tylenol. She spent several days in the hospital getting a treatment that blocked the drug from destroying her liver.

She looked so little in her hospital gown, so young and vulnerable without her makeup. She was writing a paper about Frida Kahlo for her Art History class and lay in her hospital bed flipping listlessly through a book of Kahlo's self-portraits, vivid paintings of her body, broken by a bus accident and recuperating in bed from the numerous surgeries that followed.

I was consumed with worry and guilt. I vowed to try harder to understand Alice, figure out what was best for her, and show her that I was someone she could always count on. After she recovered, she told me she was grateful for the near-death experience because it helped her get over the shyness. After the Tylenol overdose she was required to get regular counseling. At one point she was evaluated by a psychiatrist who told us he thought Alice might be borderline bipolar. He told her he could prescribe something to help her sleep and relieve her anxiety, but warned it would reduce her intensity, maybe her creativity, definitely her all-night art-making sessions.

A couple of days later when we were riding in the car she said out of the blue, "That was scary, what he said."

Alice knew that making art was integral to how she negotiated the world, so she didn't see the drugs he offered as an option. I agreed with her decision but must admit I loved the idea of a pharmaceutical silver bullet, a chemical cure for her suffering and the helplessness I felt in the face of it.

***

Shaken from the events of Alice's first year in high school, I was glad to leave town for our annual summer vacation at my mother's beach house. Alice, still sullen and withdrawn, was miserable about being trapped with the family and geographically separated from her recent romantic interest. One sunny morning when we were all getting ready to go to the beach, Alice pulled me aside and fixed me with a desperate look. "Mom, I need you to help me with a photo project but you can't ask a lot of questions or keep me from doing anything I need to do."

Though I was looking forward to a day on the beach, our relationship had been distant and strained for the last year and I saw this as an opportunity to build some trust between us, to demonstrate that I took her seriously as a person and as an artist. I agreed to her conditions. I would be the silent assistant.

We went to the small upstairs bedroom, which was stuffy, hot and humid. She had some black markers and a notebook of her writing and told me where she wanted me to write each one of the words and phrases: *life* and *death* on the bottoms of her feet; *something poisonous, delicious, forbidden* on her lower back; *I was dying but inside her I lived* on her stomach. She took various poses and directed me as I shot several rolls of film over the next few hours.

As the photographer, I was utterly absorbed in my job. But as her mother I was confused and conflicted. I felt like she had taken me hostage, and at the same time as if I was invading her privacy.

But I had another feeling that trumped the others, deeper and subtler, that kept me going through my discomfort and resentment. I felt grateful for the chance to show her that I saw her for who she was, and that I wouldn't recoil from what she showed me. She needed proof. Could I handle this, support her on her own path to becoming?

She was making the pictures to send to the person she had a crush on back home. But the phrases also referred to us, and the irrefutable truth between all biological mothers and their children, that every day after the moment of birth is about separating and that this wrenching apart into two separate people involves a perpetual act of mourning the loss of the other.

When we took a break from our photo session, I saw our reflection in the big oval mirror above the dresser. I was facing the mirror agitated and exhausted. She was facing me, back to the mirror, in her body writing, looking over her shoulder blowing a big triumphant bubble with her gum. I was holding the camera, so even though it wasn't part of her plan, I took the picture. She didn't show me the pictures I took that day. She got them developed and sent a bunch of them to her crush back home. In the fall she made prints in her high school darkroom from some of the negatives. Six months later for Christmas she presented me with a thrift shop framed 8 x 10 print of the picture I took of us in the mirror. I propped it on my bedroom dresser and looked at it often over the next several months.

To avoid the pitfalls of voyeurism and sentimentality, I stopped using images of my daughters in my artwork when I was in graduate school. But this picture of Alice and me reflected in my mother's mirror, taken candidly by *me*, in the middle of an art project directed by *her* and featuring *her* almost naked body, covered with *my* writing of *her* words, created to send to *her* first romantic interest captured the complexity of our intertwined relationship more effectively than any of my previous work. I wrote a short description of my experience of that day and combined the picture and the text in a handmade book I titled *Alice's Idea.* The project was a turning point for me as I began to see my writing as an important part of my creative practice, and as a way to help me understand, detach, be present, and keep my sanity through the next few years.

***

In Euripides' version of the story, Medea is not punished for her transgression but protected by the Gods, carried away from the tragic scene in a chariot of fire. Killing her children is an act of vengeance but it is also a sacrifice in the truest sense. She gives up what is most beloved to her in an act that cuts both ways, as self-destruction and self-empowerment, in the end connecting her to the sacred.

I'm struck by the way the photographs Alice took of me as Medea cut both ways. I felt exposed and embarrassed in relation to my colleagues and at the same time proud and powerful in the role of this tragic mythic character. Was Alice tapping into my desire to reclaim myself, the identity I swallowed during the years of marriage and motherhood? Did I need to face the Medea in me who was feeling oppressed and disempowered, to turn the tables and rise up in heroic vengeance, make the journey to the underworld and return renewed and enlightened, finally free? When Alice did that project she was almost eighteen and would soon be moving away for the summer. I knew she would eventually return to her hometown for college but with a new independence from me. This was a year of significant separation for us. At the time no one knew it would also be the year I would end my twenty-year marriage.

* * *

A few weeks after Alice graduated from high school, she and her dad both moved out. I began to read through the box of journals I filled during Alice's teen years to select passages to piece into an essay I'd been invited to write for an anthology. Alice knew I was working on the essay and asked several times if she could read it during the two years it was in progress. I always planned for her to have final veto power over any parts she objected to before it went public, but wanted it to be finished before she read it. When it was accepted for publication I handed it to her saying, "Remember you are fictionalized here in the sense that this is just my version of what happened."

She said, "I've thought about it and I don't think I'm ready to read it. I'm afraid I'll take it too personally and it wouldn't be good for me now."

I was impressed by her judgment as much as I was relieved. I actually hoped she would never read it. I don't think any child should see themselves through their mother's ambivalent eyes. Mother love is supposed to be unconditional and uncomplicated. I was also mortified. Without her okay, how could I publish it, knowing she could read it after it was published and might never forgive me? Then to raise the emotional stakes, she smiled sweetly and added, "I trust you, Mom."

By refusing to read the essay she made me entirely responsible for my words. For months as the essay went through final edits, my stomach hurt as I agonized about whether to publish it or not. One day she mentioned casually that she found the essay weeks before by my computer and read most of it. She said, "I cried hard but really like it and I'm fine with it being published."

* * *

Now Alice is twenty-three, making room-sized installations in her last year as a sculpture major in the school where I teach. As I look back on her teen years, I see the myriad ways we used art between us; sometimes as a tenuous suspension bridge, the only thing connecting us, sometimes as a mirror we held up to help us see ourselves or to show the other what we saw, sometimes as a decoy to draw attention away from what was really going on, sometimes as a semi-permeable membrane, letting in only what we could handle at the time. Art was a comfort, a test, a microscope, a smoke screen, a reward, a gift, a lesson, and a love letter. We weren't using art on purpose. It didn't occur to us that it would help. It's just something we did that happened to work.

LESLIE REID

Afterimage

A Journal of Making Art and Mothering Teens

I TURNED TO IDEAS OF motherhood, particularly maternal ambivalence, in my painting and photography, when my two sons were no longer young children, but moving towards adolescence. It was a time when I finally felt confident enough to look at my life as a mother in my painting. I had not been able to do so in their early childhood, when I had little energy, less confidence, and even less desire to think about motherhood as a possible issue for my work (any work at all seemed a major achievement) and when I clung to the belief that my concerns in art had not changed just because I was a mother. Neither did the discipline of visual arts particularly encourage such an exploration of the experience and meaning of motherhood. And so I lived through a long period of denial

Cantley: Spiral, 1996. Cibachrome, 9 × 13 inches.

Cantley VI, 1993. Cibachrome, 8 × 12 inches.

and self-censorship in my work, before I found the courage to address motherhood in painting.

The work on the theme of motherhood and maternal ambivalence began with a serendipitous moment of revelation while sorting through family photographs, snapshots really, which led to an urgent desire to explore my reluctance to dig into this, the center of my life—"digging into the wreck,"as Adrienne Rich calls it in *Of Woman Born.*

I believe that many of the difficulties artists face in addressing our roles as mothers arise from the fact that, not surprisingly, we are fearful of the deep and unspoken ambivalence we often experience in that role. We also fear the effects, both private and public, of any acknowledgment of that ambivalence. And for artists, the representation of motherhood remains especially difficult, coloured by association with essentialism, sentiment and autobiography.

I have always used photographs as source material for my painting, but I consciously eliminated all reference to my maternal life in work that dealt with the physical, perceptual and emotional effects of light. Photographs of my two sons swimming in a pond, a pond image I had used in many unpeopled paintings, triggered my recognition of the need to turn to my motherhood as the focus of my work, and led me to look at maternal ambivalence as subject.

The intensity of my response to these photographs took me by surprise. The images were ambiguous, revealing a darker side of my connectedness to my sons, one of anxiety and some dread, and a recognition of both external and internal danger.

In the photographs and paintings of the children, these ambiguities are evoked by shadow and by absence, my absence. The figures are often held transfixed in rings of water; faces are obscured, lost in patterns of light and shade. Connection between mother and sons seems tenuous at best, fragile and threatened. I am present only as watcher. A hovering and subtle uncertainty pervades each image.

The optical phenomenon of afterimage not only provides an apt description of the ever-shifting light/dark tonal aspects of my work but also represents the positive and negative, light and shadow character of mothering, especially in mothering teens. As my sons grow closer to adulthood, my perceptions of them, of myself, and of our constantly shifting and often fraught relationship have of necessity changed, and these perceptions are transforming the paintings. The narrative communicated by the light/dark images, like the boys themselves, is becoming more assertive. The often conflicting perceptions of our changing roles are bringing new emotions to the surface, appearing, almost literally at times, in the images of my sons and of the ponds and rivers that occur repeatedly in my work.

Now I am dealing with these new concerns: the challenges and perils of making art about mothering teens, and the seeming impossibility of seizing this time in my life and in my work. I feel both great need and resistance in trying to capture the chaotic feelings of release and regret that accompany this time. It is a period of breaking away and letting go, of stepping back even as I reach out a hand. My older son is now 18, a self-declared, legally independent adult male. Yet somehow clean socks and a full refrigerator remain issues. I'm still on call.

Family photos have been a critical source of reflection and investigation of my changing experience of motherhood, and the basis for my painting and drawing for some years. Now there are few photo opportunities. My sons are more resistant, especially to cameras, and are seldom home. It is harder to mark my presence or my absence, or my ambivalent feelings about the enterprise of mothering. I feel such a poignant regret, much stronger than I had anticipated, at this turning point in our lives as mother and sons. I am facing testosterone-driven individuation, and unlike that of infancy, it seems to be happening without me; I am unable to influence how, when and where it occurs. It is gathering noisy momentum. I am becoming someone other as well.

Are these changing relationships affecting my work? These inevitable changes seem to have become harder to deal with than I expected. Per-

Calumet: For a While, 2004. Cibachrome, 8 × 10 inches.

haps it is because I am living the changes even as I paint and write. My mothering role becomes more tenuous and contingent than ever through their growing separation, as does my presence as artist. Can I continue to work with these issues of maternal ambivalence as the relationship changes so dramatically? My work now seems to be coloured by a longing for a time available only in memory. The present asserts itself with harsh insistence. My sons' startlingly deep voices and large bodies fill the house.

I am more and more the watcher, a less visible presence in their lives. This creates a disturbing shift for my work. Once again I seem to be editing my mothering relationship out of the visual field. Even as we are needed, we aging mothers of adolescents become invisible, and we are expected to accept this as inevitable and necessary.

It appears that what we desire is not necessarily what we get as adolescent independence asserts itself. I need both love and my own independent strategy to reclaim my own desire. Perhaps my work as artist/mother can continue to provide some of that strategy.

No one can truly describe the extraordinary rush of emotion that comes with birth; but none of the stories I heard prepared me for the teenage individuation mothering experience. I find myself resisting while dealing with great need, impatience, hostility, grandiosity. And I am searching for the parallels in my work.

Teens are central in our culture, in so many areas driving it, in music, film, video, fashion. Yet critical writing about mothering teens is hard to find, other than the teen management or tough-love help books. It is hard to find serious study of what is arguably the most turbulent and contradictory period of our mothering lives. I have found little to dispel my growing discomfort at the seeming inevitability of my disappearance. Not only am I destined to bow out or be pushed out, but I will be viewed as the all-engulfing monster no matter what I do. The psychoanalytic literature is not very encouraging for mothers of teens. (Even Freud chose to ignore mothers and teens. I think he had an eye on his career.)

Delving into issues of maternal ambivalence in painting was such an intensely affirming act when dealing with the children when they were younger. But as the relationship shifts, ambivalence as I explored it in those works, when feelings of almost overwhelming fear and anxiety dominated, has shifted also. Fear and absence have taken on very different meanings.

How does this conflicted period translate into work? With as great difficulty as the relationships themselves, much to my chagrin, for I had optimistically assumed that here at least I could hold my own, hang onto what was properly mine: my work. But the struggles of adolescent individuation and teenage separation have accompanied me to the studio, and their images, once viewed more innocently, now seem taunting, challenging: hold onto us if you can.

The issues are still there, to examine in my work: to find the threads that still connect, if not bind, before the inevitable feelings of "too late" set in. Am I moving towards memory? Or am I already there?

But of course the answer is already within the work—my painting is not a study of my sons; it is about the critical space of the mother-child relationship. Art about children abounds in the culture right now, and has always been around, going in and out of fashion. But art about mothers has not had a very positive critical reception—when it has attracted any notice at all. Reviews are rare, and when they do occur they are often thoughtlessly dismissive. It is therefore all the more important for me to continue this critical exploration.

I have been sensitive to my sons' reactions to being used so publicly, though their identities are not obvious. While they expressed a certain shy reservation at the outset, I think that, as well as being reassured that they appear fairly anonymously, they have become quite pleased by their inclusion in my work. My desire to explore our relationship outside of the usual family arena, in works of art, provides a different kind of connection for them, one that seems to have taken on an enriching personal meaning. (They have also mentioned modeling fees.)

Cantley: Spiral, 1998. Oil on canvas, 48 × 72 inches.

Calumet: For a While, 2006. Oil on canvas, 51 × 68 inches.

At the same time, even as our relationship is intrinsic to my work, the work is separate from them. It is my accomplishment that is visible, and this has the added value, as Babette Smith has noted in *Mothers and Sons*, of allowing them to view my accomplishments apart from themselves, unrelated to raising them.[1]

It is critical for me to acknowledge my lived experience as mother in my work as painter. I believe with curator Jan Allen that acknowledgement of that experience is essential to the understanding of why art would be made at all.[2]

As for my teenagers and me, I know our relationship will endure, altered but ongoing. Perhaps it will exist as what anthropologist Sarah Hrdy has likened to a phantom limb.

It is up to us as mothers to reclaim connection, and in the new paintings of transition, it is that connectedness, mercurial, paradoxical and essential, that I will continue to explore.

Notes

[1]Babette Smith, *Mothers and Sons* (St. Leonards, NSW Australia: Allen & Unwin, 1995), 117.

[2]Jan Allen, *Fertile Ground* (Kingston, ON: Agnes Etherington Art Centre, Queen's University, Kingston, Canada, 1996), 24.

MARGARET MORGAN

Fragments

Pie

THE CRUST WAS TOO TOUGH, airless, brittle, a snap in two or in several parts, dry, thin. An overabundance of sauce, runny, too hot, overcooked. Steam spurted from the broken carapace, a burning splash on unexpected hand. Still tastes okay she said optimistically. Yes he said not entirely convinced but hungry. Later when they were fucking her brittle and hardened skin had broken all apart like something out of Patti Smith, and a flood of pleasure had overwhelmed them both, long hungered for, thirst quenched in exact synchronicity with the waking cry of their little girl, the two female voices in unison—a release and an ending, sudden, emphatic—as she, no sooner having come, then jumping to her mother's feet, slipping in the sex juice on the floor of her studio, slid into the role of care giver, tripping, breaking small bones, awkward and ambivalent, as clumsy but as indisputable as that chicken pot pie.

Red Letter Day

I measure time in toilet rolls. When I look down I am shocked to see that my child's nails are long—again. I notice the passing weeks by the sun's passage along the ridge before me. I am in that gray zone that is the speeding up of the time machine of Jules Verne, night and day blurred together, a gray zone five of indeterminacy. I pick lint from the dryer and think of Mary Kelly. I pull wads of cotton and hair from the drain, and think of, who was that filmmaker? I think of no one. I suckle. The milk is always making its presence felt, like a separate being.

So this morning I wake up and, coming into consciousness, dimly recognizing that old wooziness, feeling those sticky, drying juices beneath me, I roll over like the lumpen animal I have become: and sure enough, there, on the sheet beneath my sleep, is the small telltale spot: well, what do you know, said I to myself, look who's come to visit, my period, my bloody period. I feel the old familiar tug, for the first time in thirty-two months. Not that I'm counting, but, hey, I meant to write "counting" and instead typed "ac-counting," which tells you something of the state of my being. So, maybe I was keeping track. But in any case, as I was saying, there's an old friend at my door. We haven't been close in recent times, I've shunned her in fact, she's been a matter of mourning for me, her reds have made me blue. But not this morning, no siree. This morning I welcome her. "Spread yourself out, make yourself comfortable, all is forgiven!" say I to my old friend. I revel in the drag of a contracting uterus, the snake inside that is shedding its skin. I delight in the pull of the ineluctable, the beginning of a good four-day bleed. The last times I felt such pangs—it was years ago now—they were full of ennui and the ring of death, no baby, bo-a-baby, baby-baby, a gentle despair that slid into place as the blood seeped and oozed and drained down the toilet bowl each day after day, each month after month.

But now, not now, that blood, as if on a virgin's nuptials, is a source of delight and pride: it is my subjectivity—a self born anew, a self returned to me, a self after and beyond the breast. Ah yes, I remember me well. Here I am, still here. I ache. I bleed. I bleed therefore I am. I watch the flat of the television beyond the bulge of my personhood. I joggle my head from side to side, albeit in a futile game of cat and mouse with the too bright AM light of California bouncing off the screen. I am annoyed, but quietly delighting in the privilege of the annoyed. I refuse to budge. I revel in my corporeality. Still not attending to the stain that is at that very moment silently spreading, making its way into the soft, downy and expensive lower layers of the newly purchased mattress, I think to myself: Let it bleed! I am painting the town red. At the Nature Channel before me, I gloat: on the screen, an impassive mound of mother cat lying there with cubs attached, all squabbling and jostling among themselves—nothing to do with her—on all eight nipples. My nipple. No, mine. Mine! Mine! Mine! The kittens rule, and she is all squirting fluids and jiggling swollen pinkness. All nipple. All breast. Beast. I was myself that cat, a dripping padded thing, wads to contain the excess, my always large nipples enlarged some more and the nonexistent breast transformed into C cups and then, obscene Ds. Catwoman, a self dissolved or extended into the other, suckling partial self, which, though legally a separate entity, hangs on for dear life, waking, sleeping, shitting, crying to make the milk come, in synchronicity with you, its mother. And you with it. So, in all that time, of more than two mountainous mammalian years, whether because peri-menopausal or because my body had so wholeheartedly given itself over to the manufacture of nourishment for the infant, I never bled. Instead I flushed mildly, swelled, aged, and remained constantly, slightly, sweaty, and always, always, milky, translucent like the glass of an office door. I am the new mother of ripe middle age lactating with the symptoms of menopause.

But now here, still in bed, a bloody mess, coterminous with the decathecting, the final boredom with ~~nursing~~, no, breast-feeding (why the word *nurse*? I don't like it—it suggests illness, another pathologizing of motherhood), here, now, with that dragging, tugging, bleeding sensation—when am I me without my abjection?—I revel in the return to personhood. I am uterus, not nipple. Bleeding or no, this is me, mine. And this, on the very same day that my daughter, with as much aplomb as pride, iterates her own access to subjectivity that is the abjection of her very own shit into the Potty, into which thereafter she stared with her most curious crumpled frown clearly inherited from the forty-year-old, her father. For quite some time. We went then together, ceremoniously, to the toilet to empty the shit—her shit—into the bowl and then rinsed and rinsed and washed and washed and then ate *cooka* (cookies) to celebrate and this on the very day she, a discreet self, went for the second time to nursery school all on her own with other kids and caring strangers. So that while I bled, she seeped away too. A red-letter day for subjectivities accessed and returning. We—she and I—are still in synchronicity.

Reflection

Yesterday morning the child was perched on the edge of the bath waiting to have her teeth cleaned: peering closer, she smiled, and said, "I can see me in your eyes." I fell in love and was happy.

Later, in the car on the way to school, she asked, classically, "Where do babies come from?" I replied somewhat cryptically, thinking to myself that now was not the time for a lengthy discussion of recent technological advances, and of her own first photograph as an eight-cell organism, that usually a man and a woman make a baby: you know how a chicken egg gets fertilized (her friend Ella had hatched a flock of chicks the month before)? Well, the woman has the egg, way inside her vagina, and the man has the fertilizer, and it comes out his penis. Not exactly accurate but perhaps good enough. In her seat, reflecting upon the enormity of chicken life, she furrowed her brow and was silent.

Naming

"Naming is something like attaching a label to a thing. One can say that this is preparatory to the use of a *word*. But what is it a preparation *for*?" –Wittgenstein[1]

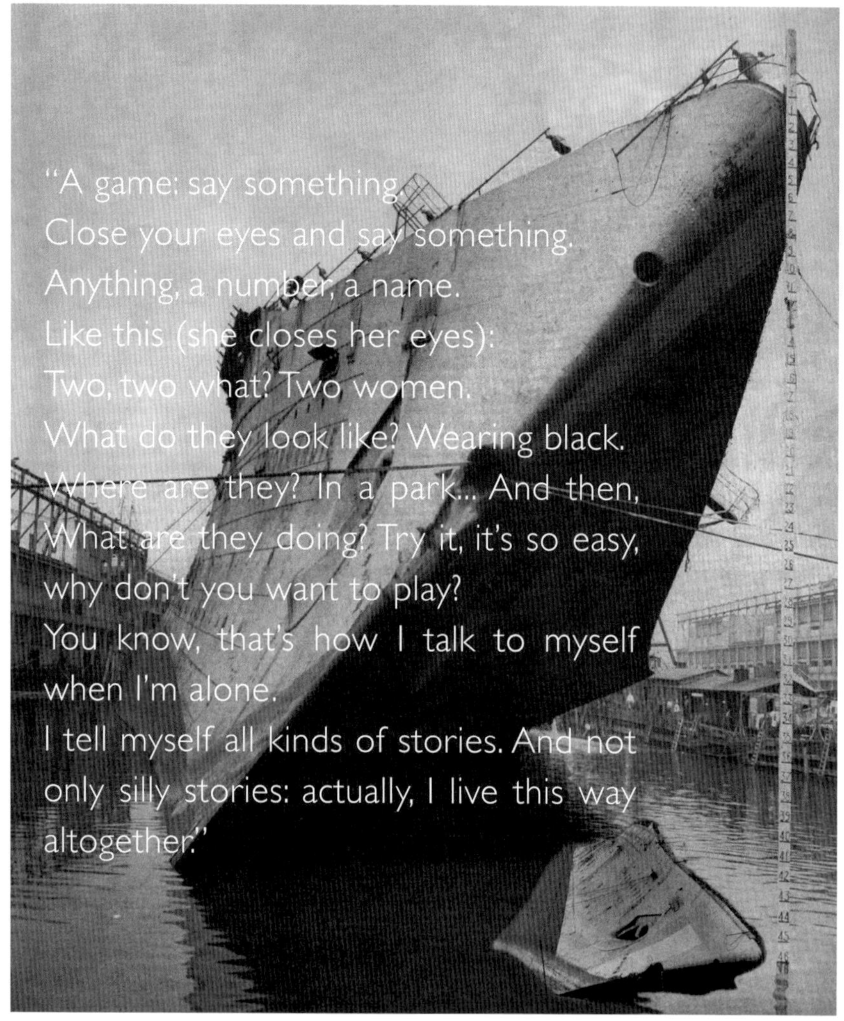

"A game: say something.
Close your eyes and say something.
Anything, a number, a name.
Like this (she closes her eyes):
Two, two what? Two women.
What do they look like? Wearing black.
Where are they? In a park... And then,
What are they doing? Try it, it's so easy,
why don't you want to play?
You know, that's how I talk to myself
when I'm alone.
I tell myself all kinds of stories. And not
only silly stories: actually, I live this way
altogether."

In 2006 Nadja Millner-Larsen completed *In the Room Without Mirrors*, a photomontage-text project about her projected relationship to the Nadja for whom she was named, the eponymous real-life character in the surrealist anti-novel by André Breton.

N a d j a

A photo-text collaboration between
Nadja Millner-Larsen and Sherry Millner

Twenty-five years ago (in 1983) Nadja's mother, Sherry Millner, completed a forty-minute video *Womb with a View*, explicitly structured as an unfinished novel in nine chapters, which considers pregnancy as a highly contradictory transitional state of being. This is how the video ends:

(sound of Fats Waller, singing *Seafood Mama*)

ROLLING TITLE:

At 9:49 AM on October 5 a healthy girl-child with the right number of fingers and toes was born into the world. After careful consideration (three days) her parents named her:

Nadja Odette Riley Millner-Larsen (N.O.R.M.L.)
and they lived happily ever after.

I. Naming

Nadja, we are told, identified with the Celtic myth of Melusine, who, due to a man's betrayal, was doomed to wander the earth forever as a monster: half-woman half-serpent. At the end of Breton's novel, Nadja is herself betrayed by her lover, and left in a mental asylum. Breton abandons Nadja upon recognizing her infallible irrationality (that serpent's tail). With her wandering mind, this doomed Nadja would never achieve the position of a stable subject within the work of art. Rather, Breton transformed Nadja's story into an art object.

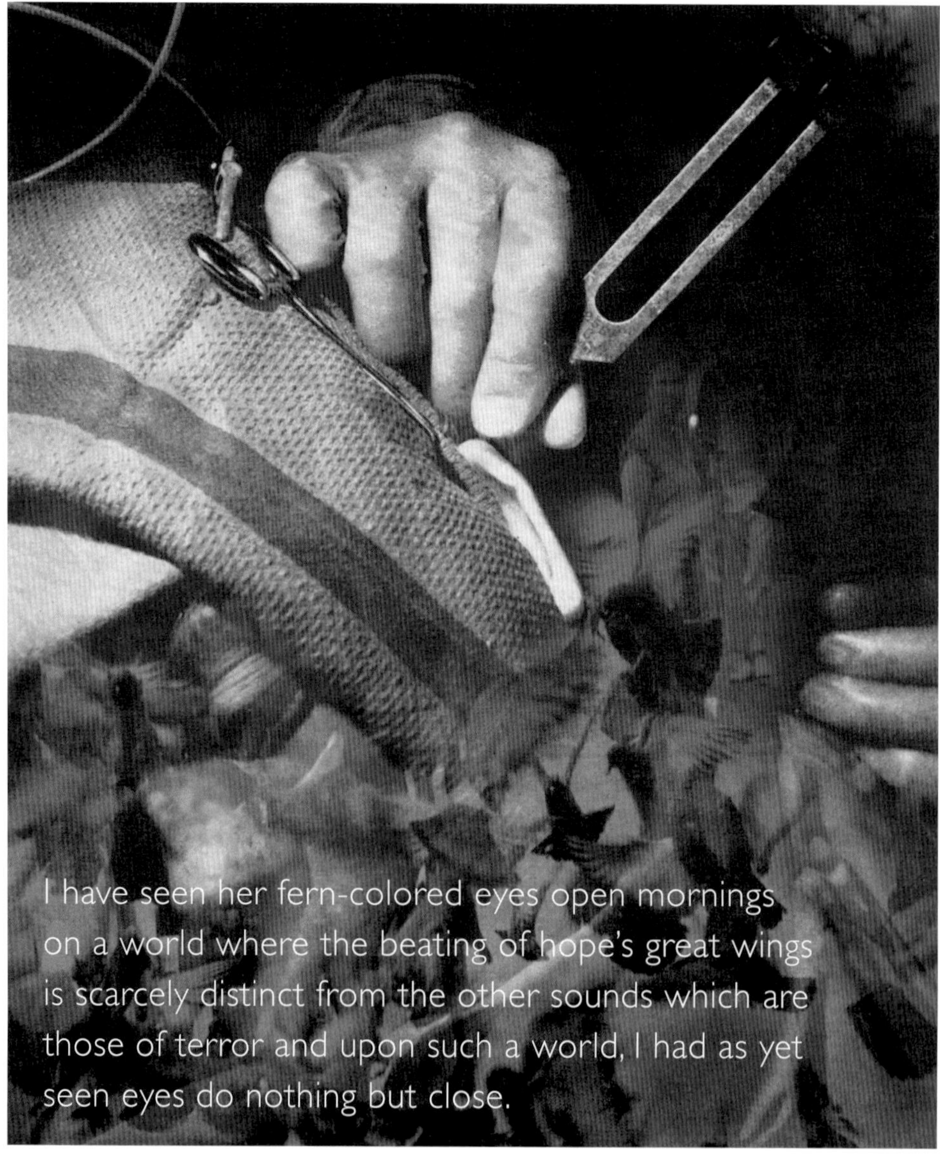

I have seen her fern-colored eyes open mornings
on a world where the beating of hope's great wings
is scarcely distinct from the other sounds which are
those of terror and upon such a world, I had as yet
seen eyes do nothing but close.

as an Aesthetic Act (Half-n-Half)

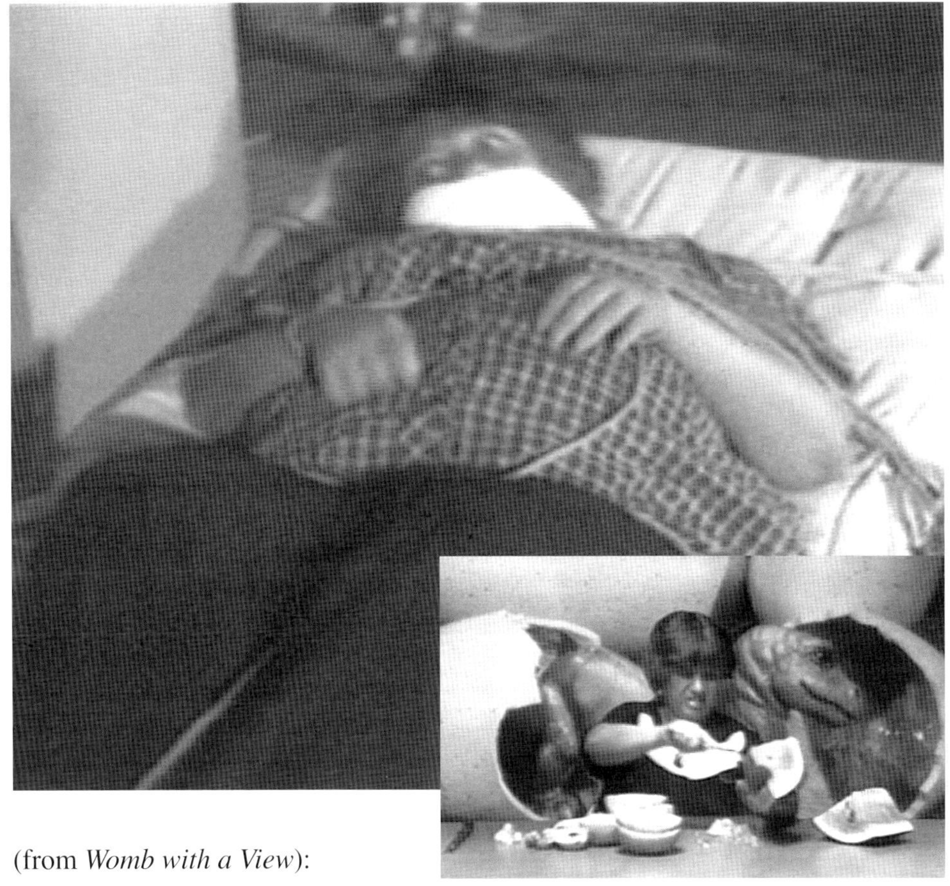

(from *Womb with a View*):

VO SHERRY: The sun blinded me....The blade advanced.

Cut to close-up of sawblade spinning. Screams of terror on soundrack.

VO SHERRY: It was a nightmare....The sun split me in two....

Camera pans over Sherry's struggling pregnant body, tied down with ropes. She strains and flails.

VO SHERRY: Half of me was an artist. Half of me was a nurturer. The sun burned into my body, into my brain. Half white light. Half red hot. A nightmare of split commitments. I keep trying not to see it as a contradiction. I won't let it tie me down. Any moment now I'll wake up.

II. Naming

"Women have had the power of naming stolen from us." –Mary Daley[2]

"…is the real Nadja this always inspired and inspiring creature who enjoyed being nowhere but in the streets, the only region of valid experience for her, in the street, accessible to interrogation from any human being launched upon some great chimera, or (why not admit it) the one who sometimes fell, since, after all, others had felt authorized to speak to her, had been able to see in her only the most wretched of women, and the least protected?" –Breton[3]

Less wretched perhaps, yet no less exhausted by the weight of femininity. Are my own visions separate from hers?

as a Feminist Act: Notes collected

(from *Womb with a View*):

VO SHERRY: The problem of naming the baby leads to the problem of naming the experience. Having a child, becoming a mother, giving birth, have often trapped women in the past.... How to rename, reclaim the experience without making the mistake of taking my whole identity from it?... When we first arrived at the birth classes we were greeted by our instructor, "Hi Mom, Hi Dad." After eight weeks I still didn't know the names of the other couples.

Nadja—the only one who calls me MOM.

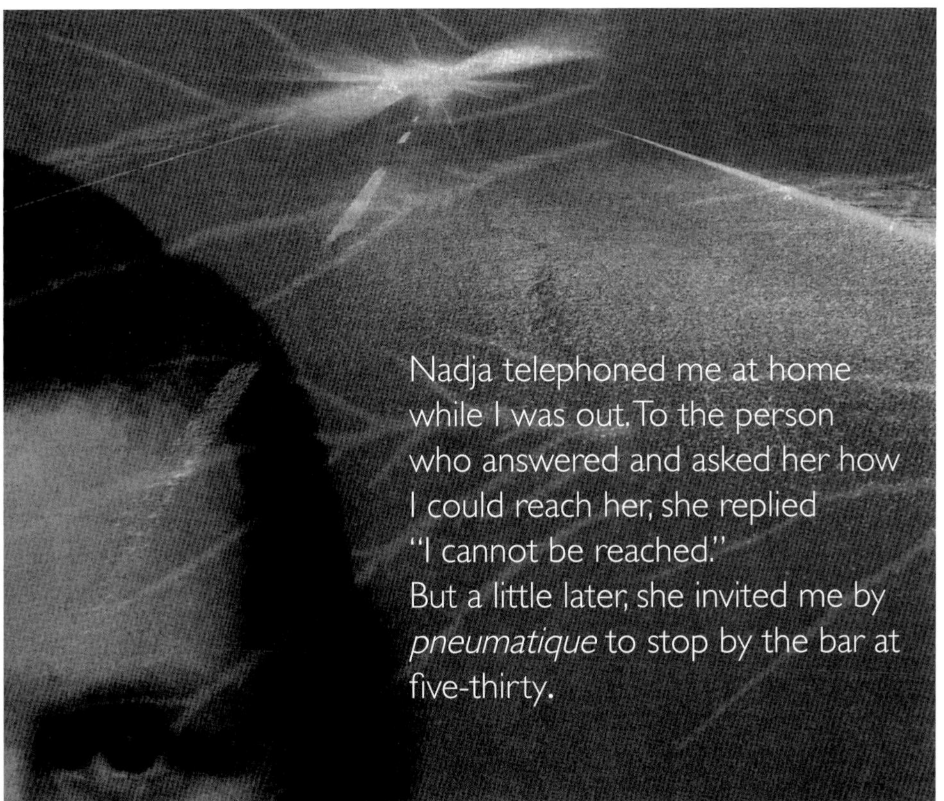

Nadja telephoned me at home while I was out. To the person who answered and asked her how I could reach her, she replied "I cannot be reached."
But a little later, she invited me by *pneumatique* to stop by the bar at five-thirty.

III. Naming

For me "Nadja" represents the process of knowing (or the unceasing desire for knowledge), similar to growing up. "Nadja's" instability as a literary character resists the idea of the name, or rather, the title. What does your transfer of this name Nadja represent to you?

This becomes a question of recapitulating a state of mind: what was I thinking when the time came to give you, our baby, a name? We'd read Breton's *Nadja* aloud. It was one of the first books we read aloud together (a practice we still follow to this day—as I write this we are reading aloud Victor Serge's *Memoirs of a Revolutionary*). Thus that name we decided to give you is bound up with what we saw as the extraordinary potential of the power of love. So what's interesting to me is this conjunction of influences, this collage of influences, that led us to give you this essentially experimental name (love, history, art, literature, memory, anarchism, the beauty of intransigence, etc.) somehow supposed to sum up the potential growth of this absolutely new and unprecedented human being-in-process.

I've come to think that handing this name over to me may represent your rejection of the authority inscribed in the process of naming. Is this the result of "the crisis of naming" acted out in *Womb with a View*?

"You'll write a novel about me. I'm sure you will. Don't say you won't.
Be careful:
Everything fades.
Everything vanishes.
Something must remain of us..."

I wished to allude through a relentless pursuit of absurdity to the fact that all naming is ultimately suspect to the degree that language abstracts from the almost alarming complexity and specificity of the real. And yet "naming" seems to define and maybe colonize the identity, the experience, even the aspirations—so, while sounding fanciful, this "crisis" itself has real dimensions and implications. Certainly it cuts

as Transference

straight through to my central struggle with the idea of motherhood altogether: the exercise of authority, from which I almost instinctively shrink and yet which is itself so bound up—in the reality of mother-daughter relationships—with tenderness, love, responsibility, nurture.

Why did you give me my name?

There are other reasons I haven't pointed out: the alluring strangeness to our ears of the two syllables, the almost tragic or perhaps just tragic independence of the Nadja whom Breton attempts and, I think, fails to capture in his book, the notion that in Russian, as is mentioned in the book, Nadja means the beginning of hope and only the beginning—which so summoned for your father and me our own, perhaps excessively complicated, approach to living a passionate existence. The more I think about this question the more reasons there are and I actually think we considered however fleetingly most of them when the time came to make that odd and oddly final decision of naming.

Why so many names? To give me a choice?

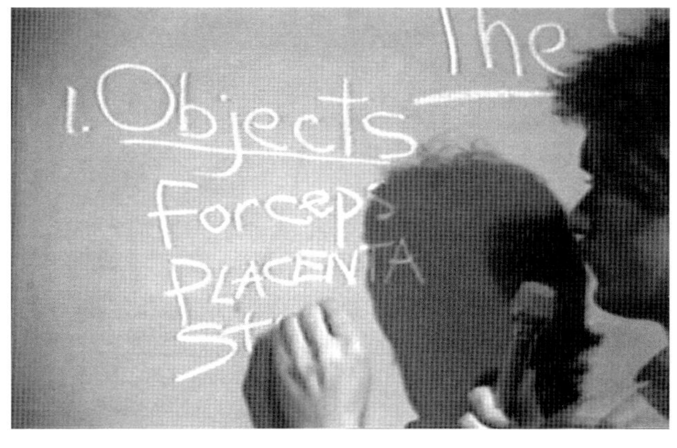

Always, always we aimed to give you alternatives as we went about "raising" you. That was our theory in a sense, a cornerstone of anarchist education theory, in fact, another way to "reject the authority inscribed in naming" as you put it. Why not give you alternatives in your own name? What if you hated Nadja? Thought it was some sort of botch or curse? So then you could become a Riley instead. (And each of your other names was also embedded with allusions for us, of course—Riley so you might live the "life of Riley.") And then there was the majorly galvanizing moment when we realized that your initials would spell: NORML. That seemed to confirm that our whole nutty process had some hidden structuring principle—so it fell right into place.

IV. Naming

Nadja represents herself as a transparency:
"The soul in Limbo."
"The thought on the bath in the room without mirrors."
Reading, and re-reading this namesake, I ask myself, why has my mother titled my reality with such a destabilizing identity—that of the transparency? The name is hardly *empowering*.
This may be why I'm so exhaustively preoccupied with the flimsy aspects of subjectivity.

Nadja's way of knowing resists mastery: she signifies an ontological process at once interactive, subjective, and dependent on chance. Like the fragmentary process of growing up, or the physical process of collage, even the interplay between a transparency and its shadow—Nadja never quite matches up with herself but (rather) refracts, falls, fails.
Nadja inhabits the space beneath and above water—a feeling rendered through the transparency shimmering like the surface of liquid beneath which a dream world exists that we may have access to if we are willing to live our everyday lives through other processes of seeing and knowing.

At the risk of exhausting the affective register, it sometimes feels rather melancholic, this always deferred moment of lucidity.
Is this my inheritance?

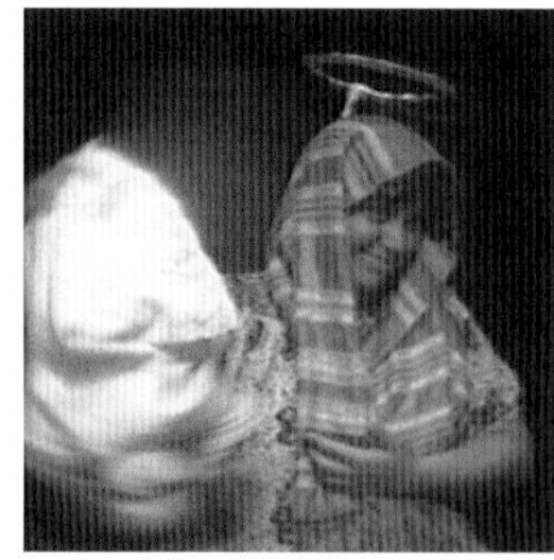

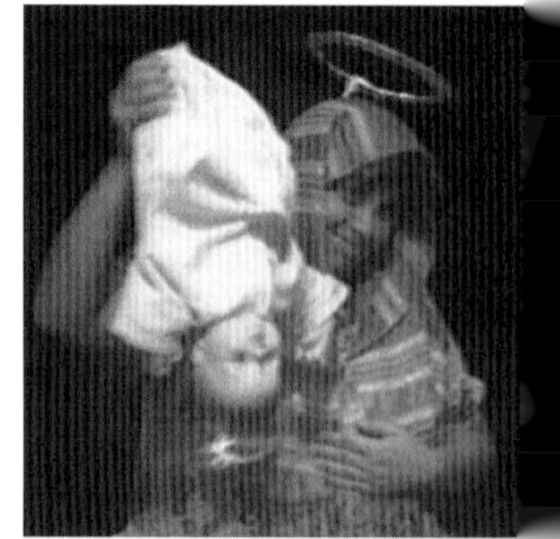

as Transparence

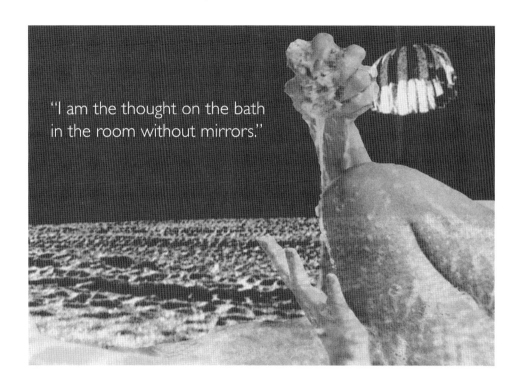

"I am the thought on the bath
in the room without mirrors."

V. Naming

Have I successfully lived your initiatory act (your first maternal action)?

Success, if that's the corrrect word choice, would mean excess—that you lived out this open "prescription" far far beyond any possible idea I could ever have had of what a NADJA would could might turn out to be and become. I don't really believe that if we'd have named you Murgatroyd you might therefore have somehow been handicapped. But, Nadja, you have so far exceeded and continue, day by day, to exceed.

What if you could rename me now?

Let's pretend I could achieve that level of imaginative power. Would a new name enable you to reshape your being in ways not subject to mere Nadja-ness? That might be fun, a game to play, in the short term, but you'd break whatever rules might gather around that new assembly of letters, soon enough. I suppose some names might get used up or persist as no more than markers of constricting stability—but more likely it's the interplay between the magic of the name and the user of it that makes the difference.

What was your first reaction to my project? Did you think of *Womb* immediately?

I thought: what a gift you are. Very few surprises in life hit you shake you with the bracingly intimate sense that maybe what you hardly ever dared hope for (and would want never to burden any child with) is there now, right in front of you. It's no longer the beginning of hope then.
And then the ground shifts—or accumulates, you might say, as I shift from "seeing" you as daughter to seeing/experiencing you as artist/equal…(and I don't mean to imply a one-way directionality but an expanding back and forth, an expanding of possibilities and of the dimensions of recognition). And then the specific project itself—your re-claiming and re-problematizing this "name"—assuming your own authority, your own authorship however fraught or contradictory, seems to me so brave and beautiful.

as Gift

In appropriating Nadja as my "subject," I have enabled her—as an idea, as a modernist myth, or a worldview—to become entangled in my own subjectivity as an artist/author. For me *Nadja* (the novel) is not so much a found object as an inherited object—inherited through the process of naming.

In the Room Without Mirrors is a gift too in that it takes me full circle, back to revisit rethink and re-live all of my contradictory feelings about (impending) motherhood from a completely different and wholly unexpected place. To have the experience, just for a moment, of a whole—the fragments connected, the meaning made manifest. Just for a moment, because the process continues....

Could naming be in some way prophetic?

If the act of naming is honestly in as many forseeable or even unforseeable ways as possible an expression of potential, then maybe it could be prophetic.

"those are your thoughts and mine. Look where they all start from, how high they reach, and then how it is still prettier when they fall back. And then they dissolve immediately, driven back up with the same strength, then there's that broken spurt again, that fall... and so on indefinitely."

Notes

[1]Ludwig Wittgenstein, *Philosophical Investigations* (New York: Prentice Hall, 1999), section 26.
[2]Mary Daly, *Beyond God the Father: Toward a Philosophy of Women's Liberation* (Boston: Beacon Press, 1973), 8.
[3]André Breton, *Nadja*. trans. Richard Howard (New York: Grove Press, 1960), 113.

All in-image quotations gathered from: André Breton. Nadja. *Trans. Richard Howard. New York: Grove Press, 1960.*

Page 338
Breton, 74.

Page 340
Breton, 111.

Page 343
Breton, 94.

Page 344
Breton, 100.

Page 347
Breton, 101.

Page 349
Breton, 86.

Womb with a View is distributed by Video Data Bank (School of the Art Institute of Chicago, 112 S. Michigan Ave., Chicago, IL 60603).

RACHEL HALL

After Long Winter

"Illness often takes on the disguise of love, and plays the same odd tricks."

—Virginia Woolf

THE FIRST TIME SHE AWAKES in the night, my daughter wants to climb into my bed. She isn't complaining yet and is rather easily led across the hall, back to her bed. *Bad dream*, I think, if I think anything at all and hunker down, back under my warm covers. Beside me, my husband breathes steadily, undisturbed. I'm asleep in minutes.

The next thing I know, a blade of bright light cuts into my sleep. The bed beside me is empty. I'm so deeply asleep I can't fathom what is happening. I call out for the light to be turned off. "Maude is sick," my husband snaps from the hallway. The linen closet creaks open. I hear him rooting around for fresh sheets and blankets. I'm fully awake now as if slapped into consciousness. And so begins a night of illness, of holding back her long hair as my daughter vomits and gags, of dashing back to her bedside and in between—the jagged dreams of interrupted sleep. In the following hours there will be much to clean: bedding, rugs, clothing, upholstery, and still the lingering smell of sickness—both ripe and sour. There is nothing glamorous about this, especially since my husband and I go about it in our pajamas, hair matted, eyes bleary, our voices sharp, edged with affront when we speak to each other.

It's three in the morning. My daughter is on the toilet, hunched and shivering. I'm sitting on the rim of the bathtub, shielding my eyes from the light. I'm ready with a bowl in case she needs to throw up again.

"I'm so sorry, Mommy," she says.

"You can't help being sick," I say, stroking her forehead. It feels hot and clammy.

"You're the best mommy in the world."

"I want to be with you when you need me," I say and am struck by the absolute truth of this statement.

At eight, she prickles easily, lobbies for more freedom, sometimes refuses our kisses, but how mild she is when ill, how sweet-tempered and lovable. And how easy it is to give her what she needs—the cool cloth, extra blankets for the chill, soothing words. I'm not glad she's sick, but there is a certain pleasure in tending to her. I love the smooth warmth of her back when I rub it to help her fall back asleep, the flush on her cheeks, her eyelashes webbed with tears, eyes glittery, bright.

"This is what ages you," my mother says, later when I call to tell her Maude is sick. Even now when it rains, my mother has pain in her left elbow from a fall she took carrying me, fever raging, from my bedroom. I ended up in the hospital where I stayed for a week with tonsillitis. From that time I have only a few fragmented memories—an IV pole I had to roll with me to the bathroom, the movable hospital bed, nurses with crisp triangular hats, though surely these memories are colored by my reading and rereading of *Madeline*. "Madeline soon ate and drank/On her bed there was a crank."

I received get-well cards from my entire kindergarten class and sweets and stuffed animals from friends and family. I don't remember, as my mother does, the mean nurses who insisted I first drink beef broth if I wanted ice cream and refused to allow my mother to stay overnight in my room. This was the late sixties in Toronto, where hospitals were still run in an exacting British style without regard for my mother's sloppy American devotion and concern. She grows livid speaking of this even now. "Those nurses were so nasty, don't you remember?" But I don't, not at all. What I recall is my mother's gentle attentions, her hand in mine, the white crescents of her fingernails reassuring in their familiarity.

My daughter doesn't end up in the hospital. She is sick for a night and part of the next day, then pale and peaked for a couple more. If serious illness is, as many writers on the subject say, like being removed to another land, then regular, run-of-the-mill sickness with its low-grade misery is a weekend getaway, a day trip, still capable of providing glimpses of another way of life, glimmers of understanding.

When we are ill, we regress, adults become children, children grow younger. We are absorbed by our aches and discomfort, care only for our needs. When my grandfather was hospitalized after his final stroke, his brief moments of lucidity were spent pleading for his pipe. "It's the only thing I've ever wanted," he said, whimpering. Though he didn't recognize me, his eldest grandchild, he allowed me to feed him ice chips

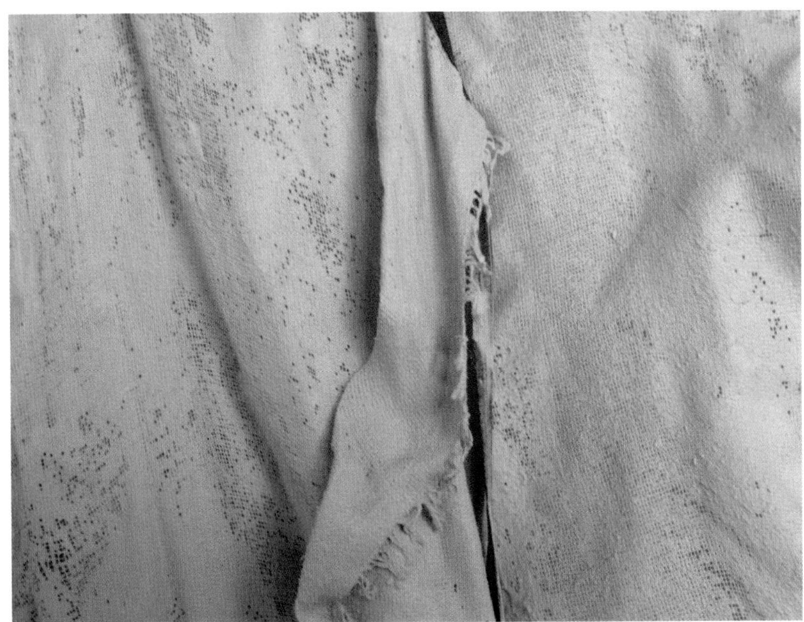

Sarah E. Webb, 2004. Top: *Mrs. P.* Bottom: *Mrs. M.*
Beeswax, cheesecloth, thread (detail), 55 × 44 inches.

Sarah E. Webb, 2004. Top: *Option 1*, 3.25 × 6 × 1.5 inches.
Center: *Option 2*, 6 × 10 × 1.5 inches. Bottom: *Option 3*, 2 × 7.25 × 1.5 inches.
Cherry wood, Queen Anne's Lace seeds, sterling silver.

from a Styrofoam cup, and moisten his lips with a small sponge, but this wasn't what he really wanted. He cried out pitifully, this huge man, who'd scared me for most of my life with his gruff pronouncements and firm opinions.

Now my eight-year-old needs me in the middle of the night as she did as an infant when my body offered her one desire. Then, I'd leap from sleep, pull her, squawking, to my breast. I've grown to miss that rare meeting of need and desire—and this, its purest form. Do I tell this story because in it I appear the good mother—selfless, gentle, kind? Certainly, it is pleasant to see myself that way, but it's more than that, too. Caring for her calls back previous illnesses, other nights when this calm evaded me.

When my daughter was between nine months and a year she suffered from chronic ear infections. At night, I'd nurse her and lay her in her crib. Soon she'd be screaming. I'd repeat the nursing and again lay her down, certain that she'd fall asleep this time. Over and over again she seemed ready for sleep, but when laid flat, the screaming began. It was screaming—not whining or whimpering or fussing; not even crying accurately describes the sound. I heard in it pain and betrayal, accusation and fear. And it might last all night. In Alice Munro's short story "My Mother's Dream," the narrator asks this:

"What is it about an infant's crying that makes it so powerful, able to break down the order you depend on, inside and outside of yourself? It is like a storm—insistent, theatrical, yet in a way pure and uncontrived... ready to crush your brains inside your skull."[1]

We tried everything to make the crying stop. I would draw a bath and nurse her as we soaked, ignoring as long as I could the increasingly tepid water. She slept propped against me. She could sleep in her car seat, the car looping the thruway or the wide suburban streets, where inside their homes happy, healthy families slept. Once returning home after such a drive, I saw a homeless man pushing his grocery cart of cans and bottles down the snowy sidewalk and I imagined I knew his story: a sick child, his job lost from staying home to care for her. His house would be next to go, then his mind. It seemed in my sleep-deprived state, if not an inevitable trajectory, then a fairly easy one to slip into.

In the morning after the sleepless nights, we'd line up at walk-in hours at the pediatrician's office, stunned by fatigue and our own incompetence in the face of our daughter's pain. She was losing weight and when not crying, seemed listless and dull. "You again," the doctor would say, taking out his otoscope, and guilt would elbow its way in, hunker down next to the worry.

Our pediatrician would put her on antibiotics and things would get better for a couple of days, but then the infection would return. The continuous medicine gave her horrible diarrhea that turned her entire bottom raw and caused the birthmark on her labia to rupture. This required more doctors, including a plastic surgeon, who spoke exclusively into her handheld recorder except to tell me not to leave Maude's soiled diaper in the garbage pail in the examining room.

So often was Maude inconsolable and in our bed, that we moved our mattress to the floor, so we could sleep without our worrying about her falling. It took up all the floor space. Our bedroom became a sick bay, our dresser top a drug dispensary littered with ointments and salves, bottles of infant ibuprofen and Tylenol, the garish pink of liquid amoxicillin. We ran the humidifier so much that the windows wept condensation.

Maude's illness was all I thought about that long cold winter, all I could manage—nothing more. I didn't write so much as a word those many months of her sickness. Instead of the novels and short stories that had kept me company my entire life, I read books with titles like *Childhood Ear Infections* and *No More Milk!* I learned of alternative remedies like holding a warm onion half to the infected ear. A nutritionist recommended we take her off the antibiotics and all dairy products. She instructed me to warm mullein flower oil and apply it in Maude's ears with a tiny dropper. And finally this is what worked. Spring came, she turned one, took her first steps, something she'd seemed primed to do months ago before the illness hit. It seemed we might all live.

Some people explain their desire to have a second child as the opportunity to use what they learned the first time around. To me, that didn't seem like a good enough reason. Though I loved my daughter, I didn't like whom I became when tired, brittle with worry, consumed with illness. I didn't want to go back to the place of illness, a place that remained vivid in my thoughts for a long time. One child was plenty.

Writing this now, I wish I could've seen past the sickness and worry. The illnesses—standard childhood illnesses—recede into the distance, a tiny speck in an otherwise healthy life. Health returns all bright and dewy, like spring after a long winter. But how could I have known then that I would one day write about those times with something akin to longing?

Like the time of the illnesses, the time I might have had another child has passed as well. My body won't cooperate, despite medical advances and innovations, a slew of specialists, pills and supplements. I won't have another child, but I do have this one, and I have this night with its tears and smells, its alarm and relief. I smooth it on like a balm.

fat & blood
(and how to make them)

a book work by Sarah E Webb,
published on the occasion of the exhibition
fat & blood (and how to make them),
September 9 - October 9, 2004
Kristen Frederickson Contemporary Art, New York
Printed at Boxcar Press, Syracuse, NY

96/100

Mrs. C

An early marriage; three pregnancies, the last two of which broke in upon the year of nursing; she began at last to show in loss of flesh and color.

Mrs. N

Meanwhile she met with energy the multiplied claims of a life full of sympathy for every form of trouble, neglecting none of the duties of society or kinship.

Miss A

Everything wearied her:

to eat
to read
to sew

Mrs. P

By and by she began to feel tired, and at last

gave way quite abruptly.

Sarah E. Webb, *fat & blood (and how to make them)*, 2004. Letterpress Artist's Book on Mohawk Superfine, ed. 100, 3.75 × 2.5 inches.

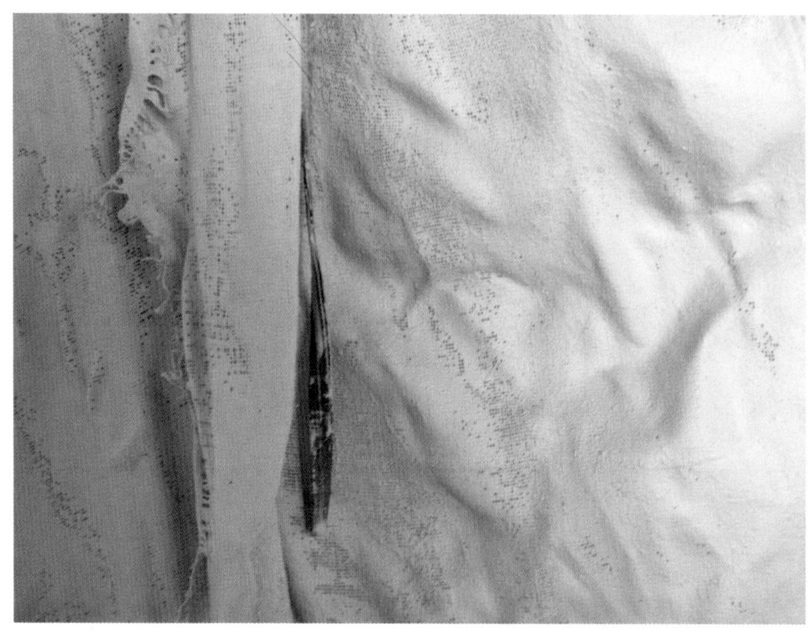

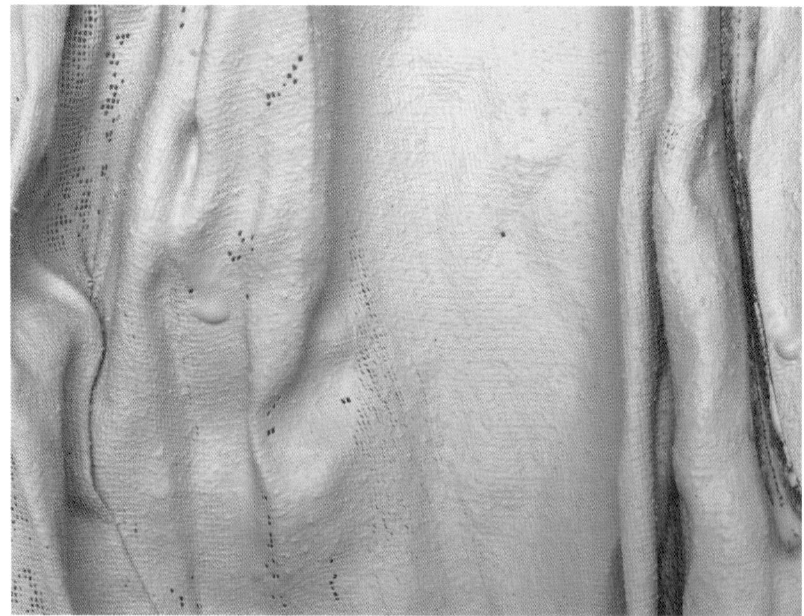

Sarah E. Webb, 2004. Top: *Mrs. C.* Bottom: *Miss A.*
Beeswax, cheesecloth, thread (detail), 55 × 44 inches.

Notes

[1]Alice Munro, *The Love of a Good Woman: Stories* (New York: Knopf, 1998), 322.

Sarah E. Webb's *fat & blood (and how to make them)* refers to the attempts by Victorian women to control their own physicality. Responding to S. Weir Mitchell's famed "rest cure," the work questions how women's bodies were seen as mere tools for the conception of children and objects to be manipulated by a male-dominated society in which women were considered merely reproductive, not productive. The central installation of *fat & blood* is comprised of nine handmade medical gowns. Using the contemporary paper gowns worn in the doctor's office as a pattern, Webb sewed their equivalent with cheesecloth and red thread, then hand dipped each gown in beeswax. Accompanying the gowns are three cherry boxes containing vials of Queen Anne's Lace seeds, an arcane method of contraception. *fat & blood* explores the shift in who has cared/cares for a women's body. The installation questions and considers the cultural impact of relinquishing the role of the midwife into the hands of the (male) physician.

—*Kristen Frederickson*

SARAH E. WEBB

Milk and Tears

Performing Maternity

> *to nurse:* to nourish at the breast: to suckle/to consume slowly/ to take charge of and watch over/to care for and wait on (as a sick person)/to rear, to educate/to promote the development or progress of/to feed an offspring from the breast/to take care of a young child/to attempt to cure by care/to hold in one's memory or consideration.[1]

IN MY TWENTIES, WHILE ATTENDING art school, I became a dutiful student of feminist art history. My eyes were opened to a (re)reading of texts and images, and I learned how traditional, patriarchal art history had literally exposed, and arguably privileged, women's breasts as objects of male desire and female sexuality. However, in my thirties, breasts embodied a different reality for me as I nursed my infant son and my mother-in-law continued her battle with advanced breast cancer. In the process of becoming a mother, I was losing a mother(-in-law). My life became consumed by the silent language of milk and tears: bodily fluids of nourishment, but also of suffering. Milk and tears converged as a liquid performance, an elliptical connection between the maternal (nursing) and medical (cancerous) breast.

The following meditation considers the origins of my installation, *Milk and Tears* (2001). I have come to understand my own work as being part of an artistic trajectory of process-based art that addresses the maternal body, specifically the work of Sarah Hutt (b. 1951) and Sarah Slavick (b. 1958). Despite distinct material preferences, and generational differences, our shared visual and theoretical affinities can be understood within the context of a process- or performance-based mode of production. That is, the physical act of making work (with text, image and object) becomes intrinsic to its meaning, frequently incorporating the repetition of gesture, handwork, touch. For each artist, "work" as process is as important as

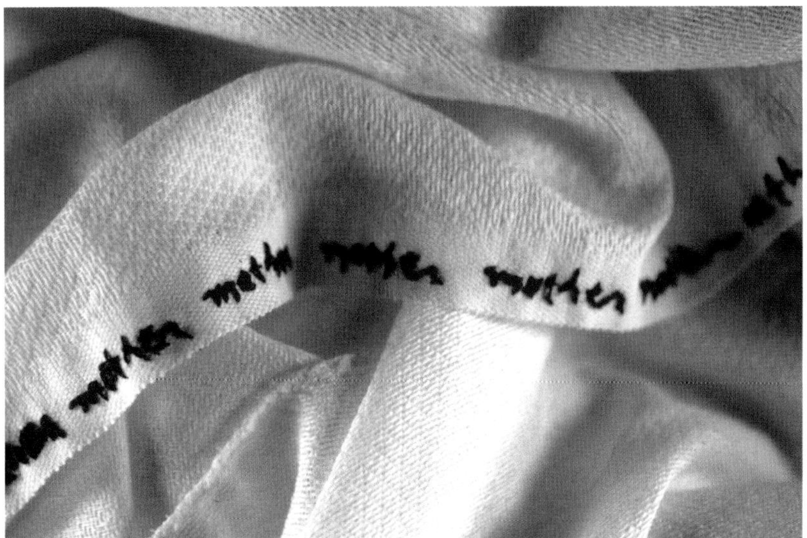

Sarah E. Webb, *Milk and Tears*, 2001. Birdseye weave cloth diapers, thread.

"work" as product, an acknowledged strategy within both the politics of performance art and feminist art history, and becomes a means to recreate the mother, the maternal body. As women, we offer our bodies to our children as nourishment, but also bring a spoon to the mouth of those too weak to feed themselves. The work of Hutt and Slavick, as well as my own, explores the collision of these two basic instincts, "to nurse" and "to nurse," by incorporating lived experience with feminist theories of embodiment and corporeality.

Charmaine Eddy has written that "corporeality is always already 'marked as' something other in our representational economies in an attempt to open up a space between the perception and representation of the cultural performativity of the body. The 'marking' of the body 'as' something other ultimately illustrates that corporeality is positioned as supplementary in and through its representations."[2] Consider the iconographic Christian trope of maternity, *Madonna del Latte*, a mother whose bodily function was restricted to the pleasure of nursing, but also foreshadows what will become a future expression of her loss and pain. If we are to reclaim the maternal body, to (re)make Mary, with what language can we speak? How can we begin to render the mother?

We form memory (and meaning) through repetition, perhaps accounting for the inexplicable sameness that pervades our family photographs: mutually constructed narratives.

It is this performance of ritual activity which both marks and unmarks the maternal body.

Within this context the maternal body and specifically the breast are readily symbolized through their absence. The cancerous breast is physically, surgically removed from the body. The lactating breast is unwelcome in public; women are instructed to be discreet. Peggy Phelan reminds us how "loss acquires meaning and generates recovery—not only of and for the object, but for the one who remembers. The disappearance of the object is fundamental to performance; it rehearses and repeats the disappearance of the subject who longs always to be remembered."[3] In the work discussed in this essay, the maternal body (the breast) is absent, but in each case a re-marking, a re-making, a re-trieving of the maternal body occurs. In keeping with the writings of Luce Irigaray, we discern a (maternal) space that privileges haptic over visual representation—the duality of touch (and the breast) as loci for both pleasure and pain.[4]

MY MOTHER'S LEGACY

Sarah Hutt's mother died of breast cancer when she was only thirteen years old. In the summer of 1994 her sister had the idea of putting together memory books about their parents for her own children. However, the task turned out not to be simple. Hutt writes, "What we found was many of our childhood memories consisted of fuzzy black and white photos taken by our mother with no explanation of who was in the picture, the place or the date. Without (our mother), the link that passes stories between generations had been broken."[5] Marilynne Robinson wrote in her novel, *Housekeeping*, "memory is the sense of loss, and loss pulls us after it."[6] And so, Hutt began to write down memories of the mother she had lost. She went through old photographs and waited for them to speak. The project began as a way to "collect (her) thoughts, then as a way to piece together memories and give it form."[7] In its final state, *My Mother's Legacy* (1995) is a 1,000-line poem. A single memory burned directly into the bottom of each of 1,000 wooden bowls. It is a text stitched with fire. Just like photographs, as we have learned from Roland Barthes, Hutt's wooden bowls bear the trace of their lost object: a presence understood by absence.

Hutt chose to use bowls as representative of her mother, whose day revolved around the preparation of familial meals—vessels capable of being filled, but also depleted. Mother as subject. Mother as object. Hutt remembers her mother turning plates over to establish where they had been made; we as viewers now perform the gesture to uncover what is no longer there. If we understand this interaction between art objects and the viewer to be one which is essentially performative, we reconstruct the woman (the mother) by reading the bowls. For Hutt, the order in which the bowls are read is not significant, as each has the potential to coax the act of remembrance, as we search for her mother and by default, our own. And so in the spirit of this chance narrative, I offer the text of a few bowls:

My mother ate cold leftovers
My mother talked to her mother every day
My mother gave us oranges in our Christmas stocking
My mother promised
My mother said only tell a story once
My mother put raisins in the meatballs
My mother twisted her rings when she talked
My mother kept her options open
My mother wanted snow white hair when she was old
My mother said I took after her
My mother said there was no secret
My mother always had a sweater with her
My mother gave me paper dolls
My mother said things turn out

MILK SHOWERS

Sarah Slavick considers her paintings to be abstracted interiors of the body made of cells, blood, milk, veins, wounds, and sutures. For the past ten years, Slavick has made large paintings on wood comprised of grids of individual, small panels. In works such as *Milk Showers* (1995), the physical working of additive and subtractive layering of paint evokes numerous conceptual and physical connections, as the panels are painted separately and then placed together as a single composition.[8] Singles are meant to exist in equal strength to the whole, while the repetition of the same task over and over is made visible. As mothers, we nurse our children, change their diapers. As small tasks they can be laborious, mind-numbing. Those tasks that define us change and alter our perceptions. Tillie Olsen wrote, “It is distraction, not meditation, that becomes habitual; interruption, not continuity; spasmodic, not constant toil.”[9] Yet, standing from a distance, one realizes the fleetingness of these acts, and, from the baby, the child emerges.

Milkvein, *Milk Showers*, and *Milkvein 2* (1995–96) arose out of Slavick's own experience with motherhood and speak to the sustenance of new life, mother's milk. Carol Mavor describes Slavick's work as "abstractions of alimentary love—milk drops like rain drops."[10] As Hélène Cixous wrote, "The voice is the mother and the mother's body: 'Voice: inexhaustible milk. She has been found again. The lost mother. Eternity: it is the voice mixed with milk.'"[11] For Cixous, mothering and theorizing are corporeally formed through lactation.[12] But the milk is also reclaimed as a voice of power (and pleasure) within the context of feminist art. If we consider breastfeeding as a performance of maternity then "leaking" becomes a visible trace of the performance. Expressing milk—milk as expression. What does it mean to have one's milk "let down" and who exactly is let down when there is no one else to nurse: the mother, the child?

Novelist Ann Enright wrote, "The milk surprises me, above all, because it hurts as it is let down, and this foolish pain hits me at quite the wrong times. The reflex is designed to work at the sight, sound, or thought of your baby—which is spooky enough—but the brain doesn't seem to know what a baby *is* exactly and so tries to make you feed anything helpless, or wonderful, or small. So I have let down milk for Russian submariners and German tourists dying on the Concorde.... What I had not expected was that there should be some things that do not move me, that move my milk. I find myself lapsed into a memory I cannot catch, I find myself trying to figure out what it is in the room that is sad or lovely—was it that combination of words, or the look on his face—what is it that has such a call on my unconscious attention, or my pituitary, or my alveolar cells."[13]

MILK AND TEARS

And so I return to where I began, to my own interest in the topic of milk and tears. Julia Kristeva wrote, "milk and tears ... are the metaphors of non-speech, of a semiotics that linguistic communication does not account for. They re-establish what is non-verbal and show up as the receptacle of a signifying disposition that is closer to the so-called primary processes."[14] Consistently, my work has been concerned with the historical construction of what is deemed "feminine" in Western culture by creating objects and installations which question, expose and rupture a traditional reading of the private, domestic sphere. I have sought to retrieve a woman's story and empower her with a voice to speak for herself. By recalling materials and methods that reference a woman's historical place, I reconsider their origin, and traditions.

My son Noah was born under the sign of Cancer, which suddenly did not seem inconsequential. On the day of his *bris*, there were two hairless heads in the room, however only one had been stripped from chemotherapy. I began to consider the breast as a site of contradiction: a site of primary nurturing, and a place of destruction. Working through the enormity of such a topic, I returned to Julia Kristeva's discussion of women's time as unique from Father time, its gestational cycles as an approach to seeing/recording beyond monumental, linear moments.[15] A child cries, and as mothers we offer our bodies in comfort. Women's time: lunar, tidal, menstrual, conceptual. Milk, tears, chemotherapy dripping into and out of the body.

And so I began to embroider, to chain-stitch a passage from Ann Sexton's poem "Dreaming the Breast" along the edge of twenty-eight birdseye cotton diapers with red thread (the color of bleeding and of healing).[16]

Mother, I ate you up. All my need, took you down, like a meal.

Within the gallery, the diapers were quietly draped in rows of fourteen like shrouds, or deflated balloons.[17] The act of stitching exposed a tangle of strings, deliberately left hanging with the promise of continued conversation—the hope of reunion. While I cannot deny the historical implications of the use of embroidery within a feminist, as well as a feminine, context, the choice to embroider became one of necessity. How else to make work conducive to living with a small child, capable of withstanding frequent stops and starts, as well as work that would be portable/packable as I regularly traveled to visit my husband's mother? Rozsika Parker observed in *The Subversive Stitch: Embroidery and the Making of the Feminine* that "embroidery has provided a source of pleasure of power for women, while being indissolubly linked to their powerlessness."[18] So too, maternity.

On the second wall I placed eight glass boxes filled with either coarse, crystallized sea salt or powdered milk. Etched into the glass were the contradictory definitions of what it means to nurse—tiny, glass nipples—*la mère/la mer*—the infinite sea between mother, daughter, and back again. Of course, the (medical) circles continue to ripple: we are instructed that being breastfed oneself, and/or breastfeeding one's own children, reduces one's risk of developing breast cancer.[19] As bodily fluids, milk and tears are metaphors of both a mother's inexhaustible love, but also of the pain to which she yields. Leaking, dripping, milk and tears stain our skin, our clothing, and our lives in between the cycle of birth and death.

Barbara Bobrow passed away January 15, 2005. I dedicate this essay in loving memory.

Notes

[1] *Webster's Ninth New Collegiate Dictionary* (New York: Merriam-Webster Inc., 1983), 812.
[2]Charmaine Eddy, "Material Difference and the Supplementary Body in Alice Walker's *The Color Purple*," in *Body Matters: Feminism, Textuality, Corporeality*, eds. Avril Horner and Angela Keane (Manchester: Manchester University Press, 2000), 100.
[3]Peggy Phelan, *Unmarked: The Politics of Performance* (London: Routledge, 1993), 147.
[4]Thank you Laura Auricchio, for pointing out the obvious.
[5]Sarah Hutt, artist statement for *My Mother's Legacy*. sarahhutt.com.
[6]Marilynne Robinson, *Housekeeping* (New York: Farrar, Straus and Giroux, 1980), 194.
[7]Hutt, artist statement.
[8]Sarah Slavick, artist statement.
[9]Tillie Olsen, *Silences* (New York: Delacorte Press/Seymour Lawrence, 1978), 19.
[10]Carol Mavor, "Too Close to See," in *Flesh and Blood* (Pittsburgh: Carnegie Mellon University, 1998), 8.
[11]Toril Moi, *Sexual Textual Politics: Feminist Literary Theory* (London: Methuen & Co., 1985), 114.
[12]Alison Bartlett, "Thinking Through Breasts," in *Feminist Theory* 1.2 (August 2000): 184.
[13]Anne Enright, "My Milk," *London Review of Books* (October 5, 2000): 29.
[14]Julia Kristeva, "Stabat Mater," in *The Kristeva Reader*, ed. Toril Moi (New York: Columbia University Press, 1986), 174.
[15]Julia Kristeva, "Women's Time," in *Feminist Theory*: A *Critique of Ideology*, ed. Nannerl Keohane, Michelle Z. Rosaldo, and Barbara C. Gelpi (Chicago: University of Chicago Press, 1982).
[16]Anne Sexton, "Dreaming the Breasts" in *The Complete Poems* (New York: Houghton Mifflin, 1981), 314.
[17]Laura Auricchio, "Works in Translation: Ghada Amer's Hybrid Pleasures" in *Art Journal* 60.4 (Winter 2001): 37.
[18]Rozsika Parker, *The Subversive Stitch: Embroidery and the Making of the Feminine* (London: The Women's Press, 1994), 11.
[19]See medical statistics at http://www.prairienet.org/laleche/detcancer.html.

SILVIA ZIRANEK

(L)IF(E), AS IN MY …

HAD I BUT WOMB ENOUGH

HAD I BUT WOMB ENOUGH, AND LIVES, THIS TWO-TIME
BABYNESS WOULD BE JUST FINE, MY BODY EASY FOR MUCH
MORE, IT'S JUST THE BRAIN SCREAMED 'STOP!' AND SLAMMED
MORE'S DOOR.

THE FIRST BOY BLONDLY LULLABIED LIMBS' DREAMS, THE
SECOND MUST-HAVED, SURGED, AN URGENT GIRL OF MOTHER'S
LOVING NEEDS; MY WHOLE REQUIRED HER.

MOST DAYS I FEEL I FACE THE FIRING SQUAD OF LIFE, AN
ALWAYS MOTHER, NEVER WIFE (YET BOUND BY PARENTAGE
TILL DEATH US PART). AT LEAST I'M MUM, AND MRS ART IN OWN
RIGHT, CONCOCTING (W)OR(D)S AND (TH)OUGHTS, AND
PR(ACT)ICES AND (F)LOWS, NO LONGER PRONE TO BOTTLED
WAYS AND TWENTY:SOMETHING BLOWS.

MY BEAUTY JEWELS JAILED MY HEART — I'M THEIRS HOWEVER
MUCH I ART.

I WOULDN'T HAVE THEM ANY OTHER ANY WAY, AND BUT I
WONDER: WHAT DID BECOME OF PRE-MUM, ALL PINK, MOTOR-
BIKING ME ME ME? ….

AND IN MY BAG I ALWAYS FIND ELASTIC BANDS, SOME SNACKS, AN
ENTERTAINING GAME LONG SINCE DECLINED — AND SNAPS
OF YOUNGER VERSIONS OF MY DEARS, FOR WINGED CHARIOTS
ADD THEIR LINES TO LOVE AS WELL AS LOVELOST LIVES.

THE FRYING PAN OF LIFE

WHAT FOOD TO FEED THE MOUTHS I BORE, I ASK THE FRYING PAN OF LIFE?
WHAT TASTE TO TAME A TONGUE UNTRIED, I ASK THE SAUCEPAN OF MY SOUL?
WHAT JEWEL TO FORK LIPWARDS TONIGHT, I COOKLY QUIZ MY SHELFY SELF?
FOR HE DOES DRY, AND SHE SAYS SAUCE, AND I NEED — I? NEED?! — MORE THAN SPICE…
EACH DAY 3 MEALS, EACH MEAL 3 MOUTHS, EACH MOUTH ITS MIND, EACH MIND ITS SOUL. HE'S FOWL, SHE'S FISH (ISH), AND I AM VEG AND FRUIT AND CHEESE (AND WINE).
THE EGG I SPOON IS EAT REFORMED: THE CLOSEST TO DEAD FLESH I TAKE.
TAKE OMELETTES — WE DO, ONCE A WEEK OR SO. THEY MAKE THEIR OWN, THEN I FRY MINE WHEN HOME AGAIN (THEY'RE OF AN AGE TO DO THAT NOW AT LAST AT LEAST). AT LENGTH HE SEETHES, HE FAVOURS HARD AND THICK AND PLAIN AND FIRM (I'VE EVEN GRILLED WHEN MOISTURE LURKS). SHE SAVES HER YOLKS FROM STERNER FLAMES, ADDS ONIONS, PEPPER, CHEESE SOMETIMES.
IT'S SAID THEY EAT MORE WHEN THEY COOK; THEY LEARN, AND THAT FOR THEM IS GOOD. AND ME.

NOT BRICK BUT BEING

ME NOT BRICK BUT BEING.
MY LIFE AS A WALL: DOOR'D, FLOOR'D, FLAWED.
MY LIFE AS A WINDOW, ALMOST; MY LIFE AT A WINDOW, OFTEN,
BUILDING THE BLOCKS OF MY ME FROM A CHELSEA FIRST
FLOOR PANE TO A BERMONDSEY NOW NO THROUGH LANE,
BOTH CHILDREN'D, BOTH MUM PLUS TWO THOUGH BEFORE I
WAS YOUNG — NOW IT'S ME DRIVES THE SCHOOL RERUN.
NOT BRICK BUT BEING, NOT WALL BUT HOLDING UP, HOLDING
DOWN, HOLDING ON, HOLDING OUT.
BORN KING'S, SCHOOLED BELLEVUE, LEFT LEEDS, GOLDSMITH'D
GLEBE, TAPPED MALLINSON, TRAPPED IN EARLSMEAD, LOVE
BOATED GRAND, ACME'D ARCHWAY, DAAD'D STORKWINKEL /
HELMSTEDTER, MUM'D BANYARD, THEN 44 > 32.
ME NOT ROOF BUT KEEPING DRY, ME NOT ART BUT TRY TO:
TALK WORD AND THOUGHT, WEAR WORD WEAR WALK, TALK
TASTE TALK MOOD, DRESS M(OR)E NOT LESSNESS, NOT BRICK
BUT BUILDING YES TO BEST TOMORROW — I DO SEE, I DO LOOK, I
DO THOUGHT, I DO FROCK, I DO MOUTH, I DO COULD, I DID THEN,
I DO NOW, I DO FOOD, I DID FIGHT, I DO PERF, I DO WRITE, I DO
BRICK, I DO BUILD, I DO LIVE, I DO (L)IF(E).
HAVE TRAVELLED.
WORK TO COMMISSION
SUITABLE FOR ALL AGES. AND GENDERS.
PINK.

TO MY JOINT MEANINGS

Z SAID

VENI, VIDI, VOCAB'D; I CAME, I SAW, I CONJUGATED: I THINK IN WORDS, I WORK IN VERBS, I SEW INFINITIVES (97%). TO DO IS TO BE, SO I WAS. THEN I HAD. NOW I AM, AGAIN.
OH BONJOUR OFFSPRING (A LIFE WITH A DOOR IS A DOUBLY ATTRACTIVE FEATURE).
AGAIN: I WROUGHT, I WIPE, I SHALL TYPE — NOT CAST. WITH SEASONING. © SCZ 2005. NOR IRON. I'D NEVER DECLINE A DECLENSION...

Silvia Ziranek performing TEN TIARAS (DOWN TO MY LAST). Photo: Meg Tait.

M(OR)E

ARE WE ALL? THEN I'LL.
MY NAME IS.
I, A FEMALE, WAS BORN IN, STUDIED AT, TRAVELLED IN AND.
AND AS FOR WORK: THROUGH WORD AND WARDROBE, MOT — WORT — AND GARDE-ROBE — KLEIDERSCHRANK NICHT KUEHLSCHRANK, HAVE INVESTIGATED ATMOSPHERE, ATTITUDE, IMAGE, IN/EQUALITY, SCALE, PURPOSE, CATEGORISATIONALISM, ISHNESS, FEMINISMUS, THOUGHTHOOD, BEING, BUYING, BREWING, BAKING, BURNING BOAT AND BUILDING BRIDGE, COLOUR, AND COCKTAILS, TEXT, AND TEXTILE, EMOTION, AND MILLINERY, AND, MAYBE, M(OR)E.
I TEND TO AND SO ON — I ARE OR (DECLINING SILENCE), RARELY DOWN TO MY LAST TEN TIARAS: ICI VILLA MOI. VERY MOI. VERY FOOD, INTERNATIONALISING WITH LIPSTICK WHILST CHASING SPACE, WHEN ANYONE CAN APRON, WHERE I DO SHOE, Z IN WHATEVER, SOON UPON AGO.

CHRISTEN CLIFFORD

BABYLOVE

How My Infant Son Became the Other Man

BEFORE I BECAME A MOTHER, I believed that motherhood would change me: my maternal instinct would smooth me, balance me, make me patient, give me a nurturing generosity. I'd become a better person but I wouldn't lose myself. I'd breastfeed exclusively but still find time to write. I'd make homemade baby food but still fuck. I had it all figured out.

I bought all the new books on mothering that I read about in *The New York Times* and *The New Yorker*—*Bitch in the House, The Mask of Motherhood, The Myth of Motherhood, The Price of Motherhood, A Life's Work, Fresh Milk*, and a book a friend recommended—*Fermentation*—the only erotic novel I could find that featured a pregnant woman. But no one else's narrative could prepare me for the next stage of my sexuality.

People always tell you that becoming a parent will change everything, but what I didn't count on was that it *wouldn't* change me. The problem is that I'm still the same person, a sex-obsessed neurotic facing a new reality: my husband and I love our son more than we love each other. It's like being in a permanent threesome, the kind where one person—not you—gets all the attention.

How do I summarize my sex life before the baby? Well, I had one. I lost my virginity at fifteen, had four partners by the time I was seventeen. I considered myself pansexual, theoretically as open to getting turned on by a coffee table as a person. I had boyfriends and a few girlfriends, some serial monogamy with lots of fucking around in between. I reveled in being provocative. I instigated group sex at parties, usually fueled by alcohol. I tried everything I could think of: oral, anal, BDSM and beyond.

I met Ken when I was twenty-five and he was thirty-four. What we had was probably typical: in the beginning it was all love and lust, fucking in bathrooms and trains, dancing all night, having sex all day, experimenting madly and believing we couldn't get enough of each other. Eventually, of course, we did get enough of each other and slowed down. We reserved weekend mornings to do nothing but fuck and eat and read the paper. Then weekend mornings became more and more about reading the paper.

When I hit thirty, we decided we were ready for a baby. Sex without birth control was hot. I hadn't fucked without a condom since I was eighteen, and the skin-on-skin friction was arousing, but so was the idea of sex as an extension of humanity, of something bigger than just us. I had one of those dream pregnancies—I exercised every day, felt great, and looked fabulous. It suited me, and I reveled in it. I had new tits that I absolutely adored. A certain type of man paid me a lot of attention. The hormones were like being on E all the time; my husband and I had sex every day. At parties I listened politely to the horror stories of couples who didn't have sex for four months after their babies were born and was privately dismissive: "That'll never happen to us."

But we were, in fact, just like everyone else: our sex life went down the toilet right away. It started with the birth, which didn't go as planned. Felix was premature, so I had him in a hospital with labor-inducing drugs, not in a hot tub with a midwife. I was in diabolical pain and shat everywhere, including standing up on the bed while barking at the nurse, "No I'm not having the baby I'm just taking a shit, put something underneath me now."

The worst part: I ripped open, requiring more than twenty stitches.

I'd never had stitches anywhere before, had never broken a bone. It was quite a shock to be injured, and to be injured *there*. When I finally got the courage to look, it was a huge relief to see that my clitoris was still there, and in the same place. But I discovered a womb with a view. The rumblings I had heard from women, not in complete sentences even, just mumblings of "never the same again"—this is what they were talking about. A swollen mass of red flesh. A gaping hole where tightness had been. I swear I could see my cervix.

I felt disfigured and damaged. I didn't cry, I shook. *This isn't happening*, I thought. *No one must know*. I blocked any thought or feeling below my waist, wore cleavage-revealing clothing, encasing my milky breasts in black lace bras under ripped-open tank tops. I became obsessed with Kegel exercises.

Eventually, I felt around and masturbated, tentatively. As I became aroused, my breasts squirted milk. That was cool. I felt like a teenage boy trying to see how far he could shoot. When I told this to one of my mommy friends, she said, "You should try masturbating while breast-feeding. It's *amazing*."

I didn't want to miss out. I went home, got out my mini-massager and settled into the Glider rocking chair with Felix, then a month and a half old, at my breast.

Then the doorbell rang.

It was the FedEx man. I buzzed him in, but he couldn't get through the second door, which sticks. So I went to the door in my bra and yoga pants and signed for the envelope with Felix still nursing. When the FedEx man turned to leave, I realized I still had the vibrator in my hand, not my keys, and the second door had closed behind me. I was now stuck in the vestibule with a vibrator and a baby. I rang the bells to my neighbors' apartments and no one answered.

I started to cry hysterically. It was sleeting and below zero and *I was barefoot and practically naked with an infant and where could I go like that and what the fuck was I doing anyway? Only a sick person tries to masturbate with a baby, for God's sake. And I'm locked out of the house and everyone will know what I was doing and …*

Noticing my distress, the FedEx man rang the bell at the house next door. My neighbor—a blue-collar father of three, fond of revving his motorcycle at eight in the morning—waved me over. I hid the vibrator under the rug and ran. He settled us on his couch with a blanket and asked if my kitchen window was locked. I whimpered "no," and he went to break into my apartment. I looked at his kids' Crayola drawings and hoped he didn't find the vibrator, or worse yet, step on it and break it.

He came back with one of my coats and asked if I wanted to finish feeding. I mumbled "No, thank you, thank you," still crying. I ran home, retrieved the dastardly vibrator, threw it in the back of my drawer and fed Felix tenderly from the other breast, apologizing to him the whole time. I vowed never to masturbate again.

But an hour later I was already thinking how hot that was of my neighbor—taking control and saving me, all knight-in-shining-armor-like, when I was so vulnerable.

That incident crystallized the whole madonna/whore thing: the feeling that as a mother, I wasn't allowed to be sexual. My black bras and obvious cleavage were meant to counteract that notion, and they may have fooled other people, but I couldn't trick myself into feeling sexual, or even sexy. I desperately wanted to subvert the image, but I was just like everyone else.

When Felix was two months old, I decided that my husband and I absolutely had to have sex. I didn't feel like it, but I was so paranoid about us losing our sex life that I started something. We fooled around on the couch while Felix took a nap in the bedroom.

I was terrified that it would hurt, that I wouldn't get turned on, that I wouldn't be able to come, that it just wouldn't work. I was scared that he was so turned off by seeing a baby come out that he wouldn't want to go in. And he didn't. He found my clitoris and stayed there. We had a gentle session of mutual masturbation and regained some sense of intimacy.

But still, no intercourse. Despite my doctor's reassurance that I was healing well, I had convinced myself that sex would be unbearably painful. At the suggestion of my shrink, I gave myself a "sex hour" while the baby napped. The idea was to experience the pain I anticipated by myself, so I would know what to expect. While Felix gurgled in my arms, I got everything out and ready to go. I put a towel in my rocking chair. On the coffee table I lined up two dildos, a butt plug, some lesbian porn, three vibrators and two bottles of lube. I was nothing if not prepared.

As soon as Felix was asleep and situated in his crib, I put in *Lez Be Friends*. But the close-ups just made me think of changing diapers. I used a lot of lubricant and inserted the narrowest dildo carefully. It didn't hurt as much as I thought it would. I was determined to get turned on, and when I did, it felt like it was happening to someone else. I came, but not in that supercalifragilistic-Prince-song-sex-relief way that I used to. My orgasm was almost in spite of itself.

At a yoga class a few weeks later, I felt my muscles, my bones, my skin, for the first time in months. I realized that I literally didn't feel my body anymore. Before I gave birth, every bump and bruise would send me to the chiropractor. Now I was sure my back was screwed up from hunching while nursing and carrying car seats and strollers, but I didn't even notice. My body was no longer mine.

I knew that no one has sex for months after having a baby (except teenagers, my doctor told me). I knew most of my mommy friends weren't having sex. Felix demanded my attention day and night. So why was I still obsessing over it? I had used sex to fill every possible hole in my life up until the day I gave birth (actually, even on the day I gave birth—I gave Ken a blowjob right before we left to go to the hospital). Now I didn't have any room left; I was full of Felix. The constant motion of early motherhood actually decreased my neuroses. I didn't have the time to worry myself sick by cataloguing my humiliations. I was doing something important: keeping this tiny human alive with milk from my breasts. My body was doing what it was meant to do. I didn't need an orgasm to slam me out of myself.

Still, I missed my husband. One night in bed, I said, "I think you need a non-sexual tour of the region, so that when we do have sex again, you know what you're getting into. Literally." I spread my legs and directed the reading light between them. I opened my sex with my fingers and showed Ken the ridge of scar tissue that stretched diagonally from the right side of my vagina to the left side of my anus. I took his hand so he could feel the area just inside the right wall of my vagina. "This still hurts. That great move you have will have to wait."

He was tentative. "I saw a baby come out of there, " he said. "It's not for fun anymore."

It was understandable that *I* didn't want to have sex, but wasn't he supposed to? My mommy friends were starting to complain about their husbands' libidos. Gisele told me she kept Ernesto happy by giving him a blowjob every three days. I knew that Ken was as busy as I was, as tired and cranky, and in shock at being a father and responsible for our little family. But I hated him for making me feel so undesirable. I hated myself for not talking to him about it. I hated that it was up to me to initiate sex. We occasionally talked about it, but even talking about sex was uncomfortable. Ken seemed completely turned off. Part of what I love about him is that he has a sensitivity that's almost feminine. Now I wanted him to be more of a man.

Seven months after Felix was born, the three of us came home from an afternoon walk. With Felix still asleep in his stroller, I said, "How about we take a chance he'll stay asleep?" We were both tentative. Ken undressed and got into bed while I went to the bathroom. I didn't want him to see my body, so I took off my jeans and socks, then got into bed and slipped off my underwear, T-shirt and bra. We didn't look at each other, just hugged hard and tight for a long time, then loosened up and kissed. I took his ass in my hands and noticed it was softer. I was glad that I wasn't the only one who was out of shape. I had forgotten that just the feeling of his cock in my hand could turn me on. He put his hand on me, opened me, found the wetness inside, rubbed my clitoris until I told him to fuck me. He put on a condom and entered me gently, missionary position. I kept asking him to look at me. I wanted not to be invisible.

It was a little uncomfortable, but not the body-wracking pain that I expected. I relaxed into the pleasure of being fucked. After awhile he came, looking in my eyes, then lay next to me and used his hand to get me off.

Afterward, I asked the million-dollar question. "Does it feel different inside?"

"Not really ... maybe a little ... To tell you the truth, it's been so long..."

We laughed. I realized I missed the afterwards as much as the sex: the hormone high, the smell.

After that night, we had sex every week or two for a few months. Then it dwindled away again. Felix grew. He needed more; I had less. Our romantic little family was actually a small corporation. We were really tired. Familiarity breeds contempt. Resentment builds upon resentment. We lost our humor.

And I realized that I love my son more than I love my husband. I know Felix's body better than I know my own. Right now, his ear is exactly as long as my middle finger from knuckle to tip. He has a patch of dry skin on his left shin. His fingers still splay like starfish, hot against my skin. I lean in too close; I want to get a whiff of his breath. When I read him a book, I surreptitiously press my lips to his hair over and over, very lightly so he won't notice and bat my hand away. He knows I'm too into him. When I feed him, he pushes my face away. He wants the breast and the milk, not the mother. I'm terrified he'll grow up to be one of those boys in high school who only look at women's breasts, not their faces. I worry that I will be jealous of his girlfriends.

Sometimes I'm afraid I go too far. I linger a little too long when I look at his little dimpled ass. I enjoy it too much when I put lotion on after his bath. I know everybody loves a naked baby; I know children are inherently sexual; I know it's normal to be turned on by your infant. One fatherhood book has a sidebar that tells new dads not to get freaked out if they get a hard-on. But this is tricky territory. Is it wrong to encourage him to touch himself? Is it okay to think of my baby when I masturbate? Is that just a manifestation of his all-consumingness? Babies are like a gas—they expand to fit all available space.

But I worry that I'll subtly cross the line, that the sexuality I share with Felix will fuck him up. (My parents never talked to me about sex; my son may have the opposite problem.) In my mind, I can fuzzily see the progression from our innocent play to abuse.

They are little, they are yours, you forget that they have their own wants and needs, you think you can do anything with them, for them, to them.

I would never abuse my child, but I understand a little those who do.

Sometimes when Felix takes his nap, I get out the Hitachi. I don't think about my husband. Nor do I think about Johnny Knoxville, or that butch dyke at the coffee shop, or being taken from behind by a faceless stranger. Right after the baby was born, I imagined mothers licking my wounds. Now I think about other men who are fathers. Sexy men, new men, but fathers. Tackily enough, my friends' husbands. They would understand the leaking breasts, the extra pounds around the hips, the moodiness.

But always, my thoughts turn to Felix. I have a hard time concentrating on my clitoris, even with all that roaring power on it. I start thinking of when his next doctor's appointment is, or how cute it is that "yellow" and "sausage" are his first multisyllabic words.

For someone who has, for better or worse, gotten strength and power from being desired, I am now operating unsuccessfully in two parallel universes. On one hand, I have never been so desired in my life. Felix ravages my breasts as no one else ever has. It's not sexual hunger, it's actual hunger. Even now, at a year and a half, he runs from across the room at the sight of them, tackles me onto the floor or couch, climbs up my body until he's within reach, then draws back and takes a good look, grins and goes in for the attack. People always say of breastfeeding, "It's sensual, not sexual." But it *is* sexual. He nuzzles and paws at me, grunts, throws his head from side to side as he latches on, his pink mouth warm on my nipple. He tries to get as much as he can into his mouth as his whole body burrows into me, his little heels digging into my thighs and still-soft belly. He kneads the breast he's nursing from with his hand to get more milk, and uses his free hand to tweak, twist and pull on my other nipple. I wonder if he's holding onto it protectively, so no one else can get it.

Who would give up being needed like that? Not me. Because the opposite universe is the one in which no one wants me. I'm a mother; I have little to no value to the outside world.

In keeping with our Felix-centered life, two months ago my husband and I invited thirty-two babies and their parents to a Valentine's baby brunch. We bought cases of cheap champagne, and the parents we know from yoga and work and the playground ate quiche and bagels, got drunk and pretended it was a kids' party. I started drinking at two. By nine-thirty, after the last guests left, I slurred to Ken, "I love Felix more than I love you."

It was the first time I'd said it out loud. I continued: "And you love Felix more than you love me. What's up with that? I want you to love me more than you love him, but I still want it to be okay for me to love him more than you."

Despite my drunkenness, he was patient. "It's different, that's all," he said. "It's a different kind of love."

"It doesn't matter," I said, then passed out. Happy Valentine's Day, honey.

My husband and I are fully in the cult of the kid. Our culture now rewards long-term breastfeeding and spending $800 on a stroller. We are supposed to sacrifice everything for our children: certainly sex, even romance. But I want to have a romantic life with my husband. I don't want to wake up when Felix is in school, or going off to college, and not know who Ken is. I want to be a model of erotic love for Felix to learn from.

I'd like to be able to say that by applying the golden rule of threesomes—play with everyone and take turns—I could come to some reckoning, but I can't. I can't resolve my sexuality changing, nor the placement of my erotic longing onto my son, nor my worries about psychologically damaging him. My husband gamely says, "It's okay, it's just all about you two for now." I try out the long view and understand that this is just a phase. I will stop breastfeeding Felix eventually; he'll get older and more independent; our physical attachment will decrease; he will probably not turn into an ax murderer as a result. I'm not sure where that leaves Ken and me. Maybe we'll wind up scheduling sex, like the advice columns tell you to. It sounds more businesslike than bold. But as I recall, a ménage à trois is difficult to negotiate: all those jangling limbs and sensitive egos, desires and expectations clashing up against one another, all that excitement and disappointment keeping each other in check.

Christen Clifford in *BabyLove*. Photo Tal Shpantzer.

LAURA LARSON

Hidden Mother

MY MOTHER EMILIE WAS BORN on September 23, 1942.

My daughter Gadisse was brought to the orphanage in Addis Ababa, Ethiopia on May 23, 2009. The doctor estimated her age at eight months, making her provisional birthday September 23, 2008.

*

The adoption agency called on June 15, 2009, the first day of my summer holiday. "We have a referral to offer you." These are the words I repeat to my friends. Not everyone understands—what's a referral? An opaque beginning to this story. The orphanage named her Gadisse, which means shelter in her native Oromo. She was found in Shashemene by a gentle man named Alemu Mamo. This is what her report says. I know she is being fed, her diaper changed, she's crawling, growing, playing. Staring at her picture, I think I detect a little smile on her stunned face. She doesn't look into the camera and the harsh light of the flash marks her official identity as an orphan. It's the only picture I have and I'm greedy for more.

*

At first, I try writing to her—a short note every few days—to bring her closer. I write to her about how much I love her and how I can hardly wait to bring her home. But, after several notes, my address of her becomes confused. Sometimes I speak to her as the child I will bring home, then as an adult, a young woman I've raised. She keeps appearing to me as a teenager. In this rehearsal of attachment, I'm already anticipating another stage of separation.

*

My mother died on April 9, 2009, of complications from the treatment of leukemia. We had an acrimonious relationship and I often went for long stretches of time without speaking to her. I fended for myself in a home that was often chaotic, neglectful and violent. From this, I earned a sense of independence that has brought me great comfort but I often worry about my ability to connect to others. I went as far away from my mother as I could and now I'm beginning to understand how my emotional distance, no matter how necessary, must have hurt her. The idea of Gadisse leaving me is already too much to bear.

*

My grandmother, Eleanor, raised my mother as a single parent, abandoned by her husband while she was recovering from a devastating car accident. They lived with my great-grandparents, and my Oma was the unquestioned head of the household. In her native Germany, my Oma had lost her young daughter Lanchen to tubercular meningitis during World War I. My mother told me stories about how she would trespass onto farms at night, stealing potatoes to feed her family. She conceived two more children: my grandmother, who became the much adored replacement child, and my Uncle Heinz. Although the death of Lanchen echoed in their family, it was Eleanor's losses that governed their home—the loss of her beauty, the loss of her husband—and these absences formed the emotional center of the family. My mother always felt marginalized to this center, the agent responsible for my grandmother's social stigma and unhappiness.

*

To my enormous relief, my parents divorced when I was thirteen and I became the daughter of a single mother. My mother understood this as deprivation for both of us and her ambivalence towards parenting turned to resentment. When I was in college, I remarked to my mother that she had been raised in a matriarchal household and she looked at me like I was crazy.

I never told my mother about my plans to adopt while she was alive.

*

This note is printed on every page of Gadisse's medical reports:

It is important to recognize that children who are available for adoption have suffered great loss. Feelings of sadness, abandonment, grief, confusion and anger may be present in various degrees. It is nearly impossible to anticipate how these feelings may manifest themselves in a particular child. Commitment, patience and the ability to access professional and lay support are important as families move through the adoption adjustment process.

Taking refuge in Winnicott, can I be a good enough mother?

*

Gadisse's story possesses the hallmarks of a fairytale: a child abandoned and rescued by a kind woman. Is she a princess who is mourned by her rightful family? Or a child escaping a cruel existence? The violence of loss beckons narrative—to distance, to quiet, to fit unimaginable experience into recognizable form. Of course, the story is much more complicated.

Poverty and poor access to health care are the primary causes that bring children into institutional care. Her family may have died. They may have been too poor or ill to take care of her. Her abandonment may have been a planned action taken with the help of a relative or neighbor, who brought her to the police after "finding" her. For these families, abandonment often means a chance for their child to have the luxury of a middle-class American life: a stable home, an education, and health care. This last possibility is almost too much to bear, to imagine their pain in relinquishing her. My family—Gadisse and I—will begin with this ineffable loss.

*

I'm buried beneath an avalanche of books about parenting the adopted child in a transracial family and I'm thrown back into familiar terrors. My belief that a book can provide the answer to everything—boredom, ignorance, loneliness, suffering—falters. Ignorance becomes appealing when I consider not only the intricacies of child development and attachment but the particular issues that face adoptive children. I fantasize that I will be her invincible mother but mostly I feel utterly defenseless and unprepared. People congratulate me on my courage and tell me I'm doing a brave and wonderful thing. But, the truth is, I feel selfish. I want her. I suspect I'll be a jealous and possessive mother, like my own.

*

Her body moves away from mine. Will she return?

*

Several weeks after receiving Gadisse's referral, I receive a call from the adoption agency telling me that she has been diagnosed with TB and has begun treatment that will last six months. In the following days, I turn to frantic networking between the doctor in Columbus and the doctor in Ethiopia, with my Washington agency acting as intermediary. There is nothing I can do. I wait anxiously for reports and photographs of her from other families traveling to Addis Ababa to bring their children home. On one occasion, a family announces they have posted pictures of her; when I check the site, I can't find her. Did I not recognize her? I am almost too humiliated to ask if she was there. And even worse, perhaps she had been removed from the nursery, hospitalized for complications related to the TB or another unknown illness? (The family had in fact not photographed her. I'm completely outraged. Have they forgotten already what it's like to wait for news?)

Several weeks later, I receive this report, with photographs, from another parent:

Gadisse ... OH, MY WORD. What a sweetheart. She kept doing the funniest scrunchy smile. I was cracking up. When I was going through pics, my sister saw her and said "Her momma's just going to fall in love with her." I can guarantee that! She's stunning.

The images show her plump and boisterous, flirting with the camera. I can see her new baby teeth through her big smile. She's got a little potbelly now and her arms, painfully thin in the first photograph, are filling out. She makes the scrunchy smile—a skeptical and playful look, an expression I recognize as one of my own. She's changed dramatically in two months and she doesn't look sick. I sob with relief and happiness.

*

I see a thinker, a coquette, a comedian, a stunning and fierce girl.

(Like Barthes' Winter Garden photograph, I will not reproduce the image here. It is only for me.)

*

To talk about my mother and Gadisse at once feels dangerous. But, I can't think of one without the other.

*

My friend Bernard, an inveterate collector of vernacular photography, introduces me to the *hidden mother*. Early nineteenth-century studio photographers employed a number of different devices to still the body for the long exposures of the camera. Sitters leaned on pedestals to steady their bodies, or their necks were held in a pincer-like brace. But, these technologies couldn't be used on the small, unruly bodies of infants. To comfort the baby in the separation entailed of a portrait, the photographer enlists the mother in a structural but visually peripheral role in the image. Her body props the infant's for the portrait, steadying and comforting. The hidden mother appears in many forms. Often, she is swathed in fabric, her concealed lap acting as a pedestal for her infant. These images remind me of dressing up as a ghost as a kid, throwing a sheet over my head and running around, arms outstretched, moaning. Sometimes the hidden mother's arm reaches into the frame from the side or her body crouches behind the chair or pram, perhaps whispering to the baby, mama's here.

*

Attachment and autonomy: the *hidden mother* speaks to the fragile balance a mother must maintain in raising a child, but the adoptive mother experiences this ambivalence through a particular constellation of desire, anticipation and anxiety. Activated by a photograph, my attachment to Gadisse was immediate and intense. But, will she recognize me as her mother? Will I be able to love her as much as her mother in Ethiopia? Will I be her hidden mother?

*

I dread the prospect of sending Gadisse into the world. But, she's already there.

*

She keeps appearing to me as a teenager.

In 2007, I began filming *Electric Girls and the Invisible World*, an experimental video that imagines female adolescence as an experience of supernatural power. It features five teenage girls—Annie, Emma, Joshelyn, Maria and Ryan—and I shot a major share of the project during the summer before four of the girls began high school. I also began the long process of adoption during its production, so these two experiences intertwine in my memory. I didn't know Gadisse yet.

Many sections of the video were scripted, but their performances relied principally on improvisation, allowing its content to be shaped by the girls' experiences and personalities. I had to shift between the part of the documentary observer, stepping back to record the girls' interactions, to a directorial mode, where I strategically shaped the material. I learned when to lead, when to intervene, and when to stand back. Over the course of eight months of shooting, the girls changed every day and these shifts, both subtle and dramatic, were astonishing to witness. Sometimes they

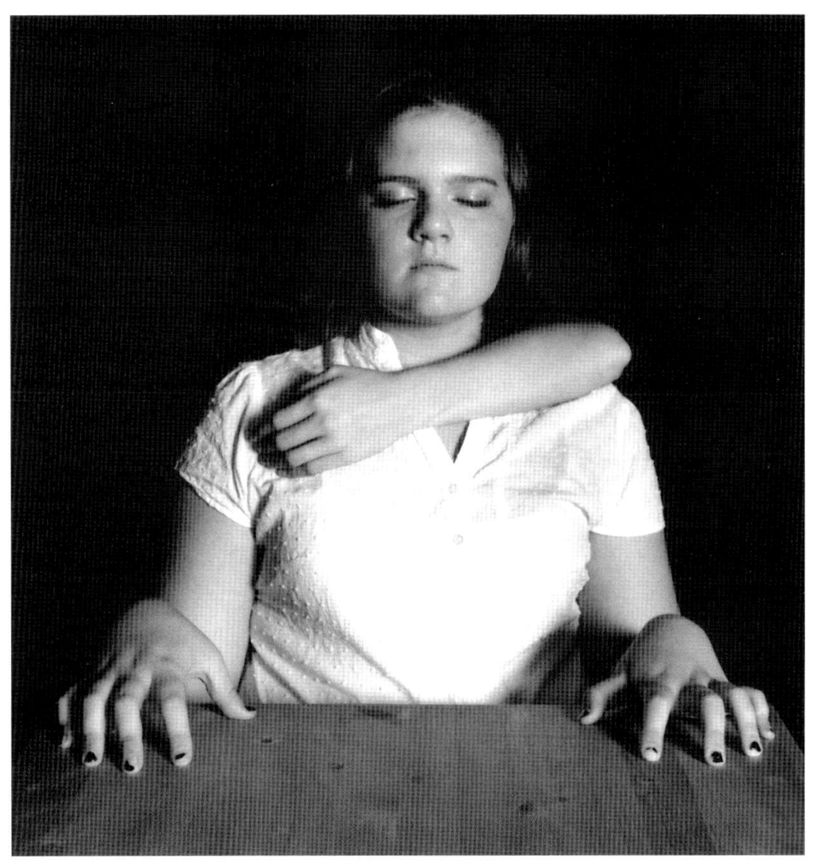

Laura Larson, *Ryan,* 2008. Gelatin silver print, 20 × 24 inches.

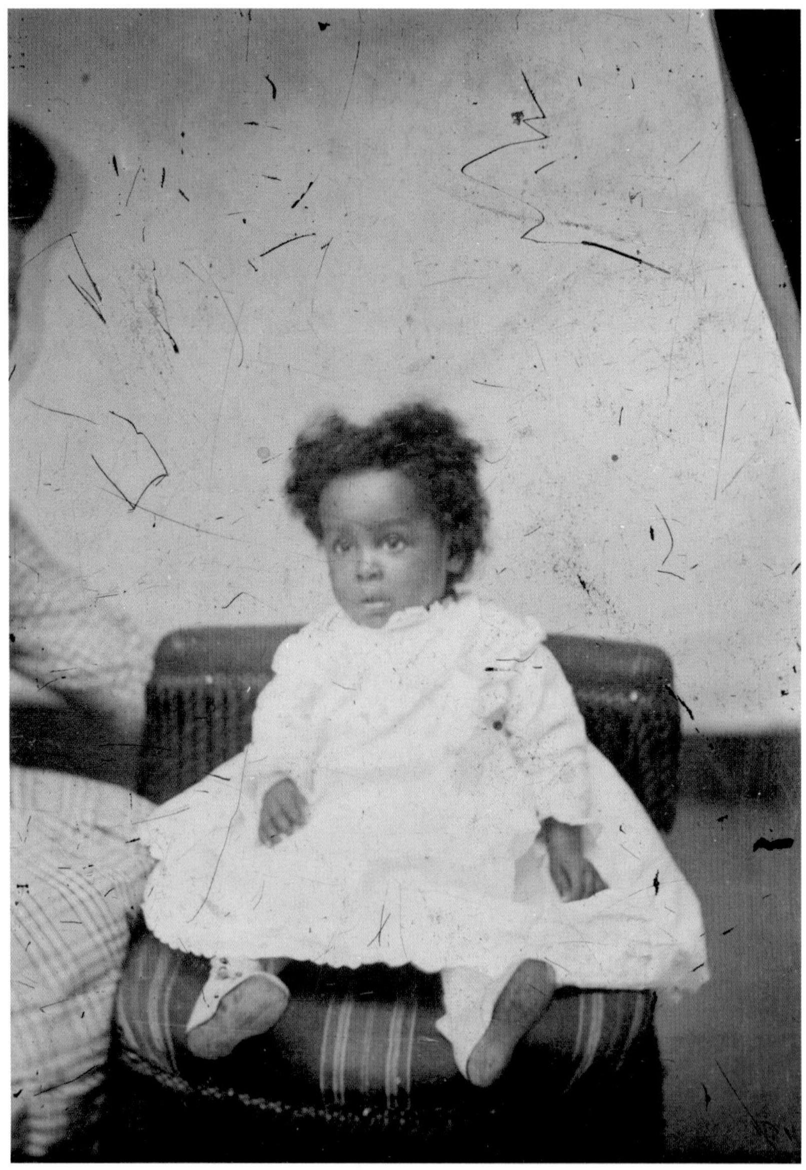

Anonymous tintype, not dated, 3.5 × 2.5 inches.

were like children and at other times, old souls. I felt flickers of maternity towards them, a quiet indication of a powerful force in me, but I had the luxury of distance.

*

The hidden mother haunts the child. She would return, even if she hadn't been lost. And, now I wait for Gadisse to come back to me.

VI.

*The M Word, Mother/mother-**

JOHANNA TUUKKANEN

From the original performance *Soft skin/harsh life.*

Physical artistic deeds 1; Milk. Photo: Pekka Mäkinen.

From the *Physical artistic deeds 1; Milk* performance. Photo: Pekka Mäkinen.

My works exist on the borders of contemporary dance, performance and live art, but are always based on strong physical presence, the gendered body and sensuality. Humour, self-irony, gentle audience interactivity and perceptive observation are present in the works. Besides the everyday life, various female myths and gender-specific realities are playfully featured; I'm a diva, a mother, a being, a humorous bio-bitch, a seduction version of Mrs. Niskavuori, a strong-minded woman

Physical artistic deeds 1; Milk. Photo: Pekka Mäkinen.

of the well-known Finnish family saga. My feministically conscious body allies with people, events, architecture and environments in various places. The logic of my physicality is based on abundance and sensuality. The bodily awareness manifested is not the body-orientedness of control but it is a mixture of bodily functions, work and euphoria.

CAROLINE KOEBEL

Berlin Warszawa Express, 2006, 19:50, color, video.

Opening narration: "In August 2004 I was in Berlin. A friend was arriving from Warsaw. I went to the East Train Station to greet her. I filmed the train pulling into the station and my friend getting off, smiling and waving as she walked towards me on the platform. Soon after I mistakenly recorded over her. I then decided to do a performance. As often as possible for the next few months I went to greet that very train arriving daily shortly after 5PM from Warsaw. I was also awaiting the birth of my child."

Für Ihre Sicherheit.

JENNIFER WROBLEWSKI

Slave to Love (detail), 2009. Charcoal on paper, 72 × 190 inches.

Since my pregnancy in 2007 I have generated two distinct bodies of work unexpectedly predicated on my dual roles as mother and artist. It has become one of my primary goals to contribute to a generational effort to reframe the relationship between artistic practice and parenting. Pre-pregnancy, my monumentally scaled drawings were generated from a spontaneous, authentic investigation of my own physicality. I used all of my body to make the marks, and they often referred to internal sensations of embodiment.

New Monuments to the AntiConcept: When Tom was four months old I began making work for a solo exhibition as part of a fellowship with A.I.R. Gallery in Brooklyn, NY. I worked at night, while he slept. As I began the new drawings, I was surprised to find that my concerns had changed dramatically. I spent all day with my son. His life experience appeared to be very direct. He didn't care about language or appreciate aesthetics. He was interested in the material of the world, learning to move himself around. He liked touching things, running his hand across a leaf or watching the trees sway in the breeze.

Almost immediately, I was drawn to found objects and materials that I glued to my new drawings. These objects and materials were mostly black and white, projecting a drawing-like resonance, but it was important to me that they could be touched. They had actual weight, they protruded from the wall, they cast shadows. The new materials activated the work, they altered and improved it.

New Collaboration: I did not intend to generate work about my pregnancy, though obviously pregnancy creates all kinds of new interior sensations. It did not feel morally comfortable or

Impala, 2009.
Charcoal, wire, beads, glitter, glue, figurine on paper, 72 × 72 × 6 inches.

Untitled, 2008.
Charcoal and watercolor on paper, 20 × 30 inches.

reasonable to use my unwitting son to generate new work. But then one day, when I was about seven months pregnant, I was in my studio working on other things, and he was moving around a lot. I could not resist the urge to make some drawings that included his activity.

I wanted to manifest a few concrete mementos of the time we had spent together in the studio, specifically. I used paper roughly the size of my torso, and I spent twenty or so minutes per drawing mapping out his movements. I annotated the drawings with notes like "pain," "kick," "twist" to help me.

50/50, 2008. Charcoal and watercolor on paper, 30 × 20 inches.

*Mother/mother-**

Curated by Jennifer Wroblewski
December 2, 2009–January 3, 2010

THE WORK IN *MOTHER/mother-** was created during the years immediately following a pregnancy or birth of a child by artists who become parents. It includes drawings, paintings, narrative and non-narrative film and video, sculpture, an artist's book, an audio piece, and embroidery.

The motivation for the exhibition was both personal and celebratory, although the work does not deny feelings of ambivalence. For her first show as a new parent, Jennifer Wroblewski created work that directly referenced her son, Tom's, presence. She wondered if other artists had experienced similar changes in their practice after having children. This curiosity compelled her to organize *Mother/mother-**. She came to the process of curating with a hypothesis and an established story of her own for which she hoped there existed parallel protagonists. It took Wroblewski about eighteen months to search out and sift through the work of the hundreds of artists who enthusiastically responded to her open call for work. The work exhibited in *Mother/mother-** was generated out of personal, idiosyncratic, unexpected byproducts of the restructuring of the physical and psychological self transitioning into parenthood. Following is a selection of work by six artists included in the show.

British artist Rachel Howfield's ongoing installation *Up Yours,* consisting of bodily emissions and human debris preserved in plastic bags, then classified and filed in chronological order on index cards, preserves and presents evidence of a life led.

Canadian Lindsay Page's series *Spawn* examines motherhood as steeped in the intensity of anxiety and exhilaration, momentous gain and the spectre of loss. It is a personal inquiry as well as public commentary on the dominant narrative of birth as celebration. The transformation of pregnancy brings promise but also the threat of the loss of control and autonomy.

Shelley Rae, an American living in the UK, photographs the concept of family, *heimat*, and the uncanny circumstances that re-awaken past visions. As in Proust's notion of involuntary memory, where childhood recollections surface after tasting something familiar, Rae elicits the viewer's memories by offering visual tasters of familiar relationships and objects. Her minimalist yet strong visualizations document the conflicts of power and gender in a domestic setting.

RACHEL HOWFIELD

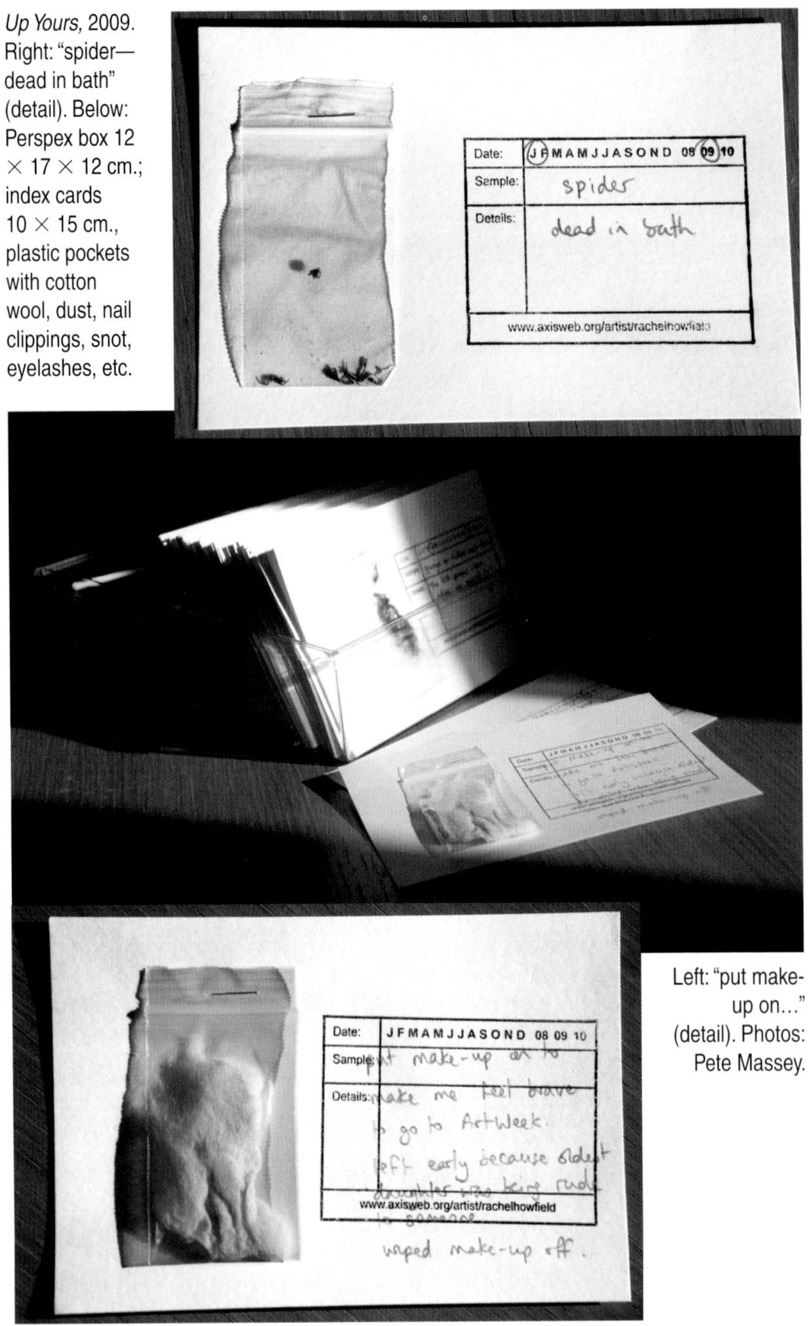

Up Yours, 2009. Right: "spider—dead in bath" (detail). Below: Perspex box 12 × 17 × 12 cm.; index cards 10 × 15 cm., plastic pockets with cotton wool, dust, nail clippings, snot, eyelashes, etc.

Left: "put make-up on..." (detail). Photos: Pete Massey.

LINDSAY PAGE

Top: "Untitled" from the series *Spawn*, 2008. Bottom: "Untitled" from the series *Spawn*, 2009. Archival pigment print, 24 × 32 inches.

SHELLEY RAE

Top: *Das Unheimliche*, 2007. Bottom: *Heimat,* 2007.
Color digital photographs, dimensions variable.

PARISA TAGHIZADEH

Top: *Kristina, 2009.* Bottom: *Wendy, 2007.* Digital color prints, 12 × 20 inches.

Portraits from the series *MOTHER* show working mothers without their children. Taghizadeh asks her subjects to choose their own environment for the shoot; this is often their work space or a place they feel best represents or defines them. The project brings the subject's forgotten pre-maternal identify to the surface as the women face the camera directly, not confrontationally, but utterly, inescapably present.

ERIKA DEVRIES

Holding, 2003–2006 (detail, spring/summer). The installation comprises over 100 individual 8 × 10 inch chromogenic printed photographs, dimensions variable.

Holding is part of a larger body of work entitled *Preschool.* The large number of photographs, and the similarities between them, emphasize as well as highlight the differences and lend the piece a film-like narrative. What becomes overwhelmingly apparent through the repetition and quantity of images is the sense of time passing, movement, and issues of control between parent and child.

KATE WILHELM

Top: *Fuck Reality,* 2009. Bottom: *Not a Work of Art.* Archival digital prints, 10 × 20 inches.

From *Two-Powered: A Diary of Motherhood and Apple Pie*: "I remember in university learning the meaning of ambivalence, from the Latin *ambi* meaning both and valence for strength or power. Literally, it means two-powered. Although I intellectualized the concept of being powered by two contradictory emotions to some extent, it wasn't until I became a mother that I truly got it." At the time Wilhelm created these photographs, it felt like an activity totally separate from motherhood, almost an escape from it. But looking back over them, she realized they expressed this experience. She found herself drawn to graffiti, broken signs, and ripped, home-made posters—messages from people seeking a voice outside the dominant discourse. She photographed places and objects that were overlooked and undervalued, that mirrored the position of motherhood in our culture, where cleavages are perfectly natural but a breastfeeding child is just too risqué for "family" establishments. The images reflect the isolation or alienation Wilhelm felt, the solitude and the stillness she craved.

VII.

Afterword

TANYA LLEWELLYN

Artist Mom

I LIKE TO TELL PEOPLE about maternal ambivalence, because it shocks them.

"You see," I'll say, "how entirely over-sanctified the idea of mother love has become in our society. The all-consuming, self-sacrificing love of a mother for her child is seen as the most instinctive love there is. The mother who expresses any emotion other than pure, unconditional love is a monster—a Medea. But of course, it's more complicated than that, especially in a modern world where working women are always forced to make sacrifices. Mothers are supposed to be saints, but we blame them for everything."

(Here the listener smiles and nods while looking vaguely troubled.)

"Your mother makes art about maternal ambivalence? Phew!" The "phew," often whistled under the listener's breath, is supposed to read: "God, that must've screwed you up."

A professor of mine once said, "No wonder you're a writer."

Having an artist for a mother is supposed to make me creative, but a little odd. And they're right. My mother always was the odd one. She wore funky purple glasses and mismatched earrings. Unlike most of the other mothers of my elementary school classmates, she had never changed her name, so that it was always jarring to hear my friends call her "Mrs. Llewellyn" without thinking. Not surprisingly, I inherited much of her "oddness"; when I arrived at summer camp adorned with a series of brightly-patterned leggings, the other girls mocked me mercilessly for my "clashing" colors. I called my mother in tears. She said, "There's no such thing as two colors that 'don't match.' Every color matches with every other color." Secretly, I blamed her and decided that her artistic sensibilities had left me sadly unprepared for the world of pre-teen pop culture.

At first, I blamed her for my social toils, and later for what I came to call "the cross of emotional intensity": feeling things too deeply. I thought I might have been happier if I had had a "normal" mother, with a "normal" job and only the most casual interest in understanding and expressing emotion. I know now how very wrong I was. What I used to call my mother's "intensity" is really the very essence of her art, of a mind that observes and experiences the world profoundly. Her self-awareness and introspection, I believe, are what allow her to grasp and channel her creativity, to mold shifting images into tangible form. I imagine it is so, to some extent, with all artists. The constant process of moving between the exterior world and the power of their interior visions must lend to their lives a shade of passion and fire, however secret. As a child there were no taboos in our household; we could talk about anything and expect real answers. Years later, it used to astonish me to discover how much was "off limits" in other mother-daughter relationships.

My mother is not just an artist: she is a feminist. I don't think the two could be separated for her, nor could they be separated in terms of their impact on me. I grew up proud to be a feminist in a way that disturbingly few young women of my generation are, ever since feminism became a dirty word (translation: "unfeminine"). To this day, I think it is extremely important for the child to understand that they do not make up the entirety of the mother's life. As a child, I always knew that my mother had her work, providing her with her own creative life that I was not part of. I may have resented it at times (what child could help it?) but still it inspired me with a great respect for her abilities. Women are trained to feel that they must give up every thought, atom, and particle of themselves to their children if they want to be considered good mothers. I believe the reverse; I believe that to do so creates a sense of entitlement in the child, who is never truly made to acknowledge the mother as her own entity.

People often ask me what it was "like" to grow up with an artist for a mother, which is always a difficult question to answer, since everyone's childhood seems normal to them. When I think back on mine, what comes to mind is the web of imaginary games that consumed me. What I can probably never fully appreciate is how carefully my mother nurtured this fantasy life, taking part when I wished her to, but never uninvited. Since it was Victorian England that I loved from day one, my mother employed her artistic talents in endless sets of paper dolls copied from old-fashioned books. Sometimes she played with me the games that I used to play in my head everywhere I went. These games were a joy and delight to her, I believe, because she saw there the freedom of childhood to exist unbound by the real. Looking back, with the self-centered memory of a child, I see my mother not as an artist per se, but as the champion of creativity who taught me how to take the stories I loved and make them my own, without which I would not be a writer today.

In later years, despite, or perhaps because of, my gratitude for her sacrifices, I came to feel a kind of guilt at having stood somehow in the way of my mother's career. I wondered if she might have been a more famous, more glamorous artist had she been able to pursue her ambitions with full independence. Her answer to this has always been that her art is profoundly indebted to the experience of motherhood, that she would not have become the artist she is today if she had not also been a mother. That is something I tend to accept without quite believing. If she wasn't making art about motherhood, I'll think to myself, aside from the extra time to devote to her art, she wouldn't be running up against so many prejudices and Freudian hang-ups. But perhaps saying that she should have chosen some "easier" art is the same thing as saying that she should have been something other than an artist, some more socially sanctioned path likely to bring in wealth and prestige. And either one would have been equally false to the thriving, rich inner life that makes her who she is—the woman, the mother, and the artist.

Bibliography

Aamalia, Jordana. "Mad, Bad Mothers and the Deviant Event: Catherine Bell and the Maternal Instinct." *n.paradoxa* 22 (July 2008): 69-75.

Alizade, Alcira Mariam, ed. *Motherhood in the Twenty-First Century*. Psychoanalysis and Women Series. London: Karnac, 2006.

Bartkowski, Frances. *Travelers, Immigrants, Inmates: Essays in Estrangement*. Minneapolis: University of Minnesota Press, 1995.

Barrett, Michèle and Bobby Baker, eds. *Bobby Baker: Redeeming Features of Daily Life*. Abingdon, Oxon: Routledge, 2007.

Bassin, Donna, Margaret Honey, and Meryle Mahrer Kaplan, eds. *Representations of Motherhood*. New Haven: Yale University Press, 1994.

Bee, Susan and Mira Schor. "*M/E/A/N/I/N/G* Forum: On Motherhood, Art, and Apple Pie" (1992). *Mother Reader: Essential Writings on Motherhood*. ed. Moyra Davey. New York: Seven Stories Press, 2001.

Benn, Melissa. *Madonna and Child: Towards a New Politics of Motherhood*. London: Jonathan Cape, 1998.

Bentz, Valerie Malhotra and Philip E. F. Mayer, eds. *Visual Images of Women in the Arts and Mass Media*. Lewiston, NY: E. Mellen Press, 1993.

Betterton, Rosemary. "Promising Monsters: Pregnant Bodies, Artistic Subjectivity, and Maternal Imagination." *Hypatia* 21.1 (Winter 2006): 80-100.

Betterton, Rosemary. *An Intimate Distance: Women, Artists and the Body*. London: Routledge, 1996.

Billops, Camille. *Finding Christa*. 1 videocassette (55 min.), 1991.

Brakman, Sarah-Vaughan and Sally J. Scholz. "Adoption, ART, and a Re-Conception of the Maternal Body: Toward Embodied Maternity." *Hypatia* 21.1 (Winter 2006): 54-73.

Brodzki, Bella. "Mothers, Displacement, and Language in the Autobiographies of Nathalie Sarraute and Christa Wolf." *Life/Lines: Theorizing Women's Autobiographies,* ed. Bella Brodzki and Celeste Schenck. Ithaca, NY: Cornell University Press, 1988.

Caporale-Bizzini, Silvia, ed. *Narrating Motherhood(s), Breaking the Silence: Other Mothers, Other Voices*. Bern; New York: Lang, 2006.

Chase, Susan E. and Mary F. Rogers. *Mothers and Children: Feminist Analyses and Personal Narratives*. New Brunswick, NJ: Rutgers University Press, 2001.

Chernick, Myrel, ed. *Maternal Metaphors: Artists/Mothers/Artwork*. Rochester, NY: The Rochester Contemporary, 2004.

Chernick, Myrel. *Mommy Mommy.* 1 videodisc (25 min.). Directed by Myrel Chernick. New York: Myrel Chernick, 1994.

Chernick, Myrel. *Women I Have Known*, Artist's book, self published, 1984.

Christophe, Francine. *From a World Apart: A Little Girl in the Concentration Camps*. Trans. Christine Burls. Lincoln: University of Nebraska Press, 2000.

Cobb, Shelley. "Mother of the Year: Kathy Hilton, Lynne Spears, Dina Lohan and Bad Celebrity Motherhood." *Genders* 48 (2008). http://www.genders.org/g48/g48_cobb.htm.

Crittenden, Ann. *The Price of Motherhood: Why the most Important Job in the World Is Still the Least Valued*. New York: Metropolitan Books, 2001.

Dally, Ann G. *Inventing Motherhood: The Consequences of an Ideal*. New York: Schocken Books, 1983.

Daly, Brenda O. and Maureen T. Reddy, eds. *Narrating Mothers: Theorizing Maternal Subjectivities*. Knoxville: University of Tennessee Press, 1991.

Darrieussecq, Marie. *Le Bébé*. Paris: Editions de Minuit, 2002.

Davey, Moyra, ed. *Mother Reader: Essential Writings on Motherhood*. New York: Seven Stories Press, 2001.

Delbo, Charlotte. *Auschwitz and After.* Translated by Rose C. Lamont. New Haven: Yale University Press, 1995.

De Marneffe, Daphne. *Maternal Desire: On Children, Love, and the Inner Life*. New York: Little, Brown, 2004.

DiQuinzio, Patrice. *The Impossibility of Motherhood: Feminism, Individualism, and the Problem of Mothering*. New York: Routledge, 1999.

Donnelly, Karen J. and J. B. Bernstein, eds. *Our Mothers, Our Selves: Writers and Poets Celebrating Motherhood*. Westport, CT: Bergin & Garvey, 1996.

Ehrenreich, Barbara and Deirdre English. *For Her Own Good: Two Centuries of the Experts' Advice to Women*. 2nd Anchor Books ed. New York: Anchor Books, 2005.

Emecheta, Buchi. *The Joys of Motherhood*. New York: Braziller, 1979.

Frankl, Viktor E. *Man's Search for Meaning: An Introduction to Logotherapy.* New York: Washington Square Press, 1963.

Frueh, Joanna, Cassandra L. Langer, and Arlene Raven, eds. *New Feminist Criticism: Art, Identity, Action*. New York: IconEditions, 1994.

García Coll, Cynthia, Janet L. Surrey, and Kathy Weingarten, eds. *Mothering Against the Odds: Diverse Voices of Contemporary Mothers*. New York:

Guilford Press, 1998.
Gaulke, Cheri and Sue Maberry. *Offerings at the Crossroads*. Los Angeles, self-published, 2005.
Gaulke, Cheri and Sue Maberry. *Marriage Matters*. Los Angeles, self-published, 2005.
Gaulke, Cheri and Sue Maberry. *Frogskin*. Los Angeles, self-published, 2005.
Gelles, Judy. *Florida Family Portrait*. Rochester, NY: Visual Studies Workshop, 2002.
Gelles, Judy. *When We Were Ten*. Rochester, NY: Visual Studies Workshop, 1997.
Gerber, Nancy. *Portrait of the Mother-Artist: Class and Creativity in Contemporary American Fiction*. Lanham, MD: Lexington Books, 2003.
Gilbert, Barbara, Barbara Rose, Sybil Milton and Alfred Gottschalk. *From Ashes to the Rainbow: A Tribute to Raoul Wallenberg, Works by Alice Lok Cahana*. Los Angeles: Hebrew Union College Skirball Museum, 1986.
Glenn, Evelyn Nakano, Grace Chang, and Linda Rennie Forcey, eds. *Mothering: Ideology, Experience, and Agency*. New York: Routledge, 1994.
Goldstein, Inbal, Igway Productions and Fanlight Productions, directors. *The Mothers' Triangle*. 1 videodisc (69 min.). Boston: Fanlight Productions, 2005.
Greenfield, Susan C. and Carol Barash, eds. *Inventing Maternity: Politics, Science, and Literature, 1650–1865*. Lexington: University Press of Kentucky, 1999.
Grosz, Elizabeth. *Sexual Subversions: Three French Feminists*. Sydney: Allen & Unwin, 1989.
Guenther, Lisa. "'Like a Maternal Body': Emmanuel Levinas and the Motherhood of Moses." *Hypatia* 21.1 (Winter 2006): 119-136.
Hanigsberg, Julia E. and Sara Ruddick, eds. *Mother Troubles: Rethinking Contemporary Maternal Dilemmas*. Boston: Beacon Press, 1999.
Hardy, Sarah and Caroline Wiedmer, eds. *Motherhood and Space: Configurations of the Maternal through Politics, Home, and the Body*. New York: Palgrave Macmillan, 2006.
Hays, Sharon. *The Cultural Contradictions of Motherhood*. New Haven: Yale University Press, 1996.
Hennessy, Rosemary and Chrys Ingraham, eds. *Materialist Feminism: A Reader in Class, Difference, and Women's Lives*. New York: Routledge, 1997.
Herman, Michelle. *The Middle of Everything: Memoirs of Motherhood*. Lincoln: University of Nebraska Press, 2005.
Hill, Marylu. *Mothering Modernity: Feminism, Modernism, and the Maternal Muse*. Origins of Modernism, vol. 10. New York: Garland, 1999.
Hirsch, Marianne, ed. *The Familial Gaze*. Hanover, NH: Dartmouth College, 1999.
Hirsch, Marianne. *Family Frames: Photography, Narrative, and Postmemory*. Cambridge, MA: Harvard University Press, 1997.
Hirsch, Marianne. *The Mother/Daugher Plot: Narrative, Psychoanalysis, Femi-*

nism. Bloomington: Indiana University Press, 1989.

Horowitz, Sara R. *Voicing the Void: Muteness and Memory in Holocaust Fiction*. Albany: State University of New York Press, 1997.

Hrdy, Sarah Blaffer. *Mother Nature: A History of Mothers, Infants, and Natural Selection*. New York: Pantheon, 1999.

Huston, Nancy. *Journal de la Création*. Paris: Seuil, 1990.

Jackson, Rosie. *Mothers Who Leave: Behind the Myth of Women without their Children*. London: Pandora, 1994.

Jetter, Alexis, Annelise Orleck, and Diana Taylor, eds. *The Politics of Motherhood: Activist Voices from Left to Right*. Hanover: University Press of New England for Dartmouth College, 1997.

Juhasz, Suzanne. "Mother-Writing and the Narrative of Maternal Subjectivity." *Studies in Gender and Sexuality* 4.4 (2003): 395-425.

Jussim, Estelle, Tillie Olsen, and Julie Olsen Edwards. *Mothers & Daughters: That Special Quality: An Exploration in Photographs*. New York: Aperture Foundation, 1987.

Kaplan, E. Ann. *Motherhood and Representation: The Mother in Popular Culture and Melodrama*. London: Routledge, 1992.

Kelly, Mary. *Imaging Desire*. Cambridge, MA: MIT Press, 1996.

Kelly, Mary. *Interim*. New York: New Museum of Contemporary Art, 1990.

Kelly, Mary. *Post-Partum Document*. London: Routledge & Kegan Paul, 1983.

Kloepfer, Deborah Kelly. *The Unspeakable Mother: Forbidden Discourse in Jean Rhys and H.D.* Ithaca, NY: Cornell University Press, 1989.

Koppelman, Susan, ed. *Between Mothers and Daughters: Stories Across a Generation*. New York: The Feminist Press, 1985.

Kristeva, Julia. "Stabat Mater." *Tales of Love*. New York: Columbia University Press, 1987.

Lacan, Jacques. *Feminine Sexuality: Jacques Lacan and the école freudienne*. Eds. Juliet Mitchell and Jacqueline Rose. New York: WW Norton, 1982.

Ladd-Taylor, Molly and Lauri Umansky, eds. *"Bad" Mothers: The Politics of Blame in Twentieth-Century America*. New York: New York University Press, 1998.

Lawler, Steph. *Mothering the Self: Mothers, Daughters, Subjects*. London; New York: Routledge, 2000.

Lazarre, Jane. *The Mother Knot*. New York: McGraw-Hill, 1976.

Lehmann, Jennifer M., ed. *The Gay & Lesbian Marriage & Family Reader: Analyses of Problems and Prospects for the 21st Century*. New York; Lincoln, NB: Gordian Knot Books; Distributed by University of Nebraska Press, 2001.

LeMaster, Tracy. " M/Othering the Children." *Genders* 47 (Spring 2008). http://www.genders.org/g47/g47_lemaster.html.

Lemieux, Kristina L. "13 Short Pieces, but Not the Whole [T]Ruth." *Hypatia*

21.1 (Winter 2006): 74-79.

Lindemann, Hilde. "Miss Morals Speaks Out about Publishing." *Hypatia* 21.1 (Winter 2006): 232-239.

Liss, Andrea. *Feminist Art and the Maternal.* Minnesota: University of Minnesota Press, 2009.

Liss, Andrea."Maternal Rites: Feminist Strategies." *n.paradoxa* 14 (2004): 24-31.

Litt, Jacquelyn S. *Medicalized Motherhood: Perspectives from the Lives of African-American and Jewish Women.* New Brunswick, NJ: Rutgers University Press, 2000.

Ludtke, Melissa. *On Our Own: Unmarried Motherhood in America.* Berkeley: University of California Press, 1999.

Lukacher, Maryline. *Maternal Fictions: Stendhal, Sand, Rachilde, and Bataille.* Durham: Duke University Press, 1994.

Luna, Alina M. *Visual Perversity: A Re-Articulation of Maternal Instinct.* Lanham, MD: Lexington Books, 2004.

Maslin-Prothero, Sian and Danusia Malina, eds. *Surviving the Academy: Feminist Perspectives.* London; Philadelphia, PA: Falmer Press, 1998.

Miller, Tina. *Making Sense of Motherhood: A Narrative Approach.* Cambridge; New York: Cambridge University Press, 2005.

Millu, Liana. *Smoke Over Birkenau.* Evanston, IL: Northwestern University Press, 1986.

Morgan, Lynn M. "Strange Anatomy: Gertrude Stein and the Avant-Garde Embryo." *Hypatia* 21.1 (Winter 2006): 15-34.

Mullin, Amy. "Parents and Children: An Alternative to Selfless and Unconditional Love." *Hypatia* 21.1 (Winter 2006): 181-200.

Nice, Vivien E. *Mothers and Daughters: The Distortion of a Relationship.* New York: St. Martin's Press, 1992.

Nixon, Mignon. *Fantastic Reality: Louise Bourgeois and a Story of Modern Art.* Cambridge, MA: MIT Press, 2005.

Novy, Marianne, ed. *Imagining Adoption: Essays on Literature and Culture.* Ann Arbor: University of Michigan Press, 2001.

Nyholm, Janet and Jerome Kaplan. *From a Housewife's Diary.* West Burke, VT: Janus Press, 1978.

Oakley, Ann. *Woman's Work: The Housewife, Past and Present.* New York: Vintage Books, 1976, 1974.

Oakley, Ann and Juliet Mitchell, eds. *Who's Afraid of Feminism? Seeing through the Backlash.* New York: The New Press, 1997.

O'Reilly, Andrea, ed. *Feminist Mothering.* SUNY Series in Feminist Criticism and Theory. Albany: State University of New York Press, 2008.

O'Reilly, Andrea. *From Motherhood to Mothering: The Legacy of Adrienne Rich's*

Of Woman Born. Albany: State University of New York Press, 2004.

O'Reilly, Andrea. *Toni Morrison and Motherhood: A Politics of the Heart.* Albany: State University of New York Press, 2004.

O'Reilly, Andrea, ed. *Mothers & Sons: Feminism, Masculinity, and the Struggle to Raise Our Sons.* New York: Routledge, 2001.

O'Reilly, Andrea and Sharon Abbey, eds. *Mothers and Daughters: Connection, Empowerment, and Transformation.* Lanham, MD: Rowman & Littlefield, 2000.

Park, Shelley M. "Adoptive Maternal Bodies: A Queer Paradigm for Rethinking Mothering?" *Hypatia* 21.1 (Winter 2006): 201-226.

Parker, Rozsika. *Mother Love/Mother Hate: The Power of Maternal Ambivalence.* London: Virago, 1995.

Peskowitz, Miriam. *The Truth Behind the Mommy Wars: Who Decides what Makes a Good Mother?* Emeryville, CA: Seal Press, 2005.

Prilleltensky, Ora. *Motherhood and Disability: Children and Choices.* Basingstoke, Hampshire; New York: Palgrave Macmillan, 2004.

Quah, Stella R. *Between Two Worlds: Modern Wives in a Traditional Setting.* Field Report Series, no. 19. Singapore: Institute of Southeast Asian Studies, 1988.

Rabuzzi, Kathryn Allen. *Motherself: A Mythic Analysis of Motherhood.* Bloomington: Indiana University Press, 1988.

Ragoné, Heléna and France Winddance Twine, eds. *Ideologies and Technologies of Motherhood: Race, Class, Sexuality, Nationalism.* New York: Routledge, 2000.

Rebhan, Gail S. *Mother-Son Talk.* Rochester: Visual Studies Workshop, 1996.

Rebhan, Gail S. *Some Light Switches in My House.* Washington, DC: Sulwalki Books, 2008.

Rebhan, Gail S. *Twenty-One.* Washington, DC: Sulwalki Books, 2008.

Retford, Kate. *The Art of Domestic Life: Family Portraiture in Eighteenth-Century England.* New Haven: The Paul Mellon Centre for Studies in British Art, 2006.

Rich, Adrienne. *Of Woman Born: Motherhood as Experience and Institution.* 1st ed. New York: Norton, 1976. 10th anniversary ed. New York: Norton, 1986.

Richards, Amy. *Opting In: Having a Child Without Losing Yourself.* New York: Farrar, Straus and Giroux, 2008.

Richards, Joan L. *Angles of Reflection: Logic and a Mother's Love.* New York: W. H. Freeman, 2000.

Sanders, Darcie and Martha M. Bullen. *Staying Home: From Full-Time Professional to Full-Time Parent.* 1st ed. Boston: Little, Brown, 1992.

Sebald, Hans. *Momism: The Silent Disease of America.* Chicago: Nelson-Hall, 1976.

Shanley, Mary Lyndon. *Making Babies, Making Families: What Matters most in an Age of Reproductive Technologies, Surrogacy, Adoption, and Same-Sex and Unwed Parents*. Boston: Beacon Press, 2001.

Sickels, Amy. *Adrienne Rich*. Gay and Lesbian Writers. Philadelphia: Chelsea House, 2005.

Suleiman, Susan Rubin. *Risking Who One Is: Encounters with Contemporary Art and Literature*. Cambridge, MA: Harvard University Press, 1994.

Suleiman, Susan Rubin. *Subversive Intent: Gender, Politics, and the Avant-Garde*. Cambridge, MA: Harvard University Press, 1990.

Suleiman, Susan Rubin. "On Maternal Splitting: A Propos of Mary Gordon's 'Men and Angels.'" *Signs: Journal of Women in Culture and Society* 14.1 (Autumn 1988): 25-41.

Suleiman, Susan Rubin. "Reply to Bauman." *Signs: Journal of Women in Culture and Society* 15.3 (Spring 1990): 656-659.

Suleiman, Susan Rubin. "Playing and Motherhood; or, How to Get the Most Out of the Avant-Garde." *Representations of Motherhood*. Eds. Donna Bassin, Margaret Honey, and Meryle Mahrer Kaplan. New Haven: Yale University Press, 1994.

Sullivan, T. Richard, ed. *Queer Families, Common Agendas: Gay People, Lesbians, and Family Values*. Binghamton, NY: Harrington Park Press, 1999.

Swigart, Jane. *The Myth of the Bad Mother: The Emotional Realities of Mothering*. New York: Doubleday, 1991.

Theill, Signe, ed. *Doublebind. kunst. kinder. karriere*. Exhibition Catalogue, Berlin: Vice Versa Verlag, 2003.

Thomas, Julia, ed. *Reading Images*. New York: Palgrave, 2001.

Thompson, Julie M. *Mommy Queerest: Contemporary Rhetorics of Lesbian Maternal Identity*. Amherst: University of Massachusetts Press, 2002.

Thompson, Mary. "Third Wave Feminism and the Politics of Motherhood." *Genders* 43, 2006. http://www.genders.org/g43/g43_marythompson.html.

Thurer, Shari. *The Myths of Motherhood: How Culture Reinvents the Good Mother*. New York: Penguin, 1995.

Trebilcot, Joyce, ed. *Mothering: Essays in Feminist Theory*. New Feminist Perspectives. Totowa, NJ: Rowman & Allanheld, 1984, 1983.

Umansky, Lauri. *Motherhood Reconceived: Feminism and the Legacies of the Sixties*. New York: New York University Press, 1996.

Van Buren, Jane Silverman. *The Modernist Madonna: Semiotics of the Maternal Metaphor*. Bloomington: Indiana University Press, 1989.

Volavkova, Hana, ed. *...I Never Saw Another Butterfly: Children's Drawings and Poems from Terezin Concentration Camp, 1942-1944*. New York: Schocken, 1993.

Waldman, Ayelet. *Bad Mother: A Chronicle of Maternal Crimes, Minor Calami-*

ties, and Occasional Moments of Grace. New York: Doubleday, 2009.

Warner, Judith. *Perfect Madness: Motherhood in the Age of Anxiety*. New York: Riverhead Books, 2005.

Welldon, Estela V. *Mother, Madonna, Whore: The Idealisation and Denigration of Motherhood*. London: Free Association Books, 1988.

Wright, Elizabeth, ed. *Feminism and Psychoanalysis: A Critical Dictionary.* Oxford: Blackwell, 1992.

Contributors

From **Danielle Abrams'** lineage of *bubbies* and *tummlers*, and African American Southern ancestors, emerges a hybrid blend of personae. She has performed nationally at museums, festivals, and performance spaces, receiving fellowships from the Franklin Furnace Fund for Performance Art and New York Foundation for the Arts. Abrams teaches in the MFA Program for Interdisciplinary Arts at Goddard College.

Kelly Barrie lives and works in Los Angeles, California. He received his MFA in 1997 from the California Institute of the Arts. His photography has been exhibited at the 2008 Biennale of Sydney, Australia, with solo shows at Miller Durazo Fine Art and Angstrom Gallery, Los Angeles, as well as numerous group exhibitions.

Maria Assumpta Bassas Vila is a mother and professor of Contemporary Art History at Faculty of Fine Arts, University of Barcelona. She also teaches in a Master of Women's Freedom Program at Duoda Centre for Research on Women (www.ub.edu/duoda) and organizes exhibitions and activities for the Contemporary Art Collection "The relationship" and other shows as a freelance curator.

Dick Blau is Professor of Film at UW-Milwaukee. His photographs have been published widely. He is the co-author of *Polka Happiness* (1992), *Bright Balkan Morning* (2002), *Living With His Camera* (2003), and *Skyros Carnival* (2010). He is currently finishing his study of family life, *Thicker Than Water: My Family in Photographs 1968-2008*.

Monica Bock is a sculptor and installation artist affiliated with SOHO20 Gallery Chelsea in New York City and Associate Professor of Art at the University of Connecticut in Storrs. She has exhibited widely in venues that include Chicago's Museum of Contemporary Art, Pittsburgh's Mattress Factory and Mobius in Boston.

Myrel Chernick is an artist and writer living in New York. She has shown her text-based multimedia installations nationally and internationally, lectured widely and curated the exhibit *Maternal Metaphors.* She is currently writing and illustrating a hybrid novel that takes place in Paris and New York.

Christen Clifford is a writer and performer in New York. She has performed at The Culture Project, PS 122, Galapagos, HERE, Joe's Pub, and The Kitchen, and toured internationally. Her writing has appeared in *Nerve, The Huffington Post, Salon*, and *Smith*. She is a recipient of a NYFA Fellowship and has been a visiting scholar at NYU.

Renée Cox is a photographer living in New York. She has used her own body, nude and clothed, to celebrate black womanhood and criticize a society she often views as racist and sexist. She continues to push the envelope in her work with her elaborate scenarios and imaginative visuals that offend some and exhilarate others.

Patricia Cué, a native of Puebla, Mexico, is assistant professor of graphic design at San Diego State University. She received her graduate degree from the Basel School of Design. Patricia's research focuses on cultural sustainability and ethics in graphic design, contemporary motherhood and culture, using experimental book formats as her medium.

Erika deVries is a visual artist working across disciplines based in Brooklyn, NY. Exhibitions and lectures include: Halifax University, Los Angeles Center For Photographic Studies, Point of View Gallery, Chicago, Gemachtschule Universitaet Kassel, LaSalle University Art Museum, Philadelphia. Erika is member of the full-time faculty at New York University. Her work is represented by Miyako Yoshinaga Art Prospects, NYC.

Denise Ferris lectures in Photography at the School of Art, The Australian National University, Canberra. The anxieties generated by photographic representations of the child in public and the milk emulsion remain research interests. Ferris' work is in the National Gallery, National Library of Australia and Canberra Museum and Gallery, as well as District Six Museum, Cape Town.

Jane Gallop is the author of several books, including *Thinking Through the Body* (1987), *Feminist Accused of Sexual Harassment* (1997), and *Living with His Camera* (2003). Gallop teaches at the University of Wisconsin—Milwaukee.

Cheri Gaulke and **Sue Maberry** met at the Woman's Building in Los Angeles in 1976, became a couple in 1979, had twin daughters in 1994, and married legally in 2008. Their lives and artwork continue to express the goals of feminist art—to raise consciousness, invite dialogue and transform culture.

Judy Gelles received an MFA in Photography from the Rhode Island School of Design. Her work is in the Los Angeles County Museum of Art and the Philadelphia Museum of Art. Her two sons work in television. Her mother, now 93, lives by herself in Maine and Florida.

Nancy Gerber holds a doctorate in Literatures in English from Rutgers University. She is the author of *Portrait of the Mother-Artist: Class and Creativity in Contemporary American Fiction* (Lexington, 2003) and *Losing a Life: A Daughter's Memoir of Caregiving* (Hamilton, 2005). She lives in Montclair, NJ.

Judy Glantzman lives and works in New York City. She is represented by the Betty Cunningham Gallery, where she has had solo shows in 2006, 2008 and 2009. She shows her work nationally and internationally in numerous solo and group exhibitions and was a 2001 recipient of a John Simon Guggenheim Memorial Fellowship.

Heather Gray is an artist living in Vermont. She has received her BFA in Sculpture with a Minor in Photography and Film from Virginia Commonwealth University and her MFA in Visual Arts from Vermont College of Fine Arts with a concentration in Photography.

Rachel Hall's fiction and nonfiction have appeared in journals and anthologies, most recently in *Crab Orchard Review, Water~Stone Review* and *New Letters,* which awarded her their Cappon Fiction Prize. She has received awards from Glimmer Train, Lilith, Nimrod and the Bread Loaf Writers' Conference. She teaches at the State University of New York at Geneseo.

Youngbok Hong is an Associate Professor of Visual Communication at the Herron School of Art and Design. She has explored the emotional engagement with narrative in interactive media. Hong received a BA in Philosophy from Ewha Womans University and an MFA in Visual Communication at The School of the Art Institute of Chicago.

Rachel Howfield is an artist interested in gender roles and identity. She exhibits internationally, and is the founding member of "APT = Artist Parents Talking" network. She lives in West Yorkshire, England, with her husband and two daughters.

Mary Kelly has contributed extensively to the discourse of feminism and postmodernism through her large-scale narrative installations and theoretical writings. Recent exhibitions include *Documenta XII, WACK! Art and the Feminist Revolution*, the *2004 Biennial*, Whitney Museum of American Art, and the *2008 Biennale of Sydney*. She is the author of *Post-Partum Document* and *Imaging Desire*.

Jennie Klein's primary areas of research lie in contemporary art, art criticism, feminist art, and performance art. She is a contributing editor for *Art Papers* and *Performance Art Journal* (PAJ), and a member of the editorial board of *Genders*. Klein has published in *n.paradoxa, Art History, New Art Examiner,* and *Afterimage*.

Caroline Koebel's films and videos are informed by conceptual art, film theory and feminism, provoking new modes of aesthetic and critical engagement with such subjects as early cinema, commodity culture, world affairs, and maternity. Koebel co-authored the stencil graffiti book *Schablone: Berlin*, and has published catalog essays on Carolee Schneemann and Barbara Hammer.

Laura Larson is an artist based in Athens, Ohio, where she chairs the Photography Program in the School of Art at Ohio University. Her most recent work considers the relationship between nineteenth-century spirit photography and contemporary practice. She is currently at work on a project about the writer Upton Sinclair.

Andrea Liss is the Contemporary Art Historian/Cultural Theorist at California State University San Marcos. Her teaching focuses on feminist art and theory, photographic theory and representations of memory and history. Her son Miles is now twenty years old and her book *Feminist Art and the Maternal* appeared in January 2009 (University of Minnesota Press).

Tanya Llewellyn grew up in New York as the daughter of two visual artists. She received her undergraduate degree in 2008 from Wesleyan University, where she studied creative writing and Victorian literature, and is planning to pursue a career in fiction. She has completed one novel as well as several works of short fiction.

Mónica Mayer (México, 1954) and **Maris Bustamante** (México, 1949) are visual artists with long-standing careers as performance artists. They have both written extensively on this subject. In 1983 they formed *Polvo de Gallina Negra*, the first feminist art group in Mexico, which lasted for ten years. Since then, they each work independently.

Ellen McMahon is an Associate Professor of Art and Design in the School of Art at the University of Arizona. She is becoming increasingly engaged in the world outside the family, recently receiving a Fulbright Scholars Grant to work as a writer/designer/artist in a wetlands conservation project in Puerto Peñasco, Mexico.

Sherry Millner is a video artist/filmmaker who also makes photoworks. Recent videos include "Graven Images" and "Partial Critique of Separation." She is also co-producer of the nomadic projection series *State of Emergency.* She is Professor of Media Studies at CUNY, Staten Island.

Nadja Millner-Larsen is a doctoral candidate at New York University. Her work rests at the intersections of Visual Culture, Affect Studies, Queer Theory and Memory Studies. While her previous research focused on mid-century underground press in New York, her dissertation explores contemporary visual re-activations of past moments in leftist radical culture.

Michelle Moravec received her Ph.D. in history from UCLA. Her research focuses on women's social movements. Her particular interests are the intersection of feminism and art, as well as constructions of modern motherhood. She is currently an assistant professor of history at Rosemont College in Philadelphia.

Margaret Morgan's practice includes video, photography, drawing and writing. Her work explores the abject from the residues of the twentieth, "American," century and its fascination with hygiene to the vicissitudes of mothering. She is included in exhibitions such as *Trash* and *A Picto-*

rial Guide to Sanitary Defects, and has written for *Plumbing: Sounding Modern Architecture* and *Women in Dada.*

Mignon Nixon teaches at the Courtauld Institute in London. She received her Ph.D. in art history from the Graduate Center, City University of New York, and serves on the editorial board of *October* Magazine. She is the author of *Fantastic Reality: Louise Bourgeois and a Story of Modern Art* (2005).

Lindsay Page is a Canadian interdisciplinary artist working in photography and video installation. Her work has been exhibited internationally and has appeared in publications including the *New Yorker* (2009), *Emergence: Contemporary Photography in Canada* (2009) and *Camera Austria* (2007). She is the recipient of numerous awards, including a 2010 Canada Council for the Arts grant.

Shelley Rae was born in Flint, Michigan, and received a Masters in Fine Art from Central St Martins College of Art and Design in London. She has exhibited photography, video and installation work internationally in Germany, Italy and the United States. Shelley lives and works in London.

Gail Rebhan is a Professor of Photography at Northern Virginia Community College. Collections include Smithsonian American Art and the Polaroid Corporation. Exhibitions include the Corcoran Gallery of Art and the Folkwang Museum, Germany. Published photographs include *Feminist Art and the Maternal* and *Reframings: New American Feminist Photographies.* Rebhan has an MFA from California Institute of the Arts.

Leslie Reid is an artist working in painting and photography, a full professor at the University of Ottawa, and has received grants and awards from the Canada Council for the Arts and the Ontario Arts Council. Her work is in major collections, including the National Gallery of Canada.

Aura Rosenberg lives in New York City and Berlin, Germany. Her work includes painting, sculpture, photography and video. She has shown her work in the United States and Europe. Her publications include *Head Shots* and *Berlin Childhood.* The work reproduced here comes from her 2008 publication, *Who Am I? What Am I? Where Am I?*

Ruth Skilbeck is a conceptual art writer and theorist based in Sydney. Her current research interests include psychoanalysis and the mother in contemporary art/writing. She is published in *Communication* and *Critical/Cultural Studies, The International Journal of the Arts in Society,* and *Pacific Journalism Review.*

Barbara T. Smith is one of the pioneers of performance and body art. Beginning in the 1960s, she began creating durational performances in which she used her own body, often at some personal risk. Her lifelong commitment to alternative spirituality anticipates many contemporary artists who incorporate spiritual practices in art making.

Susan Rubin Suleiman is the Dillon Professor of the Civilization of France and Professor of Comparative Literature, Harvard University. Her books include *Subversive Intent: Gender, Politics, and the Avant-Garde* and *Risking Who One Is* from Harvard University Press.

Parisa Taghizadeh is a freelance artist/photographer currently based in Los Angeles. She grew up in London and worked as a still photographer for arts organizations, television, and cinema. Her work deals with issues of personal and cultural identity. She has exhibited widely; most recently at the San Francisco Arts Commission and the Fowler Museum at UCLA.

Signe Theill is an artist and curator who lives in Berlin, working in photography, video, and site-specific installation. She is the curator of the exhibition *doublebind. art. children. career,* 2003-2006. Recent exhibitions include: *2009 Strictly Berlin, Photo-Performance 2008*, European Center for the Arts, Hellerau, Dresden with "Gulliver Dreaming" Video 15. Min.

Johanna Tuukkanen is based in Kuopio, Finland. Her work moves on the borders of live art, contemporary dance and performance. She was awarded the State Prize for the Arts in 2006, and has worked in the fields of art and culture as a performer, dancer, choreographer, writer, journalist and regional artist.

Sarah E. Webb is an independent curator, scholar and artist residing in Rochester, NY. Her installation- and process-based performance work has been exhibited nationally and internationally. Webb is also the co-editor of *Singular Women: Writing the Artist* (UC Press, 2003). She received her MFA from Visual Studies Workshop, Rochester, New York.

Kate Wilhelm was once a government drone who just went to work and came home to watch TV, lacking any real critical engagement with the world. Becoming a mother in 2006 changed all that. With motherhood, everything became more intense and important, and suddenly she had something to say. She lives in Guelph, Ontario, with her husband and son.

Marion Wilson lives and works in Syracuse, New York, and maintains a studio in New York City. She has exhibited with or completed public commissions for the New Museum of Contemporary Art, NYC, Kasia Kay Art Projects, New Orleans, and Dorsky Gallery, NYC. Wilson directs the Community Initiatives in the Visual Arts at Syracuse University and teaches in the Sculpture Department.

Jennifer Wroblewski lives and works in New Jersey. Her drawings have been exhibited widely. She is the recipient of a 2009 NYFA Fellowship in Printmaking/Drawing/Book Arts and has been an adjunct lecturer in the School of Art+Design at SUNY Purchase since 2006. *Mother/mother-** is her first curatorial project.

M(OR)E B(RI)E(FLY). ARE WE ALL? THEN I'LL. ELLE S'APPELLE. SIE, FRAU, WAS BORN, STUDIED, TRAVELLED, ARTED, MUMMED, ARTS. AS FOR WORK: THROUGH WORD AND WARDROBE (KLEIDERSCHRANK UND KUEHLSCHRANK) INVESTIGATES ATTITUDE, IMAGE, ARCHITECTURE, SCALE, HEIRARCHY, HUMOUR, PURPOSE COLOURS, CATEGORISATIONALISM, FEMINISMUS, TEXT AND TEXTILE, TASTE, CAMOUFLAGE, COMMUNICATION, DOMESTICS, EMOTION, BEING, SEEING, AND, MAYBE, M(OR)E.